Good luck, Rich
May you plow
those acres of
dollars some day
B.K. Hayden

HOW YOU CAN GROW RICH THROUGH RURAL LAND –
Starting From Scratch

HOW YOU CAN GROW RICH THROUGH RURAL LAND --
Starting From Scratch

Bradley K. Haynes

Greatland Publishing Co.
7 South Street
Front Royal, Virginia 22630

Library of Congress Cataloging in Publication Data

Haynes, Bradley K.

    HOW YOU CAN GROW RICH THROUGH RURAL LAND - - Starting From Scratch

    Catalog Card Number: 78-73695

ISBN 0-932586-02-3

Copyright 1979 by Greatland Publishing Co.
Front Royal, Virginia 22630

All rights reserved. No part of this book may be reproduced in any way, or by any means, without permission in writing from the publisher.

Printed in the United States of America

SUBDIVESTOR'S SUMMARY of the TABLE of CONTENTS

LESSON 1: THE SECRET OF SUBDIVESTING

In this lesson you'll learn: Secrets Long Held By The World's Most Successful Men . . . Why The Rich Make Out So Easily . . . How You Can Use Certain Known Success Principles To Build Riches For Yourself . . . Advice From A Land Pro On How *Not* To Fowl Up . . . How To Plant Your Seeds For Riches . . . How To Determine *Where* You'll Profit From Land . . . How To Purchase Your First Piece Of Rural Land . . . How Much To Pay For It In The Raw . . . The Common Thread That Links Every Self-Made Rich Man On Earth . . . Why You Must Strike When The Iron Is Hot . . . How To Know When The Success Cycle Is In Your Favor . . . Why You Should Not Expect A Fast Rise In Price By Just Holding Land . . . How A Quickie Land Deal Can Pump Out The Profits . . . The Case Against "Getting Involved" With Your Project . . . The Front-End Profits Theory — Why Your Future Should Be NOW!
Lesson Begins On Page 1.

LESSON 2: ALL ABOUT PARTNERS AND KEY MEN

In this lesson you'll learn: How To "Get In Bed" With The Right Man — Or Woman . . . How To Assess Drive And Potential . . . How To Win Friends And *Lose* People . . . The Importance Of Partners Sharing The Same General Attitudes . . . How To Avoid A Divorce — Business Style . . . Why Partners Who Like A Security Blanket Can Leave You Cold . . . How To Find The Positive Thinker — Why He Should Finish What He Starts . . . Who Was Moviedom's Worst Partner, And Why . . . Why The Job Hopper Will Always End Up In A Hole . . . Why Dealing With Friends And Relatives Is A No-No . . . How To Fill All The Slots — Subdivesting's Key Work Areas . . . How To Get 'em To Hustle For Money; For Land; The Role Of Mr. Adman; About The Sales Slot — How To Avoid Headaches And Hangovers Through "Problem" Thinking.
Lesson Begins On Page 13.

LESSON 3: HOW DO I FIND THE PROFITABLE LAND DEALS?

In this lesson you'll learn: The Art Of Creative Cruising For Land . . . The Value Of A SOURCE BOOK — What It Can Do For You . . . The Six Primary Sources For Rural Land Deals . . . Where To Find A Gold Mine Of Potential Deals . . . Why Country And Regional Newspapers Are Critical To Your Operations . . . How Someone Else's Dead Asset Can Become Your Live Wire To Profits . . . How Word-Of-Mouth Can Reveal Gold In Them Thar Parts . . . How To Plot Your Next Conquest — Doing It In The Comfort Of Your Home; Your Office . . . How To Start An ACTION FILE — Your Winning Way To Score Everytime . . . About The Dispassionate Developer — The Art Of Keeping Cool When Too Many Deals Look Hot . . . Why You Must Pay Yourself First . . . All About The *Goal* Mind; How And Why *Goal Orientation* Works — How It Can Create Wealth For You . . . The Importance Of Your STATEMENT OF PHYSICAL GOALS — An Understanding Of How The Rich Have Acquired Their Wealth . . . The "Something For

Nothing" Illusion — Why You Must Write Out A STATEMENT OF EXCHANGE And *Earn* Your Good Fortune.
Lesson Begins On Page 31.

LESSON 4: THE PURCHASE OF RURAL LAND

In this lesson you'll learn: The Importance Of Physical Make-up . . . The Ideal Ratio Of Water Frontage And Road Front To Backland . . . What You Should Know About Location, Location, Location — Why This Factor Is Critical, Even In Rural Areas . . . The Joy Of Scoring . . . My Secret Formula For Hitting The Profit Target Everytime . . . All About The Miss-stakes I've Made . . . How The Feds Sometimes Snare Innocent Developers In Sweeps For "Land Hustlers" . . . The Most Important Exemptions To The Interstate Land Sales Disclosure Act . . . How To Maximize Profits And Cut Risk To The Bone Using The FEASIBILITY CHECK LIST And QUALITY REFERENCE SHEET . . . All About Love At First Site — Why First Impressions Can Rub You The Right Way . . . About The Seduction Of Mr. Cool; Or, Hotshot Meets Hotspot . . . The Value Of Your Checks And Rechecks — How *Not* To Wake Up With A Hangover And An Empty Wallet By Bedding Down With The Wrong Deal.
Lesson Begins On Page 51.

LESSON 5: HOW TO FINANCE YOUR PROJECTS

In this lesson you'll learn: All About The Cash In Other People's Pockets — Why You Should Use It Or Lose It . . . The Power Of Proper Positioning With Mortgage Notes . . . What You Should Know About The Release Game . . . How To Play It Under A Blanket Mortgage . . . How Lots Can Be Sold Prior To Your Own Settlement — Simultaneous Hijinks In The Closing Office . . . All About Land Lusting On Credit . . . Those Neat Little

Tricks Of The Trade; Or, What's A Nice Banker Like You . . . ? . . . How The Federal Reserve System Affects Your Flow Of Funds . . . How To Find The Green Grease When Things Get Tight . . . What You Should Know About The Prime Game; Or How To Keep Your Nose "Green" In An Over-ripe Economy . . . All About Swinging Deals With Partners . . . How You Can Pay Release Fees In Notes Rather Than Cash . . . Little Known Facts About Pension Fun-ds — How To Find And Romance The Mature Partner With Ready Cash . . . Getting Funds Elsewhere — Who's Usually Willing; Who's Usually Not . . . All About Sharing The Wealth — Neither A Borrower Or A Lender Be . . . Except.
Lesson Begins On Page 77.

LESSON 6: DEVELOPING RURAL LAND

In this lesson you'll learn: How To "Shaft" A Lot To Avoid Getting Shafted By Unfair Local Ordinances . . . How To Give A "Nose Job" To An Ugly Piece Of Land . . . How To Slice Into The Land Pie For Maximum Profits . . . How To Perform The "Quickie"— Developed By Dirt Peddlers In The Sixties . . . Why Certain Lots Will Turn A Man Off — And His Wife On . . . How To Avoid A "Lot Cramp" . . . What Kind Of A Lot Will Make A Hard Customer Beg For It . . . The Hardest Piece Of Recreational Land To "Hustle" — The Easiest . . . How To "Undress" A Lot For Maximum Exposure . . . How To Get *All* The Dirt — What You Should Know About Soils . . . How To Play Godfather — Some Thoughts On Covenants And Lot Owner Associations You Can't Refuse.
Lesson Begins On Page 99.

LESSON 7: WHAT YOU NEED TO KNOW ABOUT ADVERTISING AND SALES PROMOTION

In this lesson you'll learn: Why Some Ads Succeed And Why Others

Fail . . . Seven Vital Elements Of A Successful Direct Response Ad . . . The Greatest Rural Land Ads – Exposed . . . How To Hold Attention In December As You Did In May . . . The Powerful Pied Piper Pitch That Keeps 'em Coming Back For More . . . The Importance Of The Believability Factor – Avoiding Those Corny Lines . . . What You Should Know About Long And Short Copy – Is Length Really That Important? . . . How To Promote The Double Play – Giving Away More Value For The Money And Liking The Results . . . Tickler Tips; Or, How To Get 'em To Come Out . . . How To Write A Successful "Foreclosure" Ad . . . What You Need To Know About Direct Mail "Love" Letters – How To Make Them "Fall" . . . How To Feel Like The Happy Huckster – Proven Lines That Make Your Phone Ring . . . Erotic Penmanship – Making The Right Strokes For The Right Folks.
Lesson Begins On Page 133.

LESSON 8: THE SALE OF SUBDIVIDED LAND

In this lesson you'll learn: How To Cuddle With Real Estate Brokers; Their Care And Feeding; When To Kiss Them Goodbye . . . Pricing Tricks In A Competitive Market . . . About "Land Whores" And High Pressure Salespeople – Why You Don't Need Their Services . . . What You Should Know About "Burns" (Defaults) – How To Handle Them . . . How To Profit From Your Own Foreclosures . . . The Advantages Of "Deed-Backs" From Delinquent Property Owners . . . The "Bigger Fool" Theory . . . Some Very Good Reasons For Getting In And Out Quickly . . . How To Handle Salespeople On The Firing Line: The Good, The Bad, And The Hungry . . . What To Do About Candy Store Mania – The Temptation Of Salespeople; How To Control And Channel Their Drive . . . The Pleasure Of Selling Your Own Property . . . About The "Gold" In Those Referrals . . . The Basics Of Successful Salesmanship . . . How Enthusiasm Can Tame The Devil . . . The Potency Within *You* . . . Client Foreplay . . . How Identifying With Your Client Can Improve Your Sales Life . . . What You Should Know About Closing Hints –

How To Recognize When The Customer Wants To Buy . . . How To Test Your Coy Quotient — Deferring To Your Prospect.
Lesson Begins On Page 167.

BOOK II — THE B.K. HAYNES SUCCESS FORMULA

In this book you'll learn: What Amazing Powers Lie Hidden In Just Two Key Words . . . The Source Of All Man-Made Wealth . . . A Cure For The Leanest Purse — Yet It Is The Medicine Most Overlooked . . . What Negative Emotion Is The Major Cause Of Individual Failure . . . The Fool-Proof Self-Confidence Formula Contained In The Word, A-D-M-I-T . . . Your Seven Deadly Enemies In Life — How To Conquer Them . . . What Twin Qualities Of The Great And Super Great Can Be Yours For The Asking . . . How The World's Most Successful Men Can Become Your Personal Advisors . . . Who Was The Most Supremely Successful Man Who Ever Lived? . . . About Your Lifetime Servant — Have You Let Him Grow Lazy And Inefficient Through Disuse? . . . Why A Pleasant Personality Cannot Be Manufactured — How You Can Acquire One . . . What Critical Quality Is So Essential For You That, Without It, You Are Ultimately Doomed To Failure . . . The "Fatal Fifty" Failure Habits — How Many Can You Spot Within Yourself? . . All About Leaders — Are They Born Or Made? . . . How To Acquire The Finest Insurance Policy Against Failure Known To Mankind . . . How To Determine What You Want Out Of Life And How To Obtain It . . . A Proven Step-By-Step Procedure For Reaching And Influencing The Subconscious Mind — The Controller Of All Dreams And Aspirations . . . Nature's Unexplained Law That Yields Benefits In Greater Measure Than The Effort Put Forth — How This Law Can Be Made To Work For You . . . How To Generate "Belief Power" To Drive Your Money-Making Machine . . . Your Infallible Guide To Finding The Work, Rendering The Service, And Achieving The Goals You Desire Without Sacrificing Your Peace Of Mind.
Lesson Begins On Page 195.

APPENDICES

A. Frequently Asked Questions and Answers for Beginning Subdivestors
B. Dictionary of Real Estate, Subdivesting, and Success Terms
C. Bibliography and Suggested Further Reading
D. Federal and State Regulations Supplement
E. Land Acquisition Check List and Development Forms
F. Measurement Tables and Computation Data for Land Areas
G. Mapping Structure and Information for Land Procurement
H. Soil Legend and Sample Soil Map
I. Sample Protective Covenants for Subdivisions
J. Sales Contract Forms, Credit Applications, and Disclosure Information
K. Sample Deed, Deed of Trust, and Related Note
L. Forms and Information for Servicing Notes Receivable
M. Note Discount Information and Procedures
N. Key to U.S. and Foreign Annual Interest Rates

Appendices Begin On Page 269

Foreword

HOW <u>YOU</u> CAN GROW RICH THROUGH RURAL LAND — — Starting From Scratch is not a something-for-nothing approach to a final goal of wealth and independence. It is a step-by-step guide to this goal which makes the most of your natural abilities. It will show you how to use what you've got to a much greater advantage. It will teach you ways of controlling your future to a much greater extent. No part of your rise to wealth and independence has been left out. It's all there. You must practice the initiative and strict adherence to the guidelines which are necessary for the completion of the project you will set for yourself, the reaching of your goals for wealth and independence in a short period of time without taking any great personal or financial risks.

Don't misunderstand. This is not a book of shady deals or questionable tactics. All of the points in your journey to the top are completely above-board. Underhanded dealing will most likely render the entire plan useless.

The key element is *you*. You will determine whether or not you're going to make it. You will determine just how successful you will be. With my help through this course, you will merit your just rewards, the rewards you deserve and should get in life.

Prepare yourself for an adventure in your trip to the top and then continue to prepare yourself for the adventures which are sure to follow. Step one in your journey to wealth and independence has already occured; you have purchased my course. Step two is about to begin.

Happy Adventures !!!

Bradley K. Haynes

BOOK I

THE CAN'T-LOSE
WAY TO WEALTH
AND INDEPENDENCE

THE SECRET OF SUBDIVESTING

Lesson Number 1
Table of Contents

The Unspoken Creed Of The World's Richest
  And Most Powerful Men..p. 4
The Two Potentially Powerful Thought Sources Available To Us All ...p. 4
The Story Of Edwin C. Barnes And Thomas Edison ....p. 6
Ideas, The Coinage Of Your Brain....................................p. 6
To Reap Riches You Must First Plant The Seed ....p. 7
The Common Thread Linking All Self-Made
  Rich And Successful Persons.......................................p. 8
I Told My Friends We'd All Be Rich ....p. 9
Release Fees Made Easy ....p. 10
The Definition Of *Subdivesting*....................................p. 11
The Front-End Profits Theory.......................................p. 12
Action Points ....p. 12

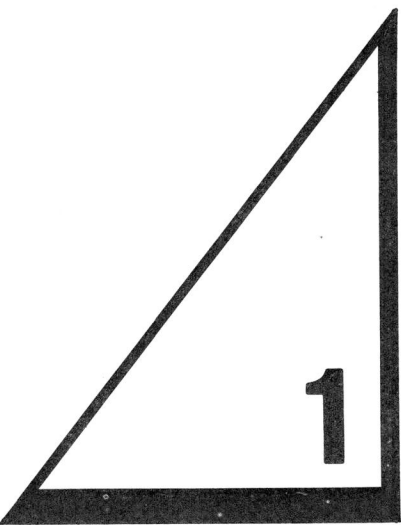

The Secret of Subdivesting

Imagine you are about to embark on a great voyage, one that will take you to lands where nuggets of gold lie on the ground and are there for the taking; where you are free from the conventional restraints and pressures of job, salary, and fear. Unusual thinking? Perhaps for the weak mind; but certainly not for the strong-willed individual who is the master of the elementary principles of mind power and success which are about to be revealed to you — secrets long known by the world's most successful men.

What do these men know that you may not know? What do I know that if you knew and could apply, would make you rich and independent?

The world's richest and most powerful men — successful personalities in all walks of life — know and consciously practice certain principles that, when mastered by you, will guarantee success. All of these men know the hidden powers of the mind, and they live by their own versions of the following creed:

> "Determined" thought, aimed at a "specific" desire, and reinforced by "persistent" effort, will result in the achievement of wealth, independence, and personal power.

When I first began my search for rural land, I wandered out of the city one rainy day without a clearly defined destination or knowledge of property values. I had not discovered the creed which I expressed above. It came to me years later, and even then it was only parceled out to me. The discovery began with an intense desire to live and work in a rural setting.

I was determined to find some land in the country where I could somehow begin a new life. Unfortunately, though I did locate a cabin and five acres that I could afford, this sort of vague determination was insufficient for the achievement of success. It was only when I was able to actually see *specific* desires and *definite* purposes that the coffers of wealth and independence were opened to me.

When the opportunity came to participate in the development of a *specific* tract of land for the *definite* purposes of making significant profits, my subconscious mind took control and fired up my life. Think about this for a moment . . . all of us have **two potentially powerful thought sources – our conscious minds** and our **unconscious minds.** Those individuals who achieve the greatest success in life are operating, so-to-speak, on both burners. Most of us do not maintain a continuous line of communication with our subconscious minds, and naturally, we fall behind. We cannot keep up with others who achieve the successes we covet and admire.

You cannot fire up your subconscious mind unless you tell this power source *exactly* what you want from it. Another line of reasoning is to think of your subconscious mind as an engine that will fire up only when supplied with fuel in the correct mixture.

When the idea of living and working in the country first began to germinate in my mind, I was without any funds to buy land or property. It was totally unclear how I could even make a living in the country. Obviously, at this time, my subconscious mind was not at work solving these problems.

Many of us would have simply dismissed such thoughts from our minds until fate and fortune dealt us a better hand. But the intensity of my *desire* was such that the *thought* did not go away; it had entered my subconscious mind. Understand, however, that the subconscious mind does not fire on all cylinders until it is fueled with the *correct* mixture. The missing ingredients in my case were the true *specifics* of my desire. I was certainly determined in my thinking, and a persistent attitude had always carried me through many dark periods in my life. Why had success eluded me?

On that rainy day excursion into the countryside, my persistence prodded luck (as it often does), and I came under the aegis of a developer whom I admired. His success helped guide my life. I purchased a river lot from him and traded it for a shell cabin situated on five acres in the same development. Soon thereafter I worked for him, and with him, on many profitable ventures. I put just $50.00 down on my first property. This step launched a career that would make me worth 20,000 times that figure.

It is sometimes amazing how small the obstacles are between you and the fulfillment of your lifetime goals. We all have a propensity for thinking more in terms of the impossible rather than the possible.

At this point, I must assume that you are determined enough to begin building your own fortune and achieving personal independence through the proven techniques I will reveal to you. It is also an assumption on my part that you are willing to apply persistent effort to accomplish these ends and that you are willing to learn and apply the "success" principles that will be given to you. With these thoughts in mind, I can get down to the specifics of how you can make more money than you thought possible in rural land and how, simultaneously, you can gain complete control over your life.

BEFORE YOU SEARCH FOR LAND, BE PREPARED.

In his book, *Think and Grow Rich,* Napoleon Hill tells the story of Edwin C. Barnes, who, as a young man, wanted to go to work for Thomas Alva Edison. Barnes was without funds to make the trip to Edison's laboratory in New Jersey. The fact that Barnes did not know Edison was an added hindrance. But did Barnes allow these difficulties to stand in his way? No! He knew what he wanted from life, and he knew why it was imperative that he have it. He knew specifically whom he wanted to work for and the location of the man's place of business. He let nothing stand in his way until he was on Edison's staff. Mr. Barnes, though he may not have known it at the time, was in possession of the key ingredient necessary to get his subconscious mind into gear. He would be with Edison though hell itself gaped and angels sang. This fierce determination, coupled with a perseverance that would make stepping stones of granite obstacles, led Barnes to Edison and later made him an associate of the great inventor. This story points up the necessity for clarity of purpose and for pinning down your goals. Assuming you know why you *want* something (wealth and independence), you must be *definite* about what you hope to accomplish including details such as, with whom, where, and during what time frame.

Since this book is written for the beginner as well as for those who have a familiarity with rural real estate, we shall begin with the idea of investing your time, your effort, and a minimum of your own money in rural land transactions. Your objective, of course, is wealth and independence for yourself.

"Ideas," said Shakespeare, "are the very coinage of the brain." An idea is intangible, yet once planted in the brain, it can grow and bear the fruit of material rewards. To mature in this manner, the idea must be nurtured by certain known principles that I will reveal to you.

TO REAP RICHES, YOU MUST FIRST PLANT THE SEED.

Begin your search for profitable deals by becoming familiar with the territory; you must plow before you can plant. You do this by acquiring some knowledge of property values in the area of your operations. *How far out and in which direction do you want to go right now? How much is property worth where you want to go? At what price is raw land being transferred from original owners (as opposed to speculators) to buyers in the areas of concern to you?*

If you're a beginner, the best way to proceed is to obtain a map of your area and determine which of your nearby counties can be characterized as rural, i.e. where people live on farms or in the country as opposed to living in the city or suburbs. Beyond the suburbs, land is always in transition from rural to suburban. Because of heavy speculation in land of this type, you should bypass transition areas if you are to correctly follow the principles set down in this book.

When my first opportunity came, it came in words spoken in the right season, and at the right moment. This combination, as the great Scottish historian, Carlyle, points out, is the mother of ages.

In 1964, shortly after purchasing my first piece of rural land, I was driving back to the city with a friend who was an ambitious young developer. I expressed a latent and persistent desire to own a piece of land bordering the Shenandoah National Park. I was as determined to find it as I was to achieve success in life. This would be a decidedly rural tract, since the parkland would never be developed. My friend knew of a farm that joined the Park; together with a mutual friend and the real estate broker, we went to look at the place. The purpose of the appointment was, as we all knew, to sell me the land. Now, since I would have been in over my head with the investment, I spoke of inviting friends and relatives in on the deal.

I felt we could develop the farm into lots and sell them quickly. I suggested this to my two friends, and at that moment, the idea that had been imbedded in my mind bore the fruit of opportunity. We did develop the land, and I quickly sold all of the lots. In fact, the venture was so successful that we formed a permanent alliance to develop and sell land throughout a wide area. Out of that association came other partnerships and opportunities for making money over a four state area.

Before getting into the economics of the first venture, let me stress the importance of something greater than the profits we made. What happened was of such monumental significance that it dwarfed all of my later accomplishments; yet the key remained a secret to me, only to resurface while I was in a period of writing and research. I was curious about all of those "millionaire" books — the ones that tell you how to become rich. I read them all. At the same time, I researched the "success" books, looking for similarities between my methods and other techniques for becoming rich and successful. I looked back over the lives of rich and successful people I had known or had read about. Somewhere there was a common thread — some invisible strand that, if found, could begin to unravel the mystery of becoming rich and successful. The common thread is this:

> **The rich and successful all know that a specific idea, planted in the recesses of the brain, nourished by determined thought and persistence, will, at some point in time, break through and yield fruitful rewards for you.**
>
> **You must, at that time, set your hands about the task of collecting those rewards or they will be forever lost to you.**
>
> **This cycle begins with a specific idea!**

This secret is succinctly expressed in the title of Napoleon Hill's excellent book, *Think and Grow Rich*. Many times the idea will grow more quickly in the mind of someone else. That is why you must surround yourself with people whose strengths will offset your weaknesses. A stunted idea, germinating in the back of your brain, could, when transplanted into the mind of a trusted associate, become a blossoming garden. When I revealed to my friend my latent desire to own a specific type of land, the idea grew more rapidly in his mind. When the idea surfaced, it bore fruit, and I set about the task of collecting the rewards. Had I failed to act when the opportunity arose, these rewards would have been forever lost to me. Chances are that another cycle would have begun with a new idea, but there is no guarantee that I would have seized the opportunity the second time around. The next time you hear someone complaining that they are plagued with bad luck, or that the "breaks" are against them, remember this little discussion about ideas. Most certainly, they didn't wish or work hard enough or long enough; and when the fruit of opportunity ripened, they let it wither on the vine.

I TOLD MY FRIENDS WE'D ALL BE RICH!!!

After a few spectacularly successful weekends, I rushed back home and shouted to all who would listen, "We'll make $20,000 each before snow falls. We'll all be rich!" I had, indeed, stumbled upon the common thread; and though this was only the beginning (there is more to becoming rich and independent than in discovering a method for making money in a hurry), the first rewards had come my way, and I began the task of collecting them.

The property was sold to us for $36,000, and two old houses were on the tract. The wizardry of the deal was that we had purchased the farm for just 10% down, or $3,600 split three ways. Now this may not sound like a lot of money for each of us to come up with, but $1,200 in those lean years was a formidable sum for me to raise. We cut that figure in half when my friend arranged for the sale to be co-brokered through his father-in-law, a real estate broker. Entry into my first deal, then, had cost me just $600.

When it came time to develop the land, we quickly sold off the two homes. The first house went for $9,500 on three acres. We took a small amount down and held the paper ourselves. (In effect we held a second mortgage.) The second home, on five acres, was sold for $12,000, with the transaction financed through a local savings and loan association.

Since we had arranged to release land from the first mortgage at a rate of $200 per acre, we paid the required $1,000 out of the proceeds of the sale and pocketed roughly $11,000 in cash, less legal expenses. From the balance, we paid back to ourselves the original $600 each that we had invested. (Note that there was no extra charge for releasing the house from the first mortgage, and that few, if any, lawyers today would allow their client to release improved property, such as houses, without a significant amount being paid over and above the per acre release fees.)

Using the seed money obtained from these initial transactions, we built access roads and surveyed the property into tracts of three to five acres. Here's a brief breakdown of the deal, showing exactly how we arrived at the cost of land — our basic product.

```
130 acres @ . . . . . . . . . . . . . . . . . . . . . . . . $36,000
less house No.1 and 3 acres   $ 9,500
less house No.2 and 5 acres   $12,000

                                            −$21,500

cost of land (120 acres)                    $14,500
cost per acre (approx.)                     $121
```

In the mid sixties, there were a few comparable sales of three to five acre tracts in the county where this development took place. We were gambling that we could sell the land in these smaller parcels. Liberal terms were offered to bring in more prospects. Our prices on the subdivided land showed a markup of about five times land acquisition cost, or an average price of approximately $600 per acre.

This transaction illustrates the principle of *Subdivesting*, which can be defined as: *Making maximum profits from a minimum investment in the development and quick sale of subdivided rural land which, in turn, can be resold at a profit.*

You'll notice that I'm *not* talking about buying rural land and holding it with the expectation that you'll make money out of it somewhere down the line. This may *not* be your way to *maximize* profits on your investment. There may be certain tax advantages to holding land for long-term capital gain, but this is a subject best left to your accountant or tax lawyer. When you become active in the development and sale of rural real estate, you will be classified as a dealer under existing tax laws. Hence, you will, for the most part, not be eligible for capital gains treatment; moreover, the premise of this book is that you will be turning land over quickly for profits, and that you will not be holding land for what it will bring you in the future.

Generally, unless you are holding property under a favorable option arrangement, you have your capital tied up in down payments, mortgage payments, taxes, and miscellaneous cost, such as repairs to fences and buildings, and the maintenance of fields and roads. The return on your investment — all things considered — may not be high enough to justify the investment and risk.

A good rule of thumb when acquiring rural land for purposes of *Subdivesting* is to buy only those properties which can be sold immediately at a profit without subdividing, and to buy these properties with a minimum outlay of capital. This is your insurance policy against something going wrong with your subdivision plans, such as newly enacted county ordinances and zoning changes.

Even the most elaborately planned scheme for making windfall profits from rural land can be bottled up by elected or appointed officials who are out to control growth and speculation.

The definition of *Subdivesting* also calls for the *quick sale of subdivided rural land which, in turn, can be sold at a profit.* If you were to chart your success as a *Subdivestor*, you would notice the profit curve flattening in proportion to the length of time you held onto the subdivided parcels. One all-important axiom to remember is that your profits come at the front end — when you first buy the property — not when you sell it. This theory may sound a bit strange to you at first, so let me explain.

When you have mastered the theory of *Subdivesting,* you will envision a plan for disposing of any project you choose. The plan will come to you immediately. You will know at once exactly how you will obtain, develop, and sell any tract of land worthy of your efforts. The plan is, in essence, the substance of your reward.

Now, I want you to think again about our discussion of ideas. Remember that you must think long and hard about something *specific* that you want — a profitable project — and that you must *practice determination* and *persistence* in obtaining this *specific* goal.

When the opportunity presents itself to you, you must set your hands about the task of collecting your reward or it will be forever lost to you.

ACTION POINTS — LESSON 1

1. Memorize the creed practiced by the world's richest and most successful men. (p. 4)

2. Select a county, area, or region in which you would like to live and work. Check newspapers advertising land for sale in that locale for average per-acre price figures. (p. 7)

3. Make a list of your strengths and weaknesses. (If necessary, ask someone close to you for help.) Begin to correct your weaknesses. (p. 9)

4. Memorize the definition of *Subdivesting.* (p. 11)

ALL ABOUT PARTNERS AND KEY MEN

Lesson Number 2
Table of Contents

Assembling Your Team...p. 15
How To Add Strength To Your Efforts
And Offset Your Weaknesses..p. 16
How To Measure Drive And Performance Ability ....p. 16
The Importance Of Partners Sharing The Same General Attitudes .....p. 17
How To Find The Positive Thinker..................................p. 18
The Importance Of Stability In Partners And Key Men............p. 19
The Story Of Fred C. Dobbs...p. 19
Think Twice About Involving Friends And Relatives
In Your Business...p. 20
Four Critical Characteristics That Measure Success Potential ....p. 21
Subdivesting's Four Major Work Areas ....p. 21
The Specialized Background Myth ....p. 22
School Background And Employment Records As
Measures of Aptitude ....p. 22
The Importance Of FINANCING AND ADMINISTRATION
To Your Success ....p. 23
Who's Qualified To Handle LAND ACQUISITION
AND DEVELOPMENT?..p. 24
Successful ADVERTISING AND SALES PROMOTION
Gets You Off The Ground...p. 25
Aim To Head Off Problems In Your
SALES OF SUBDIVIDED LAND...................................p. 27
Action Points ....p. 29

All About Partners and Key Men

One of the decisions you'll have to make early in the game is whether you'll be operating with a partner or partners, or whether you'll hire personnel to do your leg work. If you're fortunate to have a loving and helpful wife who can act effectively as your business partner, this arrangement may be very economical and profitable for you. The important point to remember in this business of *Subdivesting* — and all successful real estate entrepreneurs know this to be true — is that a large organization and high overhead will kill you. I've found that you'll maximize your profits and achieve better balance in your life with no more than one or two partners; and at the same time you should cultivate a group of trusted technical and professional advisors — much like a board of directors — who can supply you with expert advice and counsel in the areas where you may be weak. The group could be composed, for example, of a trusted lawyer, accountant, surveyor, road builder, and other specialists whose services are used in your operations.

I'm going to assume that you have the capability of getting along with people, and that you are capable of learning how to pick the right people for the job. I'll teach you all I know about selecting the right partner(s) and hiring personnel for the jobs you need to get accomplished.

When I was majoring in personnel administration in college, it did not occur to me that I would be hiring and firing people for my own businesses, or that I would be evaluating prospective candidates as partners. I've called on this training continuously in my business career, and I've learned the importance of reading about and understanding human psychology and motivation.

When you realize that key men, hired for the long term, could cost you between a quarter of a million and a half million dollars, you see the value in developing a thorough understanding of people. The selection of partners is even more critical because you end up sharing control as well as financial reward. Remember that a bad partner in business can be just as ruinous as a faulty marriage partner. Here are some pointers on how to select the right partner and key men:

1. **Look for people who will add strength to your efforts and offset your weaknesses.**

Each of us has a mixed bag of attitudes toward life; our motivations vary; we have different levels of stability, maturity, and attitudes for working with people and for performing in various jobs and occupations. Take the time to honestly evaluate your strengths and weaknesses. Once you have completed your own personal inventory of these character traits, you will be better able to judge where strength is needed in your *Subdivesting* team.

How is your drive? Are you a self-starter? If you're strong in these areas, you'll want a partner or key man who cultivates these qualities. Be sure to explore his level of perseverance and intensity. Ask about his life, his hobbies, special interests, family life, etc. He should be a hard driver in everything he touches. Your chief goal in life may be to become independently wealthy; you will not succeed without intense effort from the moment you become involved in *Subdivesting*. I do not mean that you will be chained to a life of drudgery, with little time for pleasure. I'm simply saying that, while you work at it — weekends, 6, 8, 10, months a year — you must give it your all. It is reasonable to assume that you will not make money if you do not get out and hustle, i.e. if you lack drive and self-starting ability. Your failure to generate these qualities will leave your key man uninspired, and he will react in one of three ways: (1) quit (2) take over your business (3) fail to produce enough to offset his salary.

If you are operating with partners, they will become fed up with your lethargy and dispense with you.

Here are some factors to look for when assessing a man's drive and his ability to get himself in gear for maximum performance. Ask him about his early family life. Was it satisfactory? Has he ever had to get out and hustle to make a buck? When did he start to work? Did he work his way through college? What has he done to improve his lot in life? What is he doing now to further his education? When hiring a key man or selecting a partner(s) for your *Subdivesting* team, you should stick to persons who are self-sufficient. You are not looking for people who are out of work or who are itinerant job-hoppers. You do not want problem people around you. They are a drain on your emotions; they sap your effectiveness, contribute to your weaknesses, and — regardless of any strengths they may bring you — are, on balance, less than ideal. Remember this: It is inconsistent with the technique of *Subdivesting* to attract problems. If some land deal is beset with potential traps, you must avoid it. Similarly, if after interviewing an employee, associate, or advisor, you feel he could create potential problems for you, the warning is clear — stop, back off, follow your instincts, and continue looking for someone else.

Your partner(s) or key man must share your same general attitudes toward life. Is he capable of supporting himself, or is he inexorably tied to a salary? Is he willing to learn those facets of the business for which he has little aptitude? Is his marriage secure? What examples can he give you of his persistence? What successes has he achieved? Does his past behavior show driving ambition? Are his goals sufficiently different from yours to avoid conflict and rivalry? Is his personality dissimilar to yours for the same purposes? Remember what Shakespeare said, "Two stars keep not their motions in one sphere."

You will want to associate yourself with people who possess a positive attitude. Pessimistic employees or associates can drag you down physically and mentally. They are habitual complainers. They tend to be overly critical and dissatisfied, and they will contribute to the problems you are trying to avoid. They will continually find fault with the land deals you have under consideration. They may be unduly suspicious of your colleagues and advisors. If they are inclined toward a salaried position, they may not make much more effort than that required to preserve the status quo. They may fear that your "entrepreneurial" instincts are at odds with the real world. Playing it safe could be the easy way out for them.

If you are unfortunate enough to become saddled with a negative-thinking partner, his behavior pattern could reveal a lack of concern for the welfare of others. He may come to believe that people are out to get him. Feeling this way, he could show symptoms of greediness, and he may deal unfairly and ruthlessly with salesmen, contractors, owners of property, and others to whom he must pay a price. He could end up distrusting your own advisors, such as lawyers, accountants, and surveyors. When you go to settle accounts with him, the negative thinking associate will believe you are cheating him. He may threaten you with law suits and harangue endlessly about how he didn't get what was coming to him.

By doing a thorough job at the outset of interviewing potential partners or key men, you can steer clear of the negative thinker.

How can you find the positive thinker? He should have a good attitude toward education, believing that continuing study and regular reading are worthwhile. During the interview, you should search for inaccurate thought patterns — excesses and deficiencies. Inquire about his social life. Generally speaking, moderation is the key to a harmonious relationship. Too much socializing can drain away valuable time and effort; too little social contact can turn a man's thoughts on himself, creating a different sort of person. What are his hobbies? Does he finish what he starts? Does he strive for precision? How about his health? This could be an important factor. If he has a history of periodic illnesses, are they largely psychosomatic, or are they real? What are his views toward religion? Is he an avowed atheist? If so, what higher power than himself does he believe in? Do his political views clash with your own? Does he believe every politician is a crook, or do some actually serve the people first? What about welfare? Does the interviewee believe too strongly one way or the other? Is he capable of moderation? How did he react to military service? Is he bitter about having served? What about his employment history? What is his attitude toward past employers and work areas?

By assessing the interviewee's answers and his reactions to the above questions, you will observe an unmistakable attitude pattern, one that will reveal a tendency toward either positive or negative thinking.

2. Look for stability in partners and key men.

If you're familiar with the book and movie, *The Treasure of the Sierra Madre,* you'll observe in Dobbs (played by Humphrey Bogart), a classic case of instability. You'll be quick to recognize that this is definitely not the kind of man you want as a partner. Dobbs could not adjust to anybody or anything for a prolonged period of time. Evidently he had failed in his family life; he was incapable of sustaining a friendship or of holding down a responsible job; his failure to adjust to life in general was a clear sign of his instability. Yet three rootless dreamers — hell-bent for gold in the Sierra Madre — formed an association that was doomed to failure. Theirs was a partnership, hastily organized, motivated by greed and self-service, and cloaked with mutual suspicion. By far, the least stable of the partners was the erratic Fred C. Dobbs.

By his very actions and past history it was evident that he was unreliable, undependable, and incapable of performing well under stress. He was wildly paranoid and prone to conflict and frustrations when things went wrong. His loyalty was to himself first, last, and always. Yet Dobbs was chosen as a partner because he happened to be in a flop house when the story of a gold mine was being related, and because he just happened to have won a hundred pesos in a lottery. Obviously you will be looking for a partner whose stability does not rise and fall on the basis of money alone. When interviewing or selecting a prospective partner or key man, you should constantly ask yourself this fundamental question: Does he have the necessary stability to handle the job at hand?

Be wary of the job-hopper. Too many changes in jobs or career fields could be an indication of immaturity, a character flaw closely akin to instability. Your prospect may see your offer as a quick chance to become rich, only to leave you poorer in time and effort after sampling the best of your wares. His married life could follow the same erratic pattern. The unstable person believes there is always a better deal over the horizon, whether it be a job or a woman.

You may have to probe deeply to uncover instability in many people, because written applications and superficial interviews cannot reveal how a person has reacted to prolonged periods of trouble, such as emotional upsets in his personal life or stressful conditions on the job. Some indication as to how he has handled these difficult situations may come out in conversation. He may, for example, dwell on personalities, attributing faults to past superiors or cohorts. Rare indeed is the person who admits to his own weaknesses.

It is usually not a good idea to involve friends and relatives in your *Subdivesting* activities for the simple reason that we all have a tendency to overlook and excuse the weaknesses of those closest to us. And when you're wheeling and dealing as a real estate entrepreneur, incurring debt, and gambling for those big profits, you want cool, dispassionate heads around you. Of course, you expect, by following the dictums in this book, to minimize adversity, and to avoid discouragement and prolonged conflict. Just remember that the road to wealth and independence requires a high degree of emotional stability. Some occupations and jobs are low-keyed enough that a person's unstable tendencies are seldom, if ever, revealed. You'll have more time to enjoy the fruits of your labor if you select your partner(s) or key man for the strong qualities he can bring you. Your time is valuable. Don't waste it administering weak and incompetent people who add troubles and detract from the business at hand, which is basically making more money and enjoying money more. And because you cannot deny your social conscience, remember this: There can be no charity without a medium of exchange. In our society that medium is money.

3. Look for partners or key men with aptitude for the job.

Unfortunately there are no aptitude tests which will measure the *Subdivesting* ability of potential partners or key men; nor is it entirely possible to predict the level of their success. Aside from common business sense, analytical and reasoning ability, and imagination, most people of average education who have the ability to express themselves well, and who can get along with others, should be able to succeed, providing they possess the following characteristics:

(1) Positive mental *attitude* (faith)
(2) *Motivation* to succeed (desire)
(3) *Stability* to carry through (persistence)
(4) Emotional *maturity* to lead (responsibility)

Assuming your prospective partner or key man has the required characteristics, you can then evaluate his aptitude for the job or performance category you have in mind. You'll discover that this business of *Subdivesting* can be broken down into four major work areas:

(1) Financing and Administration
(2) Land Acquisition and Development
(3) Advertising and Sales Promotion
(4) Sales of Subdivided Land

Since few persons are experts in all three of these categories, you will find yourself relying on partners or key men to fill the void. Of course, it is possible to buy expertise in each of these areas, as well as in the management of your profits and personal estate. Largely it is a matter of personal preference, depending on your operating style, your personality, the level of profits you wish to make, the amount of time and money you have to spend, and your ability or inability to work closely with others. For purposes of this discussion, I'll assume that you are seeking a partner or a key man to lend strength where you are weak and to contribute to your existing strong points. Even if your name is always on everybody's guest list, and though you're the first one chosen for every committee, you can only gain by selecting someone with the ability to get along with people and to lead and direct them. Extraordinary mental ability, though important to carry out duties at the highest executive level, is usually a secondary consideration — assuming that your man has enough general intelligence to qualify as your partner or key man. Expertise in the aforementioned work areas can be gained through training and experience. Moreover, because the techniques of *Subdivesting* are not taught in any school, specific skills can only be acquired through actual work experience and the study of closely-related subjects, such as real estate financing, direct-response advertising, salesmanship, and accounting.

Just because a man happens to have a background in a field such as banking, accounting, sales, advertising, or real estate does not mean that he will be successful, or that he will be a welcome addition to your *Subdivesting* team. Many competent and intelligent men are unsuited for the type of entrepreneurship that this business requires; often they will fail because of faulty attitude, lack of motivation, general instability, or a low level of maturity. And many highly-skilled businessmen, engineers, lawyers, and accountants fall short as real estate entrepreneurs because the security of a paycheck holds them back.

When evaluating a candidate's aptitude for becoming your partner or key man, his employment history and school record are also used to approximate ability. For example, the progress of a man's career can reveal his aptitude for moving along in the spot you have open for him. Steady advancement in a candidate's career field also can indicate intelligence, growth, and leadership ability — qualities you are definitely looking for. A review of the candidate's school record — aside from offering a clue to his intelligence — can uncover aptitudes for the specific skills you need to round out your *Subdivesting* team. For example, I've found that individuals with an educational background — preparing them to be teachers or educators — are ideally suited for the generalized nature of this business. The analytical training given to engineering students is also very useful when applied to certain aspects of *Subdivesting*. Obviously, I don't mean to imply that you should search out only those persons with aptitudes for teaching and engineering. You could, for example, desperately need a partner or key man with skills in Advertising and Sales Promotion. The candidate you choose may have studied journalism, and he may be leaving a promising career in the newspaper or broadcast industry to join you in your ventures. If you're shorthanded in Financing and Administration, a business executive with an accounting background may turn out to be your ideal man.

I want to point out, again, that it is crucial to select a candidate who can get along well with people, one who can effectively lead and direct them. Remember this: The professional and mechanical skills you need can always be purchased in the open market place. (accountants, surveyors, road builders, lawyers, advertising men, salesmen, etc.) Either you, your partner(s), or your key man must deal effectively with these people and get the most value for your dollar. Sloppy and ineffectual performance on the part of associates will show up in red ink on your balance sheet.

Whether you're bringing in a partner or hiring a key man, you should look to the candidate's record for evidence of a *positive mental attitude*, *motivation* to succeed in life, *stability* to carry through on the jobs he has undertaken, and the emotional *maturity* to lead and direct people. If he has shown *perseverance* and *determination* in overcoming obstacles to reach his desired goals, then chances are he will make a valuable asset to your team.

With a thorough understanding and honest evaluation of your strengths and weaknesses, let's take a look at the four major performance categories you will be concerned with as a *Subdivestor*.

1. FINANCING AND ADMINISTRATION

The ability to deal with banks and lending institutions, investors, sellers, and suppliers of services, such as surveyors and road builders, is critical to your success as a *Subdivestor*. Equally important is the ability to come up with creative financing for your various projects. I'll have more to say about financing in a later chapter, and I'll cite classic examples of how deals were put together using creative thinking. If you're weak in this area, you'll want to bring in a partner or key man who can handle financing. Remember, too, that once a deal is put together there is continual administration of the loan package and subsequent profits, which are usually returned to you in the form of notes or mortgages payable. These notes or mortgages are often discounted, used as collateral for loans, or collected by you or various banks for your own account. You should expand your knowledge of real estate financing if for no other reason than to preserve and protect your gains. I've found that sloppy financing and administration of notes receivable are primary causes of lost profits in the buying and selling of rural land.

2. LAND ACQUISITION AND DEVELOPMENT

Earlier in the book we discussed the critical importance of keeping an accurate record of land and land characteristics to minimize or even eliminate severe risk in the acquisition stages. Now, let's look at the actual components that such a list might include:

1. Physical characteristics of the land
2. Location, Location, Location
3. Profit and risk factors

As you know, some of the basic requirements that purchasers look for when buying land are: road frontage, water frontage, views, potable water, good soil, usable land area, etc. The type of land you select for development and the skill with which you develop the land are crucial in determining potential profits and risk.

Locating a winning piece of rural development property requires no formal training or specialized talent that I know of, other than imagination and a clear sense of what most people are looking for when purchasing rural land. Experience, I've found, is by far the best teacher. Having a background as a rural real estate agent would certainly be helpful in determining what the public at large is looking for at a given point in time. Some recreational land salesmen are also knowledgeable of trends in rural land because of their exposure to large numbers of prospects.

Assuming you have no previous background in real estate, your best approach would be to choose a compatible and competent partner or key man with the expertise you need, and to rely heavily on the SOURCE BOOK, to which I refer in a later chapter.

As a newcomer, you would also want to start with a small project having an uncomplicated financing structure, and one that required minimal or no road building. An example of a simplified project would be a forty acre tract of good land on a paved road with 800 feet of frontage. Say you and your partner(s) buy it for cash and subdivide it into four lots of ten acres, each having 200 feet of frontage. You sell the four lots and make a profit, some of which you reinvest in a second project, possibly somewhat more complicated, but potentially more profitable.

The first project required an outlay of cash — most of which you borrowed from a bank — and an expenditure for survey, advertising, and some legal expense. No great financial wizardry, sales or advertising genius, land planning, or engineering was required to produce a finished product of four lots from the raw material of forty acres. When you're ready for your second project, chances are you'll be more confident about the development aspects of larger tracts of land which, potentially, can yield you greater profits with corresponding minimum effort.

You'll learn more about Land Acquisition and Development in a later chapter.

3. ADVERTISING AND SALES PROMOTION

A simple byword for you to remember goes like this: "You can't sell 'em if you don't see 'em." You could have the greatest little subdivision going, but if you can't get the customers out to the site, you're shot down before you get off the ground. Napoleon Hill, in his book, *Think and Grow Rich*, talks of assembling a "Master-Mind" group of people who possess the talents you need for the creation and carrying out of your plans for making money.

If you have a flair for advertising or copywriting and are good at coming up with promotional schemes, this could be your main function in the "Master-Mind" group. Whether or not this is your bag, you should read or review any and all books and magazines you can get your hands on that deal with direct marketing. You'll find a list of suggested reading material on advertising in the Appendix. We're concerned, first of all, with the *direct* marketing of your subdivided parcels. This implies that you will offer your product to the consumer through the most direct method available. For example, you run an ad for a specific piece of property. You describe the property and list the price and terms. The customer comes out. Bang! — Somebody sells him. Sales, you'll recall, is your fourth major performance area.

You could be successful as a *Subdivestor* by skillfully performing in the first two work areas — Financing and Administration as well as Land Acquisition and Development — and farming out Advertising and Sales Promotion and Sales, itself, to a qualified real estate outfit in each of your operating locales. The problem here is that so few rural real estate agencies understand the techniques of direct marketing. Most handle property at a more leisurely pace than you would want. They do a lot more showing and listing. Nevertheless, I have had some success using qualified agents, who have become acquainted with the *Subdivesting* technique. If you don't plan to write your own ads and plan your own promotions, your best bet would be to locate a real estate agency or sales group of known integrity that is experienced in the quick sales of land. They would be a lot closer to understanding your concept of development than, say, an agency that specializes in homes, where a great deal of showing and shopping takes place. Remember the definition of *Subdivesting:*

> **Making maximum profits from a minimum investment in the development and (quick) sale of subdivided rural land which, in turn, can be resold at a profit.**

The word "quick" has been bracketed to emphasize, again, that you need to turn over your subdivided parcels as quickly as possible in order to achieve the level of success you desire.

In the chapter on Advertising and Sales Promotion, I will reveal the secrets of successful direct-response advertising and show you examples of ads and promotion schemes that produced quick response in record time and at minimum cost. This is a very crucial part of your journey to wealth and independence, and the methods used in promoting what you have can often make the difference between instant success and instant failure. If your ads and promotion schemes are skillfully done, the sales job is made that much easier.

4. SALES OF SUBDIVIDED LAND

In the past, many people who responded to advertisements for the sale of rural, "recreational" property were "shoehorned" into lots by salesmen using high-pressure tactics and subtle coercion as principle selling tools. Now, in an era of consumer awareness and protection, when full disclosure and truth-in-advertising are expected and often mandated by government, the transfer of property from seller to buyer takes place with far less sweat-loss and arm-twisting.

No doubt the science of selling will continue to be refined and upgraded; master salesmen will continue to be spawned; and consumers will come to appreciate more and more the artful qualities of a good and honest sales presentation by a persuasive salesperson. The fact of the matter is that most of us *want* to be sold, or we wouldn't be out looking in the first place. When we come across a convincing salesperson who has his facts and figures straight, and who has all of his arguments in proper order, we tend to listen. Efficiency is a quality that we all admire, and if we are convinced that the salesperson is rendering the fullest quantity and best quality for the money, we are more apt to sign our names to a contract and smile long after the sale is made. Remember that a thorough and effective sales job performed at the outset will result in fewer headaches for you later on.

As a *Subdivestor,* you are not only interested in the *quick* sale of your subdivided parcels — and good salespeople are essential to this end — but you should be concerned with the buyer's frame of mind *after* the sale. If the purchaser feels that he has been pressured, or if he comes to believe that his purchase was never really what he wanted, then you risk losing the sale before closing, or you face possible default on the mortgage or deed of trust. Moreover, since referrals by contented customers are a *major* source of sales, you lose time and income here, too. A faulty salesperson or sales organization can invite the very trouble you are seeking to avoid.

To minimize your troubles, you should be constantly refining your methods to weed out problem salespeople. Despite a high volume of production, if a large number of sales do not hold up, and if you find yourself drawn into disputes and controversy between salesmen, or if you're battling complaints by purchasers, then it's time for you to back off. You don't need problems. Your purpose is clear — to make a maximum amount of money with a minimum amount of effort and to survive with your integrity and peace-of-mind intact.

If you don't plan to sell your own land, and if a partner or key man is not utilized for this task, you will end up purchasing sales talent just as you would contract for surveys and road building. Regardless of who you use to sell your land, you should have a sales plan worked out in your mind well in advance of survey, and ideally, before land acquisition. The soundest way I know of for your plan to be carried out effortlessly, and with a minimum of recurring problems, is for you to select land that sells itself. You lay the groundwork for this by doing a thorough job in performance area no. 2 — Land Acquisition and Development. We'll have more to say about sales in the chapter devoted to that topic.

Summing up what I've told you so far about the people you choose for partners or a key man, make certain that you consider all of the points I have stressed when making this all-important selection. Don't rush and, above all, don't gamble. Believe me, if you do, you are gambling away your time and treasure — two things most precious in your life.

You are beginning to get a pretty good picture of what your steady trip to wealth and independence will entail by now. It's obvious that you must get started off on the right foot; so be careful when selecting the people around you. They can make or break your well-planned efforts.

Finally, don't let sympathy play any part in your selection. If this emotion becomes involved, the only one you may feel sympathy for in the near future will be yourself. Don't let friendship interfere with the making of a sound choice. Friends are the greatest thing in the world at times, but one of the worst things imaginable is to have one working for or with you who is just not capable of doing the job. Anyone who has ever had to fire a friend knows exactly what I'm talking about. You can easily hire a friend, but when it comes to firing them, the individual usually does not remain your friend for long. He may even become your worst enemy.

This area of your trip to wealth and independence is crucial. Treat the decision of hiring a partner(s) or key man with the respect this move

ACTION POINTS -- LESSON 2

1. Think about the people you know who may be helpful to you as a *Subdivestor*. If you don't know anyone with the skills and talents you need, begin your search now.

2. Memorize the four basic characteristics of a satisfactory partner or key man. (p. 21)

HOW DO I FIND PROFITABLE LAND DEALS?

Lesson Number 3
Table of Contents

The SOURCE BOOK — How It Can Be Your Key To Profits ....p. 33
The Six Major Sources For Rural Land Deals ....p. 34
Five Reasons To Subscribe To County And Regional Newspapers .....p. 34
How To Make Quick Decisions With Your ACTION FILE ....p. 36
Eight Important Items For Your ACTION FILE. ....p. 36
The Importance of SELECTIVITY In Building Wealth ....p. 37
Learning To Pay Yourself First..............................p. 37
The OBJECTIVITY FACTOR — Why It Is Crucial To Your Success....p. 38
The Importance of GOAL DEFINITION ....p. 39
GOAL ORIENTATION — Your Key To The
Accumulation And Preservation of Wealth ....p. 40
Defining Goals On The Basis of Needs And Wants................p. 41
GOAL (DIS) ORIENTATION — A Common, But Curable, Ailment....p. 43
How You Can Begin To Change Your Life ....p. 44
How Goal *Visualization* Can Be Pulled Into Play For You ....p. 45
Your STATEMENT OF PHYSICAL GOALS —
How It Can Bring You Riches...............................p. 46
The Power Of Suggestion ....p. 47
The Process Required To Implement Your Goal Plan ....p. 48
Your STATEMENT OF EXCHANGE —
You Must *Give* Before You Can *Get*..........................p. 48
Action Points ....p. 49

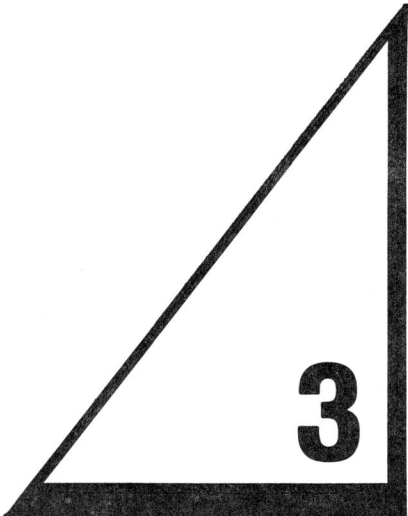

How Do I Find Profitable Land Deals?

Here are some tips on how the insiders scout for rural land deals that return those quick five-figure profits with a minimum of work. First off, every source the pros use is available to you. You simply need to acquaint yourself with these sources until you are familiar with property values. Remember this: *The real pros in rural land speculation are so busy making money that they don't have time to prospect all of these sources all of the time. You can't fail to make money if you proceed in an orderly manner and follow my instructions.*

Obtain a large loose leaf notebook and label it – *SOURCE BOOK*. All of the interesting rural land deals you come across should be entered in this book. Some of the entries will be handwritten or typed; others will be pasted-down ads, clipped from the classified sections of newspapers. In effect, the *SOURCE BOOK* will be your own charting service, acquainting you with the movements and prices of rural land. Not many pros know the value of this *SOURCE BOOK*, so you will soon move ahead of them in earnings if you faithfully maintain such a journal.

Here are the usual sources for rural land deals:

1. **The classified section of major metropolitan newspapers.**
   You should develop a habit of scanning such categories as: Farms, Farms & Land, Farms & Acreage, Country Property, Mountain Property, and Lots & Acreage.

2. **Rural Real Estate Agencies**
   Do not carry your *SOURCE BOOK* when discussing your interests with real estate brokers and salesmen. You will be immediately tagged as a "looker" and given second-rate treatment.

3. **County tax maps**
   All rural counties maintain land maps showing who owns what and how much each parcel of land is taxed. You can write to the owners of desirable parcels and inquire if the land is for sale and at what price. Indicate that you are a serious buyer and not a real estate person seeking a listing. This source will require some follow-up and record keeping, but it is often a gold mine of potential deals.

4. **County and regional newspapers**
   You should subscribe to the rural newspapers in those counties within your operating area. This will be critical to your success for the following reasons:

   a. Local auctions and foreclosures are often advertised only in these papers, and frequently a deal can be picked up at minimum cost with only few competing bidders.

   b. Most local real estate agencies advertise regularly in local papers because of the lower cost. You will get an overview of property for sale within a given area, and you can quickly spot those agencies offering consistently attractive deals.

   c. Occasionally a desirable tract of land will be advertised for sale "by owner" with a price tag below market value. Out-of-state owners, unfamiliar with local price trends, may place ads of this type. Or the owner may be anxious to sell in a hurry because he needs the money or is relocating.

d. Changes and proposed revisions to local legislation are given space in county and regional newspapers. The land you buy could be affected by new or altered zoning/subdivision requirements, health standards, soil and erosion control measures, etc. As a professional land investor, you cannot afford *not* to be informed.

e. As an "outsider" you should familiarize yourself with local issues and growth patterns so that you can accurately predict future price trends.

5. **Large Corporations and Timber Companies**
Often the largest tracts of under-utilized land within a given area are held by mining, utility, and timber companies. Railroads are also known to control large blocks of surplus land. These companies are not in the business of buying and selling land for profit, and because of their size and diversified holdings, they find it almost impossible to keep up with changing land values. The management of these companies is structured to extract something from the land that will yield a profit to the stockholders. For example, a mining company is obviously interested in mining the natural resources on its property. That's what the company does best. When the mine is played out, the company moves its operations to more profitable mining areas. From the company's point of view, the worked-over land may be viewed as a dead asset, since money from its sale could logically be put to more profitable use elsewhere within the company.

For similar reasons, a timber company may be quite willing to sell its cut-over properties at a very reasonable price; or a railroad company may decide to dispose of excess lands along abandoned rights-of-way. In most cases these properties are not in the hands of local real estate brokers. If a tract of land looks ripe for *Subdivesting,* and you find it is held by a large corporation or timber company, you can obtain their mailing address from the County Tax Assessors Office and write to their Property Management Department and inquire if it's for sale. It's worth a try. You just may turn up a bargain.

6. **Word of Mouth**
As you become acquainted with local business and professional people, such as surveyors, road builders, and lawyers, the word

will get out that you're a buyer of land. And since there will always be sellers, some more sophisticated than others, an occasional deal will come your way. Many times, after you have just purchased a piece of rural property, an adjacent owner will look you up and inform you that his place is for sale.

Make quick decisions with your ACTION FILE

Now I'm going to tell you how to make a fast decision on a property deal without leaving the comfort of your office. You can't afford the time and expense of scouting potentially profitable land without consulting your *ACTION FILE*. This file is a county-by-county breakdown of the following data:

1. County road map
2. Current subdivision ordinance
3. Soil map (if available)
4. Zoning laws (if any)
5. Area topographical maps
6. Updated county planning data (from Planning Commissions)
7. Soil and Erosion Control legislation (from SCS)
8. Current, pending, or proposed subdivision legislation (from local newspapers)

All of the above data from each county can be assembled in one file folder; and when a piece of property looks hot to you, you can often accept or reject it by consulting your files. This is the way to success and big money in rural land speculation. Not many of the pros have disciplined themselves enough to maintain an *ACTION FILE*. And here's another plus for you if you're really anxious to free yourself from the necessity of working for someone else. All businesses have filing systems; they're necessary, believe me. If you begin to assemble the above data in an orderly manner and keep your files current, you can't fail to outdistance the pros who are pulling in $50-100,000 a year in rural land transactions and making their share of fumbles.

Another secret to making money in rural land — one that many investors overlook — is that of *SELECTIVITY*. It should be obvious to you by now that, if you cultivated the five primary sources of land acquisition, that you would be swamped with potential deals. Remember this: NEVER GET YOURSELF IN A POSITION WHERE YOU *MUST* HAVE A DEAL GOING. Your good judgment — which is essential for building wealth — can vanish in times of panic.

Years ago, when I operated a large development corporation, the regional managers would bring deals to me and reason that because their salesmen had little left to sell, the corporation should locate a project for them. Here is clearly the case of the tail wagging the dog. On one occasion, we purchased some mountain land — much of it too steep for development — primarily because it was cheap, and because our salesmen and the regional manager needed to be kept productive. As you may suspect, the project was a loser, and we were forced to dump the property at close to our acquisition cost when cash flow problems crept up on us.

My point is — and if you remember this well, you'll certainly not lose those hard-won profits — that *YOU MUST PAY YOURSELF FIRST*. You can donate to charities, assist others in business, and this spirit of helpfulness can make you feel good; but if others persuade you to override good judgment in land acquisition, you risk failure.

Think of each deal you enter into as a small battle in a great war. Of course, you want to win the war — your own struggle for independence and financial security — but you must not lose sight of each and every battle. A faulty judgment on a land deal could cost you the war. I've seen it happen time and again, especially to developers who had over-extended themselves.

One fellow I know had grand and glorious dreams about creating an environmentally-sound and aesthetically-pure recreational community. Environmentalists loved the concept; architects were ecstatic over plans to harmonize their creations with the great outdoors. Developers' associations praised the venture as the wave of the future; salesmen took up the call and swore their ship would soon be coming in. The developer sailed blindly ahead, confident that his course was just and right. Suddenly, he was becalmed by planning agencies and governmental officials who felt threatened by higher density and a rising tax base. With his sales flattened, he soon ran out of cash. His ship of fortune developed leaks — too many for him to plug. His supporters, sensing impending doom, jumped ship. Suppliers came upon the listing vessel and demanded payment. Lawyers moved in for the kill. In a desperate gamble, the developer grabbed onto the bankruptcy laws and reached relative safety — though he had lost his fortune.

The lesson here, of course, is that the OBJECTIVITY FACTOR had been lost by the developer. To build wealth in rural land speculation you must not allow subjective judgment to influence the decision-making process. Consider again the definition of *Subdivesting,* your technique for successfully investing in rural land:

> **Making maximum profits from a minimum investment in the development and quick sale of subdivided rural land which, in turn, can be resold at a profit.**

Let's see how this technique could have saved the developer from going under and enabled him to greatly multiply his fortune. First of all, his profit projections were paper figures, and the ratio of net profits to overall costs was modest. His invested capital was abnormally high, with no immediate expectation of return. Quick sales could not be made because too many approvals were required from government agencies and bodies. Even if a sales program had been launched, the retail price on the subdivided lots and constructed units would have been out of line with existing property values in that area. To reach the necessary volume of sales, the developer could have turned to a high-powered, high-pressure sales and marketing organization, thereby driving up the retail price even further; but there would be no way the lots and units could have been sold at a profit in the forseeable future. And since sales made under pressure and duress are weak to begin with, the sales figures would lack the credibility to withstand the reality of fixed and recurring costs. The developer was doomed to failure.

As you can see, this example of rural land development violates the principles embodied in the definition of *Subdivesting,* a proven investment technique which, if followed correctly, is your "can't lose way to wealth and independence through rural land."

Here are the other key words you've learned so far:

1. **SOURCE BOOK** — Your charting service — an up-to-date scrap book showing you what is or was for sale; where; when; and at what price.

2. **ACTION FILE** — Your quick decision file — a county by county breakdown of data affecting the acquisition and subdivision of land.

3. **SELECTIVITY** — Your ability to choose profitable deals — a cultivated quality requiring the absence of extraneous pressures during periods of decision.

4. **OBJECTIVITY FACTOR** — Your ability to analyze deals without bias or prejudice — an acquired state of mind where decisions are reached dispassionately.

All of the books dealing with success, opportunity, and money-making stress the importance of *GOAL DEFINITION*. You obviously have some idea of where you want to go in life and how long you can spend getting there. If you've never written down your goals — both long and short term — you should begin now. Without *GOAL DEFINITION*, it will not be possible for you to achieve the level of financial independence you desire.

Back in the early sixties, when I first stumbled into rural land development, I found myself making a great deal of money and achieving phenomenal success. I was long on success and determination, but short on goals. Deals kept falling into my lap — more than I could handle by myself — and each turned a handsome profit. Money was pouring in. I literally picked up partners off the street and gave them half the pie. I had little idea where all of this was leading. All I seemed concerned with at the time was opportunity — never in my lifetime had I been given such a chance to make money.

Suddenly I had surrounded myself with a lot of people who shared the same concern — making money — and I was the fountainhead of it all. Well, one day I woke up and found that the money supply had been capped by the genius in government. It became increasingly difficult to sell or borrow on our mortgages, notes, and deeds of trust on unimproved land; and without the green grease, our corporation came to an abrupt halt. Sorry, no more land acquisition. No more fancy salaries. Overhead had to be cut to the bone. Everyone was out on the street. We'd passed *go* for the last time.

I'm going to pass on to you a valuable lesson about that experience, so that when you find yourself with a lot of profitable deals in hand you can maximize your return. The lesson for me is simply that I could have become a millionaire five years earlier had I practiced *GOAL ORIENTATION*. Five years! Think of how much money and effort I dropped because I failed to grasp this simple secret of success.

The lesson for you is that *GOAL ORIENTATION* must be firmly fixed in your mind before you can successfully apply the principles of *Subdivesting*. Establish goals and stick to them, and you'll find those profits sticking to your pockets rather than slipping away from you.

How do you go about establishing goals? How do you know where you're going if you don't know how to get there? At this point, you may know nothing at all about rural land. You may have little, if any, investment capital. How can you possibly write down any goals?

First of all, when I speak of goals, I'm talking about two distinct types, both to be set down on a long and short term basis:

(1) **Personal goals** — new car, house, beach home, airplane, farm, boat, vacation, bills paid, job promotion, etc.

(2) **Subdivesting goals** — How many deals you can handle profitably based on available and acquired capital and on the amount of time you can afford to spend.

In addition to writing down and fixing these two types of goals in your mind, you must further separate them on the basis of needs and wants. You may, for example, *need* a new car and *want* for a boat. Or you may *need* to have a profitable deal going but *want* for an opportunity much larger than you can afford. (Remember! You may *need* a deal to make a lot of money, but you should not — because of outside persuasion — be forced into feeling that a deal is *necessary*. You should never feel that you *must* have a deal going. If you sense this loss of objectivity, your first instinct should be to back off from the deal.)

For proof that GOAL ORIENTATION can work effectively for you, I refer you to any proponent, writer, or teacher of Success Motivation and to any self-made millionaire you can name. In the Bibliography of this book, you'll find a listing of books dealing with making money and achieving success. All of them state that the foundation of wealth and independence begins with the definition of goals. This is your road map. It shows you where you're going. Next is to get yourself in tune and filled up with proper motivation. If you fill your mind with the right attitudes, habits, and actions, you'll be on your way. Anything else will result in slow starts, erratic performance, sluggishness, and non-movement.

When I decided to set down goals for myself, I finally got in gear and moved ahead. Here are some specific instances of how GOAL ORIENTATION has worked for me.

1. In 1970, after fighting my way back on my feet, I decided that I wanted to take a trip around the world. In January 1971, I took my wife, my son, and my maid on an extended three month trip to three continents.

2. In 1972, I made up my mind to write a book. After spotting an article I had written, the editor of a major publishing house called me and asked that I write a book for them.

3. In 1973, I planned three vacations. I took four, one a five week tour of the Alps.

4. In 1974, I set my sights on two primary goals: The purchase of a farm and an extended tour of Africa. I returned from a fabulous trip and bought one of the best farms in the county — using none of my own capital!
5. In 1975, I wanted to raise $150,000 outside of my own income to build my dream home, complete with pool and bath house. I raised $200,000, put in seven bathrooms, and added an airstrip to my estate, complete with hanger, in addition to building the pool and bath house as originally planned.
6. In 1976, my goal was a trip to Alaska and the Yukon. I treated my family to the adventure, threw in Hawaii on a whim, and fulfilled quickie goals of beach and ski vacations. I worked less than nine months that year.
7. In 1977, I sat down at the beginning of the year and mapped out an ambitious program of leisure: Two ski vacations, three summer vacations and a fall sojourn in New York. Among the places we enjoyed were Colorado, England, Scotland, Ireland, France, Nags Head, N.C., and the Carribean. Our summer cruise took us to South America, the only major continent we had yet to visit.
8. In 1978, I decided to publish three books and to make them best sellers. Two were written by me, and all are enjoying healthy sales.

Obviously it is not enough to set your goals and to wait for them to be fulfilled. You must have the means to accomplish their fulfillment. The means I use is *Subdivesting;* but before I discovered this well-head of money and leisure time and began developing its principles, I was literally spinning my wheels in the business world. You may be doing the same thing in your present profession or job.

Consider this point for a moment. It can apply directly to your situation. Say you're a school teacher; you're fed up with your profession. You need more money and there's no hope on the horizon for obtaining the material things you desire. Bills seem to mount up faster than you can pay them. You consider getting a second job. You have a vague goal of making more money to meet your bills or maybe being able to save a few bucks for a new car, vacation, down payment on a home, whatever.

The second job taxes your energies even further. You quickly spend what extra money you make and bills continue to flutter down on you like snowflakes.

One day, in a vague pursuit of a dream, you drive out into the countryside to look at some land. You think that having a place in the country would be nice for the kids and maybe help you to relax. Of course, you really don't know how you would pay for the property even if you bought it, or how you could possibly find time to relax when you are working two jobs. You might say that you're the victim of — among other common ailments — *GOAL (DIS)ORIENTATION*. Most of your decisions lack substance — they are vague. You do not have your goals *visualized* or focused firmly in your mind. You fail in this regard, of course, because you do not feel you have the means to perform adequately or positively enough to reach any significant goals you may set down for yourself.

On this particular excursion of yours — where you are wandering aimlessly out into the countryside in search of a vague dream — you chance to meet me. You see that I am evidently happy in my work. It doesn't appear to you that what I do is work at all. I'm out in the fresh air all the time; you've noticed you can see the sky again. You see beautiful scenes everywhere. The air smells clean. You note the quiet while I'm taking you to see some country property. You observe that my work involves taking drives through the countryside and into the mountains — this is your own idea of play, not work.

You get to know me better and learn that I also fly around in my own plane, looking at the beautiful scenes from another dimension. You learn that I used to live in the city and that I once fought for a living just like you. Now I live on a farm and work at doing what I want to do, and my hours are my own. You see that I am in complete control of my life.

We talk on, and you express an interest in changing professions — maybe getting into something like what I'm doing.

A goal is crystallizing in your mind, but it is still vague like your other goals.

I decide to help you. My suggestion is that you come out on weekends to familiarize yourself with what I do and how I do it, and to earn money by selling rural property.

You should, at this point, establish two immediate goals in your mind. These goals — one long term, one short term — should be *specific*. Avoid vagueness and generalities, even if you are, in your own mind, a bit unsure as to *exactly* what you want and when you would like to accomplish the goals. Remember, goals can always be updated and revised.

Here's how GOAL ORIENTATION can be pulled into play for you in this situation. And it can mean the difference between floundering around for many years — maybe not succeeding at all — and consistent achievement of things you set out to accomplish. Your immediate long-term goal is to quit your job and to obtain a position selling rural land. Now you don't mean to eventually quit sometime and maybe go to work somewhere out in the country for someone who may be able to help you get started selling rural land. This type of thinking can accurately be termed GOAL PLODDING, rather than GOAL PLOTTING.

Anyway, you see the point I'm trying to make. You should plan to quit your job at a *specific* point in time — say a year — and you should target that date on a calendar. Good! Now you can begin getting your affairs in order. Next, you know *exactly* whom you're going to work for — or with — and where that man's office is located. (If circumstances change, you can always revise your goals.) You know *exactly* where you're going to be working. You know the town, the county, and whether your activities will take place in the country, the mountains, or at the seashore. You will, of course, have other long-term goals, but we will be getting to them later on.

Now let's go to your immediate short-term goal. Remember, you had expressed interest in what I was doing, and I decided to help you. O.K.; your short-term goal is to go to work with me on weekends and to earn a specific amount of money. Again, you should set down the amount of extra money you want to make. Take into consideration the opportunities that will be available to you as a part-timer, the amount of money you will need to set aside to make the transition to full-time in your new career field, and the amount of time you can comfortably devote to your part-time activities.

The situation I have just cited is an example of goal *visualization*. The reason it will work for you — as it has worked for me and other successful persons — is that you can actually see (visualize) your goal objects. They are not fuzzy or vague. Some success motivators encourage their students to always carry a new $50 or $100 bill around with them and to study it, fondle it, rub it against their cheek, crumple it up, listen to it crackle, etc. The theory being that you must *visualize* money if money is your goal.

Let's try right now to set down a few goals for yourself. At this time we're concerned mainly with your wants and needs (physical goals). When you have begun to practice the principles in this book, you will need to set out definite *Subdivesting* goals for yourself. Right now it's important that we set down these *physical goals* before we go on. Later in the book I'll start you on your first deal, and you'll return to these goals. As a matter of fact, you'll be constantly upgrading your goals as you achieve higher levels of success. You may also reach certain goals sooner than expected, and you'll be rethinking them. Sometimes you'll be extending the time frame for accomplishing your goals. This is to be expected. The important thing is to begin. Time and tide wait for no one.

I have made it a habit of setting down my *physical* goals twice a year — in January and June. In addition, I'm always adding mini-goals along the way. I repeat these goals orally night and day until they are achieved. Sometimes I have to modify my goals, but in nearly every case I have achieved what I needed or wanted. (We'll discuss intangible goals and character improvement in the final chapter of this course. At that time I'll give you my proven success formula, which can be applied to any career field you may choose.)

Here's how to begin: Copy your own version of the following statement and fill in the blanks with your own needs and desires, along with the deadlines for achieving these goals. Be realistic. For example, don't request a Lear Jet right away. Begin with a smaller plane. The Lear Jet can be one of your long-term goals. Don't ask for a million dollars by tomorrow. Instead ask to be worth a million dollars within, say, five years. Right now you may feel you are capable of increasing your net worth by at least two hundred thousand a year. You may want to bank at least $50,000 of that figure. If you're hung up on fancy cars, by all means ask to be driving a new Mark IV or Cadillac within, say, six months. This is a realistic goal; if necessary, you could always lease one. Remember, these goals must become obsessions if they are to be achieved. You must find a way to fulfill them. The saddest failures in life are those who lack the will to succeed. There is simply too much evidence attesting to the value of "goal-power" for this simple principle of success to be ignored or disbelieved.

Once you have filled out your personalized Statement of Physical Goals, go someplace where it is quiet, and where you can be alone. Repeat the statement orally. Do this before you go to bed at night and again in the morning. This process will be your individual affirmation of faith — faith that you believe you can achieve these goals. If you're a church-goer, you are familiar with this process. When the congregation rises to repeat orally their affirmation of faith in God, they do it unashamedly. It is an age-old technique for imbedding a belief into the subconscious mind. Unfortunately, for many church-goers, their faith tends to wane because the affirmation is repeated only once a week at most.

STATEMENT OF PHYSICAL GOALS (Sample)

On or before *(Month/Day/Year,)* I will have *(amount)* in the bank which I will earn in varying amounts and deposit accordingly.

By *(long term date)* I will have *(amount)* in the bank and will begin to invest half of it in *(form of investment)*.

My income in *(year)* will be at least *(desired amount)*.

During *(year)* I will take at least *(No.)* vacations: winter, *(No.)*; spring, *(No.)*; summer, *(No.)*; fall, *(No.)*.

By *(date)* I will resign my job and go to work with *(name)* whose office is located at *(address)* in *(city)*.

By *(date)* I will have developed a promotional idea for the sale of *(product)* which will lead to a partnership or self-sufficiency.

I will be a working partner or independent operator in *(field of endeavor)* by *(date)*.

(cont.)

On or before *(date)* I will move into a *(cost)* house in the *(section)* of *(community)*, which I have determined to be the best location for me and my family at this point in our lives.

By *(date)* I will have installed a *(pool, tennis court, etc.)* at my home.

By *(date)* I will be driving a new *(make of car)* and my wife will be driving a new *(make of car)*.

By *(date)* I will own a *(luxury item)*.

Now that you have written down your *physical goals*, it should be evident to you that you must render something in return for their fulfillment. You have asked for substantial rewards. What are you prepared to promise and deliver in return for the achievement of these goals?

All of us have certain unused or latent talents, skills, and capabilities which, in effect, amount to untapped energies. Think for a moment of your own hidden energy sources. Take inventory in your mind. This act — *taking mental stock of yourself* — is the first of three steps you must take to apply the power of *suggestion*. Your second step is to deliver this inventory to your subconscious mind through the *written and spoken word*. Write down your talents, skills, and capabilities, and orally promise to deliver them in return for the fulfillment of your goals. Your third step in utilizing the power of *suggestion* is to take *action*.

Your body can be likened to a river — sometimes placid, then flowing swiftly into rapids, and finally plunging into a deep gorge, where the swirling water is tamed and released for its peaceful journey to the great ocean. Think of all the wasted energy if the river is not used to power generators, which in turn supply you with an even greater source of energy — electricity. I make this comparison to emphasize the importance of *action* for the achievement of your goals. It will not be enough to write down your goals and repeat them to yourself if you are not prepared to follow through. *The power of suggestion will not take hold of your life until you commit yourself to ACTION.*

All of us can relate stories of men and women who have accomplished great things in their short lives. Upon close examination of these lives we see that their great accomplishments were achieved with a concentration of effort that, to idle spectators whose goals were ill-defined, looked like insanity. Those who have accomplished great things in life have understood and applied the power of *suggestion*. And since *suggestion* is the handmaiden to *enthusiasm* — a vital component in the science of influencing yourself and others — you can understand how rich and powerful personalities have achieved their substantial goals in life.

A word diagram follows which summarizes at a glance the process required to implement your goal plan:

Once the above correlation is understood, you can then draft a statement similar to the one below, wherein you promise to render certain services in exchange for the fulfillment of your goals. Your *Statement of Exchange* should be written out and read aloud immediately after repeating your *Statement of Physical Goals*.

STATEMENT OF EXCHANGE

In exchange for these rewards I will perform to the best, highest, and fullest of my ability for the benefit of those receiving my services as *Subdivestor, real estate broker, salesman of . . . whatever, contractor, etc.*

I believe that I will achieve these goals. I believe it so strongly that I can now see them coming true before my very eyes. Their accomplishment will come to me in direct proportion to my efforts expended to achieve these goals. I will be alert to any and all opportunities or plans that will lead me to the achievement of these goals. I will recognize these opportunities and plans when they present themselves to me, and I will act upon them when they are received.

I accept the loan of thankfulness for any and all benefits given to me, and I will repay that loan by bringing happiness and humble service to others less fortunate than myself.

Now that you have written down both statements, keep them handy at all times until you have committed them to memory. Revise and upgrade the statements when new goals are needed, when old ones are accomplished, and when the nature of your services changes in any way. Refer to these statements at least twice a day, preferably before you go to bed at night, and again in the morning. Remember, this must be done orally. These statements should be your constant companions; treat them as you would new born children — give them the attention they need and the absolute care, handling, and effort they demand.

ACTION POINTS — LESSON 3

1. Begin a *SOURCE BOOK*. (p. 33)

2. Start an *ACTION FILE*. (p. 36)

3. Decide how much capital you can comfortably raise for your first *Subdivesting* venture.

4. Prepare a *Statement of Physical Goals* and vow to repeat the statement at least twice a day (preferably morning and evening). You will be enlarging your statement with self-improvement commitments as you proceed through this course. (p. 46)

5. Memorize the word diagram on p. 48, which summarizes the process required to implement your goal plan.

6. Prepare a *Statement of Exchange* and vow to repeat it aloud immediately after repeating your *Statement of Physical Goals* (and ancillary self-improvement commitments). (p. 48)

THE PURCHASE OF RURAL LAND

Lesson Number 4
Table of Contents

The Ideal Ratio Of Water Frontage Or Road Front
To Back Land .... p. 53
The Basic Elements Of The FEASIBILITY CHECK LIST .... p. 54
How The FEASIBILITY CHECK LIST
Can Give You A Winning Edge .... p. 54
The Ten Components Of The FEASIBILITY CHECK LIST
And Their Top Scores .... p. 55
Fine-Tune Your Scoring With The QUALITY
REFERENCE SHEET .... p. 56
Why Certain Projects Should Be Rejected
Regardless Of A High Score .... p. 58
The Jones Farm Projects (An Analysis) .... p. 59
The ACTION FILE In Action .... p. 63
The Basic Exemptions To The
Interstate Land Sales Disclosure Act .... p. 65
The Jones Farm Project Revisited .... p. 67
How To Correctly Score A Project .... p. 69
The Importance Of First Impressions .... p. 69
Buying Property At Auction – How To Score A Winner .... p. 73
Action Points .... p. 76

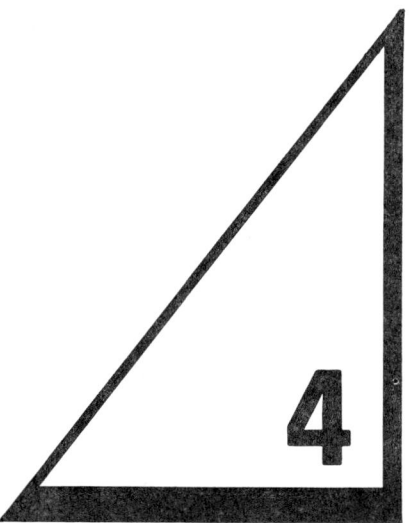

The Purchase of Rural Land

Here is a check list for the purchase of rural land that will steer you around potentially marginal projects and head you straight for the big profit-makers. Once you've passed this hurdle, your analysis will turn to a LAND ACQUISITION CHECK LIST which is revealed in a subsequent chapter.

Aside from the usability factor, the two most critical features sought by purchasers of rural land are water and roads. Is there water on the property? What kind of access will I have? Therefore, when considering a tract of land for *Subdivesting*, the more usable waterfront and roadfront, the better. The ideal ratio, I have found, is at least one mile of frontage for each hundred acres of back land. This can be your standard. Obviously, not many deals will present this ideal ratio; a few will be better than ideal; most will offer less frontage than you would desire.

The following rating system gives an optimum 100 points for the theoretically best *Subdivesting* deal in the world. A rating of 50 would give the deal a 50/50 chance of producing profits. If you could, for example, realistically rate the project at 75 or 80 points, it should be a winner. For beginning *Subdivestors,* I recommend rejection of any deal you rate below 70 points, because you may not have the experience to accurately rate your potential projects.

This rating system has been developed to give you an edge over the pros in this business, who oftentimes operate as gamblers and speculators, rather than as careful investors. They do very nicely with a system based on experience and expertise which allows them a comfortable margin of error. You cannot afford to lose. You must win every time. When you have become a huge success, you may want to throw away this course. Then you can forget my system and develop one of your own. But right now, let's see how my rating system can work for you.

The FEASIBILITY CHECK LIST is comprised of three basic elements:

1. Physical characteristics of the land
2. Location, Location, Location
3. Profit and risk factors

We have already discussed the desirability of long road and water frontage. Other important questions to be considered are: Is there any marginal or unusable land such as severe slopes, swamps, or marshland, etc? Is the soil suitable for crops? Will the soil perc? (Is it porous enough to accept sewage drainage from individual septic systems?) How much of the land is immediately productive (for grazing, cropland, timber harvest, etc.)?

You've heard it said that the key to the successful purchase of real estate is *location, location, location.* This is certainly true; however, in rural real estate, the meaning of location can be interpreted in a different light. Many people are motivated to buy rural land because it is *away* from things, i.e. located where masses of people will not disturb them. Rural locations are often sought out because of factors such as low price and a low cost of living. Such concerns — privacy, price, or cost of living — do not, however, lessen the importance of *location, location, location,* when acquiring rural land for *Subdivesting.* By even the narrowest of interpretations, any land acquisition project returns to the question of *location.* For what is the worth of a remote, inexpensive site in a low cost-of-living area if no one wants to go there?

In giving weight to government land boundary, the emphasis should be on the amount of usable land open to public recreation that borders your proposed acquisition; because this is *land you can use and land that you don't have to pay for.*

As we continue this discussion and begin to move down the FEASIBILITY CHECK LIST, you'll see that the profit and risk factors are largely determined by what you buy and where it's located. To aid the beginner in making a more objective analysis of a given project, I have compiled a QUALITY REFERENCE SHEET to be used in conjunction with the SCORING KEY included on the CHECK LIST.

FEASIBILITY CHECK LIST (SAMPLE)

PROJECT_____

DEVELOPMENT NAME _____

SCORING KEY

TOP SCORE	EXCELLENT	GOOD	FAIR	POOR
5 points	5	3 - 4	1 - 2	0
10 points	9 - 10	7 - 8	5 - 6	0 - 4
50 points	45 - 50	35 - 40	25 - 30	0 - 20

	Top Score	Points
Price & Terms	50	_____
Location	10	_____
Usable Water Frontage and/or Government Land Boundary	5	_____
Usable Road Frontage	5	_____
*Soil Conditions and Average Well Depth	5	_____
Views	5	_____
*Access and Utilities	5	_____
Development Costs	5	_____
Salability after Development	5	_____
*Ease of Entry (Development)	5	_____
Total	100	_____

*See page 58

QUALITY REFERENCE SHEET

CHECK LIST ELEMENT	EXCELLENT	GOOD	FAIR	POOR
Usable Water Frontage and/or Govt. Land Boundary	One plus mile frontage per 100 acres.	One-half plus mile frontage per 100 acres.	¼ plus mile frontage per 100 acres.	0 to ¼ mile frontage per 100 acres.
Usable Road Frontage	" " "	" " "	" " "	" " "
Soil Conditions and Average Well Depth	Well-drained. Well & septic allowed on 1 acre or less.	Moderate drainage. Well & septic OK on 3 or less acres.	Slow drainage. Well & septic OK on 5 plus acres.	Problem drainage. Unsuitable for small lot development.
Views	Appealing views everywhere.	Appealing views on about half.	Appealing views on about ¼ of property.	No appealing views.
Access and Utilities	Elec. & tel. service across prop. Beautiful access along state paved road. No esthetic drawbacks.	Elec. & tel. service to prop. line. No access problems from state-maintained road.	Elec. & tel. ready to come in. Right-of-way to prop. Some esthetic drawbacks.	No utilities available. Restricted or undefined right-of-way to property.
Location	1-1½ hours from major city. Adjoining or just outside town limits or at major resort area.	2-2½ hours from major city. Near small town or major resort area.	3-3½ hours from major city. Near hamlet or village.	4-5 hours from major city. Sparsely populated area.
Development Costs	Roads completed or roughed in on gentle terrain and/or survey completed showing lots & roads. Prop. will sell itself if advertised and shown by the average real estate agency.	Easy terrain for building roads. Boundary survey completed or easy to complete. Needs effective advertising & normal sales presentation.	Possible road building problems. No recent survey. Persuasive advertising and sales promotion needed.	Terrain unsuitable for building satisfactory roads. Only metes and bounds description available. High-pressure sales and marketing methods needed to move property.

(cont.)

QUALITY REFERENCE SHEET
(cont.)

CHECK LIST ELEMENT	EXCELLENT	GOOD	FAIR	POOR
Price and Terms	Priced below market value. Dream terms.	Priced at or below market value. Reasonable terms.	Priced at market value. Lousy terms.	Over-priced. Lousy terms.
Salability after Development	People waiting in line to buy. Exactly what they are looking for.	People say this is what they want. You feel they will buy if shown by competent people.	Maybe you could talk people into buying if you or your agent were persuasive enough.	Strong-arm methods and high-pressure sales tactics needed to move property.
Ease of Entry	Sell right now. No approvals needed by anybody.	Sell right now. Minor approvals needed or questionable.	Approvals needed now from various agencies before sales can begin.	Questionable whether approvals can be obtained.

SCORING KEY

TOP SCORE	EXCELLENT	GOOD	FAIR	POOR
5 points	5	3-4	1-2	0
10 points	9-10	7-8	5-6	0-4
50 points	45-50	35-40	25-30	0-20

*A zero in Soils, Access & Utilities, or Ease of Entry is possible cause for rejection of the project, regardless of the total score; since it is assumed that sales of subdivided parcels will never get off the ground. Your option is to go for selling the property as a whole. Your total point score will tell you whether such a move is feasible.

Years ago I came across a piece of river property that had been advertised in a local newspaper. The price sounded too good to be true for that area, and the property was described as having long frontage on a small river. I contacted the agent and, since the property was located about 100 miles from home base, made arrangements to meet him the next day at a small airport. My partner and I flew down, fully intending to buy the property if it was as represented.

I operated with a loose FEASIBILITY CHECK LIST in those days. (It was more like flying by the seat of my pants.) When we arrived at the site I immediately scored Usable Water Frontage at 5 points — the tops (total land area: 80 acres; river frontage: 1½ miles). The project was located on a small navigable river and all of the waterfront was usable. Though there were two existing farm roads on the tract, I had to score Usable Road Frontage at zero because extensive improvements would be required. I knew nothing about the soils at the time, so in my mind I scored this factor at about two. Views were O.K. — nothing exceptional; two points there, more or less. Access was from a hard-surfaced state road, but there was a right-of-way to the property through other lands. I asked whether there was electricity available. The agent didn't know. He also didn't know the width of the right-of-way. I knew, from past experience, that the local power company required a forty foot easement to run lines where none existed before. I had made a mental note to pursue this further when I arrived on the property; however, the thought slipped my mind. I gave one point to Access and Utilities anyway. Location was almost ideal — about half an hour from a fair-sized city and university town. Close to ten points here; let's say eight. Development Costs (primarily road construction, survey, sales and promotion expenses, and overhead) were roughed out in my head. Two existing roads were on the property; the survey looked relatively easy because of the long river boundary. Advertising should be short and sweet. The agent, who lived nearby, would handle sales of the subdivided parcels on a co-broke basis (5% commission as opposed to 10%). Better than even on points. Take three. The price was ideal — twenty-five points. Terms: 20% down; three year pay out. Score fifteen, for a total of forty in the combined Price and Terms category. Salability seemed like a developer's dream — five points. Ease of Entry — or our ability to get into the project fast and begin sales — was directly affected by existing government regulations on subdivisions and by zoning laws. Other factors would have been the weather, speed of survey and road construction, title problems, etc., none of which adversely affected us. We checked and found that the subdivision ordinance would permit a division into smaller tracts if no *new* roads were required. We decided to simply inprove the existing roads. On the surface it appeared as if we could get going quickly. Five points.

With 71 points out of a possible 100 going for us, I felt comfortable in proceeding with the project. Here's how the list might look in your project files:

FEASIBILITY CHECK LIST

PROJECT   Jones Farm
DEVELOPMENT NAME   Lazy River Farms

	Top Score	Points
Price & Terms	50	40
Location	10	8
Usable Water Frontage and/or Government Land Boundary	5	5
Usable Road Frontage	5	0
*Soil Conditions and Average Well Depth	5	2
Views	5	2
Access and Utilities	5	1
Development Costs	5	3

(cont.)

Salability after Development		5	5
Ease of Entry (Development)		5	5
	Total	100	71

Would a 71 point score mean that you couldn't go wrong on a deal? Not necessarily. What if, for example, you miscalculated or over-weighted the scoring in several categories? That would bring down your margin of error. You could even lose on a project if your scoring is inaccurate or unrealistic. Let me give you an example; and it is an actual case study, taken from the project I just cited to you.

We assumed, on the basis of a cursory study of the local subdivision ordinance, that the county would not interfere with our plans. But the county's interpretation of the law was at variance with our own, and a lawsuit followed. (Though we won, it cost us sales.) Take off five points. Next, our access was worse than we thought. Another lengthy suit held us up when an adjoining land owner tried to restrict our use of the right-of-way for *agricultural purposes only*. Another land owner would not willingly give the power company the additional easement needed to run electric lines to our new property owners. If we had done our homework properly, we would have scored Salability after Development at close to zero. Scratch five more points, and wipe out the single point given to Access and Utilities. When you subtract this total of 10 points from our actual score of 71, you have a marginal project — one that we could easily have rejected.

Let's stop here for a moment and review. You cannot suggest that what occurred in the former situation is an example of *Subdivesting*. It was clearly a case of land speculation. We bought the property cheap and expected to develop it quickly and make a quick profit. In reality the project dragged on for five years, and profits were minimal. Remember the definition of *Subdivesting:*

> **Making maximum profits from a minimum investment in the development and quick sale of subdivided rural land which, in turn, can be resold at a profit.**

The closest we came to this definition in our handling of the project was that we developed and subdivided a tract of rural land. Even our *Goal Orientation* was fuzzy because the partnership was new. It was formed to make profits. How much? Over what period? How long was this project to last? Did we check our SOURCE BOOK? Our ACTION FILE? No, because none existed. About the only significant homework we did was to hastily read through the local subdivision ordinance. Did we exercise SELECTIVITY? Certainly here we did something right. We were in a position to select or reject a deal on its merits. For the reasons pointed out earlier, this seemed like a sweetheart of a deal. How could we lose?

How about the OBJECTIVITY FACTOR? Here again we failed. We *assumed* that sales could be quickly made. We were stymied -- not once, but several times, all for protracted periods of time.

The FEASIBILITY CHECK LIST? We miscalculated and overweighted the points in several categories, as I pointed out earlier.

But despite the mistakes we made in this deal it was useful in building the technique of *Subdivesting* and its related principles. Let's look at yourself -- a newcomer to this theory -- and see how the example just cited could be turned around into a real profit-maker. Scrap the earlier point score. Now you're going to do things right.

You have a firm SHORT TERM GOAL of making an extra $10,000 within six months so you can become a full-time independent investor in rural real estate. (So you make it in four months, or eight, the goal is set -- that's critical.) You begin building a SOURCE BOOK, so that when a deal such as I just described comes along, you'll know it for the opportunity it really is. Your ACTION FILE is in order and up-to-date. You can make the necessary quick decision when the opportunity arrives. *SELECTIVITY* is your watchword. You're making enough money from your present activities so that you do not absolutely have to have a deal going. Creditors are not camping on your doorstep. If it's wintertime and you can't hold the property until the spring selling season, you are prepared to lose the deal. You are not pressured by your wife to move right away to that new home across town. You don't have to prove to yourself that you can make as much money as your brother-in-law. When a profitable deal comes along, you'll be ready. When you move, your head will be cool! You can be *SELECTIVE*; you can take the deal or leave it alone.

O.K., assume the river front opportunity I just mentioned comes along. You see the ad late in the evening. You'd better get moving. That kind of deal won't last long. Then you're at the door, coat and hat in hand. You remember that you don't know where the property is. In a hurry to get to the phone, you trip and fall, taking a lamp down with you. Your wife is yelling at you. The dog is barking. The kids haven't laughed so hard in years. Then you see the humor of it all. You lost your cool, hence your *SELECTIVITY*. This is not the frame of mind you must have if you expect to become wealthy and independent as a *Subdivestor*.

You gain control of yourself and place a call to the person handling the sale — say he's an agent. You'd like to see the property. Has it been sold? No? All right. How about tomorrow morning? Fine. Fine. You hang up and go immediately to your ACTION FILE. You have plenty of time. Now you're back in control.

You arrive in the morning to see the property. Your first thought last night was that you'd better sign a contract right away or lose the deal to some other sharp operator. But, after checking your ACTION FILE, you knew that you had to be prepared to go one of several ways:

1. Option it to give you more time to see if you can make more than the $10,000 you need within your 6 month goal period.
2. Buy it outright and plan to develop it with the same idea in mind.
3. Buy it outright and turn it over quickly. Shoot for the whole $10,000 profit, but settle for less on a quick cash out.

The agent tells you that the option route is out. The owner wants to sell, but he's willing to take terms with 20% down. If you're a real estate broker, you can reasonably expect that the agent is working on a 10% commission, and you can, hoping to cut your cash outlay by 5%, ask for a co-broke. (Be sure to identify yourself as a broker when you first call so that this request will not come as a surprise.) If the deal is red hot, and the agent knows he can sell it to the guy standing right behind you, you'd best be prepared to forego the 5% reduction.

What exactly did your ACTION FILE tell you that helped you reach the decision to buy?

1. From directions given to you by the agent, you spotted the tract on the county road map and area topographical map. The tract was easy to reach and was on a moderate slope down to the river (no steep land or ground in the floodplain). You saw two farm roads on the topo map.
2. From a thorough reading of the county subdivision and zoning ordinance, you learned that you could subdivide the tract into five acre parcels if no new roads were required. To avoid expensive road work and administrative delays, you were prepared to use existing roads in your subdivision scheme.
3. You knew that the county had established a planning commission, but that any division of land amounting to five acres or more did not come under their control; hence your plans would not be bottled up in committee. You could move swiftly.
4. You were flying blind on the soil conditions, as the county soil map was incomplete and unavailable to you. You were prepared to enlarge the size of your tracts if soil conditions proved too marginal for septic systems on five acre parcels. Since you knew you could turn the property over for a quick profit without subdividing, and because there was no time for soil tests, you were less concerned than usual about soil conditions. (More on soil later.)
5. You knew that the state had enacted a soil and erosion control act. After reading it over again, you knew that if your road improvements were extensive, you might be required to file a report with the county on the extent of your excavation, including drainage date, and plans for re-seeding road banks to prevent

erosion. You felt, if necessary, you could get this report ready while the property was being surveyed. The report would not hold you up. (You may want to consult an engineer.)

6. You knew, from reading the local newspaper, that no new legislation was either proposed or in the works which could leave you out on a limb midway through your development plans. However, because of the capriciousness of local governing bodies, and because you were not attuned to local politics, you were not taking chances — you wanted to get the tract surveyed into smaller parcels and put on record before the politicos changed the rules on you.

Another very important element in your initial analysis of the property was this matter of Federal legislation governing your activities. As this course is written, the Department of Housing and Urban Development (HUD) is charged with the responsibility of enforcing the Interstate Land Sales Full Disclosure Act of 1968. The Office of Interstate Land Sales has inspectors in the field who can recommend prosecution of anyone violating the rather extensive rules set down under the act; and new OILSR regulations and revisions can seemingly fill a law library.

Your best bet as a *Subdivestor* is to stay out of the way of the Federal government. It can ruin you. You can be held up so long you'll be bankrupt. I know. I've seen it happen. And it wasn't always the developer's fault. The intent of the Act was commendable, but as with similar industry crackdowns by the Federal government, a bureaucratic nightmare was created. In most cases you'll need a lawyer familiar with this agency to assist in your filing. You'll be out many thousands of dollars and be held up for long periods of time. The disclosures you make under the Act, though they may not be harmful to you, can impede the flow of sales and stir up investigators armed with potential suspensions for alleged violations. You will feel like a thief for trying to make a profit. Even the most idealistic of land developers have been made to sit in the corner by the heavy hands of over-zealous regulators who, in their own defense, are only carrying out the law.

How do you stay out of the way of HUD? Following are the most important current exemptions to the Interstate Land Sales Disclosure Act. If there is any doubt whatsoever that your project qualifies for an exemption, you should write to OILSR for an advisory opinion. There will be a charge for the opinion, but it is a cost well spent to avoid legal hassles and possible financial setbacks later on.

1. Subdivide in parcels of five acres or more.
2. Keep your subdivision under 50 lots, and avoid a common promotional plan.
3. Sell without an existing mortgage on the original tract, or under a blanket mortgage with release provisions, providing (1) the purchaser affirms in writing that he has personally inspected the property prior to signing a contract; and (2) the sales contract specifies that an unencumbered deed will be delivered to the purchaser within 120 days. Deposits on property must be escrowed and cannot be used to pay the required release fees. Most importantly, you must file for and obtain approval from OILSR of (a) your plat showing the lots qualifying for exemption, (b) the validity of your title, and (c) your sales contract. Evidence of this approval (embodied in a Statement of Reservations, Restrictions, Taxes, and Assessments) must be furnished to each purchaser prior to the sale. Within 31 days after the expiration of the calendar year in which the sale is made, the developer must file with OILSR a copy of each acknowledged statement, together with the developer's affirmation and a copy of each sales contract on the lots approved for exemption.
4. Sell lots with homes or cabins on them, or lots where you are obligated to construct such improvements within two years.
5. Sell lots to builders or persons who plan to sell to builders.
6. Advertise exclusively within the project's home county or the adjacent county, providing:
    (a) Ads are restricted to local newspapers (tourist pamphlets and travel-oriented publications are disqualified for ads).
    (b) Any billboards are located within 15 miles of the on-site office.

(c) Any sales literature is distributed on-site or in the broker's office(s).
(d) No direct mail promotion is utilized.
(e) No radio and T. V. ads appear on the air.
(f) No gifts or premiums are distributed.
(g) No dinner party and telephone solicitation of prospects is conducted.
(h) The broker's office(s) is located within the project's home county or in the adjacent county.
(i) Purchasers make an on-site inspection of the offering.
(j) A clear and specific statement is given each buyer explaining who maintains the roads and common facilities.
(k) Purchaser is given three full business days to rescind at his option.
(l) Purchaser is given a deed free and clear of all encumbrances.
(m) Offering is not located in a flood plain area, excepting those localities participating in the federal flood insurance program.

Keep in mind that any of the above exemptions can be scrapped or modified at any time. A thorough reading of the Interstate Land Sale Disclosure Act is essential to your operation, so you want the most recent copy available; this will include the latest amendments. To obtain a copy, you can write to the following address:

DEPARTMENT OF HOUSING AND URBAN DEVELOPMENT
Office of Interstate Land Sales Registration
451 Seventh St. SW
Washington, D. C. 20410
(202) 755-5860

Tell them that you're in the business of buying and selling land, and that you want to be placed on their mailing list to receive amendments and corrections to the OILSR regulations. Ideally, you should obtain sound legal advice before proceeding with any subdivision activity. Your best bet is to find a lawyer familiar with the OILSR regulations. If your state has subdivision regulations on the books, you'll want to avoid red tape at this level; so you'll need a good legal advisor (see Appendix).

O.K., so much for what your ACTION FILE told you. You feel as prepared as you can be to make a deal. It's a relatively small one — $20,000 — but just about right for a starter. You can get in for $3,000 to $4,000, depending on whether the agent will co-broke. You've got $2,000 in the bank, and you've arranged a line of credit with your banker of up to $3,000. You've got equity in your home amounting to about $10,000. You can shake all of it out on a refinancing, or you can obtain a second trust for $7,000 or $8,000. Within the next, say, sixty days you could get your hands on up to $15,000. (We'll deal with financing angles in more detail later in the book.)

You climb in the agent's jeep, and while riding over the property, you complete the scoring of your CHECK LIST. Remember, this is the time you're going to try to do things right. How many categories have been scored? Which categories will have to be modified up or down? A pocket-sized notebook is helpful at this point, and it doesn't matter whether the agent tags you as a "looker" for using it. You've already made up your mind to buy.

The agent was right on the water frontage. Your five points hold. Road front is still zero. You ask him about the soil and the average depth for wells. His answers are satisfactory; no serious problems are evident to you. The soil looks all right. You don't see any obvious signs of clay or shale (non-porous soils), or of a high water table. But then you're not a soil expert. You only know a few of the conditions that will restrict the installation of septic tanks and drain fields, and the number of individual parcels you can subdivide from the main tract. (We'll continue our discussion of soils later in this chapter.)

The agent tells you that plenty of wells have been drilled in the area, and that potable water is generally available at depths of between 100 and 200 feet. You interpret this to mean 200 to 400 feet; however, that doesn't alarm you. Even the latter figures are not excessive enough to hold up sales. People want to know whether they can drill a well. You're not in the well business. All you know is what the agent told you who sold you the property. He said 100 to 200 feet. If you repeat that figure to a customer, he can accept it, or maybe double it as you have done. If you had actually drilled a well in the area, you might have some first-hand experience to rely on. Since you're only guessing about soil conditions and depth for wells, you write down a score of two — that's less than halfway up the scale. You figure you'll hasten slowly on unknown terrain.

The views, even from the highest point on the property, are nothing to brag about. This is the first time you've been able to enter points in this category. You score two for views. At least you can see some countryside. You're not in the middle of a forest or trapped in a blind canyon.

Access is lousy. No question about it. Without more facts you have no reason to enter a score right now. Put down a question mark. How wide is the right-of-way? You need to know more because the width of the roadway could have a bearing on sales. The agent tells you, again, that he doesn't know; could be fifteen or twenty feet; could be more. He'll ask the owner about it if you're interested in buying the property. A little bell rings in your head. Is there any electric power down here? You don't see any lines. Come to think of it the agent didn't notice any either. Again, he'll ask the owner. The bell is still ringing. The local power company won't run the lines without a forty foot right-of-way. What if the price was exorbitant? What if you could not obtain additional footage at any cost? Would the utility company want to become involved in a condemnation suit? How long would that take? You could be held up for years. You need to make $10,000 in six months, remember .... Hmmm.

So you're off to see the owner. He tells you the right-of-way is twenty feet. See, it says so in the deed. Fine. Fine. What about the power lines? I didn't see any, you say. The owner tells you he just used the land for planting corn and hauling out firewood. He used to go down there to fish with the kids, but they're all grown and have moved away. New fellow bought the place next door. Tried to prevent the old farmer from going across his land, but the farmer showed him right there in the deed where it says he can use the right-of-way for agricultural purposes. Could a fellow build a home down there, you ask? Maybe two or three homes, if some of it were sold off? The farmer didn't know anything about that — maybe you could; maybe you couldn't.

You take time to review your check list. Here's your score so far:

Price and Terms	40
Location	8
Usable Water Frontage	5
Usable Road Frontage	0
Soils and Well Depth	2
Views	2
Access and Utilities	?
Development Costs	5
Salability After Development	5
Ease of Entry	?
Total Known Points	67

It's obvious to you that, even if you scored the two question mark categories at zero, you would have a better than sixty percent chance of pulling off a profitable deal. Is this point spread good enough? You think not. You need a greater margin. This is your first deal, and you have to be right or it could destroy your confidence and possibly cost you money. You go back to the FEASIBILITY CHECK LIST and see if you can logically squeeze more points out of it. Non-usable Road Frontage is a fact. Still zero. You're gambling on the Soils and Well Depth. Hold at two. Views? Could go up a point or two here. You reject the idea. Your first impression is probably correct. Access and Utilities? You're tied to a restricted right-of-way and you don't know whether you'll be successful in negotiating a better one; besides, you don't have time. You have to fish or cut bait today, now. The price is just too good. If you don't buy it, the guy behind you will. You're at the head of the line. This is the last ticket, and it's a front row seat.

You hurry down your list — rejecting an impulse to pick up a point or two in Development Costs and Price and Terms — until you're at the bottom. Ease of Entry? You'd have to do some checking with the county to verify the data in your files. But this is Sunday. There's simply no time. You could score the category at, say, two. That would be safe if they tried to hold you up. But what good is Entry if you can't solve the right-of-way problem? You could, however, pick up a full five points in Ease of Entry by selling the property as is, pick up a quick profit and run. Let others worry about the potential problems. You've got to get in and out fast. That's your game. That's how you operate. That's how you'll multiply your profits. You cannot afford to buy raw land and sit on it.

Suddenly you have the answer. You'll buy it and turn it over for a profit. You'll maybe mark it up $10,000. Buy at $20,000; sell at $29,500. However, you'll take the best offer that comes along within a specified period — say, sixty to ninety days from date of purchase. You still have the $10,000 goal in mind, and you'll have to shake out what profits you can from the first deal to continue toward that goal.

If a buyer comes along right away with a decent offer, you'll accept it. Meanwhile you'll pursue efforts to obtain a more satisfactory right-of-way, keeping in mind that if it's too costly, or impossible to obtain within a short period of time, you'll still profit from the deal.

This simplified example shows you the type of analysis you must make on each and every deal. In actual practice, you'll learn to make a thorough land acquisition analysis and work from a written contract check test. We'll discuss these considerations in detail when we get to the chapter on Land Acquisition and Development. I've learned from experience that if you go into a project with fuzzy-minded goals and sloppy thinking, you end up being controlled by the deal rather than vice-versa. And I don't need to remind you that you're reading this book to build wealth and independence. To do this, you must be in control of every deal. The seller, local governments, and federal agencies, all like to think of themselves as being in control. Let them think whatever they want. You can either play by their rules or stay out of the game. But when you do decide to enter the game, you go in knowing you can win. This is the primary difference between speculating in rural land and *Subdivesting*. Learn it well.

One day my friend, who builds homes, came to me with news of a piece of land that his associate had for sale. First the good news: It was located in the estate section of a prosperous county and had a price tag below market value for that area. Then the bad news: It had two high-tension power lines running through it, and the area was strewn with low-cost government-subsidized housing.

Now, since true worth is most assuredly discovered by the expressions on one's face, you can imagine my dilemma. My friend's associate was anxious to dispose of the property, and he asked me if I'd be interested in looking at it for possible development. I told him I would be glad to take a look and give him my opinion. When we went to look at the property, I was not immediately impressed. (Point to remember: First impressions of land and rural property are not to be discounted, since these same impressions will have great influence on the estimates and opinions of your customers.) Once past the unsightly homes and power lines, the land presented itself as a pleasant forest with lively streams and evidence of wildlife. There was some fairly steep ground, but on the whole most of the property was usable.

I told my friend and his associate that I would need additional information in order to accurately evaluate the property for possible development. Foremost in my mind was clarification of a recently revised subdivision ordinance. Being somewhat more lenient than the old ones, the new regulations allowed for relaxed private road standards which could cut down considerably on development expenses. There was some question in my mind whether, under the new ordinance, tracts of over five acres were exempt from regulations altogether. I told the seller that I'd like to talk to someone knowledgeable about the new regulations, so off we went to see a local surveyor who sat on the County Board of Supervisors. Yes, the man said, the County still wanted to approve all private roads, even though the standards had been relaxed. The new ordinance had been passed, I learned, because developers had been lining the scenic county roads with low-cost government subsidized housing to circumvent the requirement that all new roads had to meet state specifications. I learned further that any new roads were also subject to review by the county under the state-sponsored Soils and Erosion Control Act. The deal became muddier by the minute.

Still, I told the seller, I would go back and put the project to the test of my rating system. It seemed to me that the rating would come out slightly above fifty, and under the ground rules I had established for myself, this margin would be insufficient for me to enter into the deal.

Let's go through the rating process again to see how you would rate a deal of this type. First, consider your *Price and Terms.* Remember, this category is fifty percent of your point spread. A good rule of thumb is to weight price at 25 points and terms at the same figure, although you should allow yourself flexibility for unusual deals such as high price and dream terms, or dream price and no terms. If terms were lousy, ready access to cash from banks and other sources could, for example, give greater weight than 25 points on a particularly good deal. Most deals, though, will not present themselves in these extremes.

For this case study, I rated the *Price and Terms* category at 25 points. In a simplified analysis, I figured the price was right, but the terms were lousy. (29% down with a second trust and the balance of the first trust due in full within eighteen months) I would have to refinance, and this process could still leave me with a short-term second trust and an interest rate of between twelve and fourteen percent. Next, on to *Water Frontage.* Since there were abundant streams on the property, I gave a full five points to this category. *Road Frontage* was minimal — one point here. *Soils/Well depth:* 3 points. (Though I knew from experience that there were good soils in this part of the county, I did see some shale along the steeper grades. Well depth, I knew, would be within reasonable limits.) There were no *Views* to speak of. Score one point for the open areas along the power lines. *Access and Utilities:* 3 points. The property fronted on a state-maintained road, but local telephone and electric lines were absent from the interior of the property. (Extensions could mean extra charges to the developer.) I rated *Location* at 2 points. The property was located at the far end of the county, and though it joined a large estate, the proliferation of low-cost housing in the area brought the point count down. The *Development Costs* — mainly roads and survey — could be higher than I would like, despite the relaxed regulations on private roads. I went for two points here, out of a possible five. *Salability After Development:* 3 points. I felt we had a slightly better-than-even chance to produce some readily salable tracts, mainly because of the streams and our usual generous terms. In the last category — *Ease of Entry* — I felt we had a less-than-even chance of getting into the project fast. Score 2 points here, for a grand total of forty-seven points. Clearly the project was a loser in my view, and I had to reject it.

A while back I heard about a very attractive piece of property that was about to be auctioned off. I had seen the property the previous summer when it was being programmed to be a unique planned-unit development. The concept was commendable, but it floundered and died for want of adequate funding. Now it was being carried to the courthouse steps.

I had a single week to analyze the project as a potential profit-maker using my *Subdivesting* technique. The FEASIBILITY CHECK LIST for this project follows, along with a discussion of how I arrived at the point score. The project was a winner.

FEASIBILITY CHECK LIST

PROJECT   Ridgeline Farm

DEVELOPMENT NAME   Horse Country Estates

	Top Score	Points
Price and Terms	50	?
Location	10	9
Usable Water Frontage and/or Government Land Boundary	5	5
Usable Road Frontage	5	2
Soils and Well Depth	5	5
Views	5	5
Access and Utilities	5	5
Development Costs	5	4
Salability After Development	5	5
Ease of Entry (Development)	5	5
Total known points	100	45

The first thing you should notice about my scoring is that I had entered a question mark in the *Price and Terms* category. When you are preparing to bid on property at auction, the actual price of the tract is, of course, unknown to you. If the price is too high you will not be interested in buying the property because, obviously, as a *Subdivestor,* you do not feel you can make a sufficient profit on the project. For this reason, the *Price and Terms* category on the FEASIBILITY CHECK LIST has been rated at fifty points. Even if all other categories could be scored at the maximum, you would still have only a fifty-fifty chance of making a sufficient profit if you paid beyond your limit for the property. If you were not bidding at a public auction — where cash in full is required at settlement — you could conceivably come out ahead by scoring the maximum in all other categories and picking up 25 points on property with dream terms — say, with no money down; or with an interest-only arrangement.

In my analysis of the aforementioned project, I knew that if the price were right, I could end up with a total of 70 points — certainly an ample amount for the experienced *Subdivestor;* and the required minimum number of points for the beginner. Obviously my point score could climb even higher if I could arrange satisfactory refinancing prior to closing (25 points had been reserved for price; 25 points for terms). With the price factor being crucial to entering this deal, I knew I had to set an upper limit on what I could pay for the property. If bidding went beyond this point, I was prepared to drop the project.

First I set the ideal price at which I would like to purchase the property. Next I speculated on what I thought it might bring. Then I put a price tag on what I would pay for the property in competitive bidding. This latter figure was about 10% higher than my ideal price. If bidding went beyond this 10% margin, I would drop out.

Remember now, that I had 45 points in my pocket. I stood to gain a profitable project if the property could be purchased at my price. This figure would yield me the 25 points I needed to bring home a winner.

At the auction the bidding was spirited until it passed the ideal price stage; then fewer hands were in the air. Finally, as the price rose to within a percentage point or two of my outer limit, the only other bidder dropped out. The property was mine at the price I wanted to pay. I had practiced the SELECTIVITY factor. I was still in control.

Let's analyze the scoring process for a moment to see how I arrived at the first 45 points. There were several streams on the property and, consequently, the majority of subdivided parcels would have water on them. I went for a full five points under Usable Water. Next: Usable Road Frontage. An existing entrance road gave me the opportunity to subdivide immediately on both sides. However, because the tract had no state road frontage, I hedged this category at two points. Soils and Well Depth brought a full five points because the County Health Department had already approved septic systems for two acre parcels under the original concept. There were several springs on the property and evidence of underground water at reasonable depths could be corroborated by adjoining property owners. The depth of their wells varied between 80 and 175 feet. Views of the countryside and distant mountains were superb. I felt five points was justified.

Although a short right-of-way existed to the property, electric power lines were already in place. A real plus was the access road into the property. White board fencing lined the roadway, and this feature gave you the feeling you were entering an elegant estate. All in all, the Access and Utility category deserved the maximum number of points. Location was close to ideal, considering the project's closeness to a major city and its proximity to town. Located on the town limits, it shared a boundary with a subdivision of expensive homes; and central water had been piped to the farm entrance. Again, the full point count. Development Costs would be lower than usual because of the preliminary road and survey work accomplished by the previous developer. Advertising, too, would be below the average since the property was expected to largely sell itself. This factor — Salability after Development — was the project's real strong point. I scored it at the maximum. Ease of Entry was helped along by the preliminary spade work of the prior developer. Since we planned to develop five acre parcels, we could not be held up by a local ordinance controlling most development of tracts below five acres. Soil and Erosion Control data would be needed, but this information had already been filed and approved. We would simply pick up on the roads where the other developer left off. I scored this category at five, for a total of 45 points.

And, as I pointed out earlier, when the price turned out in my favor, I picked up 25 points for a grand total of 70.

Again, I want to point out that only through this type of analysis can you hope to reach logical and sound decisions on whether to go ahead with the many deals that seem, at first, to be very appealing.

Do not make a hasty or hurried decision, because a mistake at this point can set you back a long way. Be certain to use the FEASIBILITY CHECK LIST on each piece of property under consideration. I repeat: Do not rush into a land deal! That is a certain way to make mistakes, and you will notice that the whole concept of my plan toward wealth and independence is to make as few mistakes as possible and, preferably, no mistakes at all.

ACTION POINTS -- LESSON 4

1. Practice looking at land and rating each potential project using the FEASIBILITY CHECK LIST, SCORING KEY, and QUALITY REFERENCE SHEET. (p. 54-57)

2. Check your ACTION FILE to see if all data is in for your proposed areas of operation; if not, follow up. (p. 62-64)

3. Write for a copy of the Interstate Land Sales Disclosure Act. Request to be placed on the HUD mailing list for OILSR (Office of Interstate Land Sales Registration) regulation changes. (p. 66)

4. Before purchasing any piece of land, make sure you've gone through your Land Acquisition Check List (see Appendix).

HOW TO FINANCE YOUR PROJECTS

Lesson Number 5
Table of Contents

The Least Costly Way Of Raising Money For Your Projects	p. 79
How To Figure Release Fees	p. 80
How Mortgage Position Affects Your Operations	p. 80
Why You Should Avoid Third Mortgage Notes And Land Sales Contracts	p. 81
The Option Route – Try It, You'll Like It	p. 82
The Importance Of Establishing Credit With Banks	p. 83
How To Get A Bank To Pay You To Go Into A Deal	p. 84
The Importance Of Liquidity To Your Success	p. 84
Should You Sell Your Notes Or Borrow On Them (An Analysis)?	p. 85
The Workings Of The Federal Reserve System	p. 86
The Prime Rate And The Discount Rate Explained	p. 86
An Explanation Of Your "Base" Investment In A Lot	p. 87
Raising "Signature" Capital – How It Can Pay Off For You	p. 87
Offering The Seller A Premium In Notes In Lieu Of Cash	p. 88
Turning Your Short-Term Obligations Into Long-Term Obligations	p. 89
The Principal Advantage Of "Selling" Notes To Pension Funds	p. 90
More Ways To Gamble With Other People's Chips	p. 91
Where Purchase On An Installment Contract Might Benefit You	p. 92
Eight Alternative Sources Of Financing	p. 93
Action Points	p. 96

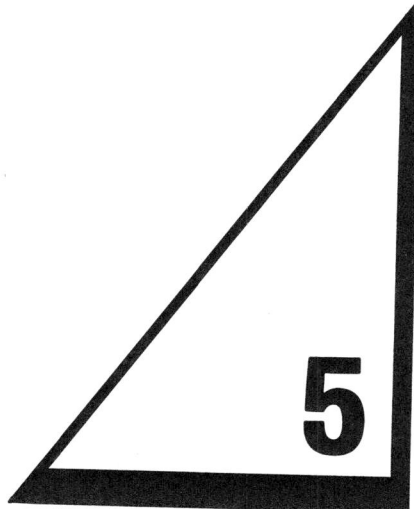

How to Finance Your Projects

Once you have located a winning project, your major concern is supplying the green grease to get it rolling. Here you have a number of choices, beginning with owner financing and conventional mortgage loans. Then there are the more costly sources of money, expressed in the form of various investor entities and partnership arrangements, all cutting themselves in for a healthy "piece of the action."

Probably the least costly way of raising money is to obtain long-term owner financing with convenient release clauses. Ideally, you'll want to put very little of your own money into the purchase. Then you can sell off parcels using a portion of the proceeds of each sale to "release" lots from the blanket mortgage. Again, ideally, you'll want to pay these releases in a non-cash form. One way is to transfer mortgage notes (obtained from your buyers) to the holder of the blanket mortgage. Let's see how this form of owner financing might work in one of your *Subdivesting* projects. The example I'll use is a case history from one of my developments.

I had purchased a tract for development along the Shenandoah River and was well into the sales program when an adjacent land owner approached me and asked if I would be interested in buying his farm. Early in the negotiations I told him, yes, but only if I could pay him in interest-bearing notes secured by land. These notes would carry my personal endorsement, and in the event of default, I would replace any note with one of equal value at the time of default.

The owner agreed to the deal, and I transferred forty thousand dollars worth of notes to him in exchange for his farm. Many of these notes were in secondary position (second trust), since they had not been released from the first mortgage. The notes were secured by lots in other developments, and I was under no obligation to release them from the blanket mortgage until I was paid in full, or until such time as I sold (discounted) them to lending institutions or investors. When the notes are sold, release fees (incorporated in the sales contract and deed of trust) are paid to the seller, who then relinquishes his first trust position on the lots to be released. The individual lots, of course, are shown on a plat produced by a licensed surveyor, and reference is made to this plat in each deed of release. For each released acre, or portion thereof, you must pay a specified amount of money to any mortgagor(s) with a preceding position.

A standard release fee may be a figure 1¼ times the per acre sales price on the entire tract. In some cases, your mortgagee may insist that lots with existing road frontage, or waterfront lots, be released only upon a proportionate release of back lots. A higher release fee is also usually required for lots with existing improvements, such as houses and barns.

When you are selling with a prior lien(s) on your property, keep in mind that until release fees are paid, the installment buyer who purchases a lot from you holds a deed encumbered by at least a first trust (owed by you) and a second trust (*owned* by you). In rare instances you could end up selling a lot where you take a third trust position. This could occur if the seller already had a mortgage on the property when he sold it to you, and he agreed to take back a second trust against the property so that you could make the purchase with little or no money down. Satisfactory release arrangements would have to be negotiated with both trust holders in order for you to deed your subdivided lots to individual purchasers. You could, of course, sell on a "land sales contract" (where your purchasers must pay you in full in order to obtain a deed). But these contracts — along with third trust notes — make very shaky collateral when you go to borrow money on them. A further source of concern could be any state legislation governing the sale of property wherein a "land sales contract" is used. Virginia, for example, has enacted legislation imposing stiff requirements on the part of developers utilizing this method of transfer.

As a *Subdivestor,* you should avoid going into deals where you must take a third trust position, and shun the "land sales contract" entirely when selling lots. (There are, however, some very distinct advantages to purchasing land under a "land sales contract" or "contract for deed," and I will discuss these advantages later.)

Now let's return to the case history cited earlier. After transferring the forty thousand dollars in deed of trust notes, I obtained a clear title to the river front farm; and since I owed nothing on the property, I took a first trust position when I sold off the lots. This meant that I was free to sell (discount) my more credit-worthy notes to raise money for development expenses.

The deal was attractive because it did not require any cash down. I did, however, put up forty thousand dollars in notes. This reallocation of my assets was largely offset by the notes coming in from quick sales of the river front lots. In fact, I was surveying, building roads, and selling before I even closed on the farm. When I went to settlement, I scheduled simultaneous closings on many of the lots. I picked up first trust notes in exchange for notes of lesser quality, thus strengthening my liquidity and financial position. Understand, however, that the second trust notes would have to be released by me somewhere down the line. This could be done through payment in full of the blanket mortgage, through release payments made when the lot owner paid off his obligation to me, or when I sold these notes for whatever reason. The key ingredient here — as in most successful real estate deals — was using O.P.M.(other people's money). And you can obviously see that this money must be put to productive use if you are to build wealth and independence.

What do you do if you don't have any notes to trade for property? (Admittedly, trades of this type are rare, but they are certainly well worth trying.) Let's carry that question a little further and ask, "How can I get into a deal if I don't have the money to tie up a piece of land and to pay for development expenses?"

Rather than setting down all your options at this point, let's continue to look at some case histories of deals that required little or no money down. I'll even show you how I was paid to get into deals. Not only did I use O.P.M., but I started out with cash to spare.

The first deal I handled on my own was a classic example of buying land with practically no money down and deferring all of my development expenses.

In 1966, I had spun in and out of several profitable projects and was looking around for a tract of land to develop. Waterfront property has always been a good bet, so I contacted all of the local realtors, finally coming up with a 40 acre riverfront farm that, at the time, was on the market for $18,500.

The realtor handed me a plat of the farm. I told him I would look at it and let him know if I was interested. I also learned that the present owner, a local investor, had paid approximately $15,000 for the place.

The seller wanted to cash out, but he agreed to sell me a 60-day option on the place for $500. He further agreed to accept half of the option money upon signing of the contract and the other half within 30 days. The entire $500 was to be applied to the purchase price, if I decided to close on the property. The seller agreed to let me survey the tract and build a road during the option period.

My first move was to get a surveyor out in the field to plot the boundaries. Simultaneously I had contracted for some heavy equipment to build a road and to improve the access road. Within two weeks I had a plat showing the new road and the subdivided lots. By this time I was making sales and scheduling closings with a local attorney. (So far I had paid out only $250 to get the deal rolling. Everything else was done on the cuff.) When it came time to close out on the property, all of my lots were sold. I had twelve hundred dollars in down payments and a cash sale which would net me four thousand dollars at the closing. To cover the balance of the purchase price on the property, I borrowed on my notes receivable, with the intent to sell them shortly after closing. Here's how the picture looked when the deal was wrapped up and all expenses paid, only sixty days after I had first optioned the property. Overhead was negligible since I operated out of my home.

ROLLING RIVER FARM

Sales: Cash . . . . $ 5,200
          Notes 46,800
Total Sales $52,000

Less:		
	Land cost	$18,500
	Roads	4,000
	Survey	1,800
	Advertising	500
	Commissions	1,200
	Legal expenses	300
	Cost of Money ($46,000 X 20% discount) . . .	9,200

Total costs $35,500

Net Profit 16,500

THE IMPORTANCE OF ESTABLISHING CREDIT WITH BANKS

Here's a neat little trick to raise money for the down payment on a hot project and to gain some spending money in the bargain. Of course, this procedure will not work until you've established a reputation with the banks as a reputable and reliable developer.

You've tied up a sweet tract of land with a small amount of earnest money. Your contract provides for the necessary releases, including a certain amount of land released for the down payment. You've specified in the sales contract exactly what lots will be released at closing. You next send your surveyor out in the field to survey this portion of the property into lots. Before closing, you contact your friendly banker and line up a loan using these lots as collateral. Now, since the subdivided lots are worth more per acre than the acreage price of the property as a whole, you obtain enough at closing to cover your down payment and, possibly, a few extra thousand for expenses.

When the project is underway, and if the lots securing your original loan are sold, you may be able to sell these notes to the bank to shake out even more cash. And remember, these lots were released as consideration for the down payment — hence there are no release payments to be considered.

I've used this financing angle to get into a number of projects when I found it more advantageous to hang onto my hard-won capital. Once you've built up a reservoir of capital, it is essential that you stash a portion away in passbook savings accounts. The interest you receive will probably not keep up with inflation, but more to the point is the financial clout your ready cash will give you when you go to borrow money. Banks, as you may have noticed, like to loan money to individuals who don't need it. A strong appearance of liquidity will enable you to get into far more deals than would otherwise have been possible. Again, the key to financing is found in other people's pockets. Use their money to make money. Your aim should be to increase your net worth each year and to avoid the dilution of your own capital.

To preserve your capital position and liquidity, you will want to exhaust all alternatives available to you before you dip into your own cash for down payments and development expenses. If you can borrow on your notes, or sell them, to get into a profitable deal, by all means do so. There are advantages and disadvantages to each tactic and you will have to make a decision that best serves your goal plan, profit picture, and operating style.

A typical loan arrangement where you use deed of trust notes as collateral, might be structured as follows:

1. You need a twenty thousand dollar down payment to enter into a profitable deal.

2. You approach your friendly banker and offer to collateralize the loan with forty or fifty thousand dollars in notes currently being collected for you in his bank.

3. The loan is made for three years, with payments on the notes being used to curtail the loan. (In effect you are assigning the notes to the bank for the period of the loan.)

Aside from definite tax advantages (you are not taxed on borrowed money, and you can deduct the interest), you retain control over your notes when the loan is paid off. The major disadvantage to this method of raising capital is the large amount of collateral required in proportion to the amount borrowed.

An alternative is to sell your notes to raise money for down payments and development expenses. A sample schedule follows of what your note purchaser's yield might be on the sale of various interest-bearing notes. (See Appendix for detailed information.)

TERM	72 mos.	84 mos.	96 mos.	108 mos.	120 mos.
BAL	$6,000	$7,000	$8,000	$9,000	$10,000
ANNUAL % RATE	9.06	9.37	9.67	9.95	10.21
DISCOUNT	10%	11%	12%	13%	14%
YIELD	12.98	13.18	13.42	13.69	13.96

The discount rate charged by banks when making loans is, of course, directly influenced by the cost of member bank borrowing from the Federal Reserve System. This institution is the central banking organization of the United States. Historically, the FRS has been given the function of influencing the flow of credit and money. Generally, when banks have plenty of money to loan, businesses find the rate attractive enough to expand. Consumers can also obtain money at lower rates for the purchase of hard-ticket items such as automobiles and appliances. Too much credit, however, can lead to unacceptable inflation rates, and the nation's economy suffers.

When the FRS wants to tighten or expand credit, it can exert its authority over member banks. For example, the FRS can increase its reserve requirements for members, thus drying up available loan funds. It can go into the open market and buy or sell government securities as a means to increase or decrease bank reserves. Checks used to pay for these securities are usually drawn on member banks, thereby depleting bank reserves and restricting the supply of money available for loans. The *sale* of government securities by the FRS has the opposite effect and can increase the amount of loan funds.

As a *Subdivestor,* your first inkling of a money shortage could come when you hear about increases in the prime rate or *discount rate*. When banks raise the lending rates chargeable to their "prime" customers, a tightening of credit is underway. Usually this increase is tied to a rise in the *discount rate* set by the FRS for its member banks. You could find loan money harder to come by and certainly more costly to obtain when the FRS is busy battling the fires of inflation. When you sense this battle looming, re-think your operations to provide for adequate cash reserves; and tighten your grip.

The movement of our economy can be likened to a roller coaster ride. No sooner do you reach the top than you're heading for the bottom at a rapid clip. Remember how you were able to release your grip on the bar when the ride was on its way up? On the way down, you'll recall, you were holding on for dear life. Don't be caught unprepared by an impending money crunch. The lack of adequate funding can sink the finest of projects and ruin your credibility with lenders. This is not the "Can't Lose" way.

The obvious advantage to selling notes is the immediate cash you receive without tying up a disproportionate amount of your collateral. Disadvantages to selling your notes include loss of interest, reduced proceeds due to release payments, discount penalty, and tax consequences (selling usually triggers income). The tax consequence is even more pronounced if you have a fairly low base investment in the lot secured by the note. In accounting terms, base is measured by the proportionate allocation of fixed expenses — roads, surveys, advertising & promotion, overhead, etc. — assigned to a particular lot. Theoretically, the lower your base investment, the higher your profit; hence the higher your taxes on the sale of the note. It makes sense, therefore, that wherever possible, you should first sell those notes in which you have a higher base. Your accountant can supply you with this information.

Ideally, you should raise enough cash from each project to recoup your down payment and to pay all development expenses. As a *Subdivestor,* using the techniques outlined in this book, your profits will, in almost all cases, be returned to you in the form of notes secured by mortgages or deeds of trust on the subdivided lots.

RAISING "SIGNATURE" CAPITAL

When I first started in the development business, I had two partners. To get into a project, each of us went to a bank and borrowed $2500 on our signatures. We used $6,000 for the down payment, leaving us $1500 for seed money. The lots sold quickly, and the project proved very profitable. Once underway, the project generated sufficient operating capital from cash sales and down payments. At the end of the project, we split up the notes, and each of us assumed responsibility for a portion of the balance due on the mortgage.

If you're entering into a one-shot deal with partners, the best way to handle the blanket mortgage after all the lots are sold is to sell enough notes to pay the mortgage off in full. Each partner is then assigned his share of the remaining notes. It is his responsibility to collect and administer his own notes. If the note(s) goes bad, that particular partner ends up with the lot to resell. To exercise fairness when splitting up notes, each partner must be content with taking a portion of those notes having marginal credit and/or erratic payment records. When distributing notes before the blanket mortgage is paid in full, you have another factor to account for. Each partner will be concerned about the amount of per acre release fees required to free his notes on the lots for possible sale. If, for example, one of the partners contemplated selling his notes, he would not want to be saddled with a large number of notes secured by large acreage lots. A note sale would simply reduce his end of the blanket mortgage at a faster clip. It may not yield him the amount of cash he is looking for.

Of course, if you remain in business with your partner(s) you may have sufficient notes in the kitty to substitute for notes in default, or to allow for substitution in other situations.

Another variation of the technique of partners borrowing on their individual signatures is when the partners borrow money jointly. Years ago, my partners and I entered into a very profitable venture by raising $10,000 each from ten different banks and lending institutions. We borrowed the money, in most cases for a year, with varied methods of repayment. The partners and their wives all signed the notes, and that was the only collateral required. In a few months we had sold all the lots. Before the year was up we had paid off the blanket mortgage and the ten separate loans through cash sales, note sales, and in some cases, by borrowing on the notes. We ended up with a substantial profit — again, by using other people's money.

OFFERING THE SELLER A PREMIUM IN NOTES IN LIEU OF CASH

A favorite financing trick of mine is to offer a seller interest-bearing notes instead of cash when it comes time for a release fee or mortgage payment. Let's see how this might work.

You find a deal you can get into for 20% down. Right away you make a deal with the broker to take his commission in notes secured by the subdivided parcels you will create. That leaves you 10% to come up with. First you try an interest-only tactic to avoid having to dip into your pocket for that amount. If the owner balks at taking interest only on the mortgage for 3 to 6 months, you offer an existing mortgage note with a good payment record. You know you would have to discount this note at the bank to come up with the balance of the down payment, so you're money ahead if the seller agrees to the deal. Of course, it's almost a certainty that the seller will require a first mortgage note, completely free of liens and encumbrances; but you're still money ahead if the seller takes it at face. Further, you attempt to show the seller how it is in his interest to take mortgage payments and releases in the form of notes secured by the individual lots you will be creating out of his property. Chances are the interest rate charged to your buyers will be higher than the interest you have agreed to pay the seller. If he balks at this proposition, offer him a premium of, say, 10% if he agrees to take notes. That may be a cheaper way of meeting your cash obligations to him than discounting notes at the bank. In effect you will be transferring an $11,000 payment in notes for every $10,000 you owe. To raise $10,000 in cash, you may have to sell $12,000 in notes, so you're a thousand ahead.

In summary, your strategy should be to cover as many of your short-term obligations as possible with longer term obligations. As a *Subdivestor,* your stock in trade is mortgage notes. You need all the cash you can generate to cover land acquisition costs and development expenses. Never make the mistake of making deals for cash when alternatives are available. Sign on the line — whether it be to a bank or a seller — to obtain the capital you need. Never dip into your own kitty unless you've exhausted all other sources. Failure to conserve cash can cost you a bundle later on, especially in periods of tight money, or when emergencies arise. There are plenty of financial buzzards out there who will offer a thirsty developer a welcome slug of cash in hard times, but they'll pick your bones in return. My experience has shown that, as a *Subdivestor,* you should balance your actual net worth with at least 10% in cash or comparable liquid assets deposited in banks and lending institutions. *Never* allow these assets to be pledged as security for any loans you may make. Borrow on your signature and other less liquid assets.

CLOSELY-HELD PENSION FUNDS AND RETIREMENT ACCOUNTS AS A SOURCE OF READY CAPITAL

Once you've established yourself as a reputable and conscientious operator, with a proven performance record, you may want to tap into the vast reservoir of capital earmarked for the sunset years. As you may know, pension funds and retirement accounts exist in a myriad of entities and their resources are committed to a wide range of investments, these being low-risk ventures, and bearing relatively low rates of interest.

If you can locate a pension fund which is actively seeking a higher return on its investments — one that is not shy about the real estate market — you can pitch a version of the following deal.

In recent years my *Subdivesting* activities have been a never-ending source of delight to the Internal Revenue Service. They enjoy grabbing immense chunks of my profits. In some years the eyes of the wolf seem rounder than others, so I am extra cautious about leaning my taxable profits. One way is to "sell" notes to pension funds. I've put the word sell in quotes because, in actuality, the notes are *assigned* to the fund. They do not actually take possession of the instruments until some mutually agreed upon future date. Usually a trustee, such as a bank or lawyer, will be assigned to hold and possibly administer the collection of the notes. In other cases the trustee will assign the administration of the note package to you, with the understanding that a specified monthly payment will either be paid by you to the fund or its assigns, or deducted from a bank collection account for the benefit of the fund. The obvious advantage of "selling" notes in this fashion is that, because the fund does not take immediate possession of the notes, you do not trigger large amounts of taxable income when it would not be to your advantage. The fund will, of course, factor their yield into the proceeds you receive from the transaction. Their rate, however, is generally below the interest rate charged by banks.

Another version of this transaction can be worked for your own account. With IRS approval, your own retirement account or pension fund may be allowed to invest in the notes that you generate. You receive the two-fold benefit of gaining a higher rate on invested funds, while at the same time freeing up a latent source of financing for some of your projects. Remember though, this funding technique will probably only be allowed where a number of employees are covered. The transaction must also be "at arms length," while using a trustee approved by the IRS.

In summary, follow all the steps I have set forth for the process of financing, and follow them to the letter whenever possible. Avoid the use of your own capital whenever possible. Make use of other people's money; and do it on a regular basis. As you begin to build up a financial platform or base, you may have a tendency to change or slightly alter your financing methods. Here you must proceed cautiously. Do you have precedent for the new financing structure? Does the deal benefit all parties concerned? Is your exposure to risk compatible with your goal plan?

If the formula you used in the primary stages of financing has worked well for you so far, then there may be no reason to change, especially when the change involves using more of your own capital. Remember, each tested and proven method used to gain wealth and independence requires commitment and consistency. These methods and formulas are not to be used just at the starting phases of the journey toward wealth and independence, but are to be used during every step and in all future transactions after you have attained your goals. A proven method is just that — it has been *proven* to be effective in all types of applications and in the face of all types of adversity.

MORE WAYS TO GAMBLE WITH OTHER PEOPLE'S CHIPS

PROBLEM: You come across a "can't lose" deal in rural property, but you're short of cash because of other commitments. You could make a bundle if only you could hold the deal on the back burner until you're ready for it.

SOLUTION: Try for an "installment contract," or "land sales contract," under which you'll gain possession and use of the property after making a token down payment. Legal title will follow when you've refinanced or when you make final payment to the seller. (Again, because of legal complications, I do not recommend transferring your subdivided lots under this arrangement.)

PROBLEM: You learn of a farmer who is planning to sell his highly developable farm, if only he can find a home to his liking. Local brokers have been badgering him for a listing and it seems like every sharp real estate operator in the area has tried for an option on the place. The farmer is stubborn and won't move until he has found the home of his choice.

SOLUTION: Agree to buy the farm at the farmer's price (assuming the deal is golden) and offer him an "installment contract" where you would take possession, say, within a year. Try to structure the contract so your down payment will be rendered upon possession. You will want, of course, the right to prepay when it comes time to refinance and develop the property. If there is an existing mortgage on the property, you will want assurance that this encumbrance can be cleared when you retire the "land sales contract."

PROBLEM: You're drooling over a choice piece of rural land where potential clients should be as prolific as corn stalks and profits will (pardon the pun) be coming out of your ears. The seller is reluctant to grant an option on the property; nor does he want to sell for all cash, because of the tax consequences. He decides to sell, taking 29% down and holding a mortgage paying him $500 per month. You don't have 29% to put down, but you can make larger monthly payments until you refinance.

SOLUTION: You offer him an "installment contract" rather than a conventional mortgage or deed of trust arrangement. You give him a token amount down and agree to pay $800 per month until the next calendar year, at which time you intend to pay him off. He agrees that you can prepay when the deal will have qualified as an installment sale, thus reducing his tax bite.

PROBLEM: You find a seller who is willing to take an interest-only note from you for the balance of the purchase price. (1% of the principal per month is standard.) Say the note is for $100,000 and your interest payments are running $1000 per month. You want to cut down on the amount of your interest payments in the near future without making a new note and risking a higher rate of interest.

SOLUTION: Get the seller to agree to break the larger note down into four smaller notes. This allows you to reduce your monthly payments when you find it advantageous or necessary to apply large amounts to principal. The seller also gains under this arrangement since, if and when he decides to sell your note(s), he'll find four small ones easier to sell than the larger note. If you go this route you must insist upon a prepayment privilege without penalty; this gives you maximum flexibility in your operations.

The information I've given you so far on financing rural properties describes the methods I've used to achieve wealth and independence. However, you may want to take advantage of other ways in which rural land can be financed — techniques which may be more applicable to your particular situation. While most of the following financing sources are not suitable to my *Subdivesting* techniques, they do deserve mention here so that you will be completely aware of all of the financial means available to you.

1. Insurance Companies — This lending source is normally interested in the larger properties and in loans amounting to one million dollars or more. They usually work through mortgage brokers, and almost any type of project can be financed through them, with the exception of single-family residences. Insurance companies usually go after large office buildings, shopping centers, and high density apartments and housing complexes. The interest rates can vary tremendously, depending on loan demand in the market as a whole and the availability of loan funds within the company itself. Costs will vary between companies, and several sources should be checked

for quotes. A mention of the fact that you've been to other companies for quotes may have an impact on your final interest rate because most of these companies are very competitive. The type of borrowing we're discussing here is usually of a long-term nature and is not easily adaptable to the technique of *Subdivesting*.

2. Savings and Loan Associations — Savings and loan associations are the largest lenders in the financing of single-family dwellings. They also handle apartments and high density housing and prefer loans in this latter area of not less than $100,000. They will go as high as $800,000 and higher in some specialized instances. Savings and loan associations are very location-conscious and will tend to carefully scrutinize any properties they are asked to finance. While they do make some loans on commercial, industrial, and shopping center properties, they prefer to finance the single family type housing. They rarely make loans to purchase unimproved properties such as the rural land discussed in my *Subdivesting* methods.

3. Larger Pension Funds — This type of financing will include union and retirement funds for groups such as civil service workers, teachers, and others. Normally, the larger properties are preferred, with loans being made in the million dollar category. Like savings and loan associations, they are conservative lenders. They'll closely examine the property, as well as the individual or individuals requesting the loan, before granting it. They make loans of all types but prefer not to invest in unimproved properties and recreational projects. As I've mentioned, your best bet for funding your project is to contact them with a solid note investment package. Such funds are not likely to become involved in the financing of a "quick in and out" rural land project. Pension funds are not regulated like banks and savings and loan institutions; consequently, they can custom-tailor loans for individual enterprises.

4. REITS — REIT is an abbreviation for Real Estate Investment Trust — these investment entities generally finance large properties in the

seven figure range. They normally lean towards commercial, industrial, and shopping center projects, and in the past they have advanced money for construction loans. Rates are normally higher because they take greater risks with their money. They work only through mortgage brokers. If you are considering this means of financing — although it is not really suitable to my method of *Subdivesting* — be extremely careful, because these trusts have had an erratic performance record in recent years, and you may find yourself out on a limb if they fail in their commitment to you.

5. Trust Funds — Banks normally control trust funds, but they can also operate under the supervision of individuals and families. These funds can be a source of financing to *Subdivestors*, because the trustees may be seeking relatively risk-free ventures on which to loan money at higher than normal rates. Your past performance and financial standing will be key factors in obtaining loans from this source. Though you will pay more for these loans, trust funds can offer an alternative to over-utilization of your bank credit lines.

6. Private Individuals — Private individuals are often excellent sources to call on for quick financing. They usually make only short-term loans at rates which may vary from slightly higher to very much higher than established lending institutions. Depending on the risks taken, and on what the market will afford, private sources loan money on almost every type of property; although, in recent years most seem to prefer speculation in the high-flying single family housing market. Unfortunately, the less sophisticated can end up taking a bath when the boom years come to an abrupt halt. The manner in which these speculators work is varied, but many will work through a mortgage company, real estate broker, or loan broker. Most loans are for less than ten years. Private individuals offer excellent opportunities for establishing fees, terms, and loan amounts which are more suitable to individual preference, because a certain amount of wheeling and dealing can be brought into play

with these lenders. Be prepared, however, to pay through the nose for this type of loan.

7. Seller — Here's a way that is well-suited to my method of *Subdivesting*. Not only can the seller be an excellent source of money for carrying the second deed of trust but he can also — and usually does —provide lower rates in first mortgage financing.

Owner financing involves the least amount of risk, and while the seller may not always be willing to finance your activities, you should try for options, interest-only arrangements, and small down payments whenever possible. Remember that satisfactory release payments will have to be built into the contract and deed of trust or mortgage.

8. Private Syndicates — Real estate syndicates are organizations formed to invest in real estate. Syndicates can be found in the form of a trust or a partnership of a limited, general, or corporate nature. The investors are offered many practical advantages in real estate investment with a relatively small outlay of capital. Tax and legal advantages are usually favorable. A real estate syndicate takes much of the risk away from the individual and spreads it among several or many individuals. A syndicate arrangement can be an excellent way to get started, but remember that any profits are lessened by the greater number of investors.

ACTION POINTS — LESSON 5

1. Begin a supplementary reading program dealing with real estate financing techniques and strategies. (See Bibliography.)

2. Review your credit relationship with various banks. Cultivate those banks offering overdraft privileges and lines of credit against charge cards, such as the American Express Gold Card. Review the equity

you may have in your home. (You could have a second and third trust option; you may want to refinance or give a second trust on your home as down payment on a *Subdivesting* project.) The key here is to have access to money when you need to take advantage of a deal.

3. Order copies of amortization schedules for both simple interest and "add-on" loans. (See Appendix.)

4. Follow the financial pages in any major metropolitan daily and/or the *Wall Street Journal.* Keep abreast of the prime rate and the discount rate charged member banks by the Federal Reserve System. (Your *Subdivesting* strategies will change with the state of the economy and the availability of money at reasonable rates.)

DEVELOPING RURAL LAND

Lesson Number 6
Table of Contents

How To "Shaft" A Lot To Avoid Getting Shafted
By Unfair Local Ordinances .... p. 102
Avoid Hassles Through The "Middle-Of-The-Road"
Approach Toward Growth .... p. 102
How To Give A "Nose Job" To An Ugly Piece Of Land .... p. 104
How To Slice Into The Land Pie For Maximum Profits .... p. 106
Three Human Qualities That Are Required
To Develop A Subdivision Plan .... p. 106
How To Perform The "Quickie" —
Developed By Dirt Peddlers In The '60's .... p. 110
When The "Quickie" Form Of Development
Will Work Best For You .... p. 111
Why Certain Lots Will Turn A Man Off — And His Wife On! .... p. 113
Open Space Vs. Wooded Land —
Why A Mixture Of Both Is Best For You .... p. 115
How To Avoid A "Lot Cramp" .... p. 115
Why Your Lots Should Look As Good On Paper
As They Do On The Ground .... p. 117
What Kind Of Lot Can Make A Hard Customer Beg For It? ...... p. 117
Waterfront Lots — Why They Should Be Priced
Much Higher Than Back Lots .... p. 119
The Hardest Type Of Recreational Land To "Hustle" —
The Easiest .... p. 119

An Unbeatable Combination When Selling Recreational Land . . . . . .p. 122
How To "Undress" A Lot For Maximum Exposure . . . . .p. 122
How To Double Your Money And Keep Development
Expenses To A Minimum . . . . .p. 126
Playing Godfather — Some Thoughts On Covenants And
Lot Owner Associations You Can't Refuse .p. 126
What You Should Know About Soils And Building Sites . . . . .p. 128
The Septic System And "Perc" Test Explained. . . . . .p. 128
Avoid Problems By Using The Septic System Check List . . . . .p. 129
The U.S. Soil Conservation Service (SCS) —
How They Can Help You . . . . .p. 129
Further Considerations About Building Sites . . . . .p. 130
Action Points . . . . .p. 131

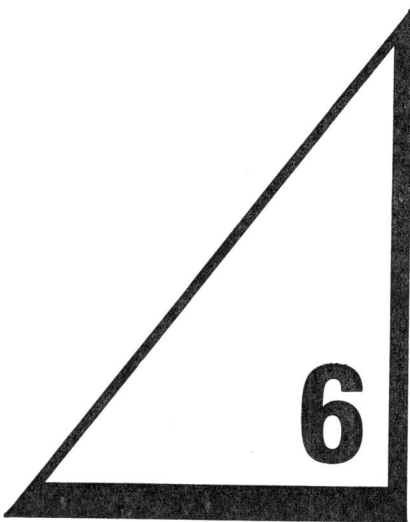

Developing Rural Land

What does it require to turn out a finished product from something rough? The ingredients are a mixture of talent, knowledge, skill, and imagination. In the development of rural land you'll usually find a number of people contributing to this mixture. You, of course, will generally oversee the operation. Your surveyor, your road builder, your sales and marketing people, all will contribute to the finished product.

The product, in this case, is a project of developed lots. Your concern is that they shall be marketable, while not detracting from the beauty and aesthetics of the landscape. Governmental restraints and economic factors often are the overriding considerations when determining the profile of a given development.

In this lesson, you'll learn a few of the "angles" I've used to bring home handsome profits from varied tracts of land. In some cases I could envision immediately how the development would turn out. In other instances, I had to work hard in bringing together the correct mixture of talent, knowledge, skill, and imagination.

Much of this lesson is devoted to turning disadvantages into advantages when developing rural land. Your goal is to transform a diamond in the rough into a sculptured jewel of beauty and profit.

HOW TO "SHAFT" A LOT TO AVOID GETTING SHAFTED BY UNFAIR LOCAL ORDINANCES

Rural counties are becoming increasingly more cautious about permitting the subdivision of land within their jurisdiction where new roads do not meet certain state specifications. The county fathers are obviously concerned about complaining property owners who, at some point in the future, will want their roads maintained by the county and state. Many counties have effectively "bottlenecked" small lot subdivision almost entirely through harsh road-building requirements, thus preserving the "estate" quality or agricultural characteristic of the area. Often there is an ongoing battle between the "anti-development" forces and the "pro-development" advocates. As a *Subdivestor*, it is usually not wise to align yourself politically with extremists on either side of the argument. Loss of objectivity is something — as an investor and speculator — you cannot afford. Your attitude should be, "Just lay out the ground rules. I'll play the game according to the book."

When the "book" calls for all newly subdivided parcels to front on existing state roads, or on roads brought up to state specifications, you can principally consider only those projects in that particular county where you don't have to build new roads. Most likely, the county subdivision ordinance will specify minimum frontage requirements, such as 100, 150, or 200 feet, before any parcel of land can be cut off of a larger tract. Not all larger parcels will readily lend themselves to a subdivision where each lot fits neatly along a state road. Your problem will be to develop a subdivision scheme that provides access to the back land, while still conforming to existing county regulations. You accomplish this end by providing a "shaft" or corridor from the state road to your interior property.

In this particular subdivision, the lots along the state road were used for the construction of government-subsidized housing. Aesthetically, this subdivision arrangement leaves much to be desired; however, the economics of rural land subdivision often do not provide for the enormous expense of building roads to state specifications. It is interesting to note that this county modified its ordinance to allow for less stringent road

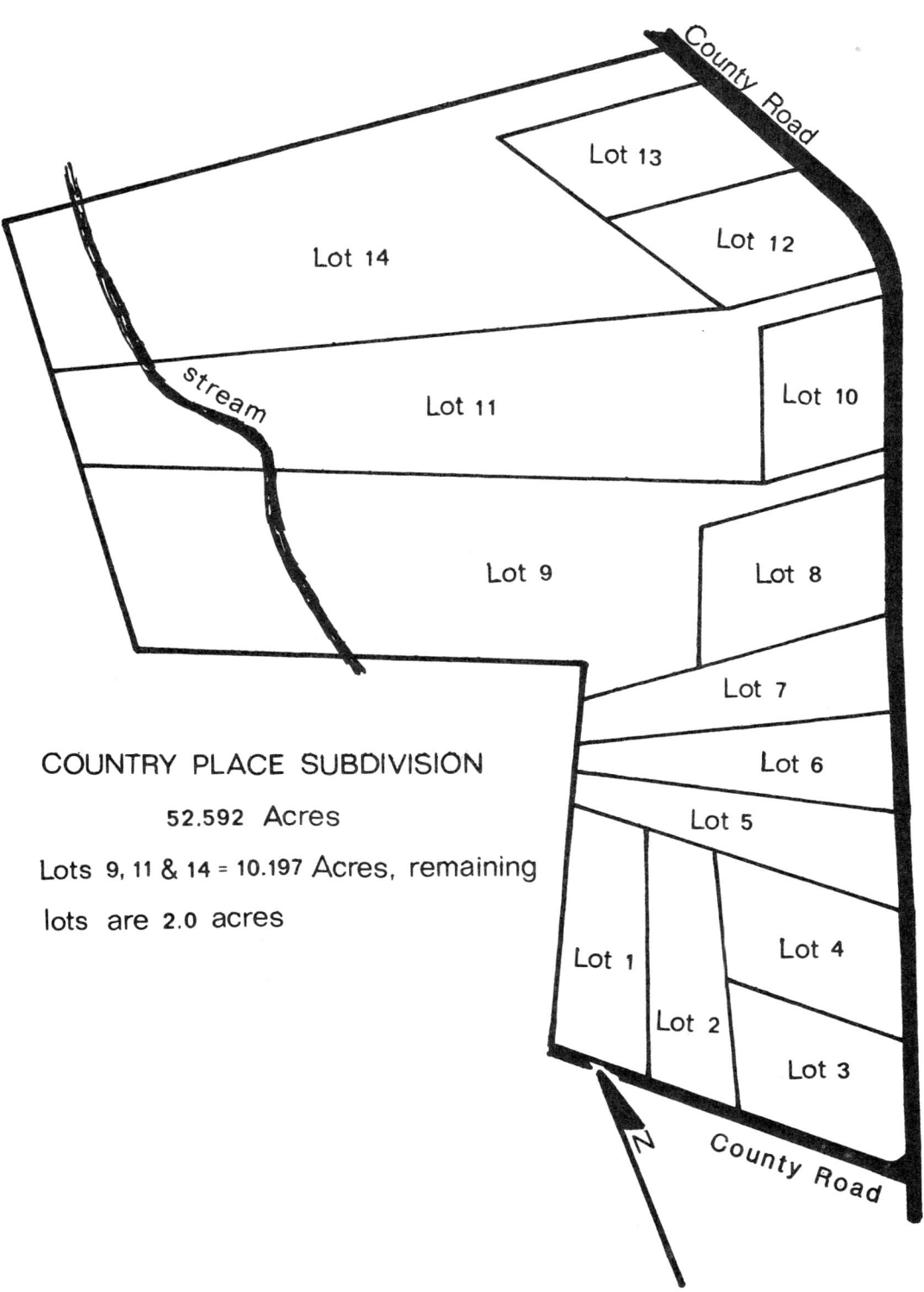

requirements in certain situations. This more enlightened and flexible approach to the problem made it possible for developers to consider other alternatives, such as constructing low-cost housing on sites further away from the scenic rural roads. Land developers could also give greater attention to more aesthetically-pleasing plats and lot design.

HOW TO GIVE A "NOSE JOB" TO AN UGLY PIECE OF LAND

When we first went down to look at this piece of land, we were immediately turned off by the entrance. Here was this potentially profitable (but overgrown) tract of riverfront, where the river could not be seen from the road, and which had absolutely no attractive element along the state roadway. All we had to work with was a dirt path leading through some ordinary pine trees in a sparsely populated section of the county. Clearly, before we could get customers off the road and down to the river, we would have the problem of turning them back on after they had been turned off by the approach. A secondary problem was in providing access to the river so that we could open up her true beauty to the customers' anxious eyes.

Here's how we solved both problems, thus generating much quicker sales and higher profits than would have been possible with the old "scarred" face.

At the highway we cleared some trees to provide an expanse of open area. The entrance road was considerably widened and adorned with an attractive log fence and gate. A rather rustic "estate-type" sign was hung along the road to impress anyone approaching or passing by. The impression was that some "rich dude" must be holed up in his country estate. Just a little cosmetic work at the entrance, and we had altered our prospects' frame of mind.

We improved the entrance road all the way down to the river and, where the road came closest to the river, we provided a picnic area and concrete boat ramp, complete with fireplace and picnic tables. The area was cleared and given cosmetic improvements as well. This is where our salesmen greeted and oriented the prospects. When the customer could see for himself what a little clearing could do for a piece of overgrown property, he was in a more willing frame of mind to purchase what we had to offer in this development.

We grossed out at close to three times land acquisition cost on this project. This was mainly possible because, under the county's subdivision ordinance, lots of three acres or more were exempt from stiff road building requirements. Another factor accounting for the high gross was the predominance of navigable waterfront on the property. We could ask for, and get, higher prices for the lots. Waterfront has always been like gold, and this was no exception.

BEFORE

AFTER

HOW TO SLICE INTO THE LAND PIE FOR MAXIMUM PROFITS

In 1975 a farm in Pennsylvania came to my attention. My partner and I drove up to the property and began negotiating with the owner.

For more than an hour, after walking the property and analyzing its profit potential, we "dickered" on price and terms. Then I left. I went back to the car and sketched out a proposed subdivision, wherein the farm buildings could be comfortably cut off onto four of the lots, and where all of the parcels would have existing state road frontage.

My partner inspected the plan, reached into his pocket for a check, wrote out a deposit, and handed it over to the owner. We paid exactly what was asked for the property — and agreed to an all cash deal!

The owner had handed us a "can't lose" deal on which, unconsciously, I had worked my secret formula. That farm in rural Pennsylvania was worth over twice what we paid for it. *But not to the seller!* A clear-cut success and profit formula was needed to uncover the hidden wealth, but neither the owner nor I knew how quickly those substantial rewards would surface.

The owner was glad to sell the farm for his asking price. My bank was taking a big chance by going into another state to finance one of my deals with little money down. My banker never dreamed his investment would be returned to him in a few short months at a rate that would surpass the bank's most profitable ventures.

What the bank really invested in was *past performance!*

The clean little Pennsylvania farm, the buildings, and the ten acre lots, were incidental. The quick and easy profits from that farm were returned to us after I had unconsciously mixed the secret formula using several ingredients that are critical to success.

What do you think you'd need to know to convert an attractive subdivision of ten acre lots into immediate and profitable sales? Here is a case study of inspired imagination, experience, and specialized knowledge, all blended together to produce a specific desired result. We all have imagination in one form or another; for images are the brood of desire. The owner desired to sell his farm for a profit, just as we sought material gain.

However, our inspiration was for greater relative profits, and our imaginations lifted the potential of the farm far beyond the expectations of the seller. This factor, combined with know-how (gained from experience) and specialized knowledge (gained from learning) led us, as would a treasure map, to the hidden wealth on the farm.

Let's go over final point scoring on the FEASIBILITY CHECK LIST to see why we considered this farm to be a real money-maker.

Usable Water Frontage and/or Government Land Boundary

Half of the subdivided lots would have some year-round surface water on them — either a stream or pond. Score this category as *Good* — three out of a possible five. (Access to sub-surface water was excellent.)

Usable Road Frontage

Two miles of usable state-maintained road frontage (1½ miles hard-surfaced) gave this beauty a top score of five for five — *Excellent*.

Views

Exceptional views from almost every lot. *Excellent* — top score of five.

Access Utilities

Dream access along state paved road; electric and telephone lines in place. *Excellent* again - A big five.

Location

It was two hours from Washington and Baltimore; seventeen miles from a good-sized town, and five miles from a village. Score Location as *Good,* not *Excellent*. Points = Eight out of ten. Because of the scenic drive to the property (largely by freeway) along with the beauty of the surrounding countryside and access to nearby state hunting lands, I stayed on the high side of the "Good" category, which ranges from 7-8 points.

Development Costs

No road building necessary. Survey costs would be low because of the extensive road frontage and because most of the land was open, thereby making it easier for the surveyors to complete their work. The land would sell itself if we could get people to the site. A qualified salesperson lived on site and could handle prospects generated from classified advertising. Score this category as *Excellent;* four out of five points. If a boundary survey had been available, I would have added a point to the score.

Price and Terms

I felt the property was priced below market value, and when the existing farm buildings were sold off, our land cost would be within reasonable limits. We could easily mark up the price on the lots to a required figure from two to two and a half times land cost. A ten acre lot, for example, costing out at $500 per acre, might be priced at $9950 to $12,500. We knew there were multitudes of people out there who would pay this price for an attractive ten acre unimproved farm. Terms were lousy — all cash. We would have to bring in outside financing and pay 12-14% interest for a short-term loan. Some of our own cash would have to be used. The deal was not *Good*, only *Fair*; but it was on the high side of *Fair* because I had located a bank that was ready, willing, and able to loan me the maximum and to cooperate on the subsequent purchase of the mortgage notes we took in from the sale of subdivided lots. I scored this category at thirty.

Salability After Development

No question about it, the property would sell. It had just about everything going for it. Even the location of buildings on the property was such that they could be split off onto several lots. This would not pose undue hardships when attempting to get maximum price from the sale of these improvements — figure five out of five points.

Ease of Entry/ Soils and Well Depth

There was a problem here. The county required every subdivision to be approved by the local board of supervisors and the health authorities.

HOW TO SLICE INTO THE LAND PIE
FOR MAXIMUM PROFITS

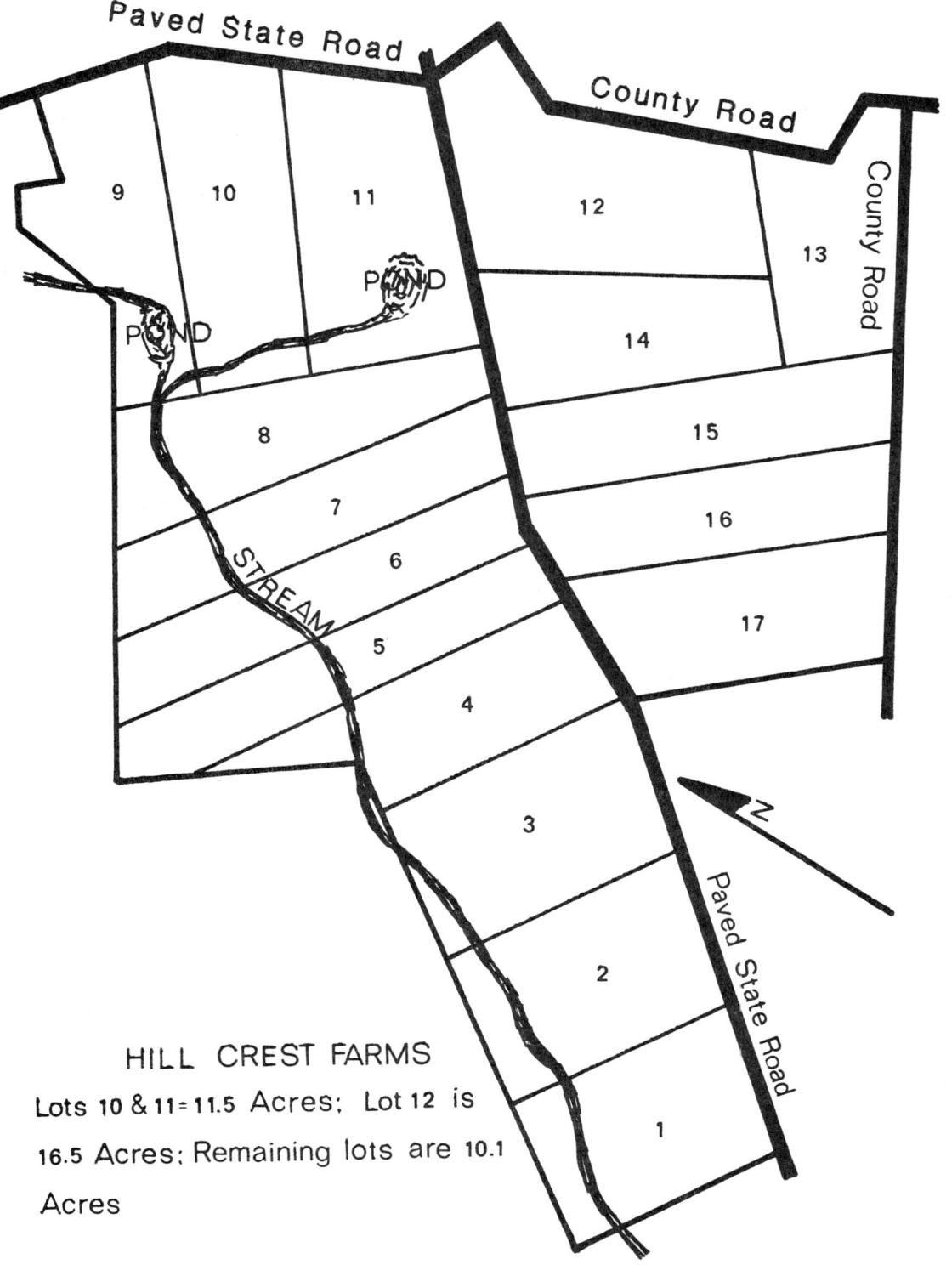

HILL CREST FARMS

Lots 10 & 11 = 11.5 Acres; Lot 12 is 16.5 Acres; Remaining lots are 10.1 Acres

The state was unconcerned about any subdivision of more than ten acres, and the project was clearly out of the purview of HUD. The county, we knew, was mainly concerned about new road construction and health standards. Since we were not planning new roads, and because of the excellent soils and the large lot sizes, we anticipated no problem in getting our plat approved. We would, nevertheless, be delayed from thirty to sixty days. Point-wise, we'd go for the high side of the *Fair* category — (2) in Ease of Entry and all the way (5) on Soils and Well Depth.

Final Score = 72 Points — A Winner!

HOW TO PERFORM THE "QUICKIE" — DEVELOPED BY DIRT PEDDLERS IN THE SIXTIES

In the early days of the recreational land boom — late fifties to late sixties — large amounts of land were being cut up and sold in rural areas even before survey, road-building, or even before the seller actually acquired title to the property himself. I recall walking along many a river bank measuring lots with a tape and nailing stakes into the ground. "Options" would then be sold on the staked-out lots, with closing scheduled after survey. And even today simultaneous closings are being used by some developers. As far as I know, they can be completely within the law.

The "Quickie" can be likened to a sleight of hand trick. One minute you're the owner of a piece of undeveloped property, and the next minute that property has been transferred and deeded to a number of owners in a different form. Here's how the "trick" works:

You go out in the country and option or contractually agree to buy an attractive and underpriced piece of farmland or riverfront, etc. on which you will not have to build roads, or where road building is of little consequence. You have scored it above 70 on your CHECK LIST, and the project is not covered by local ordinances or government regulations. You cut it up in your mind, then on paper; and finally you bring a map to your favorite surveyor and ask for a preliminary plat based on your rough drawing. If the deal is small enough, the surveyor can have a boundary survey, along with a preliminary lot and road layout, weeks before your own closing. (You have obtained permission to survey and, possibly, to build roads before closing. The surveyor has agreed not to bill you until after he has supplied a final plat. You have at least 30 days on any road construction bills as well.)

While you are an equitable owner (your name is only on the contract; not on the deed) you advertise and sell lots based on the preliminary plat. You are reasonably sure that the final plat will not differ to any great degree from the preliminary plat (acreage sizes on the individual lots will not vary more than a few tenths of one percent), and you schedule simultaneous closings. The final plat will come to you prior to your own closing, and you can judge whether any of your lots vary in size or shape from what was promised to your individual buyers. You use money collected and due at closing from your buyers to apply to your own down payment requirements.

This type of arrangement usually requires an understanding closing attorney who can cooperate with your own lawyer. As pointed out earlier, mortgage releases must be executed when your buyers either pay you in cash or pay off their notes to you. Your mortgagee will, upon payment of a pre-arranged per acre fee, then apply that amount to your mortgage note with him.

The "Quickie" is becoming more and more difficult to perform because of mounting county, state, and federal legislation. Its obvious advantage is the fact that you end up buying land and making profits with a minimum of disturbance to your own pile of chips. Not every tract of land will be suitable for this "trick," nor can you pull it off at will. Time and circumstance must be right, and you must have a cooperative seller. Usually the "Quickie" works best when you are selling lots that are in great demand. To avoid misunderstandings, always level with your clients and tell them you have not closed on the property yourself, and that you will be scheduling a simultaneous closing.

A while back we acquired a tract of land at public auction on which all of the preliminary county approvals had been obtained. We re-subdivided the property so that it was out of the subdivision ordinance (5+ acres were exempt) and proceeded to sell without having turned a spade

HOW TO PERFORM THE "QUICKIE" — DEVELOPED BY DIRT PEDDLERS IN THE SIXTIES

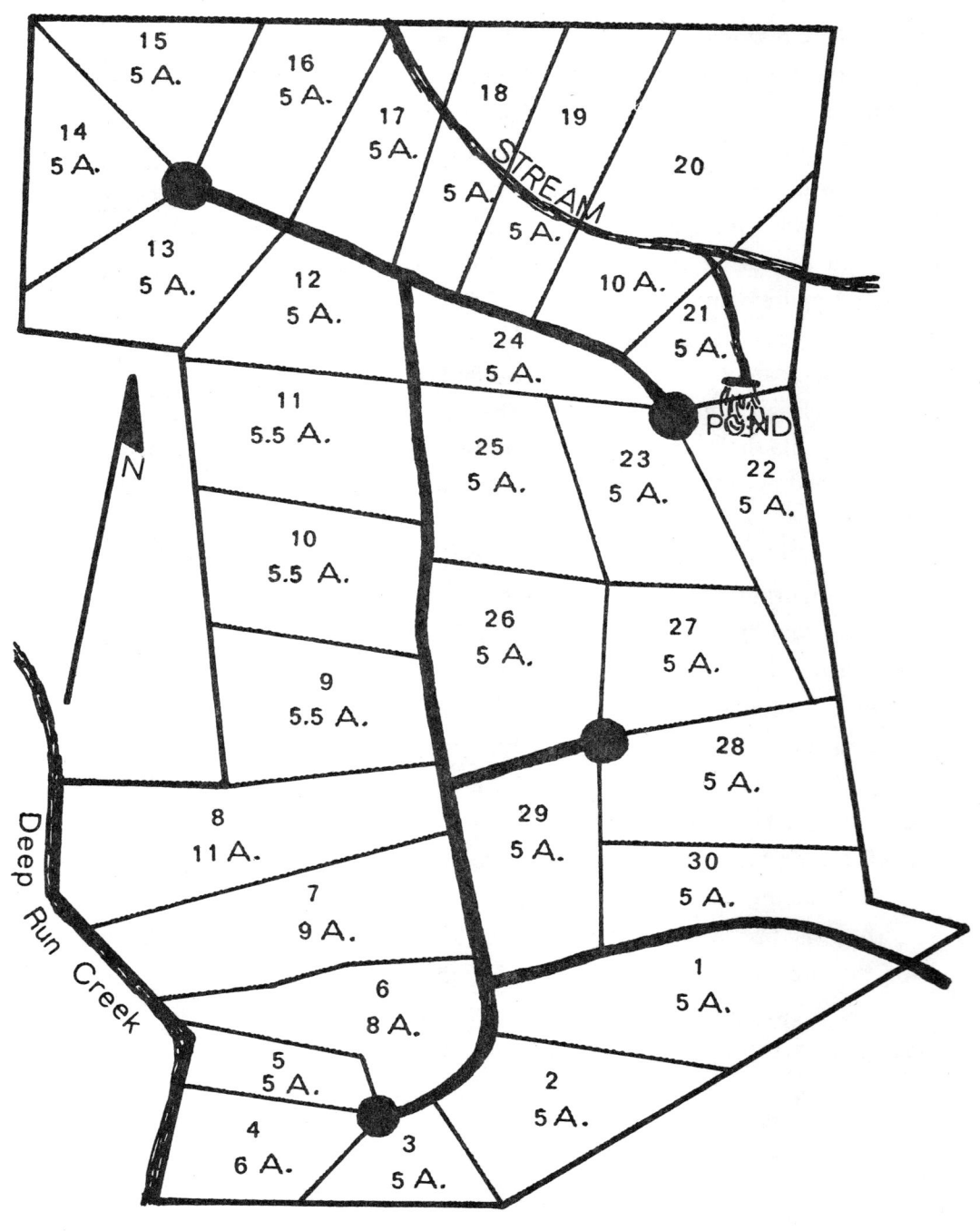

of dirt for the roads. The property was essentially sold out the first weekend, and simultaneous closings were scheduled. (In the interim we had arranged refinancing through our bank.) Our customers closed on their property before the roads were completed, although they did have a guarantee that the roads would be completed to their satisfaction or we would refund all monies paid in, plus closing costs. The property was extremely desirable, modestly priced, and well-located for resale purposes. We experienced a minimum of problems with the project, despite this unorthodox approach.

The "Quickie" has often been performed when the seller of the individual lots hasn't officially agreed to buy the property he is selling. This is possible when the developer has "optioned" the tract he is planning to cut up. He has invested a minimum amount of money in the property and, when offering it for sale in smaller parcels, is "testing the water" to see if his deal is really hot. Again, if you attempt this "trick," I would advise you to level with your prospects to avoid misunderstandings and possible allegations of fraud. If you're a licensed real estate agent, many states require you to reveal the full extent of your interest in any property you are offering for sale.

Remember this, however: You are entitled to make a profit from any investment in real estate as long as you do not violate the rights of others. Where there is no law or contractual agreement to the contrary, you can sell or assign all or any part of your option or contract for the purchase of real estate. When structuring deals of this type, it is best to consult with a competent legal advisor to ensure your compliance with all laws governing the development and sale of land.

WHY CERTAIN LOTS WILL TURN A MAN OFF — AND HIS WIFE ON!

In most cases, the purchase of rural property is a joint decision, made equally by husband and wife; however, the man usually takes the lead in negotiating for land. He may have certain preconceived ideas about *exactly* what he is looking for; he may have vague ideas; or he may be open to several possible alternatives. As a rule, his wife's opinion is rumbling around somewhere in the back of his mind and, though he may

appear in control of the situation, he senses if he makes an arbitrary decision he will be penalized in some way later on.

Sometimes the wife's opinion will surface early in the negotiations, and she'll jockey for control. The man may hold back and say: "Well, if she likes it, it's all right with me." The wife may chirp, "Now, George, you have to like it too." Or she may lay you flat out with, "I don't think you have anything I like."

You, as the seller, may reply to the little lady with amused tolerance, "Well, exactly what is it you would like, ma'am?"

Chances are what she wants is everybody's dream site in the country; still, she's reasonable and will settle for a facsimile. Most of the women I've talked to about land — particularly housewives — are turned on by rural lots where they can at least glimpse some semblance of civilization. They want to see a house or two and feel that there are people close by. Maybe they experience loneliness during the week and don't want to carry that feeling with them when they visit their property in the country on weekends. Men, though, often react in a totally dissimilar manner when shown property from which they can see their neighbors. As a rule, for them, the more privacy and seclusion, the better. Again, this feeling may be an outgrowth of their activities during the week. When the weekend rolls around, they may have had their fill of people, having comingled and hassled with the human animal on the job and on the way to and from their work.

Men, too, are often turned off by open lots where they can see a lot of weekend chores ahead, such as mowing the grass. Women, though, seem to love open spaces. Perhaps this is a throwback from being cooped up in the kitchen all week. Agoraphobia (fear of open or public places) does not seem to affect women as much as men, and the reverse — claustrophobia — could be more peculiar to women than to men. On weekends, many men would be quite content to bury themselves deep in the forest; whereas, for the wife, such a lot could represent an extension of her weekday confinement.

Your familiarity with such fears can be a big help when selecting, subdividing, and selling property. The most successful rural land developments by far, are those that offer a mixture of open and wooded land. Regardless of high point count on the FEASIBILITY CHECK LIST, I know that if I do not have a mix of trees and open space I'm going to lose a few sales.

HOW TO AVOID A "LOT CRAMP"

Occasionally you'll come across a tract of land which would be ideal for your *Subdivesting* activities, if only you could figure out what to do with an irregular chunk of land. The troublesome portion may hamper your scheme to subdivide off of existing state-maintained roads by forcing you to (1) "dump" the nefarious tract at a less than desirable price, or (2) confine the width of your primary subdivided parcels to less than desirable proportions.

Your first consideration in creating a subdivision plan is to come up with the most pleasing profit picture possible; secondly, you should strive

HOW TO AVOID A "LOT CRAMP"

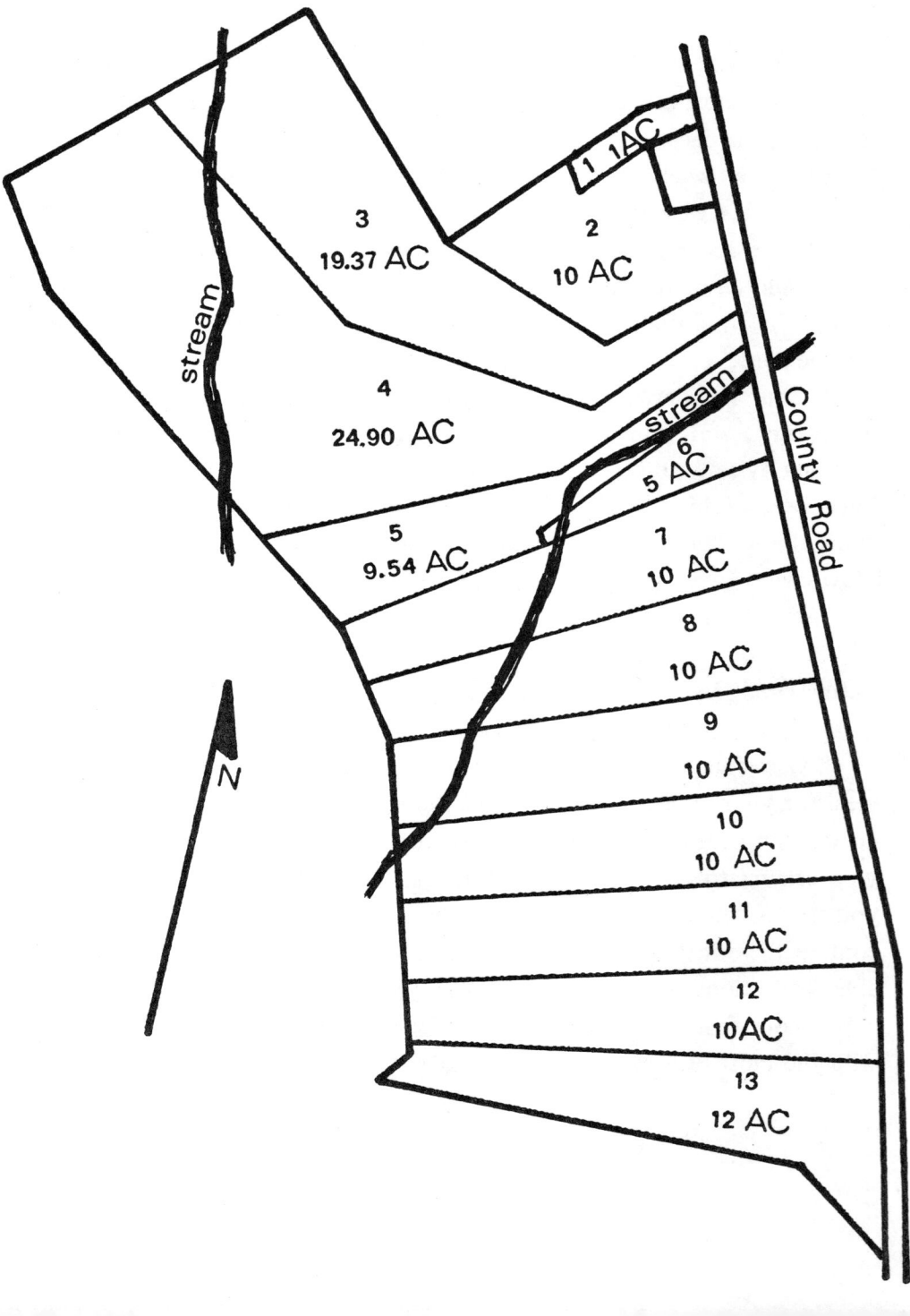

for a maximum of attractive looking lots. As a rule, lots that look good on a subdivision plat are more likely to appear engaging when viewed on the ground. You should never sacrifice overall design by "slenderizing" or cramping all of your lots when only a portion of the property is "overweight."

This plat shows how several parcels can be "shoehorned" into an irregularly-shaped piece of land, without narrowing the road frontage on the majority of lots.

WHAT KIND OF LOT CAN MAKE A HARD CUSTOMER BEG FOR IT?

When subdividing and selling rural land, you occasionally come up against some very tough cookies — savvy investors and "hagglers" who'll want the shirt right off your back. A favorite tactic is to "bad-mouth" your offering in hopes you'll come down enough in price so that they can steal it. These money-masters think you're making a killing and that you should give away a piece of your pie to a hungry friend. Never mind that they, themselves, in their own investments, are wringing out the last bead of sweat from their working capital.

Hard customers, however, are not really that hard to deal with when you understand their rules. A couple of their guidelines go something like this: (1) *Cash talks*, and (2) *Everybody's got a price.* They like to dangle the "carrot" of cash in front of you and watch you sweat for it. A steady ploy is to make a ridiculous offer, expecting you to scoff at it and then come back and settle somewhere on their turf. Frequently they'll sign a contract for a piece of hot property and throw in a few "clinkers" so they can extend the closing or maneuver for a better deal when your parade of customers has passed.

One thing that activates the adrenalin in hard-bargainers, is the sweet aroma of making a quick and easy profit. Nothing is more potent in transforming the roaring lion into a meek and humble sheep than the sight of potentially profitable deals slipping through their paws into the mouths of less savvy consumers. The "lion into lamb" trick usually occurs when

you have a waiting room full of anxious buyers for a handful of desirable lots, such as waterfront. You don't have to shave the price or diddle around with ridiculous offers. Hard bargaining simply won't work when you've got customers standing in line to buy.

Cloaked in fleece, the fierce trader will enter your mainstream of customers and politely attempt to remove your choicest lots from the jowls of your eager clients. Better that these eager beavers suffer awhile and pay a higher price later on. Of course, such nobility calls for a modest discount and possibly some re-structuring of the financing. But you, the developer, won't mind, will you? After all, those silly people out there waiting to be shown around are, in the majority, ingrates who would sop up your time with no intent to buy. Yes, your fleecy friend would be very appreciative if you would tell the others to get lost while he can get his "generous" offer down on paper. The standard conclusion to this story is that the "wolf" sheds his cloak of fleece when your customers have been sent away and he promptly proceeds to intimidate and wear you down with outrageous demands. Without your backlog of customers, you are, at that time, more likely to go belly up for him.

The smart *Subdivestor* will price his scarce lots sufficiently higher than his back lots so that he will not immediately lose his drawing card to smart investors cloaked in fleece. You'll be wise, also, to resist giving excessive discounts on lots which cannot be duplicated. Remember this: When hard customers come around looking for a shaving on the price of gold, they pay the quoted price that day — just like everyone else. Your waterfront lots are like gold. Hard customers make bold beggars when all seem rich.

THE HARDEST TYPE OF RECREATIONAL LAND TO "HUSTLE" — THE EASIEST

The term, "Recreational Land," can be applied to a broad spectrum of property ranging from high-density lots in planned-unit developments, to large tracts of rural acreage. The so-called "hustling" of land, however — as described in Martin Paulson's excellent book, *The Great Land Hustle* — is primarily the baliwick of hard-sell land companies and their wheeler-dealer salespeople. Whenever you have a remote subdivision involving thousands of lots, you are bound to have a tough sales problem — one that opens up the use of questionable sales and promotional tricks and the manipulation of lot prices and land values. These remote recreational subdivisions, many with nonexistent or bladed-in roads, offer the hardest type of land for the legitimate operator to sell.

As a *Subdivestor*, you would, in all likelihood, never become involved in the development and sale of tiny lots in the "swamps" and "deserts" of this country. You may, however, be confronted with a problem remnant in one of your subdivisions — a tract of land too big, too irregular, too steep, etc. to quickly and easily sell. If your development plan required you to be burdened with such an albatross, then so be it. But be forewarned that lots with problem sizes and shapes are a drain on your operations. They should be kept to a minimum or eliminated altogether in the development stage.

In the early seventies, my partner and I acquired a tract of land to develop in a negative-growth rural county. We had planned a subdivision

THE HARDEST TYPE OF RECREATION LAND TO "HUSTLE"

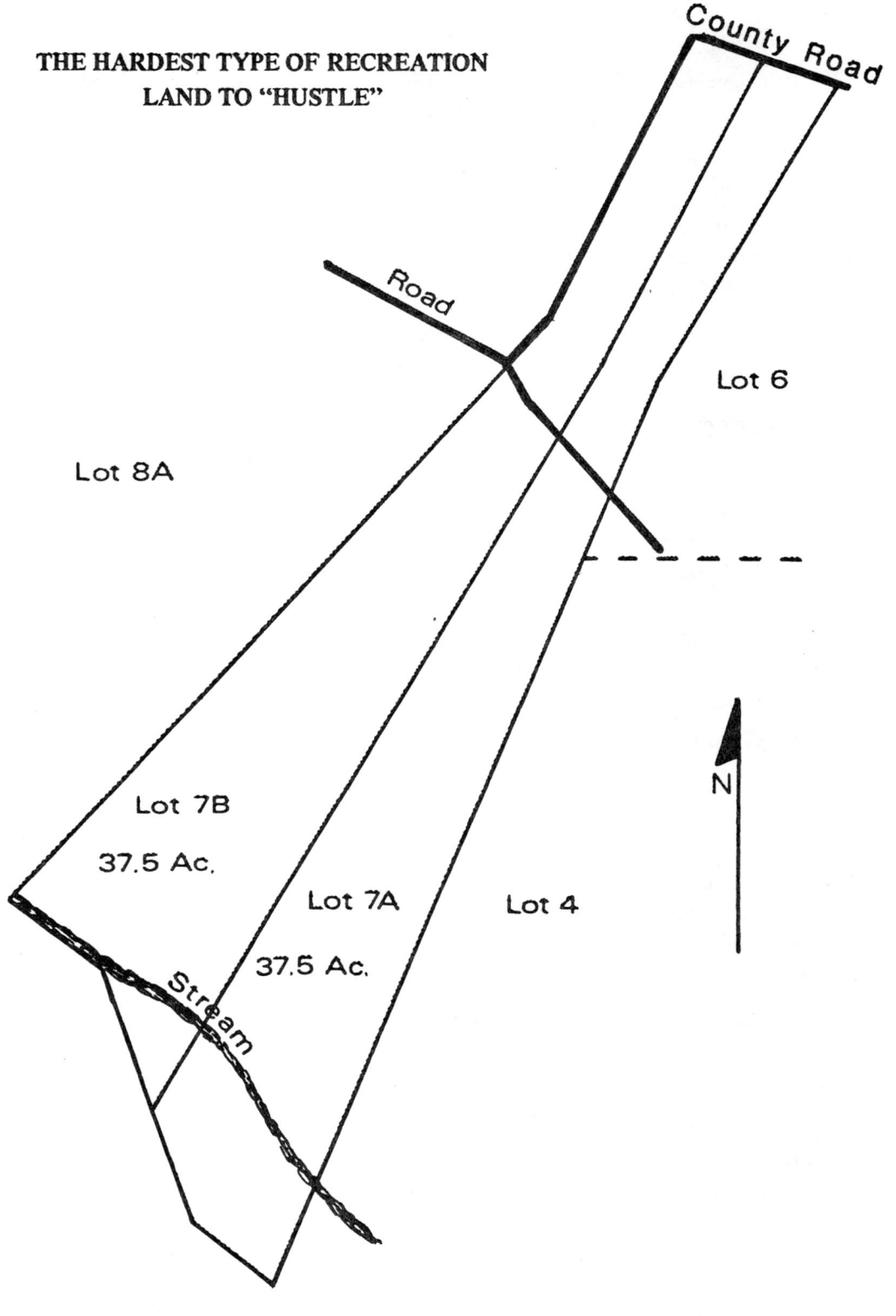

THE EASIEST TYPE OF RECREATION LAND TO "HUSTLE"

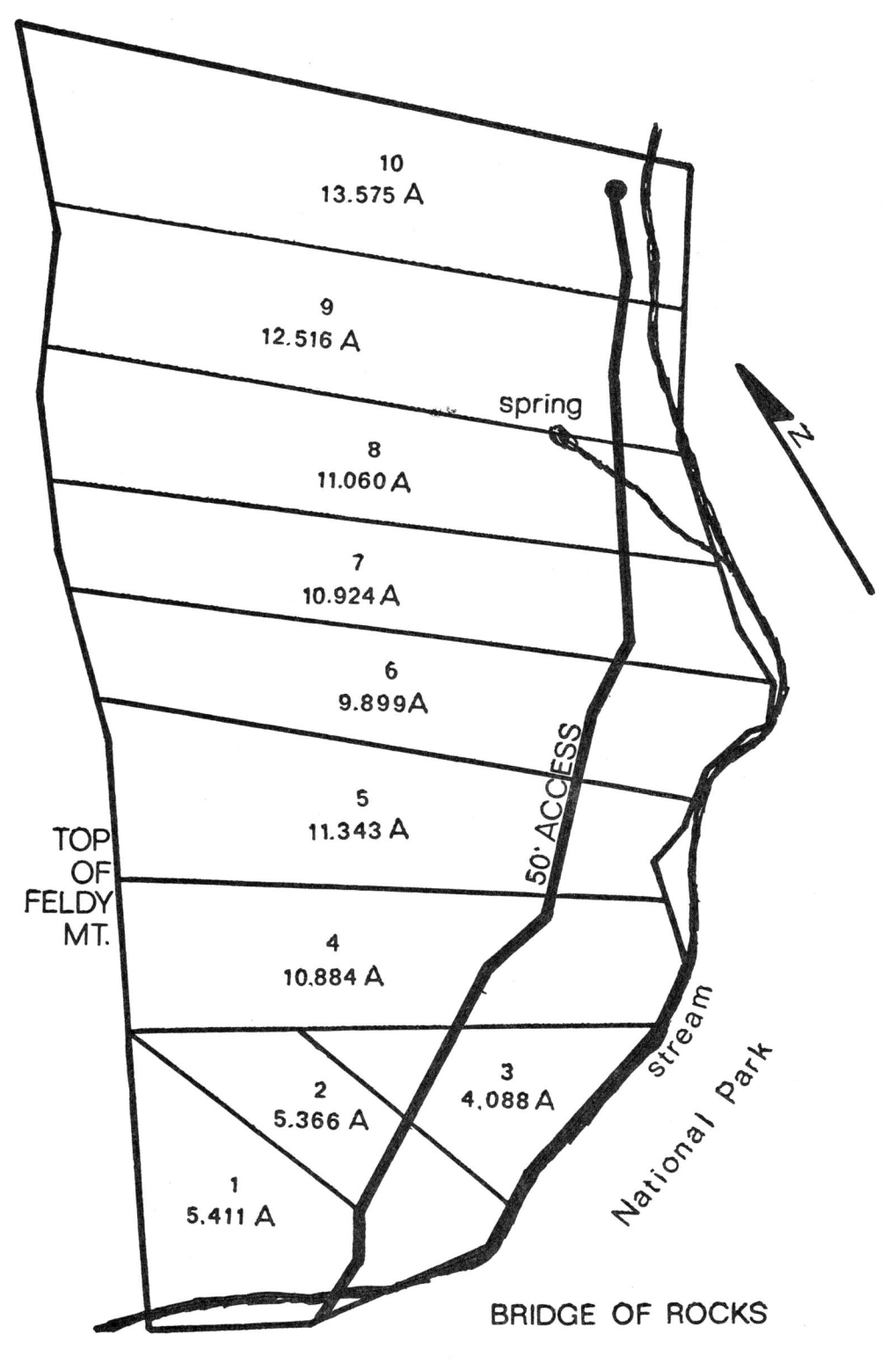

of ten acre lots, but before we could get the project underway the county changed the ground rules on us, and our original plan had to be scrapped. To avoid building expensive roads to state specifications, we ended up with some monstrous lot sizes and a few peculiar shapes that required years to market and sell.

Careful attention to the principles and techniques in this book should help you avoid being "second-guessed" by local governmental authorities out to control growth and speculation in land. On the first plat you can see a division of land that does credit to neither the developer nor the county. Even before the tract was subdivided, the property as a whole was awkwardly shaped. We had a devil of a time selling these two parcels — even when they were sacrificed at a price close to what we paid for the tract as a whole!

The easiest type of recreational property to market and sell is a reasonably priced, well-located tract of about 5-10 acres that borders a year-round fishing stream or navigable body of water and also backs up to usable government land, such as a National Park or Forest. Chances are that, if you bought the property right, you can keep the price for individual 5-10 acre parcels within reasonable limits. Larger lot sizes can cut down on sales volume, and parcels below five acres may be unsuitable for individual well and septic systems. In addition, smaller lot sizes may present sales problems and open you up to possible governmental regulation. The second plat shows a subdivision where people stood in line to buy from us. They can throw their fishing lines into the stream from their cabin decks or wade across the rocky waters into a 300-square-mile National Park and wildlife sanctuary.

Well-located acreage, water, natural amenities, reasonable price and terms — these qualities make for an unbeatable combination in recreational land.

HOW TO "UNDRESS" A LOT FOR MAXIMUM EXPOSURE

My partner saw an ad in the paper for a tract of land up in West Virginia. It was a small deal — 50 acres — and the price seemed reasonable enough. Generous terms were also promised. And when we learned that the property had "long road frontage" we decided to go up and have a look. We had been informed that the property was mostly open land, with a stream running through it.

One of the big economic issues at the time was the high cost of beef, and we knew that many in the land-buying public had turned their thoughts to open land for possible grazing. Our files on that particular county were incomplete because we had never been enticed that far west before. Nevertheless, when we looked at the property, there was something about it that did not immediately meet the eye. It was like looking at an attractive woman adorned in old-fashioned clothing, her eyes hidden behind glasses and her tresses swept up in a bun. I imagined how I might "undress" the tract to reveal its true beauty and potential to prospective "suitors."

To the casual looker or average prospective buyer, the property may have appeared to be just an ordinary tract of overgrown mountain land — possibly a little too far from the city — with a few run-down buildings on it. The price was about $17,000, or roughly $340 per acre. Twenty percent down, and the balance over seven years at 8% would handle the deal.

We were helped along by a recent survey which, incidentally, failed to indicate the existence of several springs and smaller streams; this was to our advantage as well. Road frontage was adequate, but a cemetery on one corner of the property had made about a third of that unusable. Our information showed that the county administrator and the local health authorities wanted to scrutinize any subdivision requiring new roads. Another requirement was that subdivisions of less than five acres must have roads built to certain state specifications. These restrictive factors had already ruled out any project calling for new road construction and small lots (3-5 acres). Overriding my whole analysis, however, was the requirement for a promotional angle. More about that in a minute.

To rate this property as to its potential for development and sale, I immediately went to the FEASIBILITY CHECK LIST. Using the check list elements as a guide, you can see how my analysis developed on this tract of farmland.

HOW TO "UNDRESS" A LOT FOR MAXIMUM EXPOSURE

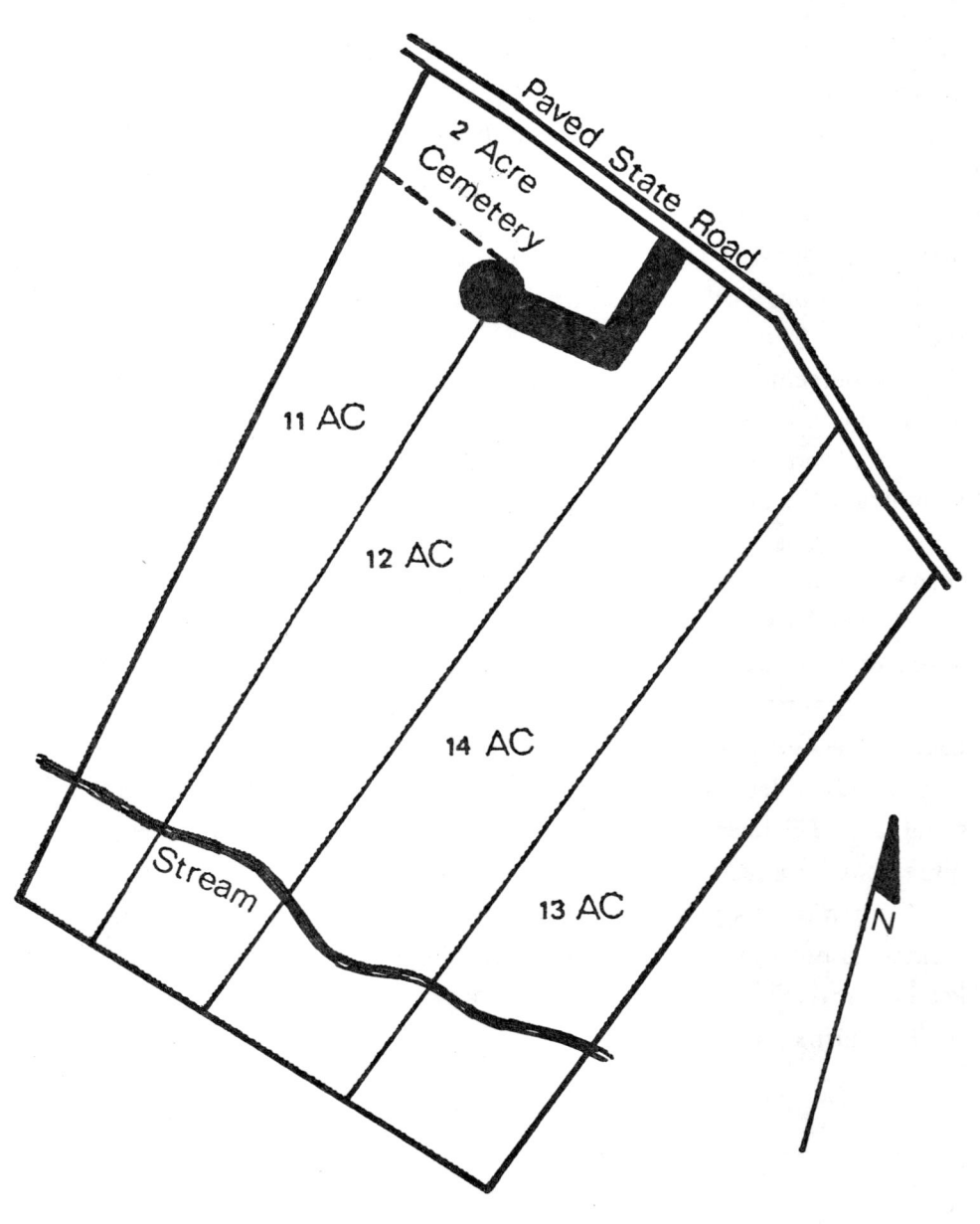

CHECK LIST ELEMENT	QUALITY SCORE	FIRST POINT SCORE	REVISED POINTS
Price and Terms	Good	40	40
Location	Fair	6	6
Usable Water Frontage	Good	3	3
Usable Road Frontage	Fair	2	2
Soils and Well Depth	Good	3	3
Views	Good	3	3
Access & Utilities	Good	4	4
Development Costs	?	?	3
Salability	?	?	3
Ease of Entry	Good	4	4
Total Score	(known)	65	71 (actual)

Development costs were left hanging on the first scoring for want of a promotional angle. Salability After Development — an element directly related to the promotional factor — was, in consequence, also up in the air. I couldn't honestly rate anything about the project in the *Excellent* category, yet I was only five points away from bringing in a winner. The key to a profitable project was clearly the promotional angle. Here's what I had to go on: Four lots, ranging in size from 11 to 14 acres, three of which bordered a hard-surfaced road, with the remaining one being granted a right-of-way over the adjoining lot. Lot? No. The word didn't have enough character to it. I needed more exposure. Tract? No. Farmette? Closer . . . Farm? Yes, that's it! I didn't have four lots, I had four beautiful little farms tucked away in the mountains of West Virginia. That was the angle I was looking for. I then proceeded to "undress" each lot to see what hidden beauty lay beneath a cursory view of the property. When I had completed my evaluation, I could honestly pick up at least six points on the FEASIBILITY CHECK LIST; enough to throw the project into the winner's circle.

Here's how the four small farms were advertised for sale and quickly sold: (We doubled our money and kept development expenses to a minimum.)

CHEAP MOUNTAIN FARMS IN ROMNEY, WEST VIRGINIA AREA

$9950

FARM No. 1 — Low priced farm with all farm buildings. Huge, 2-story barn has elec. Stable with grain bin; chicken house; garage with concrete floor. Partly fenced. On hard-surfaced road. Stream crosses property below barn. Another stream in back pasture. Splended homesite on knoll. Distant views of long, green mountains. 12 acres.

$8950

FARM No. 2 — Mountain pasture with pond, stable, and two streams. Stirring views of W. Va. mountains. On hard road joining cattle farm. Woods in rear of property where 2nd stream can be dammed up. 14 acres.

$7950

FARM No. 3 — One horse stable on exceptional hill country farm. 2 streams. Hard road frontage. Stunning views of green mountain upon green mountain. Huge old trees near homesite on hill. 13 acres.

$6950

FARM No. 4 — Just about the nicest laying farm in our inventory. Gentle, rolling hills off of hard road. Magnificent homesite with stream in back. Far-reaching views. Fenced on two sides. Joins cattle farm. 11 acres.

PLAYING GODFATHER — SOME THOUGHTS ON COVENANTS AND LOT OWNERS ASSOCIATIONS YOU CAN'T REFUSE

Duty is a troublesome master that cannot be dodged; sooner or later you must come back and settle the account. As a *Subdivestor*, you owe to your purchasers the responsibility for imposing sensible restrictions on how the property you convey may be utilized. For example, if you fail to establish minimum-size requirements for new construction within your subdivision, you may undermine property values by allowing cottages to co-exist with substantial homes. Laxity in defining construction guidelines can lead to all sorts of architectural evils, such as half-finished jerry-built homes, cinder block facades, mismatched roof lines, nonconforming outbuildings, shacks, and other eye sores. Your failure to rule on mobile homes at the onset could cause an unsightly mix of permanent homes alongside the more temporary variety. A junk yard or other commercial evil could suddenly crop up to haunt you and to destroy resale values if you did not specifically prohibit such ventures. Roads within your development could be left unattended and could become rutted and strewn with pot-holes if you failed to provide, in a set of restrictive covenants accompanying your deeds, for a property owners association and annual road maintenance dues.

In the Appendix you'll find a sample declaration of covenants. Usually you will try to gear your restrictions to the surrounding neighborhood and to anticipated development trends in that area. If you are a beginner and unfamiliar with the type and scope of restrictions you feel will be applicable to your subdivision, then you could locate a similar subdivision, and pattern your covenants after those on record in the county courthouse in that subdivision's Deed of Dedication. This is merely a starting point, and you may want to revise these restrictions if you feel some of them are unsuitable for your development. Your lawyer can assist you with this task, and you'll be glad you attended to this chore before the first lot was sold. People seem to have an aversion to accepting restrictions on the use of their property after the property has been conveyed to them. At the time of closing, however, they usually feel as if restrictive covenants are quite sensible.

When all or most of the lots within your development are sold, you should — if road and common facility maintenance are to be provided for — appoint officers of a property owners association or a nominating committee to select candidates for the various offices. (The nominating committee may, if expedient, nominate themselves and get on with the job of collecting and administering annual dues.) Enforcement of the restrictive covenants following your departure from the scene is then left to the property owners. Lawsuits for violations of these covenants can usually be initiated by a single lot owner or by the association acting on the behalf of a majority.

WHAT YOU SHOULD KNOW ABOUT SOILS AND BUILDING SITES

Not long ago you could go out into the countryside and pick up a few acres without worrying about sewage disposal. It was assumed by country folks that three or five acres, for example, would be more than ample for a septic tank and drainfields. Health authorities in the rural counties were "good ole boys" who never leaned on folks if they had a little ground around them.

Trouble started bubbling out of the ground when developers began cutting up the countryside and turning city folks out to build on wall to wall lots. A common question of the day was, "What's a septic tank and drainfield?" For the uninitiated, here is a definition of the system:

Septic tank — A concrete tank to collect solid wastes. The tank is buried underground and is connected to a field of individual disposal trenches. When full, the tank is pumped out by a septic tank service truck.

Drainfields — The area where absorption of liquid wastes occurs. Perforated pipe, surrounded by gravel and connected to solid piping from the septic tank, is laid in trenches of specific depth, length, width, and number — mainly dependent upon the size and use of the building or buildings being serviced by the system.

Another question now in vogue among prospective rural land buyers is, "Will this land perc?" The prospect rightfully wants to know if a percolation test has been performed on the property or, if not, will the results of such a test be satisfactory and positive. Very simply, the test is performed by allowing water to remain in a dug hole for a specified length of time to verify whether the soil will satisfactorily absorb liquid wastes at permissable rates per hour. A primary fear of health authorities is that, in impermeable soil, the liquid could rise to the surface and pollute wells and nearby watercourses. Before a building permit is issued, local health authorities can require the developer, builder, or lot owner to dig test holes of a specified number and depth, or they can perform this task themselves. The local health department has the authority to approve or deny building permits based on the results of this percolation test. Because of the many variables connected with interpreting these results, there is the usual appeals process, whereby you can have the test reviewed at the state level. If the soil is not mapped in your project area, you can profit by hiring a soil scientist to evaluate the soil in question. Local health authorities may be arbitrary and underskilled in evaluating soils, and you could miss out on potentially profitable deals by allowing opinion to sway fact. Never obligate yourself for a property deal until you know there will be no major problems with the soil. Such problems can come back to haunt you later on.

SEPTIC SYSTEM CHECK LIST

1. Avoid high water table areas; swampy ground; flood plain.

2. Avoid steep, rocky ground. (Trenches are difficult to construct and seepage is possible.)

3. Avoid proximity to wells and springs. (Stay 100 feet or more away and, preferably, locate the system in a downhill direction.)

4. Avoid building the system closer than 50 feet to lakes, rivers, and streams.

5. Avoid constructing disposal fields uphill from house. (A costly pumping system must then be installed.)

6. Avoid sticky, clay-like soils that resist drainage. (Usually these soils have a black, gray, or mottled surface.)

7. Avoid shale or bedrock areas where liquid wastes can seep through to contaminate springs and wells. (Septic system construction is also expensive in these areas.)

Soil information is readily available through the U. S. Soil Conservation Service (SCS), which has been measuring and mapping the nation's soil since the beginning of this century. The information has been broken down by counties and is available free from local SCS offices in the form of soil surveys. Each type of soil is coded as to name and class. By studying the survey and relating it to your project area, you can determine soil characteristics such as drainage, acidity (fertility), texture, structure, slope, stoniness, and the presence of subsurface rock or shale. If your county does not have the published data, it may be in unpublished form on maps and aerial photos. The local SCS office or county agent can help you to interpret this data. (See map in Appendix.)

SOME CONSIDERATIONS ABOUT BUILDING SITES

As a *Subdivestor,* your concern with the existence of suitable building sites will be a measure of your success. Long after you have sold off the individual lots you will have to live with your conscience and with the schedule of payments. Even if you have sold your mortgage notes, you can still be held personally liable in the event of default. The safety and suitability of building sites, therefore, should be dealt with before you sell the property, not after.

Generally, if the land is not suitable for individual septic systems, it will not support a great many building sites. Sites with high water tables and flood-prone areas are particularly risky for subdividing. Soils with clay content can give the homeowner trouble because of their expansion and contraction characteristics. Not only do septic systems operate marginally in such soils, but the very foundation of the home can be threatened.

Hillsides without adequate vegetation can also prove hazardous for building construction, due to erosion during heavy rainfall. Shallow areas subject to erosion have the same problem.

Earthquake-prone sections of the country and mountain areas where large areas of subsurface rock are present pose peculiar problems of their own. As a general rule, you do not want to subdivide land near a fault. Some counties have, because of subsurface rock, allowed alternatives to the septic system, such as beneath-the-ground holding tanks and waterless toilet-waste disposal systems. However, nationwide acceptance of alternative systems is a long way off.

ACTION POINTS — LESSON 6

1. Look through the plat books in a rural county courthouse for property that would lend itself to subdividing.

2. Get to know the record books in a typical county courthouse. Look up a deed, deed of trust (mortgage), and plat on a particular tract of land. (The clerk will get you started.)

3. Become familiar with the tax map, showing who owns property in the county and the size of each parcel.

4. Consider the economic and social climate of the country today. Think of a promotional angle that is in tune with this mood. Concentrate your efforts on locating tracts of land lending themselves to advantageous promotional concepts based on this mood.

5. Look up a typical set of restrictive covenants in the deed records of a rural county courthouse.

6. Become familiar with the septic system check list on **p. 129**.

7. Visit the Soil Conservation Service (SCS) office in a rural county to familiarize yourself with the local soil map and SCS operating procedures.

WHAT YOU NEED TO KNOW ABOUT ADVERTISING AND SALES PROMOTION

Lesson Number 7
Table of Contents

The Seven Vital Elements Of a Direct Response Ad	p. 137
The Seven Key Words For You To Remember In Ad Writing	p. 137
How To Enhance Believability In An Ad	p. 138
One Of The Most Powerful Appeals Known In Advertising	p. 139
How To Establish Value In An Ad	p. 140
Why Premiums And "Inducements" Should Be Related In Some Way To The Offer	p. 140
Why You Should Strive For Honesty In Ad Writing	p. 142
An Ad Where Every Sentence Works To Sell The Property	p. 143
How To Sell Off Old Home Places And Tenant Houses From Your Projects	p. 144
Why Historic And "Old" Properties Can Be A Gold Mine For You	p. 145
The Principal Job Of The Headline In An Ad	p. 146
How To Sell Off An Old Barn	p. 147
The Lasting Appeal Of The Words: "First Offer!"	p. 148
An Ad So Powerful That Others Tried To Copy Its Magic	p. 149
The Dynamic Appeal Of Waterfront	p. 150
Long Or Short Copy? — Why Either Will Work	p. 151
How To Successfully Advertise Your Foreclosures	p. 152
The Biggest Pulling Ad Of All	p. 153
How Direct Mail Advertising Can Accelerate Sales	p. 154
The Effective Use Of Direct Mail Letters And Display Advertising	p. 155
A Concept For The Sale Of A Bankrupt Development	p. 156
How To Sell Bargain Properties To Your Existing Mailing List	p. 159
How To Sell Additional Property To Your Existing Lot Owners	p. 161
The Magic Of Conceptual Thinking In Ad Writing	p. 166
Action Points	p. 166

What You Need to Know About Advertising and Sales Promotion

Some years ago, the editor for a prominent publisher saw an article I had written about effective real estate advertising in a competitive market. He suggested that I write a book to expand this central theme, but I was hard at work on a novel at the time, and the project never developed. My research into effective advertising and my ad writing has, nonetheless, continued unabated.

In this chapter you'll learn the money-making secrets of direct-response ad writing that have made fortunes for wealthy advertising men and entrepreneurs — men whose backgrounds and success stories I have carefully analyzed over a number of years.

The secrets are stored in the minds of the world's best writers of mail order copy and, like the combination to a safe, the secrets are referred to in the proper order and are utilized with great skill by master direct-response ad writers who must motivate people to immediate action. You may recall the story of the industrialist who complained to his staff, "I know that 50% of my advertising dollar is being wasted, but the problem lies in knowing which half." In mail order advertising, there is no such room for error. The ad writer rises or falls on the strength of his appeal.

A successful appeal produces immediate orders and coupons. If the ad flops, the result shows up in a lighter sack for the mailman and possibly another kind of sack for the ad writer.

As a *Subdivestor*, your advertising begins before you ever lay your hands on a piece of property. If you think you'll have a hard time selling the subdivided parcels, chances are you've made a mistake(s) somewhere up to the point of purchase. You may have paid too much for the property in the beginning, resulting in a price barrier between your parcels and the buying public. Your SOURCE BOOK or store of knowledge about property values could be deficient. Possibly there was a serious gap in your ACTION FILE, causing a major change in your subdivision plan, or a delay in its implementation. The trouble may have begun when you were influenced to purchase a piece of property by extraneous pressures, resulting in your loss of SELECTIVITY. Maybe your FEASIBILITY CHECK LIST was inaccurate or hastily prepared, and the property turned out to be more difficult to sell than you had anticipated. Finally, you may have purchased the land under bias or prejudice — you may have "fallen in love with it" — thus losing the OBJECTIVITY FACTOR.

The purpose of this chapter is to provide you with enough advertising savvy to sell your parcels quickly and efficiently providing you've mastered the principles of *Subdivesting* and learned to use the tools set out for you in this book.

O.K., let's go right to the heart of the matter and examine why some ad appeals succeed and why others fail. For a thorough discussion of successful advertising copywriting I recommend a thorough reading of any or all of the books or advertisements listed in the bibliography. You'll benefit particularly from the books by John Caples.

You've noticed that a good chef always manages to come up with the right ingredients in the proper proportion to make his dish entice the palate. The same holds true for direct response copywriters. If they leave out a vital ingredient, or if they mix in too much of this or too little of that, then the ad is substandard. What are the secret ingredients of a successful direct-response ad, and in what proportion do you use each of them? First the ingredients:

THE SEVEN VITAL ELEMENTS OF A DIRECT RESPONSE AD:

1. STOP THE READER
2. HOLD HIS ATTENTION
3. CREATE DESIRE FOR YOUR PRODUCT
4. MAKE HIM BELIEVE THE TRUTH OF YOUR OFFER
5. CONVINCE HIM THAT HE IS GETTING A BARGAIN
6. GET HIM TO COMMIT HIMSELF TO ACTION
7. GIVE HIM A REASON TO ACT NOW

The seven key words for you to remember when writing and analyzing direct response ads and campaigns are: STOP, HOLD, DESIRE, BELIEVE, BARGAIN, CLOSE, NOW. As we examine the ads to follow, you will get a feel for the proportion of copy devoted to each of these vital elements. Of course, not all ads will contain all seven elements. Let's see how many we can find in some of my most successful ads.

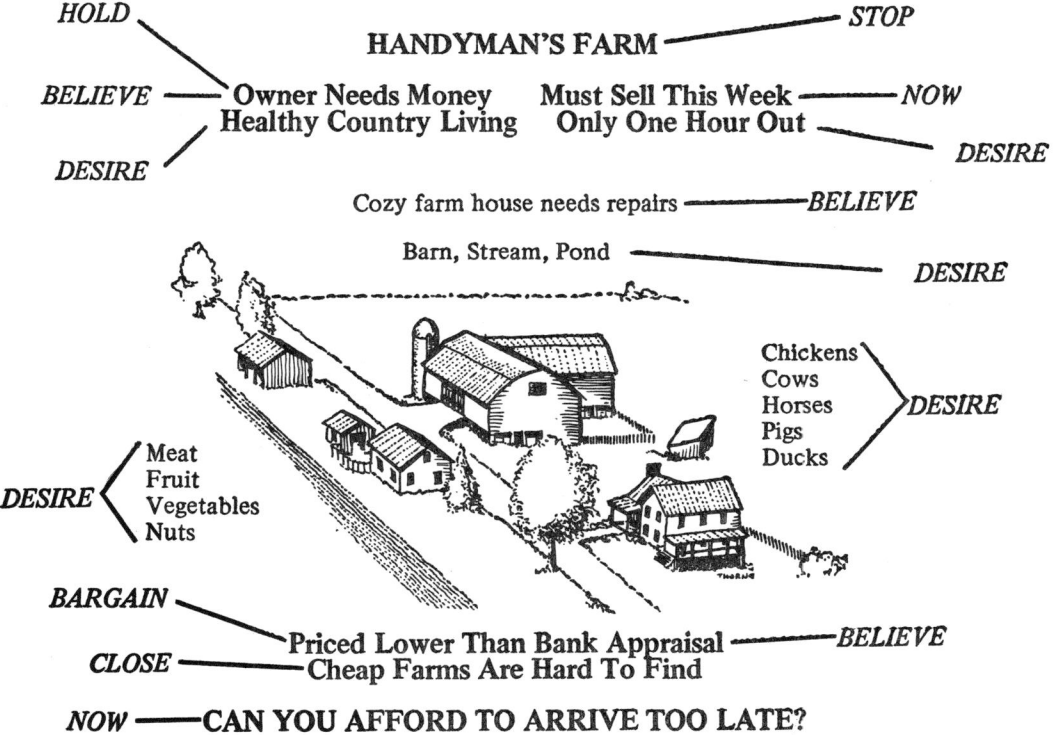

138 How You Can Grow Rich Through Rural Land

Portions of the ads presented in this chapter are shown as they actually appeared in newspaper print. Errors were not edited in order to give the reader a more authentic view of how these ads actually appeared.

7 KEYS FOR A SUCCESSFUL AD

For the price of a few acres in the country, we'll give you 14 acres for $195 down & throw in a blacktop road.

CHARLOTTESVILLE, VA. (vic.) — With the current inflation rate stealing $100 per month out of a $15,000 annual income, you can't afford not to get your money's worth. Sink your money in productive soil while you can get so much for so little, and before easing of gas crisis accelerates rush for country land. This low price will rise this summer. Property is level to rolling woodland, with garden areas and a small stream in the woods. You'll own 316 feet along a hard-surfaced state road, and you'll have a choice of several excellent building sites now served with electric power. A number of old roads run through the interior, where a 1-1 1/2 acre lakesite could be constructed at low cost. This tract is in a superior location just up the road from the James River at Warren's Ferry, and is only 25 minutes from Charlottesville. Considering the location, the large amount of acreage for the money, and the generous terms which allow you to borrow money at the prime rate, this tract should have excellent investment potential while providing you with permanent or recreational homesites, plus an iron-clad hedge against inflation. In summer, price goes up to $8500. Tie up now for trial period at just $7995. If you decide to buy, pay as little as $195 down. $118.36 per month for 96 mos. at 10% annual percentage rate. Discount for cash.

B. K. HAYNES CORP.
555-1212

- Stop the reader with your headline. (also shows value) — **1. STOP**
- Hold attention with startling fact. — **2. HOLD**
- Begin building desire and reason to act now. — **3. DESIRE**
- More desire
- Believability enhanced by specifics about property. (Avoid generalities) — **4. BELIEVE**
- Convince reader he is getting a bargain. — **5. BARGAIN**
- Call for action. — **6. CLOSE**
- Reason to act now. — **7. NOW**

Country Property

**More for your money
Less than a tankful round trip
Rich man's lakefront estate yours at po' boys $5950 — terms to suit.**

STANARDSVILLE, VA. — Try this park-like tract at no risk. Camp in the woods or on the grass beside 12-acre lake. You'll find it ideally suited to your needs or money back. Live here year round. Country club just 5 mins. away. Charlottesville 25 min. south. Blue Ridge views. 8 times more land than you would expect for such a low price. Almost 4 acres. Where else? $5950. Name your down payment. Reasonable terms to suit your needs.
Haynes-Anderson Associates
555-1212

Headline stresses value.

First sentence heightens interest and believability — "No risk."

Put your reader on the property to stimulate interest.

Believability reinforced by offering money back.

Bargain emphasized by comparing 4 acre tract to ½ acre sites selling at same price.

Commitment asked for — "Name your own down payment."

Action called for by question, "Where else?" inferring that the bargain won't last long.

Country Property

At just $58 per month this old barn is free!

Charlottesville, Va. (vic) Cheap mountain farmette for cabin or camp now, home later. Pasture & woods with stream and old barn. Clean living in John Boy's country. Views alone worth more than low price. Just 30 min. to Charlottesville. 3 acres. $3950. Bring $150, then $58.57 mo. 96 mos. 10.46% rate.
**HAYNES-ANDERSON ASSOCIATES
555-1212**

Comments

Gain attention here through the use of one of the most powerful appeals known in advertising — offering something for nothing. The inference here is that because the land is so obviously underpriced, the old barn is practically a gift. Desire and believability are also present in the ad. This is largely accomplished by associating the property with a popular and respected TV show. In the end the reader is asked to bring a specific amount of money to tie up the property.

COUNTRY PROPERTY

---

1 hr. D.C. area on Rt. No. 66
Commute! Low cost riverfront farm on Shenandoah $9750!

FRONT ROYAL, VA. — Dissolution of planned unit development. Nearly nine acres of riverfront farmland going for less than cost of quarter acre development lot. Commuters! Save thousands in advance of Rt. No. 66 completion (Now on final leg). Deep river property has stream and 220 foot waterfront on scenic river noted for fishing and canoeing. Situated downriver from Thunderbird Museum and Archeological "digs." Priceless artifacts now being uncovered from pre-historic Indian settlement along river bank. Rich bottomland for crops, cattle, horses, first home, vacation cabin, camping, home business, investment, retirement. Fish and swim from your own dock. Watch the timeless river carry canoes up river. Big adventure under big skies. Broad, sweeping, prairie-like scenes, and above you are the Massanutten Mountains, vast walls on the horizon, sustaining the Shenandoah. This river is the life-line of the Blue Ridge and the Shenandoah Valley. Make a new life for yourself before you have to pay two or three times this price: Just $9750. Bring min. $75 to hold. $75 due at closing. FREE THIS WEEKEND TO INTERESTED VISITORS! FRONT ROYAL VISITOR'S KIT AND FREE SINGLE ADMISSION TO THUNDERBIRD MUSEUM AND AMPHIBIOUS "DUCK" RIDE ACROSS SHENANDOAH TO ARCHEOLOGICAL "DIGS" (Can be seen from this property).

555-1212
Haynes-Anderson, Trustees
7 South Street
"At turn to Skyline Dr."
Front Royal, Va. 22630

Comments

In this ad we were disposing of a bankrupt development which had been sold to us following foreclosure. The ad shows you what you can do with the comparative pricing angle to establish value. Another obvious plus for the ad is the location — the property is commutable. Whenever you have the twin-barreled benefits of first and second home use, don't be shy in pointing this out. Here again we have an abundance of natural attractions to play on in building desire. Believability is established in the first sentence when we reveal the reason for selling. Readers are turned off by such vague statements as "must sell" or "sale of." Why must the owner sell? What kind of sale? Why is the property being sacrificed? Be careful with your giveaways. They must be tied directly to the offer or they'll dry up response. This inducement is appropriate because it is of direct benefit to anyone considering locating their primary home in the area.

MOUNTAIN PROPERTY

Wardensville, W.Va.
USE MILLION ACRES AT 5-ACRE PRICE!

Ruggedly beautiful trout pond area. 5 1/2 acres deep inside G.W. Nat'l. Forest minutes from new remote mountain lake and huge natural trout pond. Hunting tract with 360 ft. forest boundary snuggled on narrow trail just off state road. Scattered old apple trees from out of past. $3950; Terms $55 down; $55 month. 8% annual percentage rate.

CALL B. MARTIN, 555-1212

Buy River Farm At Price of House

Hurry on this one! Clean and attractive 4 bedrm., 2 1/2 bath. Well built farmhouse on approx. 17 acres with over 100 ft. frontage on South Fork Shenandoah River, south of Luray about 2 hours D.C. area. Lovely setting framed by mountains of the G.W. Nat'l. Forest. A paradise of fruit and chestnut trees, lush garden in yard, farm pond below house, several excellent out bldgs. including stable and barn. Fruit trees, garden. Sturdy house has basemt., kitchen, dining room, living rm., util. rm., storm windows, 2 enclosed porches and asbestos siding. Oil heat. Tip-top shape throughout. Plenty of grass for horses or cows and a Huckleberry Finn riverbank for lazy fishing and adventures down stream. $22,750, some bank financing.

B. K. HAYNES REAL ESTATE
Front Royal, Va.   555-1212

Comments

One of the most effective ways I've found to promote value is to dramatize the low price in the headline. By inviting comparison with other property of known or calculated value, the reader can judge for himself whether the offer is a true bargain. The two ads shown here are winners because they seize the reader's attention and hold it throughout the ad as he seeks verification of the claim made in the headline. Of course, the claim must be valid or you lose credibility. Unless you can logically support your claims you gain the reputation of a real estate operator who is always yelling "Wolf!"

> **MOUNTAIN PROPERTY**
> About 2 hrs. D.C. Area
> **Save 50% on waterfall forest joining Shenandoah Nat'l Park!**
>
> ELKTON, VA. — County denies zoning change for smaller lots. Now you can steal 37 valuable & unusual acres for 1/2 of proposed sale price. You gain 1/2 mile of Parkfront on Dry Run Falls trail. Continue through Park to Falls & South River Picnic Ground on Skyline Drive. Now you can be one of the few to have a roaring waterfall - a natural wonder - in your backyard. Bathe in Paradise this summer. All strange and beautiful forestland, once part of the Park. A wildlife sanctuary, suitable for cabins, retreat, campsites, investment. On excel. access road, just out of town. Recent survey. Once in a lifetime opportunity. Share this find with friends. Sacrifice: $500 per Acre, local bank financing over 10 yr. period; considerable discount for cash.
>
> **555-1212**
> **B. K. Haynes Corp.**
> **Madison, Va. 22727**

Comments

Earlier in the book we discussed the critical importance of using the ACTION FILE and the necessity for keeping it current. This ad shows you what may happen if you have land in inventory and a sudden change in zoning takes place before you can get your property developed. While this ad was very effective in liquidating the property because of its bargain appeal, it was also true that we lost profits by failing to keep up with the machinations of local governing bodies. The ACTION FILE was devised to prevent mistakes like this from recurring. Believability is helped along because the ad is honest. Desire is fostered by appealing to the "back to nature" enthusiasts and again, by offering a discount, we were able to cash out on the property.

> **COUNTRY PROPERTY**
> Dirt cheap Penna farmstead for security, fun, food, profit $59 mo.
>
> McConnellsburg, Pa (vic) — No need now to pass up that great country place because you thought you couldn't afford it. Years from now you'll look back and marvel that you bought this farmstead so cheap. Nothing mediocre about this property. This is five and one quarter acres of green Pennsylvania farmland, the best that money can buy. Low in cost, yes. But all of it is rich, productive, and usable land, located in safe area along winding paved country road. Pond across road for fishing and swimming. This is not ordinary land, but valuable state road property where you can build a home or cabin, use mobile home, camp out, grow your own food, raise livestock, or plant Christmas trees and watch the money roll in. The perfect sock for dropping dividends into your future. Now you can breathe clean air on weekends and vacations. Move here later. Cowan's Gap State Park is just up the road. Raystown Lake - 27 miles long - is only 20 min. away. Magnificent views of Tuscarora Mountains. Public hunting grounds all around. So cheap and easy to buy, we wish we could find more. Here's how to finance: $4800. Bring $100. Then own this great country place for just $59.55 mo., 120 mos., 9% simple interest. Save interest, hundreds more, with cash offer.
>
> **555-1212**
> Haynes-Anderson Assoc.
> Star Route 1, Box 15
> Hustontown, Pa. 17229

Comments

This ad sums up in the headline what the majority of readers are looking for in country property. It obviously hit home too, because the property sounded easy on their pocketbooks. Notice how it is established at the outset that a low price is no reason to suspect that the property might have limited usability. One way to build up the value of property is to enumerate its potential uses. Notice in this ad how every sentence works to sell the property. There are no flowery adjectives. When descriptive words are used they must be tied directly to a definite benefit. See how the word "winding" is used to highlight the advantage of road frontage. Study this ad to see how it draws you into the picture through hard-working, positive sentences.

> **FOR RECREATION OR RESTORATION**
> # OLD MOUNTAIN FARMS
> ## $6,500-$8,500
>
> **ELKTON, VA.** — Pre-Civil War ghostly run down house from out of the past. About 10 acres on cool, fast moving stream. Located on mountain along trail leading in Shenandoah National Park. See property from Skyline Drive. Long range views from high meadows. Cherry trees and wild roses throughout. Hand built rock walls, spring water, well shaded. $6,500, min. terms, $600 dn., $87.39 mo. 84 mos. Discount for cash.
>
> **FRONT ROYAL VIC.** — In historic Fort Valley, South of Elizabeth Furnace. Unusual 3 bdrm. farmhouse, relic of the past. Dug well, all year stream. No plumbing. Weather worn out buildings nearly 6 acres, pasture with unlimited views of valley and mountains of the G.W. Nat'l Forest all around. Few feet from trout stream. On state road. Can be remodeled into vacation retreat or hunting lodge. $7,500, min. terms 25% down, $88.85 mo., 84 mos. Discount for cash.
>
> **ELKTON, VA.** — Joins Shenandoah Nat'l Park. Good 3 bdrm. farmhouse on 5 acres back in mountains. 2 barns, stream through property. Borders state road. Tract sets in mountain hollow where waterfall plunges over 200 ft. in 2 descents. Falls trail just back of property, splendid views. Lots of green pasture. Stone throw from swimming lake. $8,500 min. terms 29% dn., $93.52 per mo. 84 mos. Discount for cash. Adjoining 5 acres available.
>
> 8% Annual Percentage Rate
> Guaranteed Worth More in Trade By
>
> **B.K. HAYNES REAL ESTATE**
> "Home of Safe Land Investment"
>
> **RARE FINDS! INTERESTED PARTIES SHOULD CALL EARLY**
> **555-1212**

Comments

The "Old Mountain Farm" approach is a sure-fire way to sell off the home place and tenant houses from your development. In the ad above we were disposing of the old homes in three separate developments. The walk-in traffic from this ad was substantial, and a large number of tracts were sold through the drawing power of these "Old Mountain Farms." As you can tell from the prices, this sale took place back in the sixties when property was a lot cheaper than it is today. Notice how we've utilized the 7 vital ingredients of a successful direct response ad: (1) stop the reader, (2) capture his attention, (3) make him want to see the property, (4) encourage him to believe in the offer by holding nothing back and giving a "guarantee", (5) establish value (through pricing), (6) call for action, and (7) give reason to act now.

> **Old Mountain Schoolhouse**
> **E. Blue Ridge Mtns. 90 mins. 495**
>
> Abandoned 1 room schoolhouse on 5 open and wooded acres back in mountains along rushing trout river. Antique structure once alive with childrens' laughter now creaking and sagging under the strain of time. Giant hemlock tree guards this ancient ghost and shelters childrens' shortcut path along the road. Old books, organ and handhewn school desks tell story of self-sufficient mountain community cast aside when the boys and girls went away. From the schoolhouse you can see the ageless mountains and hollows from which the children came. Several mountain families remain in this ghost town, abandoned general store within sight of school. Shenandoah Nat'l. Park and Virginia Game Commission have claimed most of surrounding mountains. 2 swimming lakes nearby. $4800; Min. terms: $200 down; $55 month $4100 cash.
> **555-1212**
> **HAYNES-ANDERSON ASSOC.**

Comments

Occasionally you may come across a truly unique piece of property that lends itself to more poetic treatment. This sort of approach however, should be used with discretion or the reader will think you're just playing with words. This ad was written back in the late sixties when the quest for recreational property was in full bloom. Now you'll notice the emphasis of most advertising has turned more to value and usability, rather than to intangible considerations such as prestige of ownership and hoped-for amenities. This ad would work in the face of these changes for the same reason that many antiques are more valued than new creations -- all of us seem mastered by the earliest, the oldest, and the longest.

> **MOUNTAIN PROPERTY**
> **Throw line in trout stream from 10 acres joining Park $6989**
>
> SHENANDOAH, VA. — Recent trade with Shenandoah Nat'l. Park frees up valuable cabin/campsite back along South Branch Naked Creek. Unusual site, back in recesses of Park, now offered with unrestricted access. Located below Baldface Mtn. Overlook on Skyline Drive, and just off Big Ugly Run Fire Trail. Excellent improved road. Elec. avail.; 350-ft. Park and trout stream boundary. Wade across stream into 300 sq. miles of Parkland with huge trees, unbelievably beautiful trails, crashing waterfalls, and quick, darting wildlife at every turn. Fish for breakfast from your cabin deck or lawn chair. Rare find! Seldom does trout stream property come back on the market. Don't miss out. Just $6989. Bring only $89. Then pmts. of $89.12 mo., 120 mos., 9.46% rate. Make cash offer.
>
> **555-1212**
> **B.K. HAYNES CORP.**
> "More Land & Value for the Money"
> Cor. Rtes. 29 & 230, Madison, Va.

Comments

The purpose of the headline is to catch the reader's eye and pull him into the ad. We start out right away in this ad to put the reader right where we want him — on the property, preferably having an enjoyable time. Believability begins with the first sentence, and continues throughout the ad as specific location factors and statistics are given. Notice how an abundance of natural attractions can be used to paint an enticing word picture. Of course, the real strength of the offer was the unique combination of Park front and trout stream frontage. Response to the ad continued long after the last tract in the development was sold out.

> **Largest Barn Doubles What Your $ Can Buy
> & Helps You Make a Living in the Country $22K**
>
> RAYSTOWN LAKE, PA. — (Area) Probably Fulton County's largest and most immaculate barn. Replacement cost estimated at $50,000 or more, exclusive of land. Now pick it up for a song, plus ten acres, plus two huge grain silos. Over 6,000 sq. ft. on two stories alone, plus third story loft. Property fronts 467 ft. on state paved road. Massive L-shaped building has shiny gambrel roof fenced corral, water, and lights. Cows grazing in accompanying ten acre pasture. Name your pleasure and use: farm barn, remodeled house or house & barn combination, warehouse, dinner theatre, garage, church, meeting hall, recording studio, art studio, antique shop and warehouse, museum, school, restaurant, horse stable, etc. One of life's rare bargains. More space for the money than you will ever hope to find. If you need space, you will benefit from a quick inspection trip. Just $22,000 on terms. Make cash offer to cut price further. Call for appt.; pictures, directions:
>
> **555-1212**
>
> **HAYNES-ANDERSON ASSOC.**
> Star Route 1, Box 15
> Hustontown, Pa. 17229

Comments

Got a barn you want to get rid of? Here's an ad that paid off in telephone calls weeks after it was sold. The twin appeals evident in the headline were that the reader was not only getting a bargain, but that somehow he would be helped along more quickly toward his dream — that of giving up city living for a more satisfying life in the country. The value of the barn seems obvious, and potential uses and sources of income are listed to stimulate desire. Believability is virtually assured when construction costs are compared with an existing completion price of less than $4 per sq. ft. Because we knew the barn photographed well, thus assuring people of its value, we elected to offer pictures as a lure to action. By asking for a cash offer, we were able to cash out quick and concentrate on marketing the raw land.

COUNTRY PROPERTY

Just 25 min. Charlottesville
First Offer!
All you want in low-cost productive farmland

CHARLOTTESVILLE, VA. (VIC) — Affordable, easy-to-own ten acres for fun farm, retirement, investment, and self-sufficiency. Level to rolling cropland, pasture fields, valuable oak forest, bold stream, mountain views, 400-ft. on rural state road; 1317-ft. depth through park-like woods with lively creek. This junior-sized farm has it all if you're looking for an ideal low-priced country homesite or mobile homesite where taxes are low, where it's safe, and where you can find shelter from inflation. You may have spent years searching for just such a survival tract. You can own this farm now, without waiting and watching inflation take your savings. Just $9950. Bring min. $75; $75 due at closing. Then $128.17 mo., 120 mos., 9.75% rate. Make cash offer.

555-1212
HAYNES REALTY
Rte No. 1, Charlottesville, Va. 22901

Comments

Whenever you have a legitimate "First Offer!" it could turn out to be a winner at bringing in the calls. People like to have a first look at things — no matter what it is. This ad was extremely effective in selling every lot in the subdivision, including tracts of larger and smaller sizes. What is there about the ad that pulled in response week after week and caused other real estate people to copy it? Aside from containing the 7 vital ingredients of an effective direct response ad, you'll find the answer in the headline. Here is a classic case where selectivity in land acquisition paid off. Nearly every tract had most of the features that city folks were looking for in rural farmland.

COUNTRY PROPERTY

Farmstead Bargain!
All the Features you want at sacrifice price
$9900 Bring $100

McCONNELLSBURG, PA. — First offer by health-conscious owner, who spent years searching for ideal farmstead: Pasture, woods, cropland, stream, paved road, mountain views, safe area. Now recession forces sale at bargain price. Have you ever seen all these recommended features on a ten-acre tract? If so, expect to pay dearly - up to twice as much in good times. Rich Pennsylvania soil. 10-acre farmstead measures approx. 500 x 300 on black top road. Plenty of road front to sell off part to help pay for your farm. Meandering stream through woods in back. Enough green land to support yourself. A ready resale. Sweeping views of 2 mountain ranges. Pleasant drive through clean air country. Less than 2 hours away by interstate. Experts predict you'll need a survival tract in the country. A lasting value that will outdistance inflation. Don't miss out by being late. One of the best buys for the money we've ever seen. Just $9900. Bring $100. Pay $400 at closing. Own for $119.08 mo. 120 mos., at 9% simple interest. A cash offer will steal this tract! Call for appt.

555-1212
HAYNES-ANDERSON ASSOC.
Star Route 1, Box 15
Hustontown, Pa. 17229

Comments

What was the secret of this successful ad? What was so powerful about it that caused other real estate people to copy it and attempt to use its magic for their own properties? My own analysis shows that it uses every one of the 7 vital ingredients of successful direct response advertising mentioned earlier. The ad stops the reader with the bargain appeal and draws him immediately into the picture. Desire and believability are painted into the ad because the property is the closest thing to ideal that the reader could hope for. The reader wants to believe this word picture because he knows he could spend years looking around and still not find the ideal, affordable "place in the country." Enough specifics are given to support the truth of the offer. He is thankful that someone has found the ideal place for him and now must give it up. Action is called for by citing "experts" who appeal to the self-preservation instinct. Immediacy of response is helped along by the powerful bargain theme which convinces him that, unless he acts fast, he may lose out on an opportunity that may never come again.

COUNTRY PROPERTY

**2 hrs. south of D.C. Beltway
50 miles west of Richmond
Now you have the chance to own a
homestead on the river - bring $95!**

LOUISA, VA. — Believe it or not, there is still some low cost waterfront acreage around, right here in central Va. Where else can you find five acres on a navigable warm water fishing stream for so little money? Cash in on a vanishing commodity, whatever your reason: relocation, cheap camping, home; cabin or trailer site, inflation hedge, back to nature, retirement place, profit maker. Five wooded acres right smack on South Anna River. Swimming, canoeing, fishing at your leisure. Twenty-four South Anna tracts sold in just a few short weeks. You'll be just minutes from central Va.'s largest lake, Lake Anne, 9600 acres. Uniformed buyers pay this price and more for a dinky waterfront lot on South Anna. If you can find five cheap acres on the river within 50 miles of a major city buy it! Major newspaper spots this area, near Richmond, in magic investment ring. You'll soon be looking at a $10,000 price tag for riverfront here. All waterfront we've sold over the past 10 years has gone up significantly in value at resale. Bargain five acres! $4995. Bring just $95. Own for $63.28 per mo. for 120 mos. at 9.46% A.P. rate. Slash price with cash offer. FREE THIS WEEKEND. TO CUT ADVERTISING COSTS, FREE FLATBOTTOM BOAT FROM SEARS OR WARDS with this tract.

**555-1212
HAYNES-ANDERSON ASSOC.**
501 So. Royal Avenue
Front Royal, Va. 22630

Comments

If you've got a development of small tracts with a dynamic appeal like waterfront, you'll want to play that appeal up for all it's worth. Most readers, of course, are aware of the high price of waterfront property, so you can't go wrong if you can offer them an opportunity to buy something they've always wanted, but never thought they could afford. This ad had continuing appeal because it gave the reader some news. The headline piqued his interest and activated his thoughts. An initial impulse that the headline might just be another advertising slogan is dispensed with by clearly stating that the reader could begin to own waterfront with only $95. How many of the 7 basic appeals can you find in this ad? Why do you think the free offer at the bottom was so effective?

> **COUNTRY PROPERTY**
> **Tree Farm! $7950**
> Charlottesville, Va. (vic)
>
> A steal! 15 acres of wildlife woodland. 358 ft. on paved road. Pvt. road to building site. Suitable for camping, mobile home, cabin, or private dwelling. James River access. Owner sacrifice. $7950. Terms: $950 dn. $99.81 mo. 108 mos. 10.33% rate. Make offer for cash and adj. 25 ac. with small stream. $11,950.
>
> **B.K. Haynes Corporation**
> Front Royal, Va.
> **555-1212**

Comments

Here is an example of an effective small ad that could have been written by a non-dealer who just happened to have a tract of land for sale. Notice the suggestion of immediate use and the low price which make up the punchy headline. The bargain appeal and call for immediate action are dominant throughout the ad.

> **Front Royal, Va. 1 Hr. Beltway**
> **SMALL, CHEAP FARM**
>
> Run down 3 B.R. frame farmhouse with bath. Excellent barn. 8 ac. with bold stream and wooden bridge. Sweeping mountain views from upper pasture. Just off Rt. 66 interchange. $11,950. Min. terms: $950 dn. $133.47 mo. 120 mos. 8% Annual percentage rate. Adj. acreage avail.
>
> **B. K. HAYNES REAL ESTATE**
> Front Royal, Va.
> **555-1212**

Comments

Sometimes you can fall into the trap of writing too much or trying too hard to promote a piece of property. Your failure to keep your ad copy simple and direct could make the reader wary about the offer. A good exercise in ad writing is to let the copy sit for a day or so after you first type up an ad. Go back to it with a fresh look, and ask yourself whether you really need to say all you've said to bring out qualified prospects. This ad says very simply, "Here's a small, cheap farm you can buy, and it's close in. You'll have to do a little work to fix it up, but the price is certainly right and it's easy to own. More land is available if you want it." The ad has simply transferred onto paper the thoughts and longings of a great many potential buyers. And when you can do this, you don't need a sales pitch to bring the customers out.

> **Mountain Property**
> **CHEAP MOUNTAIN FARM**
> Albemarle County Line - Bldgs. alone insured for more than asking price! Depression price on small Walton country farm back up in Blue Ridge. Raise cows, chickens, pigs, veg., keep horses. Just 30 min. from Charlottesville & U. Va. 9 rm. frame farmhouse (no bath) has spectacular views of Blue Ridge and Nat'l. Park. 2 story log barn. Garage & machine shed. Stream through pasture. Fruit trees. Woods. Pond site. White board fencing. 10 ac. with more land avail. $26,950. $5,000 dn. $1,950 in Jan., $5,000 in spring. Then pmts. of $196.16 mo. for 120 mos. 9 3/4% annual percentage rate. Cheaper yet if you can do with 5 acres.
>
> Haynes-Anderson Assoc.
> 402 Park Street
> Charlottesville, Va.
> 555-1212

Comments

This ad shows you a successful format for selling off farm buildings. Catch immediate attention using the appeal of finding an inexpensive little place in the country where you can make dreams come true. Value is shown here in the very first sentence. Notice how believability is built into the ad through the use of specifics, including the admission that there is no bath in the house. To help the reader visualize the farm and to strengthen desire, reference is made to the Walton TV show. Visual associations of this type tell far more than a plethora of flowery sentences. The ad asks for a direct commitment of specified amounts of money so that nothing is left up in the air. If the reader is unable to make that much of a commitment right now, he is enticed by a smaller option.

> **Make $ on Foreclosures**
> Owners of valuable mountain property lose thousands due to recession. Their loss, your gain. Pick up some property for a song. Some with no money down, take over payments. Samples: Shenandoah, Va. CABIN ON RIVER, $6989; $89 dwn' Elkton, Va. 10 ACRES WOODS, 2 FARMETTES WITH STREAMS, ONE 9 ACRES, ONE 5 ACRES ALL THREE UNDER $5000. WITH CREDIT REFS. YOU MAY NEED ONLY $50 DOWN ON SOME PROPERTIES. Madison, Va.: LARGE CABIN ON 3 ACRES, $6995. 5 ACRE RUN-DOWN MTN. FARM, $4975. 3 ACRE WOODS, NO DOWN PMT. REQ. LITTLE AS $75 ON OTHERS. MANY HAVE LONG-TERM TO RUN AT CHEAP INTEREST RATES. PAYMENTS AS LOW AS $1 PER DAY. Write for free list. People stealing bargains every week. INCLUDE PHONE NUMBER OR CALL FOR SPEEDY APPT. Not a gimmick to sell land, values are real. Phone or write Mr. Haynes or Mr. Gallihugh, B.K. HAYNES CORP., Cnr. Rates. 29-230, Madison, Va. 22727. 10 years experience selling & re-selling mtn. land.
> **555-1212**

Comments

During the oil and gas crisis of 1973-74, foreclosures multiplied when people became worried about the sudden shortage and high price of gasoline. Some consumers panicked; others felt that they could not keep up the payments on their property. This ad ran for months during that period and successfully wiped out every foreclosure in inventory. Later variations of the ad included the free offer of my "Land Buyer's Guide" to those who wrote or called in for our list of "Distressed Properties." This approach can pay off during any gas crisis.

Comments

Sometimes a piece of property you consider to be of little value can be made appealing by giving it an imaginative, fresh look. The "Gray Ghost" described here probably pulled more responses than any other single ad I've written. Notice here how a potential disadvantage (old shack) has been turned into a definite advantage (historic old farmhouse).

COUNTRY PROPERTY

**Rare Gems in Blue Ridge Mountains
Near Madison, Va.**
**Land Treasures of Virginia
Gray Ghost**

Reduced for immediate sale. Ghostly run-down mountain farmhouse left behind in Blue Ridge foothills. Pitiful 3 room outcast lingers in overgrown fields shadowed by an encroaching forest. Grim decaying structure pulled from the earth by rock chimney and hand-hewn beams. Old shed gasps for life in weeds. 6 acres wildly beautiful scenery. Small stream, spring, and swimming lake hidden in woods just steps away. $4950. Minimum terms: 10% down. $68.58 month. 84 months. Cash discount. 5 ACRES ON TROUT STREAM. $2950. Minimum terms: $50 down. $45.21 month. 84 months. Cash discount.

B. K. HAYNES CORP.
Madison, Va.   **555-1212**

While all of the ads discussed so far in this chapter are meant to serve as good examples of the proper way to advertise your rural tract of land, it should be understood that every one of these ads appeared in newspapers in just the form that you see them (with the exception of the phone numbers) and were *most successful* in producing immediate results for me. By following the example of these advertisements closely, you will be able to arrive at hard-hitting, believable immediate response advertisements that are guaranteed to produce results.

DIRECT MAIL ADVERTISING

To accelerate sales, you may want to conduct a direct mail program in addition to your direct response advertising. Small ads like these can be effective in building a mailing list at minimum cost. It is much easier to sell a client who has received mail from you prior to the time he responds in person to your ad. The mailing should tie in directly with your newspaper advertising and list specific property offerings. If a client on your mailing list has not purchased a piece of property from you within a year, he should be "cleaned" from your list. This is not to say that he will not reappear by simply responding to another of your ads or by writing in and requesting that your mailings continue. We've sold clients who have been on and off our lists for years. However, this list must be periodically "cleaned" if your direct mail program is to operate at maximum efficiency. Be sure not to encourage the reader to write for information when, in the same ad, you are asking him for an immediate response. This approach, I've found, weakens your ad. Your direct mail program is a separate entity that calls for different guidelines.

LAND TRAP? Send for FREE Land Buyers Guide, B.K. Haynes Realty, Dept. B, Front Royal, Va.

CHARLOTTESVILLE, VA. and ROMNEY, W.VA. 10 small farms you can buy under $10,000. For free list call/write Haynes-Anderson, Assoc., 501 South Royal Ave., Front Royal, Va.

DIRECT MAIL LETTERS AND DISPLAY ADVERTISING

As a *Subdivestor,* the only type of sales letter that you will want to send out is one designed to bring the client straight to the closing point. You are after an appointment, a commitment to purchase, or an offer of purchase. You can accomplish this by effectively building into your letters the same seven elements of successful immediate response advertising that you strive for in your ads.

Your mailings should be restricted to those clients on your mailing list. You're either asking for a new sale or (in the case of your existing property owners) an additional sale. Your success as a *Subdivestor* is dependent upon *quick sales of the subdivided parcels which, in turn, can be sold at a profit.* You must get in and out of deals as quickly as possible, while still making an overall profit. To do this, you may have to take a loss on certain parcels, but this will be more than covered in the tide of profits flowing from the project as a whole.

You are not interested in random prospecting for clients using methods you may find in general real estate sales and in much of the land development industry. You should envision yourself as, first, an investor and, secondly, as a developer. *Subdivesting* does not call for the administration of a sales and marketing force; nor does the technique require a large staff. If no one associated with you has the expertise to perform a certain task, then the job should be farmed out. You should not, for example, bring in a staff person if their only function is to write direct mail letters and handle advertising chores. They must be capable of performing along the broad spectrum of *Subdivesting* in order to justify a key position.

Let's look at a few situations where you may need an immediate response letter written or a display ad designed for the newspapers. In Situation No. 1, you and your partner have been in business for a while and you've just acquired a large tract of land as the result of a foreclosure sale. You are now at the development stage where you'll be offering a variety of five to ten acre tracts. Your mailing list is quite substantial; it includes both existing property owners and prospects who have responded to your ads and mailings but who have not, as yet, found what they are looking for in land. You've retained a local real estate agency with capable salesmen to handle sales on a commission basis, and they've been properly oriented to your way of doing things. You told an advertising art agency how you operate and what you were offering, and they've prepared a classic ad that should produce a steady flow of clients. Problem: You need an effective immediate response letter written for all the people on your mailing list, and the ad agency is not qualified to write the letter. They recommend a free-lance immediate response writer. You contact him and acquaint him with your way of doing business. Subsequently, he knocks out a letter that should do the job.

I don't recommend locking yourself into an ad agency for a commission on your volume of newspaper advertising. You may have to pay 15-20% of the ad cost, plus production expenses. Your best bet is to use free-lance writers and art studios that work on an hourly or fee basis. You save the agency commission and maintain maximum flexibility. If you find yourself using a lot of display advertising and immediate response letters, you'll soon learn which free lance writers and art studios are most effective in relaying your concept to the buying public. In the Bibliography you'll find source information on where you can buy free lance writing and advertising art work.

Situation No. 1

NAME OF FIRM

Address

Dear Client:

Recently, just outside the town limits, an entire bend of the Shenandoah River went on the auction block. This property is unique in that, on the property, archeologists are currently uncovering artifacts from one of the earliest known Indian settlements on the North American continent.

A resort development had been planned for this river bend, and hundreds of thousands of dollars had been expended on a museum and in land planning. Quarter acre lots were scheduled to sell for $10,000 to $15,000.

Now, small farms 20 to 40 times larger than these lots are being sacrificed for less than the developer's price on a single lot. For example, you can steal a five acre farm just outside of town for as low as $5,900. You can choose a five acre riverfront estate for as low as $9,950. You can check with any realtor in town, and find that small farm-sized plots of land are priced much higher throughout the Shenandoah Valley region. This property can be purchased on just about any terms. You can name your own down payment.

This fall, we will be offering the property as primary homesites to people from the Washington D.C. area who wish to relocate to the country and commute to their jobs. Right now, it is estimated that about ten percent of the local residents now commute. Route 66, a nonstop interstate freeway, will soon be completed from Front Royal to the Washington metropolitan area. Commuting will be commonplace. Land prices around Front Royal are expected to double.

Prior to offering this property for sale to metropolitan residents, we will be offering the choicest land to local persons with a discount of up to 10%. If you would care to inspect a five or ten acre farm on or at the Shenandoah River, please tear off the enclosed appointment form and mail it to me before November 15, 1976. If you select a farmstead this weekend, during the preliminary stages of survey, you will receive a $200.00 promotional rebate. You will receive this $200.00 deduction in addition to the up to 10% discount which is only available for a limited period to all local residents and prospective residents of this area.

For your protection, so that you may have ample time to make up your mind, a money back guarantee is in effect until January 1, 1977.

Let me hear from you soon. If you have ever looked for small acreage for a primary, secondary, or retirement homesite, or for investment, I sincerely believe you will find this opportunity too good to pass up.

Best Wishes,

B. K. Haynes

P.S. SPECIAL, THIS WEEKEND ONLY. Check out the farmsteads at Thunderbird. If you are interested in viewing the Indian artifacts found on the property, we will pay the costs for two admissions to the Thunderbird Archaeological Museum and the "duck" ride across the Shenandoah River to the "digs".

THIS OFFER IS OPEN TO ALL WHO ATTEND THE SALE. Please stop by our office on the corner of Routes 55 & 340 (on the left at the turn from Washington D. C. to the Skyline Drive and Thunderbird Museum).

REMEMBER! FIRST TO COME GET FIRST CHOICE.

CALL COLLECT NOW FOR A SPEEDY APPOINTMENT AND RESERVATIONS FOR THE MUSEUM AND "DUCK" RIDE. NEVER HAS THE VALLEY BEEN MORE BEAUTIFUL. THE MUSEUM WILL SOON BE CLOSED EXCEPT BY APPOINTMENT, AND THE "DUCK" RIDE WILL CEASE IN COLD WEATHER. SO CALL COLLECT NOW: (703) XXX-XXXX; if no answer (703) XXX-XXXX.

. . . .

THUNDERBIRD FARMS APPOINTMENT FORM

– TEAR OFF AND MAIL –

I WOULD LIKE TO INSPECT ON (DATE) ....

I WOULD LIKE TO INSPECT AT (TIME) ....

NAME ....

ADDRESS ....

CITY ....

STATE ....ZIP ....PHONE ....

In Situation No. 2, you and your partner have purchased a farm and the subdivided tracts are now ready for sale. The parcels you have to offer are just what a great many of your clients have been looking for. You've researched the locale where the farm is located, and you've come up with a bevy of interesting facts which should help sell the property. You are fairly familiar with what is happening to the consumer's dollar, and you are aware of his hopes, fears, and aspirations. With this knowledge in mind, and using the seven basic elements of successful direct response advertising, you compose a letter and prepare a pictured summary of your strongest parcels, and mail the offering to those clients on your mailing list *who have not, as yet, purchased land from you.* You realize that these people are probably scanning the newspapers every week looking for property. They'll probably see the classified ad you intend to run. You understand the positive impact an immediate response letter could have if it were received when the client had seen or was about to see your offering in another medium (newspapers). The recognition factor would definitely aid sales.

You and your partner have only a dozen tracts to sell, including the old farmhouse, so you intend to handle sales yourself, and sell mainly on weekends. You've found a cooperative real estate agent in the area who can handle weekday appointments for you. Calls are taken at your home or office and appointments are relayed to you at the farmhouse, where you now have a phone installed for weekend use. Your letters are out, your ads are placed, the property is what people are looking for and can afford to buy. The next step is to finish with the project as soon as possible and get on to something else.

SITUATION No. 2:

NAME OF FIRM

Address

YOU ASKED US TO KEEP IN TOUCH...

Charlie Anderson, my partner, suggested I write to you personally about some kept-back land in nearby Pennsylvania that should make money for you.

This farmland, on Cascade Creek, a mountain trout stream, is also ideally located for your personal safety just 12 to 14 minutes from Cumberland, Maryland, a healthful, scenic area, having the lowest crime rate in the entire state.

By 1976, the Middle Atlantic states are expected to have the highest population density in the country. Experts are now advising that, to protect your family's well-being and economic future, you should secure a low-tax place in the country; a piece of land, preferably with fish-producing waters, having some grassland, a woodlot, and soil suitable for tilling. Ten acres, they submit, is more than adequate for your family's food needs.

Even if you have no immediate plans for re-locating in the countryside, you should know that thousands are getting out daily, forcing up the price you will pay for farmland by an average of 20% yearly. Because your land will be unique: hard road, year-round fishing stream, woods, pasture, tillable ground, near cosmopolitan city, you should be able to find ready buyers, sell at a profit if you wish.

If you make $15,000 annually, this year you will lose $1200 of your hard-earned cash to inflation. This land could help get your money back — then some. *You should buy growth lands.* A conservative estimate is, because of inflation, one-half the value of your pension, savings account, or bonds, will be wiped out over the next 20 years. *You must hedge aggressively against inflation.*

As proof of the values listed here, you may ask any real estate broker offering land within two hours of your city if he has comparable property in his files. The answer in 90% of the cases will be "no." Should he have a similar tract, the price will be considerably higher, and bankers will not finance your purchase. They are now putting their money out at 10% interest, and on much shorter terms than we give to you here. *You actually pay the lowest mortgage rate currently available.*

In any event, we will refund your money within 30 days of purchase, regardless of reason.

If you're looking for a weekend place, you should know that industry figures show 50% of the recreational homesites sold in this area are ¼ acre or less in size and cost an average of $5,000 each. Fortunately, you will stand far above the crowd.

Your real estate investment strategy should include a defense: not just recreational property, (and this land is prime) but all-purpose land, purchased right, suitably leveraged, and having an ultimate higher use — hence built-in profits — such as farm-type land.

I would like those of you who asked that we keep in touch, to visit us in the mountains this weekend. Your short journey will take you along major highways, and this land will enable you to benefit from the best of two worlds: unparalleled scenery, and swift access to principal metropolitan areas from Maryland's narrow western strip.

To ensure your financial success on this journey, we will allow you a 5% reduction from the prices shown here, because we will save that amount in advertising. *But you must visit us early!*

Call us collect today so that we can adequately prepare you with plats and directions. On weekdays you may call: (703)XXX-XXXX. Weekends call: (703)XXX-XXXX.

With great financial success to you,

Bradley K. Haynes

P.S. Fall colors appear sooner here, in Pennsylvania Dutch country. Use this land all year. Just two miles from your property you'll find the 500 acre, 5-mile-long, Koon Lake, with its adjacent 3,000 acre state hunting forest. You'll be located directly in the ski belt, with Blue Knob Ski Area in Bedford, just 15 minutes away.

SITUATION No. 3

You've just purchased more land adjacent to the property described in Situation No. 1. Since that project is now essentially sold out, you feel that there is a market among *existing property owners in that development* who may be interested in acquiring an additional tract for investment or other purposes. In addition, you realize that a potential market exists among friends of property owners who may have missed out on the first opportunity. Your second immediate response letter is aimed at property owners and their friends. Its composition turns out to be a dual effort between you and the free-lance writer who performed so well for you the first time around. The letter performs for you as expected, and you make enough from early sales to recoup your down payment in the property.

NAME OF FIRM

Address

Dear Client:

This area is on the verge of its greatest of all real estate booms — a huge explosion in raw land prices — a boom so large it dwarfs anything that has gone on before.

You may have seen this vast boom when it first began to roll; many of you snapped up acreage on the Thunderbird tract so fast that it was essentially sold out in six months.

Since that time, the crowd has begun to sense this boom in the making. This fall they've been rushing in. Why? One reason is the imminent completion of Route 66 — the non-stop freeway from the D. C. area. The crucial portion from Marshall to Front Royal is nearing completion, and the paving contract has been awarded by the State Highway and Transportation Commission. This section will be opened in 1978, and work will soon begin on the short final leg.

Here's some inside information that will give you and your friends a head start in the rush for raw land around this area. When Thunderbird was sold at auction, it was returned to two separate groups of mortgagees. Group A owned Section No. 1, where the archeological digs are located, and this is the thousand or so acres that was sold out this spring. Group B reclaimed Section No. 2, along the ancient stream bed, where evidence of the earliest known community in North America was first uncovered.

Section No. 2, laced with streams, and fronting on the Shenandoah River is now available to you and your friends for the first time. If you were in the first land rush to Thunderbird, you undoubtedly shared the archeologists' feelings that you were on to something extraordinary.

Here's how a Washington Post writer, reporting on the Thunderbird phenomenon, described the land rush . . . "It's easy to see . . . why land-hungry city folk would want their own five acres on this green hillside looking over velvety fields and woods to the shining arabesque of the river and Massanutten Mountain looming beyond. And it's easy to imagine how eagerly they put down their deposits on the . . . wide lots stretching down through the uplands and across the floodplain to the river."

The secret of Thunderbird gradually came out as the first property owners let in their friends, and now the news is spreading far and wide.

You've probably said the hell with all the shared ownership of woods and recreation areas and Olympic-sized pools. Most of you want your own acreage where you can create your own environment.

Because the entire Thunderbird tract was sold at a foreclosure sale, it was returned to mortgagees whose interests and commitments were no longer tied to Thunderbird. Section No. 2 came into our hands at about half the per acre cost of bulk land in the Front Royal area.

> *This means that your cost and the cost to your friends is about one half of what you would expect to pay for ordinary acreage in this area, none of which offers the archeological significance and natural attractions of the Thunderbird site.*

If you're an investor, it's easy to see how Thunderbird can give you a head start on raw land profits. You obviously know that people will be coming to this area in great numbers because of the new highway. You have this rare opportunity to get there first and to be sitting on some very choice land when they arrive. It's not hard to imagine a five acre farmette that you purchased for $6,400 being worth $14,000 - $15,000, when Route 66 brings the Washington area down to a one hour's drive from Front Royal. It's entirely possible that a riverfront farmette that you purchased today for $12,450 could, because of the new highway and inflation, double in value when the commuters arrive.

Inflation is, of course, a great spur to rising property values. This is so because, in terms of today's dollars, the same land you buy at Thunderbird today may cost you twice as much in years to come. Your savings could actually buy you less tomorrow than would the same money today, if today's funds were invested in raw land at a destination point like this area and Thunderbird.

Today, in this region, five acre homesites in Rockland, near the country club, are selling for $25,000 and up. In the Browntown road area, a five acre site would cost you a minimum of $15,000. Both of these areas, like Thunderbird, are desirable residential sections on the outskirts of town.

If you're looking for an inexpensive acreage homesite in the country, where you can eventually consolidate your first and second homes, keep this fact in mind:

> *A main reason for housing inflation is that land prices have multiplied six times in the past 20 years and now account for an unprecedented 25% of builders' costs.*

For those of you who missed out the first time, there's no reason to let this opportunity slip through your fingers if you're short of cash right now. You can buy with inflated dollars and bind the property with as little as $50 down. The interest you pay over the life of the mortgage is, of course, tax deductible.

Don't worry about the security of your investment, either. Those of you who now own land at Thunderbird know that the land is deeded to you at closing. You own it. You don't have to pay off the mortgage for it to be yours. You cannot lose it if you miss a payment, or if your payment arrives late.

You can also profit from your land at Thunderbird while waiting for Interstate No. 66 to connect Front Royal with the Washington area. If your land is wooded, consider the wealth of firewood available to you. Local people are also waiting to clear your land if you give them the timber. If you own pastureland or tillable acreage, consider leasing it out to local residents interested in garden space, grazing land, or the hay crop.

Because your property is located at Thunderbird, its potential is automatically doubled because of its unique location along the Shenandoah River at the George Washington National Forest, and because of the archeological discoveries being made there.

You cash in on the excitement of exploration and discovery, in addition to the canoeing, fishing, swimming, hunting, hiking, camping, riding, etc. that people drive hours from their homes to find. These twin features — archeology and recreation — are the magnets that will continue to draw potential buyers to the Thunderbird site.

Rarely has there been such an opportunity for you to acquire a low-cost acreage homesite this close to the Washington area; nor will this opportunity ever come again.

We expect that these new lands will be sold as quickly as they are placed on the market. In the first section of Thunderbird we had a waiting list, because sales were outdistancing surveyors.

To encourage an early sellout so that advertising, promotion, and overhead costs can be kept at a minimum(with resultant savings being passed along to you in lower land costs)we are making the following offer:

BRING THIS LETTER WITH YOU TO OUR OFFICE AT 7 SOUTH STREET AND RECEIVE A
$500.00 REBATE
THIS $500.00 REBATE IS $300.00 MORE THAN THE AMOUNT GIVEN TO NEWSPAPER READERS WHO RESPOND EARLY TO THIS OFFER. THIS LETTER IS TRANSFERABLE TO FRIENDS OF YOURS WHO MAY WANT TO TAKE ADVANTAGE OF THIS LIMITED OPPORTUNITY.

Please fill out the attached Advanced Information Form and we will be happy to give you (or friends) preferential consideration and advanced information on properties coming up for sale at Thunderbird. We will call you as soon as new plats are available so that you or your friends can preview the new lands for sale prior to the general public.

Here again are current minimum prices on five acre estates in comparable residential areas around Front Royal. These three areas are about the best places to live if you settle here:

ROCKLAND AREA	BROWNTOWN ROAD	THUNDERBIRD
$25,000	$15,000	$6,900

Here's how easy it is for you to tie up a five acre estate at Thunderbird now. (As opposed to waiting and buying through a resale broker.)

Sales price: (minimum)	$6,900
Less your rebate: -	$ -500
Your Price:	$6,400

Minimum terms: Bring just $50 now; $50 at closing. Then payments of $82.62 mo., 120 mos., 9.84% rate.

NO REASONABLE CASH OFFER REFUSED. ABOUT 25% OF ALL PROPERTY OWNERS IN THE FIRST SECTION OF THUNDERBIRD PAID CASH.

Simply detach and return the following form and we will supply you with information that will give you or your friends a head start in the rush for raw land around this area.

Sincerely,

B. K. Haynes

. . . .

ADVANCED INFORMATION FORM — PLEASE DETACH AND MAIL TO: HAYNES-ANDERSON, TRUSTEES   7 SOUTH ST. PHONE: 555-1212

☐ Yes, I want to be informed as soon as new properties become available for sale at Thunderbird.

☐ Yes, I will be coming to your office in advance of survey to preview the new section. (Plats expected in late October.)

NAME:_____   ADDRESS:_____

CITY:_____PHONE: _____

Follow these advertising suggestions as closely as possible. By all means feel free to modify the ideas to suit your own situation. The main point to remember when advertising and promoting your properties is that conceptual thinking will help your sales.

Conceptual thinking, in simplified terms, means selling the sizzle and not the steak. Think about a raw steak. Not very appetizing, is it? But take the same hunk of meat, place it on a charcoal grill, and allow the juices to hit the hot coals. Now you have a sizzle. That's your pitch. You sell the taste and smell, not the meat itself. You sell the concept of a cuisinic delicacy.

What the product can do *for* the client is more important, advertising-wise, than the product itself. It's what the land can do *for* your customer that's critical in your ads. The land itself is secondary.

ACTION POINTS – LESSON 7

1. Memorize the seven vital elements of a direct response ad.

2. Begin a "Great Ads" file by clipping appealing ads from newspapers and magazines. Find examples in these ads of the seven vital elements.

3. Augment your current studies by reading books and periodicals related to advertising. (See Bibliography.)

4. Make a list of the seven vital elements in ad writing. Under each category write down three sentences from the course ads which exemplify each point. Finally, make up a sentence of your own to demonstrate each element at work.

5. Find the seven basic elements or appeals in the ad on

THE SALE OF SUBDIVIDED LAND

Lesson Number 8
Table of Contents

Advantages To Selling Your Parcels Through
An Effective Local Agency ....p. 170

How To Handle Real Estate Brokers And Salesmen ....p. 170

How To Determine The Interest Rate You'll Charge
Your Installment Lot Buyers..................................p. 171

What Is The Minimum Down Payment You Will Require? ....p. 172

How To Deal With Foreclosures ....p. 172

How To Brake Defaults By Your Minimum Terms Buyers ....p. 172

The Argument Against Using A "Contract For Deed"............p. 172

What Can Be An Acceptable Rate Of Defaults For You? ....p. 174

How To Pay Brokers And Commission Salespeople...............p. 174

Make Your Profits Through Quick Turnover....................p. 176

Seven Basic Reasons For Getting In And Out
Of Your Projects Quickly ....p. 176

How You Brief Your Salespeople Makes The Difference.........p. 177

The Salesman's Orientation Package — A 14 Point Check List ...p. 178

Site Signs — Do They Bring In Sales? ....p. 180

Mining For Referrals..p. 180

Tips On Selling Your Own Land ....p. 182

Persistence Pays Off ....p. 182

Have You Demonstrated Enthusiasm?...........................p. 183

Have You Preconditioned Your Clients To Buy?................p. 183

Have You Gained The Client's Confidence? ....p. 184

Frequently Asked Questions You Should Be Able To Answer .....p. 184

Have You Successfully Identified With The Client?...........p. 186

Closing Signals — Increase Your Sales By Learning
To Recognize Them ....p. 187

Have You Deferred To Your Prospect?.........................p. 188

Action Points ....p. 188

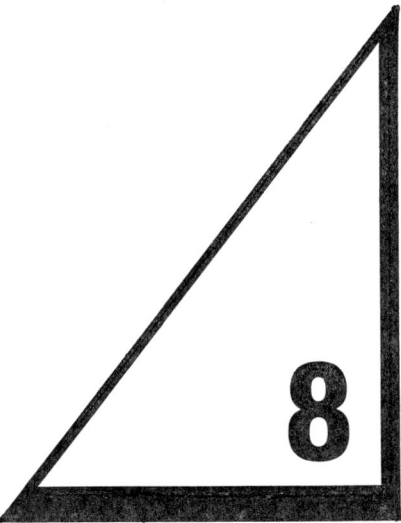

The Sale of Subdivided Land

This is not going to be a chapter on salesmanship, because that topic is broad enough to cover many volumes. I must assume that you, or someone associated with you, has enough of an aptitude for sales to take the lead in getting your subdivided parcels sold in a hurry. There are several ways you can go on this:

1. List your properties with a real estate agency
2. Hire self-sufficient salesmen
3. Sell it yourself

When I first started out in this business, I wrote my own ads and direct mail letters (I still do) and sold my own property. On most projects I had more clients than I could handle, so I persuaded friends and acquaintances to help sell on a commission basis. Some made more sales than others, and this was largely due to greater determination and overall sales ability. As you might know or suspect, most master salesmen are usually taught the art or science of salesmanship. Seldom do you find a "born" salesman who is also a devoted student and passionate researcher of the laws of selling and success. To the born salesman, selling seems to come easy, but that does not necessarily make him a better salesman than one who has taken the time to master salesmanship as a profession — one that calls for concentrated study and effort.

If you have little interest in sales, there is still the motivation of selling your own property and profiting from a product that you created (subdivided lots) which will bring out the best of whatever sales ability you have to offer.

Another shot in the arm for the non-salesman can be the presence of large numbers of potential clients who respond on site to look at and to buy what you have to offer. If you've picked the right land, developed it right, and advertised it right, super salesmanship will be the least of your worries. But in any case, whether or not you decide to handle your own sales, your knowledge of sound and effective sales principles can still benefit you, because you'll want to know:

HOW TO HANDLE REAL ESTATE BROKERS AND SALESPEOPLE

As a *Subdivestor,* I seldom go out and sell my own properties. I do, however, talk with clients and prospective clients all the time so that I can keep up with changing tastes and attitudes.

A good liaison with effective real estate brokers and salesmen is critical to your operation for a number of reasons. First of all, a properly oriented and motivated real estate agency will, while selling your properties, remove the headaches you would have in administering a sales force. You thus gain more freedom and flexibility in your operations. Remember: Every sales problem that is thrown back on you increases your burden in life. In *Subdivesting* your aim is to minimize problems while maximizing profits. When the urge hits you to take a vacation in the South Seas, for example, you just may want to leave right away. If you only have your secretary to administer, you'll have that much more control over your own life.

Obviously, the real estate agency you choose to handle your properties in a given area must have expertise in selling rural land. It would be foolish to list your properties with a friendly city broker whose offices are far removed from your project. The distance factor is too much to overcome, and city salesmen will not give their full time and attention to rural properties. Even in rural areas you'll be better off choosing a country broker or realtor whose specialty is rural land (as opposed to town properties), and one whose sales team is reasonably aggressive.

Your prospective clients can be identified as primarily city folks looking for a place in the country. Their motivations include: recreation, retirement, investment, relocation, or agriculture. Whatever their motivations — a site for a home, cabin, mobile home, business, or camp — most of your clients nourish deep-seeded feelings that there is something sacred about owning a piece of land, and although their immediate goals may be unclear, most expect to either use the property or profit from its resale. In the interim, some will build; others will visit their property on occasional weekends and on vacations. Some may never return, and these owners are primarily investors and speculators who will later either resell their property or list it for sale with a local agency.

One of the principle advantages you have in using local real estate people for your projects is that you can supply service after the sale, while establishing a reputation for handling land that appreciates in value. Documented evidence of realtors and brokers who have returned profits to your clients through resales can be a persuasive tool when opening new projects; and you'll get some return sales from satisfied investors.

The technique of *Subdivesting* requires you to offer property for sale on an installment basis. Your big attractions are low down payments and generous monthly terms to purchasers. Where interest rates are not fixed by law, the rate of interest you charge to purchasers should be scaled upward in inverse proportion to the amount of down payment. The larger the down payment, the lower the rate. The following sample pricing schedule was used for one of my past projects:

Lot No.	Price	*Dn. Pmt.	Mo. Pmt.	Terms	Annual % Rate
9	$4,750	$100	$66.29	108 mos.	10.33
33	2,950	100	37.99	120 mos.	10.21
34	3,750	100	52.03	108 mos.	10.33
43	5,250	100	68.65	120 mos.	10.21
74	6,900	100	90.66	120 mos.	10.21

*An acceptable $100 *minimum* down payment could be payable as follows: $50 upon signing the contract; $50 due at closing. With 10% down the interest rate would drop to 9.58 A.P.R. With 25% or more down, the rate was reduced to 9% simple interest.

This kind of pricing flexibility is necessary to help sell out your projects over a minimum period of time. Obviously, your number of potential clients would be limited if you sold only for cash or if you required a large down payment. Selling with no down payment is not advised. Your clients must make a cash commitment at the outset or you're looking for trouble. Down payments of 1% are less than desirable because of the increased likelihood of default by purchasers having little equity in the property. In addition, banks and other lenders do not like to loan money against this kind of note; nor are the notes salable until an equity build-up occurs and a history of regular monthly payments has been established. Use your parcels requiring 1% down as traffic builders. Your more desirable parcels should command at least 10% down and carry a lower rate of interest.

HOW TO DEAL WITH FORECLOSURES

An effective way to bind the 1% client to the property is to charge all closing costs to him. This could amount to several hundred dollars above the down payment, and for all practical purposes this outlay of funds acts to brake a potential default. For many years we have charged all the closing costs to installment purchasers. This more than offsets the legal costs involved in foreclosure proceedings.

Lawyers in the past have debated the ethics of charging the purchaser for the preparation of the deed (normally a seller's expense); but since you'll assume a certain risk by giving an immediate deed and offering property on such generous terms, you may feel justified in charging all the closing expenses to the purchaser. Other charges to purchasers include fees for preparing the note and deed of trust, recording costs, lawyer's settlement fees, title opinions, and title insurance.

As a *Subdivestor*, I have purposely avoided using the "land sales contract," or "contract for deed" when selling property. Under this arrangement, the purchaser is not given title to the property until it has been paid for in full. And while this method of transfer does preclude foreclosure proceedings in the event of default, it is associated with high pressure sales tactics. Consumer advocates, rightly or wrongly, often zero in on this procedure to show how customers can be bilked out of their lots by missing payments or by being late with their installments. Most land sales contracts contain a statement that purchasers can lose their property and all of their equity upon default. Under the deed and deed of trust arrangement, the property in default must be advertised in the local paper for a period of time before being offered at a foreclosure sale. These proceedings vary from state to state so you should check your local statutes in consultation with an attorney. In Virginia, for example, the delinquent purchaser has at least two chances to redeem his property — once while it is being advertised, and again at the sale itself. He must, of course, foot the bill for advertising and legal expenses and suffer potential damage to his reputation and credit rating. You'll want to point out these disadvantages to the delinquent note maker in an effort to encourage him to deed the property back. You stand to gain hundreds of dollars by avoiding foreclosure expenses.

If the property does eventually reach the courthouse steps in a foreclosure auction, it could conceivably bring a bid higher than the amount owed on the property. If the bid price is high enough it could even pay all expenses and yield a return of equity (even profits) to the delinquent property owner. If the bid price is lower than the amount owed, then the seller (you) must absorb the cost of foreclosure. But you regain possession of the property, and if you've done an efficient job of *Subdivesting,* you should be able to resell the parcel for as much or more than the original price. Over the years I feel that, on balance, we have profited significantly from foreclosures. First of all, we have collected principal and interest payments on the note. Secondly, we have been able to sell a great many foreclosures for a higher price the second time around. These factors have far outweighed the expenses of bringing seriously delinquent property owners to foreclosure.

It may seem paradoxical to be discussing the tactics of profit-making while simultaneously taking up the subject of property foreclosures. After all, if the principles of *Subdivesting* are valid and properly applied, they should minimize problems. Why sell property on which you'll later have to foreclose? Before I answer that question, I want to return briefly to the definition of subdivesting:

> **Making maximum profits from a minimum investment in the development and quick sale of subdivided rural land which, in turn, can be resold at a profit.**

In order to sell out your projects quickly and profitably, you must (assuming you've done your other homework) offer attractive prices and traffic-building terms. Whenever you have large numbers of clients purchasing property on a minimum-down-payment basis, you're going to have a certain number of defaults.

Experience has shown that you would be doing very well if your foreclosure and/or deed-back rate is 5% or less of sales. A rate above 10% is cause to re-think your operations to find out why you are getting a large number of defaults. (This analysis precludes sudden economic turmoil or national disasters such as a gas crisis or war.)

Operating with a 5% default rate, you would expect that for every hundred parcels sold you would have to foreclose or request a deed-back on five lots. These five lot owners would have paid the closing attorney for his time and effort. You will have gotten a token down payment and usually a number of sporadic monthly payments, most of which have been applied to interest. These funds should cover your pro-rata out-of-the pocket costs, such as advertising.

HOW TO PAY BROKERS AND COMMISSION SALESPEOPLE

On these minimum terms deals you should pay the salesman no more than half of the down payment and half of the monthly payments received until his commission is paid in full. In some cases you can wait until the salesman has earned a certain figure in commissions and transfer a deed of trust note to him as payment in full. If a default occurs before his commission is paid out, the salesman may re-assign the note to you if you've guaranteed payment, or he may foreclose on his own. This procedure is helpful on projects yielding a low percentage of cash.

The salesman's commission is usually 4 to 7%, with the broker getting a 1 or 2% override, depending on his responsibilities. This rate schedule assumes that you pay for all the advertising and generate all the leads. Obviously, if the broker has responsibility for all aspects of sales and marketing, his commission is considerably higher. Some high-pressure marketing groups take 40% or better off the top to move land in recreational subdivisions. They, of course, are responsible for all related sales and marketing bills.

As a *Subdivestor*, your best course of action is to handle as much of these specialties as you can in-house. Never give away more than 10% for strictly sales and sales supervisory services. Remember: Your purchasers should be able to resell for a profit without too many years passing by. When you're attempting to pass along sales and marketing costs of 40% or better, your pricing structure simply does not have room enough to sustain resales for profit, and some parcels may even yield significant losses when sold after foreclosure.

Here is a sample salesman's commission schedule, which was used on one of our projects:

COMMISSION DATA FOR SALESPEOPLE

Commissions — Min. Down ($100.00) to 9% down = 4% commission for salesman
10% to 24% down = 5% commission for salesman
25% or more down = 6% commission for salesman
Cash (within 10% of original price) = 7% commission for salesman

(cont.)

Pay out of Commissions — Commissions are paid upon closing.
        Minimum down = ½ of down payment; then ½ of each month's payment until commission is paid.
        10% down or more — full commission

MAKE YOUR PROFITS THROUGH QUICK TURNOVER

Aside from the potential profits you can make from foreclosures and deed-backs, one distinct advantage you gain is the opportunity to generate potential clients through the advertising and promotion of these "distressed properties." It is only human nature to see potential self-serving opportunity in the mistakes and misfortunes of others. (See the chapter on advertising for ideas on promoting sales of foreclosure properties.)

As a *Subdivestor*, you should not build up a large inventory of undeveloped land. You want to get in and out of your projects as quickly as possible; and there are some very sound reasons for operating this way. First is the necessity for your money to be working for you all the time. The quickest way to wealth and independence from your investments in rural land is through turnover. Sure, we can all point to examples of speculation in raw land that yielded tremendous profits in the long haul. And in the chapter on financing we'll discuss some instances where it may be to your advantage to sit on a chunk of undeveloped land. Capital gains treatment is one distinct advantage. But there are decided disadvantages, too, foremost of which are those conditions over which you have no control. In *Subdivesting*, you must strive to minimize these conditions and to maximize those situations where you are in control. When you are sitting on a large amount of unsold and undeveloped land, you are vulnerable to the following adverse conditions:

1. A slowdown in the economy which could dampen sales. Such a slump could occur nationally or in any region of the country.
2. Sudden changes in local ordinances or zoning laws which could, by slowing county growth, wipe out anticipated profits.

3. An upsurge in competitive offerings which could lessen response to your own subdivided parcels.
4. Pressure from environmental groups to restrict development. Such pressure could be felt at the state level through the enactment of land-use legislation.
5. Added taxes caused by reassessment of land values in the county or township.
6. Changes in utility rates and minimum-use requirements which could add thousands of dollars to development costs.
7. Changes in national monetary policy which could restrict the availability of loan funds, increase the rate at which you can borrow money on your notes, and decrease the net proceeds on notes you sell.

HOW YOU BRIEF YOUR SALESPEOPLE MAKES THE DIFFERENCE

O.K., you've got a subdivision plat and you're "ready for bear." You feel that you've got exactly what the public wants. You know how to advertise and promote the property, but you've decided that you want your weekends free; so you're going to farm out the sales and follow-up to a local realtor. He's lean and hungry, and his salesmen are already licking their chops over the bodies you're going to bring into the realtor's office. This situation is good. Hungry men and women try harder. Soon, however, if things go right, you know these sales people will get fat again and slack off on their jobs. Your job is to get them properly briefed at the outset, so that after they are fed a few commissions they won't get lazy. Lazy salesmen tend to forget that there's more to making a sale than just writing up a contract and collecting a commission. Spell out in advance just what is expected of salespeople, from their initial contact with a client, through the contract stage, on to closing, and beyond — until the money is in the bank and the note is ready for collection.

"But," you say, "that's the broker's job. Once I turn over my property to a real estate broker and agree to pay him a commission, I don't expect to babysit deals through to closing." Not so! Real estate brokers and realtors can be very busy people sometimes. A lot of deals may be passing through the house at any given period. Your offerings may have to compete with the multitude of listings being actively promoted or buried by the real estate house, and even though you are supplying the clients, you may not have full claim on a salesperson's time. You could even be slicing off 2% to the broker for supervising your deals, only to find that the broker is not catching critical omissions or errors on the sales contracts.

It's amazing how many people hand over their property to a realtor or real estate broker expecting that magically, somehow, the property will be sold. Most of the time, if the realtor or his salesmen do not have an immediate buyer, the property ends up in the files of a multiple listing service. Only the really salable properties get advertised to any great extent. (An exception being an occasional "goodwill" ad placed to pacify a screaming seller whose property listing is gathering dust in the broker's files.)

If you've decided against administering your own sales force, hiring your own salesman, or selling your own property, you must supply certain fundamental information about your project to the real estate house, and you must be prepared to follow-up on sales. Here is some of the information each salesman must have from you:

1. A plat of your subdivision prepared by a licensed surveyor; a map showing the specific location within the county and, if practical, a topography (topo) map (available from Soil and Conservation Service-SCS; see Appendix).
2. Advertising and promotional materials related to the project.
3. A list of restrictive covenants, if any, that you will have recorded along with any deed you give to each subdivided parcel (see Appendix).
4. Approximate amount of annual real estate taxes and costs of utility hookups, if any. Include names, addresses, and phone numbers of companies supplying service.
5. Fact sheet describing points of interest near your project, and listing the advantages of owning property there. If your

(cont.)

property is located near a town having a Chamber of Commerce, you can usually obtain a list of schools, churches, shopping centers, public transportation, hospitals, etc. The closer you are to these conveniences, the better for sales.

6. Financing sheet, showing the full price of each parcel, the amount(s) required down, the interest rate(s), the amount of the monthly payment, the term, and the discount for cash (fixed by law; see Appendix).
7. The commission breakdown, showing who gets what, when, and how.
8. Sales procedures sheet, outlining exactly what duties are expected of each salesman handling your properties.
9. List of environmental or other restrictions on the property which are outside of your control. For example, use of the property may be restricted by a scenic easement or the lack of mineral rights.
10. Color photographs of the area where your project is located; and, if advantageous, photographs of features on the property offered for sale.
11. Complete legal information about the project, including whether you have a title opinion or title insurance, and the type of deed you will grant (see Appendix).
    (a) What are the costs for title insurance or title opinion?
    (b) How good is the deed you will grant?
    (c) Is there a blanket mortgage on the property?
    (d) How much are the release fees?
    (e) How much are closing costs? Where will settlement take place? When?
12. Health report, if any, on whether a building permit can be readily obtained.
13. Copies of your own contract (See sample in back of book).
14. Check list for those items to be submitted to you along with any contract. Such items may include: Credit report, deposit, attorney's disclaimer (purchaser agrees to select your closing attorney), request for rezoning, etc.

In addition to the aforementioned points, it may be of some value to erect a sign on your project showing who is handling sales, along with their address and phone number. While I've never obtained many sales as a direct result of a site sign, I think that on some occasions, such a sales aid may be useful. An obvious example is where you are offering property for sale along well-traveled routes and near some popular natural or man-made attraction, such as a lake or ski area.

You'll find, too, that in popular destination areas a small market will exist for your lots from builders. You'll probably have to subordinate your interest to a bank and wait for your money, but it may be in your best interest to sell your slower moving properties to a builder(s); especially if such sales enable you to get out of the project within the time frame you have set for yourself.

One of the acknowledged facts in the land sales business is that there is "gold" in referrals. In your pricing structure, you should offer a discount (usually 5%) for second lot purchases, with the benefit accruing to either the initial lot purchaser or to his friends. An exception to this offer could occur when you have more customers for a particular type of property than you have available lots. In most projects, for example, the waterfront will sell more quickly than the back lots, and a discount for multiple lot purchases may be unnecessary.

The fact is that a significant number of your sales will come from friends and relatives of satisfied customers. Your sales people should be encouraged to "mine" for referrals; but since you may have little control over the personalities and sales abilities of sales people, your best bet is to make it attractive for the first customer to bring in additional buyers. Aside from the discount you may offer for multiple purchases, you can also grant other concessions such as foregoing monthly payments or interest charges for a short period of time. It is important to remember, however, that some concessions to the purchaser for bringing in additional clients may be interpreted as violations of various regulations or laws governing the sale of real estate. To be safe, check with your attorney and avoid establishing a set pattern for these "kickbacks."

All of us can point to sports celebrities, politicians, performers, and prominent men in business who reached the top by never giving up on their goals. We can also cite a great many more failures who abandoned their goals when, at the last moment, a more vigorous effort would have yielded the sought-after rewards.

Remember this: If you've gotten your project to the point of sales and for some reason(s) you're having difficulty moving the property, you must define the problem and act to correct it. This may sound simplistic, but a great number of people fall short of success because they fail to identify problem areas, whether in business or in their own physical make-up. Sometimes it seems easier for us to look elsewhere for solutions to our problems. It may seem sensible to bring in experts, but you cannot trust your life and fortune completely to the advice and counsel of experts.

Years ago, when I operated a real estate brokerage office, I was visited on a regular basis by developers who wanted their properties sold. They had heard that I was quite successful in the land development business, and they felt that somehow I could magically transform their projects into instant winners. Only on rare occasions did I take on these projects. In almost every case, mistakes were made in the acquisition or development stage so that marketing and sales were burdened with abnormal difficulties. All of these projects could have been quickly sold out, but fundamental changes were necessary in the development concept. Marketing and sales would then have had less of a load to carry.

You may find, if sales become a problem to you, that you slipped up somewhere earlier in the game. A thorough review of your operations is then in order. You can take heart in knowing that you're going to make some mistakes. All of us are prone to errors. Your task is to be aware of them and to minimize their occurrence. Only *you* can do that. It is essential, therefore, that the *persistence* you demonstrated in bringing your project forward be continued until the last lot is sold. Again quoting Shakespeare, "An enterprise, when fairly once begun, should not be left until all that ought is won."

TIPS ON SELLING YOUR OWN LAND

While it's true that carefully chosen property, which is priced right and easy to buy, will go a long way toward selling itself, you should not forget the basic elements of salesmanship when showing your property to prospective clients; and if you've followed the procedures in this book, your sales job will be half-accomplished. Now, let's look at some of the elementary rules of selling and ask yourself if you've mastered the basics of getting your properties sold quickly and profitably.

A. Have you been persistent?

Persistence is, of course, probably the most basic tenet of salesmanship. If you've carefully and diligently followed the principles set down in these pages and are now embarking on your own sales program, you have demonstrated a degree of persistence. Think for a moment of what Shakespeare said about this quality:

> *See that first the design is wise and just. (your project)*
> *That ascertained, pursue it resolutely. (get it developed)*
> *Do not for one repulse forego the purpose that you resolved to effect. (Sell it quickly, remembering your goals and the definition of Subdivesting.)*

It's obviously not enough to bring your carefully conceived project through the development phase to the point of sales and then sit back and expect profits to start rolling in. We've already discussed the necessity for following up on your sales people, whether they are in your employ or in the charge of a real estate broker. By similar degree, you'll have to monitor your own performance if you intend to sell your own property. Stick to your goal plan. Get your property sold quickly and move on to another project. *Think* goals, and you will achieve them. I've certainly seen enough evidence of how *persistence* in real estate development and sales has battered down obstacles to success. History is shot through with examples of success against seemingly impossible odds. It was Napoleon who said, "Hard pounding, gentlemen; but we will see who can pound the longest."

B. Have you demonstrated enthusiasm?

It is a proven fact that enthusiasm is contagious. One of the oldest allegories demonstrating the power of enthusiasm is found in Greek mythology. Orpheus, a gifted singer and musician, played his lyre and sang with such artful persuasion that even savage beasts came running to listen. His miracles were such that trees followed him, huge boulders moved for him, and his beached ship was returned to the ocean. A fearsome dragon lay down and slept at the sound of his voice. Pluto himself, god of the underworld — keeper of Eurydice, whom Orpheus passionately loved — was charmed by Orpheus into allowing the hero's sweetheart to return to her home on earth.

Think back on those times in your life when you've truly been enthusiastic about something. At those moments you were trying to sell somebody on a book, a movie, an automobile, a cause, or whatever. The sales job you were performing on your listener wasn't difficult at all. You believed in whatever it was you were selling. You either owned it (automobile), experienced it (movie), or espoused it (cause). You'll remember how your enthusiasm rubbed off on your listeners. Try to visualize how their eyes opened wider and how their ears seemed more attuned to the sound of your voice. Many of your listeners, no doubt, were influenced by your enthusiasm to the point where they purchased a similar product, sought a similar experience, or joined the cause you were espousing.

You are obviously enthusiastic about your project. You've found it, pushed it along, and now it's ready for sale. The kind of enthusiasm you generate will be real and genuine, because it is *your* product, *your* experience, *your* cause. You are not working for someone else, possibly selling a product in which you have less than full confidence. It's your baby. You're proud of it. Your enthusiasm, if consciously encouraged, will transfer readily to your clients and result in quick sales of your property.

C. Have you preconditioned your clients to buy?

Preconditioning actually began when you first acquired your property for development. Clearly it is (or will be) the type of property that people are looking for, and it is priced attractively enough for people to buy without a great deal of hesitation. If you've correctly followed the procedures in this course, you should have a product in which your clients have already expressed a passing interest. Close attention to your advertising copy should help you to translate this interest into positive responses (appointments). When the prospect arrives, his mind should be reasonably receptive to your sales presentation.

D. Have you gained the client's confidence?

Know your product! This is one of the axioms of selling. Unless you have a thorough knowledge of what it is you're trying to sell, you will falter when questions are asked. And since your hesitation or equivocation serves notice that you do not have sufficient or satisfactory answers, you leave the door open for the client to say no to the sale. The chances are, however, that you will be in full possession of all the necessary answers to maximize sales. Your *ACTION FILE* has provided you with specific information about the area; your *FEASIBILITY CHECK LIST* has given you considerable research and expertise about the property you are conveying. You have been schooled in land acquisition and development by personal experience. You are sufficiently briefed in those aspects of financing and law that pertain to the property you have for sale. All in all, you are better equipped with knowledge than any salesman you may hire. Here are some frequently asked questions about the transfer of rural land that you should be able to field readily:

1. Can I obtain title insurance and/or a title opinion? How much are closing costs? What kind of deed will I get?

2. Will I receive a clear title? What encumbrances, if any, exist against the property? Are there any restrictions on what I can do with the land? Are there any easements?

3. How will the property be financed? What is the difference between simple interest and "add-on" interest? How much

interest will I be paying over the life of the loan? What happens if I prepay? What are "points?"

4. How much are the taxes on the property?

5. How deep will I have to drill for water? Can I get a health department permit? Will the land "perc?" Where do I go to get a building permit?

6. Can I get electricity? Phone service? What will my charges be?

7. Do I get riparian rights (on waterfront property)? Will the property flood? How far back from the water can I build? Will I have access to the lake, river, etc.? Can I swim? Fish? Use a power boat?

8. Who maintains the roads? How much are road maintenance fees? Who collects them? How often are they paid? Will I get snow removal?

9. Can I subdivide? Down to what size? Where do I go for permission to subdivide?

10. Can I put a mobile home on the property? What size house do I have to build? Are there any other building restrictions?

11. How far away are schools, hospitals, shopping centers, cities, towns, cultural activities?

12. Do you know of any good local builders? Well drillers? Who can I get to put in my septic tank and drain fields? Who can I get to mow or clear my lot?

13. Where can I get some free seedlings for my lot? Can I dam up that stream in back? Will the government stock my pond with fish? Can I fence in my land?

14. Can the government take some of my property to widen the road? What happens if I don't think their price is fair? Do I have to grant a right of way to the utility companies? Will I get paid for it? Can they go across the middle of my lot? How close to these right-of-ways can I build?

15. Where can I get a good lawyer?

E. Have you successfully identified with the client?

The prospect is, of course, aware that you're trying to sell him something. He also knows that you're in business to make a profit, and that you are not giving something away, or suffering a loss, regardless of what impression he may have been given. You do, however, have a distinct advantage over the average salesman in competing for your client's hard-won money. The prospect is buying directly from the owner. Ostensibly there is no salesman's commission. You can help the prospect buy the property at a lower cost. You can accept an offer and make a deal on the spot. If the prospect has openly expressed any interest at all in your property, you can build on this interest until it becomes a commitment to buy. A downfall of many real estate salesmen is the break in communication that occurs when an offer must be relayed from buyer to seller and back again.

Since you are dealing with the prospect on a one-to-one basis, you must carry through on this matter of identification. Possibly you advertised your property as "for sale by owner." In the prospect's mind he may already see an opportunity to shave the price. He may already feel more comfortable about talking with you about the property. That way he won't have to get mixed up with a salesman. He's thankful that he won't have to be put through the wringer just because he has a natural drive to buy some land in the country. You're obviously going to try to sell him the property, sure; but you're just like he is in a way. You're not a salesman or property agent.

When the prospect arrives, you should put him at ease by trying to find additional points of similarity between the two of you. What interests do you have in common? Are you from the same area? Only by feeding back questions to the prospect can you find those points of mutual identification. By degree, each step in this discussion of joint interests brings you and your prospect closer to an agreement. He realizes you still are anxious to sell the property. But then *he* wouldn't have come out if he wasn't looking for land to buy. The two of you (don't forget the wife) hit it off. You seem to have a lot in common. He now understands how you operate — that you always leave room in the deal for others to make a profit. The land you're offering is just about what he's been looking for. He's tired of searching for the ideal tract. It just doesn't exist. He makes you an offer. You accept. You've made a friend. He may refer his friends. It's possible he may end up buying from you more than once.

F. Did you recognize any important "closing" signals?

One of the biggest sales problems you will face when handling your own property may lie in the closing process. Despite the fact that many prospects are prepared to buy on the spot, they may vacillate and hedge when it comes time to make an immediate commitment. Evidence of this latent indecision, or caution, often comes in the form of comments such as, "I'll be back later with my wife," or "I'll think it over and call you." The professional salesman, of course, is wise to human nature and realizes that the "be backs" and "thinkers" will, in all probability, never return. Many of these "missed sales" are the direct result of an ineffectual sales presentation that missed the mark with the prospect. He may have signaled his intent to purchase during your discussion with him; yet, because of your inexperience, lack of self-confidence, unenthusiastic sales presentation, or other failings, you may have neglected to pick up on a certain comment that could lead to a sale.

Here are some typical questions your prospect may ask, along with suggested answers which will lead most directly to a closed deal. Questions such as these are "signals" for you to stop your sales presentation and move toward getting a contract signed.

1. "How much will you take for all cash?"
    Answer: "For how many lots?"

2. "How much will my monthly payments be?"
   Answer: "How much can you afford per month?"

3. "How much will I have to put down to get a lower interest rate?"
   Answer: "What interest rate are you looking for?"

4. "What's the smallest down payment you will accept?"
   Answer: "How much do you want to put down?"

5. "Do you have any other land for sale?"
   Answer: "Do you want the best I have to offer? This is it."

6. "Can I think about it until next weekend?"
   Answer: "Do you think this is the property you want?"

G. Have you deferred to your prospect?

It is important to keep in mind the power of humility in turning prospects into buyers. No one likes a seller who comes on too strong. One who brags about how great his property is, and how there is no way in the world you could go wrong by buying from him, turns people off.

Remember, whenever a sales pitch is made, someone is always sold. You either sell your prospect the property you have to move, *or* the prospect sells you on the fact that he will not be sold. When you're the one doing the selling, "Sell. Do not be sold."

ACTION POINTS – LESSON 8

1. Begin watching the classified and display advertising of real estate agencies in your prospective area of operations. Later you may want to make personal visits to determine whether any of these agencies can effectively handle some or all of your sales in their area.

2. Check the foreclosure ads in rural newspapers where you plan to operate. If a large number of lots and parcels are being advertised, find out why.

3. Get to know the real estate sales commission rates in your area of operations.

4. Begin assembling a salesperson's information package, using as a guide the 14 point check list on pp. 178-179

5. Locate and study a typical rural subdivision in your area; then prepare your answers to the real estate questions on pp. 184-186.

6. Familiarize yourself with the closing signals on pp. 187-188.

BOOK II

The B. K. HAYNES
"Can't-lose"
Success Formula

BOOK II
THE B.K. HAYNES "CAN'T LOSE" SUCCESS FORMULA

Lesson Book II
Table of Contents

Napoleon Hill's Chief Observations About
The World's Richest And Most Successful Men ....p. 199
Meaningless Experience — How It Can Hold Up Success ....p. 200
SCRIPT And FLAME — Two Mystery Words With Amazing
Money-Making Powers. ....p. 201
Success Rule 1: SAVE At Least 10% Of Your Earnings ....p. 202
Measure Your Financial Success By Your Liquid Assets ....p. 202
Success Rule 2: Have CONFIDENCE In Yourself ....p. 204
The Abysmal Failure. ....p. 204
The Critical First Step In Building Or Rebuilding
Confidence In Yourself. ....p. 205
The Necessity For Prayer And Autosuggestion In Your Life. ....p. 206
A-D-M-I-T — Your Self-Confidence Formula. ....p. 207
Success Rule 3: Develop Self-CONTROL ....p. 208
What Is The Role Of Power In The Accumulation
And Retention Of Wealth ....p. 208
The Seven Basic Fears — What Are They? Why Must
You Conquer Them?. ....p. 209
A Demonstration Of Hypochondria By Napoleon Hill ....p. 210
How Unwarranted Fears And Inflamed Emotions
Reduce Your Tolerance For Pain ....p. 211
The Four Essential Components Of Everyone's Life ....p. 212
The Living Tools For Operating Your Life ....p. 213

The Seven Positive Emotions; The Seven Negative Emotions ....p. 213
The Fear Of Poverty — Does It Motivate Men To
Achieve Great Wealth? ....p. 213
Six Symptoms Of The Man Who Fears Poverty.................p. 214
How To Defeat Fear Of Criticism ....p. 215
How Others Can Gain Control Of Your
Mind Through Criticism ....p. 217
Success Rule 4: Develop CONCENTRATION And Persistence......p. 217
How Concentration And Persistence Can Breed Genius............p. 217
The Three Critical Steps For The Nourishment, Development,
And Application Of The Powers Of Concentration ....p. 219
Success Rule 5: Learn To COOPERATE With Others...........p. 220
The Main Cause Of Practically Every Human Failure ....p. 220
Why A "Master-Mind" Alliance Is Crucial To Your Success ....p. 220
Famous People Who Owe Their Success To
Cooperation With Others..p. 221
Seven Invisible Guards Who Will Guard Your Leadership Role ......p. 222
Success Rule 6: Practice The Golden RULE ....p. 223
The Ten Basic Motives Behind All Of Our Actions ....p. 224
Success Rule 7: Use Your IMAGINATION ....p. 227
Imagination Rules The World ....p. 228
Success Rule 8: Develop A Pleasant PERSONALITY ....p. 229
Why The Building Of Character Is Essential To
Improving Your Personality ....p. 230
Is It "Just Your Character" That Determines How You Act? ....p. 230
The Role Of Fantasy In Developing A Pleasant Personality.........p. 232
A Concise Definition Of Personality ....p. 233
Ten Steps For Developing A Pleasant Personality ....p. 233
Success Rule 9: Practice TOLERANCE and Patience ....p. 234
Intolerance — Can It Be Inherited?..................................p. 234

196

The Three Institutions Through Which Social Heredity Operates ....p. 235

Father Forgets — A Stirring Essay On Impatience................p. 236

Success Rule 10: Learn To Profit From FAILURE...............p. 237

Abraham Lincoln — A Failure?................................p. 238

Those Who Profited From Failure.............................p. 239

Ralph Waldo Emerson — An Excerpt From His Great
Essay On Compensation ....p. 240

Why You Must Never Accept An Experience As Being A Failure ....p. 240

The Fifty Major Failure Habits — Why You Must
Purge Them From Your Life..................................p. 241

Shakesphere's Wise Words About Circumventing Failure..........p. 243

Self-Help Quiz Can Help You Banish Feelings Of Failure ....p. 243

Why You Should Not Harbor Desires That Are Too Many,
Too Confusing, And Beyond Your Training To Accomplish........p. 244

Advice From John Paul Getty.................................p. 244

Success Rule 11: Learn To LEAD..............................p. 244

Are Good Leaders Born Or Made?.............................p. 245

Why Is Effective Leadership So Critical In The Military? ....p. 245

Three Basic Questions To Help You Develop Leadership Qualities ...p. 245

Thirty-One Effective Leadership Qualities......................p. 245

Great Business Leaders Who Understood
The Real Virtue Of Money ....p. 246

An Understanding Of Life's True Rewards ....p. 247

Success Rule 12: Think ACCURATELY........................p. 248

Thirteen Inaccurate Thought Patterns..........................p. 249

Accurate Thinking — On What Three
Basic Factors Does It Depend ....p. 250

The 26 Enemies Of Accurate Thought — Why You Should
Destroy Their Build-Up In Your Mind........................p. 250

The Four Basic Ways To Increase Your Income ....p. 250

46 Questions To Purge Your Mind Of Inaccurate Thought Patterns . . p. 251
Success Rule 13: Have A Definite AIM In Life . . . . p. 253
The Eight Steps For Reaching And Influencing
The Subconscious Mind. . . . . p. 254
The Motive Factor That Always Preceeds Action . . . . p. 256
How To Build Desire. . . . . p. 256
How To Build Belief — Its Important Relationship To Desire . . . . . . p. 257
Advice From Andrew Carnegie . . . . p. 258
Success Rule 14: Go The Extra MILE. . . . . p. 258
The Most Common Cause Of Failure. . . . . p. 258
Advice From James J. Corbett . . . . p. 258
Perhaps The Most Persuasive Reason For
"Going The Extra Mile" . . . . p. 259
Nature's Unexplained Law About "Going The Extra Mile". . . . . p. 259
Should You Look Out For Yourself First? . . . . p. 260
A Simple Definition Of A Fool . . . . p. 260
Success Rule 15: Act With ENTHUSIASM . . . . p. 261
Why Enthusiasm Is The Key To Action. . . . . p. 261
How Benjamin Franklin Tracked His Enthusiasm . . . . p. 261
How Self-Discipline And Faith Can Help You To
Become More Enthusiastic . . . . p. 262
How Autosuggestion Can Build Enthusiasm . . . . p. 262
Belief Power — An Essential Ingredient For
Generating Enthusiasm . . . . p. 262
The Three Factors Necessary For Sustained Enthusiasm. . . . . p. 263
An Enthusiasm Formula For The Achievement Of Your Goals. . . . . p. 263
The Most Enthusiastic Person Who Ever Lived . . . . p. 264
Advice And Conclusions From Napoleon Hill. . . . . p. 265

The Can't Lose Success Formula

The story is told of Mozart who, when asked for advice by a young composer, addressed himself to the creative process. "You must begin with simple compositions — songs for example," said the great composer.

"But, sir, you began composing symphonies when you were a child."

"True," said Mozart, "but I asked no one how to begin."

Mozart, of course, was a genius, and geniuses are not often rich. Most of the world's great fortunes have been built by men who began through trial and error, and who, by following a great deal of advice (good and bad) found that their success covered a multitude of blunders. Napoleon Hill — the great writer and astute observer of the world's richest and most powerful men — came closest to distilling the secrets of becoming rich into a workable formula for others to follow and practice. Two important observations he made were:

(1) An intangible impulse of thought can be transmuted into material rewards by the application of know principles.
(2) Knowledge is only *potential* power. It becomes power only when and if it is organized into *definite* plans of action and *definite* ends.

If, through mental telepathy, you could reach out and pull from the air those thought impulses of the world's richest and most successful men, and if you were able to file them away for easy reference, you would quickly observe that the known success principles practiced by these men totaled less than twenty. Now it does not seem a formidable task to commit such a small number of success principles to memory. But what is the worth of carrying around a lot of principles in your brain? Study and evaluation, as we know from our school days, is no substitute for action.

Returning to point number two above, it is critical for you to realize that unnecessary knowledge and meaningless experience can be serious roadblocks along your way to wealth and success. Learning, like inflated money, can reach a point where it is almost valueless to you in reaching your specified goals. The wise man is the one who soon realizes that he cannot know everything. As for the value of experience, remember this: Experience is often overrated by the old and entrenched, who are suffering from the successive disenchantment of the things of life. There is no proven correlation between higher education or tenure in one's calling and the accumulation of great wealth. Only the great principles of life endure, and these you must commit to memory and habit. By cultivating the success principles about to be revealed to you, your habits become quite different from those who have failed; and by recognizing this difference, you take the first step on your way to wealth, independence, and success.

In college, the word, SCRIPT, often meant the form in which you were to answer a written examination. It is also derived from the word SCRIPTURE, which is a sacred book or writing, more commonly known in the Christian world as the Bible. The word, SCRIPT, then, could mean answers written down that you should live by. SCRIPT is a powerful word — a code word in this case — formed from key letters of nine proven success principles. When understood and put into action, these nine principles will supply you with over half of the known ingredients for achieving success, wealth, and an independent life style.

The second principle code word you should commit to memory — and subsequent action — is the word, FLAME. Fire is the most tangible of all visible mysteries. It is visible combustion; a bright light to lead the way; voracious, all-consuming energy; the sun; the sustenance of life on earth.

Hidden in the word FLAME, are the six remaining primary principles discovered by Napoleon Hill as being endemic in the rich and successful men he researched, studied, analyzed, and interviewed during his lifetime. The word FLAME can be your guiding light to the treasures at the far end of the tunnel. The word SCRIPT can only serve as your map and guide to the tunnel's entrance, and you can only proceed as far as daylight can penetrate. Together these two amazing key words — SCRIPT and FLAME — can unlock a storehouse of treasures such as your mind has never seen. Wealth, however, is shy and timid; it won't come to you. It is totally the antithesis of poverty, a condition which, in its bold and ruthless way, can overtake wealth when it accumulates without well-conceived and carefully executed plans. To observe this truth you have merely to recall the parable of the profligate son and to observe the flight of wealth around the world from the twin evils of inflation and communism.

When you have mastered the principles contained in this chapter, you will have the power to accumulate all of the wealth you desire. Chances are, however, that you will become somewhat moderate in this quest since another of life's great principles teaches us that the most priceless of riches is *peace of mind*. In Og Mandino's inspiring book, *The Greatest Salesman in the World,* he tells of the rich merchant's remark to the aspiring young camel boy who would become a wealthy and successful salesman. "So far as material wealth is concerned, there is only one difference between myself and the lowliest beggar inside Herrod's palace. The beggar thinks only of his next meal, and I think of the meal that will be my last."

With these moderating thoughts in mind, and with the knowledge that whatever thoughts you send out will come back to you greatly multiplied to bless or to curse, let us proceed to unravel the secrets of success — fifteen in all — hidden within the words, SCRIPT and FLAME. Once you have identified these crucial ingredients of success you must commit them to memory and habit. Remember now, that these principles are not just expedient thoughts for this hour alone; they are laws from and for the ages. The rich and successful live by these laws, and the truly successful people in this world have acquired a state of mind in which they are convinced of their success. They consistently achieve the goals they set out for themselves. Those who fail, remember, are those without the ability to reach their goals in life, whatever they may be. And failure has never been known to overtake the person whose determination to succeed is strong enough.

To become rich and successful you must follow the example of those you admire. (Successful human achievement, of course, does not belong to the rich alone.) Pursuits soon become habits, and habit and imitation are the source of all working, all apprenticeship, all practice, and all learning in the world. Your objective should be to form good habits and to become their slave.

(S) CRIPT   SUCCESS RULE 1 — SAVE AT LEAST 10% OF YOUR EARNINGS

The rich and successful all know that by sowing the seeds of frugality, they will reap the benefits of personal independence. Benjamin Franklin, widely known and respected for his pursuit of frugality, said that the way to wealth is as plain as the way to market. It depends chiefly on two words — industry and frugality. He believed in wasting neither time nor money and in making the best use of both. Without the savings habit, coupled with determined effort, success will be stunted; with them, your efforts will bear fruit.

When you think about it, you soon realize that money is the medium by which all earthly success is measured. Banks want to be assured of your liquidity before loaning you money. Money in the bank means personal freedom. In Clason's excellent book, *The Richest Man in Babylon,* the rich man, Arkad, gave this advice: "Counsel with wise men. Seek the advice of men whose daily work is handling money." The way to wealth is not along the avenue of your accumulated capital. It lies along the road to other people's money. I found the road to wealth when I began setting aside a portion of all I earned and resolved to keep it. I know of no better way to keep a score of your financial success, other than to base it on the liquidity factor. How much do you have in liquid assets? How much did you have yesterday? How much will you have tomorrow? Financial statements can be deceptive and open to widely varying interpretations. Net worth figures are often inflated and meaningless when the goddess of opportunity arrives at your door. Her favors are sold at once. She has no time for the man of inaction who must assess his investments.

A carefully conceived and executed savings program can cure the leanest purse. It is the cornerstone of all budgets. It is faithful to the requirement that your money be put to work. Wise management of your savings can protect your principal from the ravages of inflation. Remember the sacredness of your principal. Dissipation of principal is a primary source of failure and can lead to a loss of personal independence. Whenever possible you must use other people's money to make money. In your younger years — and considering the inflationary aspects of our times — it appears more frugal to have as little equity in your home as possible. Your liquidity is more impressive to bankers than the intangible benefits of equity in one's home. Remember, also, that borrowed money comes cheaper when your capital is gaining interest from the lender. Eventually you will want to own your own home free and clear of all encumbrances. Without a solid base of operations in your later years, you risk a loss of personal independence. To augment this end, you'll find that a savings habit will lead to the assurance of a future income — the primary goal of rich and poor alike, and the foundation of our social security system. Unfortunately, this system has become a mere dream and illusion, and is totally incapable of advancing the lifestyle of anyone practicing the principles revealed in this book. The only way you can advance toward wealth and personal freedom is to increase your earning ability. Though your "necessary expenses" may go down with your declining years, so can your income be reduced. The trick is to confine these "necessary expenses" to certain budgetary limits — say to a maximum of 90% of earned income. That leaves 10% of your earnings for yourself. Don't spend this 10%, even if the bargain is good. Just as you must condition yourself to avoid the illusionary schemes of con men, you must avoid the weakness of dipping into your savings to satisfy current desires and "opportunities." If the "opportunity" appears too good to pass up, stop to think about the odds against you when you abrogate the principles you espouse. It is human nature to vacillate and allow opportunity to escape when the time is ripe to accept it. If the "opportunity" is wrong for us, we become stubborn in our quest for it. Once you have accepted the habit of savings, cling to it as did the old mariner who held tight to the last plank of his ship amid storm and darkness.

S (C) RIPT   SUCCESS RULE 2 – HAVE CONFIDENCE IN YOURSELF

Most of us could use a little more self-confidence in our lives. As we observe others of greater or more imagined success, we tend to zero in on this characteristic of self-assurance. When prominent personalities appear before us, we often feel we are viewing persons of sublime self-confidence. Self-conceit, if it exists to a large degree in a prominent personality, is often not perceived at all. What we see is an intense identification of that person with his object or work. Common fears such as danger and death can seem beneath the concern of the personality. The person's quest or immediate effort could appear almost insane to the common eye, and we are awed by what we perceive to be an almost superhuman will of accomplishment. Think for a moment of Lindberg preparing to cross the Atlantic alone; DiMaggio extending a hitting streak that appears safe for 500 years; Gary Cooper alone at High Noon. Self-confidence is the first requisite to great undertakings. Only when many of your hopes have failed, and when your fears have passed unrealized can you expect to build self-confidence. You are the judge of how your own internal forces relate to the outside world. It would seem, then, that you must first come to know yourself – strengths and weaknesses; all of your hopes and fears.

Consider the worst of the human conditions – The Abysmal Failure. He is incapable of earning much money. He is continuously quarrelsome. Nobody does anything he suggests. In sports, he is clumsy and slow. All of the hobbies he ever tried were flops. He can't get along with his own family. He's lousy at work and admits he shouldn't get paid for what he does. He can't talk anybody into anything. Everything goes wrong for him. If it were not for bad luck he'd have no luck at all. He gets conned into sucker schemes. Kids shake him down for money. He's convinced everyone is looking down on him.

Now, since it is unlikely that anyone reading this book considers himself an abysmal failure, we can surmise that there is hope for anyone to raise their level of self-confidence. Fear and doubt, of course, are the real reasons why people lack confidence in themselves. (I'll identify the basic fears for you in later pages and we'll deal with them in more detail at that time.) Right now you should know that the absence of fear, and not higher education or high I.Q. is the major cause of individual success. It would seem that our Abysmal Failure was beyond hope because of his cancerous fears. Only a miracle could possibly save him. But miracles, being the pet children of faith, have been known to occur; and fear is the major reason why the Creator, or Infinite Intelligence, does not always respond affirmatively to prayer. Belief in a higher being than yourself (faith) is an absolute first step in the building or rebuilding of confidence in yourself. Even the worst failures and reprobates in our society can find their minds and lives reshaped by a newly-found and abiding faith. It is the linchpin in the development wheel of character and self-assurance. In the process of developing self-confidence, your mind will be given certain exercises to perform. The role of faith in this process is to enlighten and guide the mind.

The first exercise I want your mind to perform is quite simple. You must simply ADMIT to yourself that there is a Higher Being (God, if you will) or Infinite Intelligence greater than any man on earth, and that you have the same opportunity as anyone else of communicating and forming an alliance with this miraculous source of all energy and life. Every successful man has received help from unknown sources, so don't think for one minute that self-confidence comes solely from developing your own internal forces. Napoleon Hill writes of the form of self-hypnosis called *autosuggestion*, a mind exercise through which the subconscious is influenced to act automatically on your wishes and desires. It is a powerful force for personal achievement, especially when coupled with prayer (your means of contacting God, or the Infinite Intelligence). Through effective prayer, you express a fervent and persistent plea for help in attainment of certain hopes, desires, and definite objectives, which you admit you cannot attain through your own efforts alone. To be effective, prayer, like autosuggestion, must be continuous and must not be utilized only in moments of misfortune. Your entreaties will then be motivated by fear — a negative emotion. Your mind must be in a positive frame for autosuggestion and prayer to work for you. In prayer, you ADMIT to yourself and to Infinite Intelligence that you need help. You cannot achieve these hopes, desires, and definite objectives by yourself or in concert with other mortals alone.

Prayer and autosuggestion are similar in that, effectively used, they are capable of working "miracles." In effect, you convince yourself that you can accomplish certain things through the assistance of unseen and unknown powers. You have *faith* that you are not alone. For Christians, this expression of faith has taken on more personalized dimensions because of the splendid example of Christ — the supreme example of self-confidence and success.

It is self-defeating to set goals and to express hopes and desires to yourself twice a day without making account to Infinite Intelligence through an expression of faith (prayer). You must ADMIT to the existence of this Higher Being and beseech his help in overcoming those obstacles that block out the attainment of whatever hopes, desires, and definite objectives you seek. When ravaged by adversity, unpleasant circumstance, failure, and physical pain, you must ADMIT that there are unseen hands at work planting the seeds of equivalent benefits. Never get discouraged. Refuse to accept as inevitable any circumstance you do not desire. Soon this form of mental exercise will condition your mind to accept as inevitable those "miracles" that can transform your life from one of failure to success. Mental attitude is probably the most important determining factor as to what results you will receive from prayer and autosuggestion.

Now you must have noticed the number of times I used the word, ADMIT, in this brief discourse; and you've seen that I have capitalized it like the previous key words, SCRIPT and FLAME. The word ADMIT is comprised of key letters in my formula for raising your level of self-confidence. When working to develop this essential principle of success, you can remember the points on which to concentrate by referring back to the word, ADMIT.

A-D-M-I-T = YOUR SELF-CONFIDENCE FORMULA

A = Autosuggestion — Your doorway to the subconscious mind where, through the process of self-hypnosis, your desires, hopes, and definite objectives, if held persistently, will express themselves in some practical way. The subconscious mind, through its link to Infinite Intelligence, will bring forth rewards, benefits, and fulfillment in direct proportion to those things which one thinks about most often and believes are attainable.

D = Definite Goals — All individual achievement begins with a definite purpose and a plan for its accomplishment. The subconscious mind will not act upon vague ideas, plans, or purposes.

M = Mental Attitude — A contagious state of mind which communicates itself from one person to another without spoken words, signs, or actions, by the medium of telepathy; therefore it should be positive. Thoughts mixed with feelings of emotion tend to attract similar or related thoughts.

I = I Can! — The firm belief that whatever the mind can conceive and believe, the mind can achieve. Knowing exactly what you want and going after it with enthusiasm and total commitment, thus becoming alerted to opportunity. You are what you want to be. You act as you want to act. Here's how a wise poet has expressed this thought:

> If you *think* you're beaten, you are.
> If you *think* you dare not, you don't.
> If you like to win, but you *think* you can't,
> It's almost certain you won't.
>
> If you *think* you'll lose, you're lost,
> For out of the world we find,
> Success begins with a fellow's will —
> It's all in the *state of mind*.
>
> If you *think* you're outclassed, you are.
> You've got to *think* high to rise.
> You've got to be *sure of yourself* before
> You can ever win a prize.
>
> Life's battles don't always go
> To the stronger or faster man,
> But soon or late the man who wins
> Is the man WHO THINKS HE CAN!

T = Truth and Justice — Your realization that nothing can be received without giving something of equal value in return and that every adversity, every unpleasantness, every failure, and every physical pain carries with it the seed of an equivalent benefit. Whatever you do for another by the thoughts you send forth, so shall you reap. Love always rebounds to the benefit of those who express it, even though it may not be reciprocated.

S (C) RIPT   SUCCESS RULE 3 – DEVELOP SELF **CONTROL**

There once was an orator in ancient Greece of whom it was said, "I'm sure he could govern the earth, if only he could control his tongue." The observation could be advanced by stating that the command of one's *self* is the greatest empire a man could aspire to, and consequently, to be subject to our own passions is the most grievous slavery. Bad and ignoble rulers throughout history have shown us that the man who least governs himself is least fitted to govern others. The world seems to make way for and follow the man who has gotten himself together and who knows where he's going. When the going gets tough, the man in control of self gets going. His "power" is derived from organized and intelligently directed knowledge about the components of his mind and body, as well as a thorough understanding of man's basic fears and emotions.

In developing the principle of self-control, you should know that power is required for the accumulation of money. Power is also necessary for the retention of wealth. Whenever a wealthy individual or an immense corporation fails to exercise self-control, they will experience an erosion of their power base. Often this occurs when either loses control of their ego, and when they view themselves as beyond the law. In almost every instance, the abused power is being exercised, not by the owners, but by trustees and directors of invested funds or by holders of the public trust.

If you would aspire to build up great wealth on earth you must first understand the very essence of life and concentrate on the elimination of the seven basic fears:

1. Fear of Dying.
2. Fear of Growing Old.
3. Fear of Becoming Ill.
4. Fear of Pain.
5. Fear of Losing Someone's Love.
6. Fear of Being Poor.
7. Fear of Being Criticized.

FEAR OF DYING

Life has often been likened to energy which, along with matter, cannot be destroyed. Life can be destroyed, but, as with energy, life also changes form, beginning with a germ cell, through birth, and seemingly ending with death. However, death, it can be argued, is merely a transition stage, wherein, unlike energy, no new form emerges. If your soul lives on after death, then surely your soul does not age. You possess eternal youth. If this transition does not occur, then what remains after death is a long and abiding sleep, and sleep is not one of man's basic fears. If you fear a fiery Hell, or the devil himself, then conversion to, and practice of, the Christian faith can assure you of eternal salvation.

FEAR OF GROWING OLD

Old age to many of us may seem a long way off, but when the yellow leaves of life appear, it will be too late to do anything about it. Control of self means the conquering of this fear by preparing for the eventuality and enjoyment of old age. When you see an old man of good humor — friendly, equable, and content — you can be sure that his youth was wisely spent. Patience, justice, and generosity were among the coins he placed on life's counter. He doesn't try to return his spent years for the fresh merchandise of youth. He does not dread the sunset. He is like the evening of a fine day. Shakespeare left these words for those who would prepare now for the years ahead:

> Though I look old, yet I am strong and lusty;
> For in my youth I never did apply
> Hot and rebellious liquors in my blood;
> Nor did not with unbashful forehead woo
> The means of weakness and debility:
> Therefore my age is as a lusty winter,
> Frosty, but kindly.

FEAR OF BECOMING ILL

Napoleon Hill, in his classic book, *You Can Work Your Own Miracles,* tells of an experiment he conducted during one of his lectures to demonstrate the imaginary physical ailment known as hypochondria. A number of "stooges" were pre-selected by Dr. Hill to approach a "victim" during intermission and inquire about his health. One would rush up and say something such as: "You look pale. Is anything wrong?" Another stooge then came along and insisted that the victim sit down before he collapsed. A third stooge subsequently appeared to confirm the diagnosis; "You look as if you're going to faint. I'd better get you a glass of water." By this time a crowd would have gathered, and stooge number three would add, "Make room, please. This man needs a place to lie down. He's about to pass out."

If the victim was still on his feet, it would not be for long. The role of the fourth stooge was to grab the victim by the arm and exclaim to all assembled, "Someone call a doctor, quick! This man needs attention."

In all cases where this experiment was performed the "victim" became convinced of his illness. In fact, one young man required hospitalization, and the doctors inherited the difficult task of convincing him that his illness was psychosomatic and brought on by a hoax. Following this incident, Dr. Hill abandoned the experiments. He had proved beyond doubt that ill health can be "willed" on someone by his own mind, and the comments and actions of others are not necessarily required to bring this about.

FEAR OF PAIN

If your pleasure is gathering roses, you soon lose the fear of thorns. Pain seems to stalk pleasure like a shadow. To know pleasure is to know pain, otherwise you would pursue pleasure unto your death. Active and pleasurable sports require pain to bring rest; the birth of a child is preceded by pain. Rest or hospitalization is nature's way of restoring your energies. Fear of pain (mental and physical) is, of course, different from living with pain; however, abnormally-held fears can greatly aggravate those real pains we must learn to live with. One of the best defenses against an abnormal fear of pain, and against pain itself, is a comprehensive program of mind conditioning based on the information supplied in this book. A mind out of control with unwarranted fears and inflamed emotions, is easy prey for the fangs of physical pain. The self-discipline you will gain by conditioning your mind for the acceptance of pain will serve you well when pain is to be experienced and when it actually occurs. Men in the heat of battle, primitive women in childbirth, the early American Indian, all have learned to live with pain beyond what we consider to be human endurance. Football players have at times been hit so hard while carrying the ball toward the goal that they have been classified as unconscious — nature's stop-gap for pain endurance — yet they push on for a touchdown. How? When interviewed, many of these athletes have stated that, upon being hit, all reality was gone. Their minds could not conceive pain. All that mattered was to reach the goal line ahead. This done, the clouds of emotion appeared and pain was experienced. At this point each athlete began to lose control over his own mind — the one thing of which the Creator had given him complete charge.

History has proven that the great and successful leaders of mankind, in all their endeavors, have mastered the fear of mental and physical pain. If you would come up from failure you must overcome this fear. Realize, however, that unless your mind is properly conditioned, even the simple toothache will try your strongest power of will. But the sting of pain, like the edge of pleasure, is blunted by the mind long prepared; for the hurt and the balm are diluted by the waters of patience.

FEAR OF LOSING SOMEONE'S LOVE

The fear of lost love is said to be the cause of more murders and suicides than all other reasons combined. More enterprise and accomplishment have been thrown to the wind over this fear than all of man's efforts to date. Fear of lost love has changed more minds, influenced more people to do wrong, and scared more personalities, than all the despots the world has ever known. To obtain peace of mind, and to begin mastering this fear, you must properly interpret and relate to the following basic law of nature:

When something is taken away from you (love) the seed of an equivalent benefit will be left behind to grow.

Once love is lost, sorrow can bring about reforms over such undesirable traits as arrogance, selfishness, vanity, and self-love. An abnormal or unjustified fear about losing the love of someone close to you can undo all of your efforts to achieve success. If you are afraid to go up to this fear and speak to it, the fear will not fade away. This lack of courage can bring about feelings of failure; your work performance can be lackluster and substandard; melancholia can poison your ability to think accurately.

Whether the fear is real or imagined, the result is the same — a loss of control over your own mind — and the floodgates are opened to the Seven Negative Emotions: Hate, Envy, Greed, Fear, Superstition, Revenge, and Anger.

Consider the four essential components of your life:

1. Physical concerns
2. Mental attitude
3. Social involvements
4. Spiritual needs

When any of these components is imbalanced, there is disruption in your life. Fear of lost love is an insidious disease that can disrupt a healthy mental attitude, thus impeding progress toward your goals. You must stop to attend the wound. The other components of your life are burdened by the imbalance. Prolonged anguish can aggravate the wound and cause deterioration of the other three components, thus undermining the structure of your life. Only when love is actually lost, or your fears established as unfounded, can you begin to shut out the predominance of negative emotions over positive emotions and allow the fresh current of desire, faith, love, sex, enthusiasm, romance, and hope to enter your life. These positive emotions flow and recede inversely to an imbalance in any of the four basic components. Your living tools for operating your life are: *Body, brain, heart, and soul.* They work best for you when they are continually refined and maintained in perfect order.

The Seven Positive Emotions are:

1. Desire
2. Faith
3. Love
4. Sex
5. Enthusiasm
6. Romance
7. Hope

The Seven Negative Emotions are:

1. Hate
2. Envy
3. Greed
4. Fear
5. Superstition
6. Revenge
7. Anger

FEAR OF BEING POOR

A rich man was once asked, "Are you afraid you'll ever lose all of your money?" He replied, "Poverty is uncomfortable, I've been there. But the best thing that can happen to a young man is to be tossed overboard to learn to sink or swim for himself. If he conquers the fear of poverty now, it won't haunt him when he becomes rich."

In this world you'll find contentment among rich and poor alike, but he that *fears* he will be poor can never be truly rich. At first glance it might appear as if the self-made rich of this world were motivated by an intense desire not to become poor. The often cited quotation, "I've been rich and I've been poor, but, believe me, rich is better," is more an afterthought of famous personages than a statement of motivation. Obviously it is better to have money than to be without it. The self-made rich and successful person views poverty as no more than an unwelcome shadow; certainly not the ghostly apparition of the security-conscious individual. If you would rid yourself of this fear you must first understand that it is more shameful not to know how to chase poverty away than it is to bear poverty. The poor can at least revel in their privilege to be happy and unenvied; to be free of analysts and guards, and to take from nature's bounty what the great and wealthy are compelled to purchase in the name of pleasure.

As a rule, rich and successful persons do not fear poverty because this fear is the antithesis of one of the ten basic motives — material gain. It is the want of material things, not obsessive concern about being poor, that spurs individual enterprise. One of the great truisms in life is that he who fears to suffer, suffers only because he fears.

In the daily papers, and on television news programs, you read and observe the lives of rich and poor alike. The truly poor of this world certainly do not like their plight, but they appear resigned to it and hope for something better out of life. They don't suffer from a fear of poverty, because they are there already. As a young boy I remember the trucks pulling up to our row house delivering groceries because we were on "relief." I recall shuffling to the stage of auditoriums at Christmas time to receive gifts donated to the poor. As a young teenager, I remember exchanging my art work for necessary clothing. Just as the foot is the measure of the shoe, so are the real wants of nature the measure of enjoyment. I was poor because I wanted for necessary things. When I received these things I was happy. The same measure can be applied to the rich — they can be poor, also, though in a different way. Things may not bring them happiness. It is unlikely, however, that the person who achieves wealth through his own enterprise will be hamstrung by a fear of poverty.

Following are six symptoms of the person who fears poverty:

1. Indecision
2. Doubt
3. Indifference
4. Worry
5. Over-caution
6. Procrastination

The lesson here is that you cannot achieve great wealth if you do not rid yourself of these symptoms and if you worry too much about being poor.

FEAR OF BEING CRITICIZED

Criticism can be likened, in a poetic way, to an arrow winging straight and true toward a target in the air. You're soaring like an eagle through rolling clouds until struck by the fatal dart. The shaft quivers in your heart while, still, your ambitions, hopes, and dreams cry out for greater heights. How great, you feel, must be those feathers which propelled the steel that returns you to your nest. Greater, surely, than your own plumage, which now drinks the last drop of blood from your bleeding breast.

Resolve here and now to soar still higher when the real and imagined barbs of criticism strike you in the breast. It is simply not possible to pursue the great heights in life when you are burdened with worry over what other people think, do, and say. Opinions are the cheapest commodities on the face of the earth. If taken in quantity they will lead to cancer of the soul and undermine your power of will. Criticism, like advice, is freely given away, but watch that you take only what will not destroy you. Somehow life seems to favor those who know precisely what they want to accomplish and what they *do not* want to achieve. If you aspire to grow tall in life, you'll catch much wind of criticism. Remain steadfast, says nature, and you shall have strength and wisdom sufficient for all your needs.

One of life's interesting observations is that the great and famous, though subject to an unremitting gale of criticism, can continue to do pretty much as they please; while those of lesser capability and achievement find their growth stunted and bent to the will of the gale. A successful person is like the strongest tree which sprouts and grows tall and straight despite the howling winds around it. We see this in all walks of life — entertainment, sports, politics, science, business, religion, etc. The stronger and more determined the figure, the less he will bend to the winds of criticism.

Fear of criticism and shallow goals are found in the swamp of failure. If you hesitate to free yourself, or if you follow a false channel, you risk spending your life trapped in the bogs. The channel to wealth and personal independence requires you to set your goal — not for small rivers and tributaries, but onward to the great ocean itself. If others would think this goal unreachable, and if they would discourage your attempts with disparaging remarks and conflicting effort, you must press on, else your fondest hopes and dreams will perish. When you succumb to a negative environment, such as excessive criticism and "nagging," you risk altering the chemistry of the brain to the point where you will lose all ambition and sink deeper into the swamp of failure. Remember that a quitter never wins and a winner never quits in the face of criticism. *Definiteness of purpose* and a *burning desire to succeed* are your best weapons against this awesome fear. It can blow away the blossoms as well as the caterpillars from your tree of growth. All of your hopes, desires, and plans can fall to earth if your mind becomes weakened by the fear of criticism.

Your mind becomes conditioned to withstand criticism by developing roots in the subconscious. Here is the procedure for setting down these roots and influencing their growth:

1. WRITE OUT A DEFINITE STATEMENT OF YOUR GOALS.
   This statement will be ineffective against criticism without these six little specific helpers:
   "I had six honest serving men, they taught me all I knew. Their names were What and Where and When and Why and How and Who."

2. DEVELOP AN INTENSE ENTHUSIASM WITHIN YOURSELF OVER THE ANTICIPATED ACHIEVEMENT OF YOUR GOALS.
   You must become emotional about this. Get yourself excited — Sing, Dance, Talk to yourself — See results. You must practice, practice, practice, until you can feel intense enthusiasm and joy of achievement. Remember! Criticism has never opened a good show, nor closed down a bad one.

3. REPEAT THE STATEMENT NIGHT AND DAY AFTER EACH OF YOUR "ENTHUSIASM" SESSIONS. BELIEVE

THAT YOUR GOALS WILL BE ACTED UPON IN RETURN FOR SERVICES YOU WILL GIVE. EXPRESS GRATITUDE.
To see yourself receiving rewards and achieving your goals, you must, through commensurate effort, promise and deliver something in return. The undying strength of this pact is your insurance against the undermining influence of criticism.

Remember this: The Creator has given you the power of controlling your own mind. Through the fear of criticism you relinquish this power to others who may, in turn, successfully direct it to whatever ends they may choose. Your only limitations are those which you set up in your own mind (through fear) or permit others to establish for you (through criticism).

S (C) RIPT SUCCESS RULE 4 – DEVELOP CONCENTRATION AND PERSISTENCE

Andrew Carnegie, the inspiration for Napoleon Hill's classic self-help book, *Think and Grow Rich,* had this to say about the habit of concentration: "Concentration is my motto – first honesty, then industry, then concentration." Carnegie, the founder of the company now known as U. S. Steel, was, along with Henry Ford, one of the most successful and influential industrialists of his day, as well as one of the world's richest men.

Concentration and persistence breed genius. If you can get back on your feet after being knocked down a dozen times by failure, you have proved yourself capable of accomplishment beyond the norm. Thomas Edison failed 10,000 times before inventing the incandescent light. Isaac Newton traced his discoveries to intense concentration. Concentration and persistence have lifted mankind to the stars and back, conquered disease, produced awesome weapons of destruction, and have finally duplicated the process by which the human egg is fertilized. Intense concentration and persistence are the major reasons unbeatable feats of human skill and endurance continue to be broken. These qualities are behind the election of our presidents, the success of our major stars in the theater and the arts; they are the solace of self-made millionaires, and the sustenance of all great novelists.

Sam Snead, the great golfer, had this to say about concentrated effort: "Concentration is *so* important! You've got to be able to shut out everything except the shot you're taking at that moment. You have to *know* that the ball is going into that hole." Snead has won more regular P. G. A. tournaments than any other golfer and is listed in the Guinness Book of Records for shooting the lowest score in tournament play — an incredible 59! Another record-holder, the amazing ball player, Pete Rose, applies such a steady and undissipated effort to win that his hitting streak of 44 straight games captured the imagination of an entire nation; and when he fell short of DiMaggio's magic mark, Rose went on to proclaim he would concentrate on becoming the greatest hitter in baseball.

If you think the powers of concentration and persistence are available only to the great and super great, consider that Rose and others like him have had to fight serious deficiencies to reach the top. Rose has this to say about coming from behind:

> "There are a lot of guys with tremendous talent . . . guys with more size and speed and power than I've got — and guys with faster swings, or quicker wrists, and things like that. But I think, with what I've got, I get more out of it than any other player in baseball. I get the most out of whatever talent or advantages I have. I don't have outstanding speed, but I beat out more infield hits than anybody else with that kind of speed and I make more of the tough catches. And I don't have a good arm either, but I throw out more runners than anybody else with an arm like mine."

Concentration on the task at hand is critical to your success. Few things are impractical in themselves. More people fail because they fail to apply themselves than do those who lack the means to get ahead. I attended school with the great country and western music star, Roy Clark, and I recall the intense effort and concentration he applied to whatever he was doing, be it baseball or "pickin." He has probably mastered more musical instruments than anyone in his field. In his early years, winning contests and awards became a habit with him. He simply would not give up. When failure and imminent tragedy stalked him, he concentrated the powers of his mind toward ridding these shadows from his life.

The incredible powers of concentration, nourished and developed, applied relentlessly toward the achievement of specific goals, are behind the success of every great person in history. Even despots and dictators such as Hitler, were intense thinkers who refused to be dissuaded by more rational, though less intense, thought. The three critical steps for the nourishment, development, and application of the powers of concentration are listed below:

1. DEFINE AND PURSUE SPECIFIC GOALS
   Most problems, well-organized and defined, are already partially solved. Move positively once your goals are clearly defined.
2. DEVELOP FAITH
   Follow the precepts of the Nazarene who said, "Ask and it will be given to you; seek and you will find. Knock and it will be opened to you. For everyone who asks, receives, and he who seeks, finds, and to him who knocks it will be opened."
   Matthew 7:7-8.
   "For truly I say to you, if you have faith as a grain of mustard seed, you will say to this mountain, 'Move from here to there,' and it will move; and nothing will be impossible to you."
   Matthew 17:20.
3. ADOPT A POSITIVE MENTAL ATTITUDE
   Think success! A greater part of our happiness or misery depends on our disposition and not on our circumstance. "I can't," is an idea — not a fact. Success is achieved and maintained by those who keep trying.

Finally, remember this about the power of concentration. Just reading about solutions to problems and looking at success will not bring success. Nor will success come to those who merely understand what they read and perceive about success. However, success will seek you out if you *act* on what you learn about it.

S(C)RIPT   SUCCESS RULE 5 -- LEARN TO COOPERATE WITH OTHERS

The great industrialist, Willard F. Rockwell, Jr., carries a quote from a psychologist in his wallet. It reads, "Don't forget that every human being has this motto tattooed on his chest: *I want to be important."* In your struggle to become rich and successful, remember that the whole (your life) is equal to the sum of all the parts (those around you) and is greater than any one of the parts (you). If you expect to win in the ball game of life, you must have the cooperation of your players. Don't play your own games with them or walk all over them. A humorous story to emphasize this point comes to mind.

> A pretty young lady walked into a sporting goods store and ordered all the equipment necessary for a baseball game, including a baseball, a bat, a catcher's mitt, and a catcher's mask.
>
> "Are you sure you want all these?" asked the salesman. The girl nodded. "Yes, I do. My boss said if I'd play ball with him we'd get along fine."

In the average business endeavor, a relatively small percentage of people end up shouldering responsibility for the success of the enterprise. The others are physically there, though their minds and spirits may be elsewhere. Many take from the enterprise more than they contribute. Your success is dependent upon your identification and proper remuneration of the *producers,* rather than the *reducers.* Surround yourself with people who have the talents you lack and pay them well. Success is a cooperative effort and is seldom achieved by men operating for and unto themselves. Lack of harmonious coordination of effort is the main cause of practically every human failure.

Think of the Allies at the beginning of World War II. Their ranks were badly split by dissension and factionalism. Only a supreme organizer and master of the cooperative spirit could pull them together. General George C. Marshall -- himself a great leader of armies -- selected Eisenhower, a young military officer whose forte had been in getting people to work together toward a common goal. He had never before commanded armies in the field, but he was a genius at organizing cooperative effort.

Think of Sir Edmund Hillary on Mount Everest, falling to his death only to be saved by his trusted Sherpa guide, Tenzing Norgay. Norgay knew the crevasses on Everest; he knew its best campsites, its peaks. He was the best man for the job at hand. Without him, Hillary would never have reached the top.

These stories point up the need for you to assemble a team of co-operative, enthusiastic, and energetic people around you if you hope to reach the pinnacles of success. Napoleon Hill referred to the assembling of such a group as forming a "master-mind" alliance.

The formation of just such an alliance is responsible for the success of the world's most famous hotel and motel chain — Holiday Inns, Inc. The founder, Kemmons Wilson, when asked about the principal reason for his success replied, "I guess I'm just smart enough to surround myself with the necessary brains and technical know-how that I don't have." Wilson, named by the London Sunday Times as one of the thousand most important men of the 20th century, never hesitates to point out in speeches and interviews that his success is due largely to other people — most notably his wife and mother.

Another famous practitioner of the "master-mind" alliance theory was Henry Ford. Once, during a libel suit instituted by Ford against a Chicago newspaper, the defense attorney opened Mr. Ford to scorn and ridicule over his lack of formal education. "Listen," Ford told the lawyer, "I have not built this company by cluttering up my mind with general knowledge just so I can answer foolish questions. By pushing the right button on my desk I can bring an expert into my office to answer any question I want to ask about running my business in the most profitable manner for all concerned."

Behind the men who have built up great fortunes with the help of others stand six indispensable and invisible guards. These guards are at the disposal of the leader of the "master-mind" group and are principally responsible for his leadership role. The absence of any of these guards will weaken and eventually destroy the alliance.

1. The Guard of Mental Peace.
2. The Guard of Good Health.
3. The Guard of Faith and Hope.
4. The Guard of Financial Success.
5. The Guard of Love.
6. The Guard of Wisdom.

The Guard of Mental Peace

Call on him to purge your mind of the seven negative emotions: Hate, Envy, Greed, Fear, Superstition, Revenge, and Anger.

The Guard of Good Health

He protects one of life's great riches. Without this guard you cannot effectively lead; for no man will long follow suffering and the spectre of death.

The Guard of Faith and Hope

He keeps the spiritual path open for you and shows you how, through prayer and autosuggestion, you can make direct and immediate contact with Infinite Intelligence. He shows you the way to a positive mental attitude.

The Guard of Financial Success

He keeps money worries away from you by "balancing your books." He's responsible for seeing that you give something of equal value for all monies received and expected.

The Guard of Love

He helps you to lead everyone you meet onto a higher plane than when you found them — to do unto others as you would have them do unto you. He makes you understand that you can never speak of yourself without loss, for your accusations of yourself will always be believed, your praises, never.

The Guard of Wisdom

He is responsible for the "mustering" of the other guards. His primary duty is to exchange failure and unpleasant circumstance for commensurate benefits. He reminds you that men relate themselves to one another in whatever capacities they may be associated because of a motive or motives. Without this guard you may forget that there can be no permanent human relationship based upon an indefinite or vague motive, or upon no motive at all.

Cooperation does everything when it is perfect. It satisfies desires, simplifies needs, foresees wishes, and becomes a constant fortune. The desire to be great, to be recognized, and to have riches and personal power is a healthy desire; but when a man proclaims his greatness to the world it is an indication that he has left his ego unguarded, that it has taken possession of him. Friends and associates alike will soon abandon the man who proclaims his own greatness, for it is evidence that he shields some fear or inferiority complex.

When you reach out for cooperation, remember that one hand alone cannot applaud.

SC (R) IPT   SUCCESS RULE 6 – PRACTICE THE GOLDEN RULE

There appears to be no more valid rule for mankind to live by than the Golden Rule. Nevertheless, a lot of fun has been poked at it. There is the story of the mother scolding her young daughter after overhearing her and a few friends plotting revenge on a playmate following a fight. The mother kindly took the young conspirator in tow and admonished her, "It seems to me you're going to do to Mary just what you don't want her to do to you. I don't think this is the Golden Rule -- is it?"

"Well, mama," said the youngster, "the Golden Rule is all right for Sunday, but for everyday I'd rather have an eye for an eye and a tooth for a tooth."

Obviously if you sow actions based on the "eye for an eye" attitude, so shall you reap a wrong habit. Sow wrong habits and you reap bad character. Sow bad character and reap a dark destiny.

Behind all of our actions are the Ten Basic Motives:

1. Self-preservation
2. Life after death
3. Freedom of body and mind
4. Recognition of self-expression
5. Material gain
6. Emotion of Love
7. Emotion of Fear
8. Emotion of Sex
9. Emotion of Anger
10. Emotion of Hate

Behind all rich and successful persons lies a full understanding of these basic motives. Ideally — considering the fact that the mind is the one and only thing over which the Creator has provided man with the privilege of self-control — we would like to master these motives and to use them only for the good they will do for us. Using Jesus Christ as the supreme example of one whose motives were beyond suspect, we can, at best, strive to emulate his example when evaluating our motives.

Jesus Christ was the greatest motivator the world has ever known. His example sets the standard for success in its true form. He is the ultimate practitioner of the *Golden Rule*. When he spoke, men listened and believed. His followers were legions. Even Pontius Pilate hesitated to disclaim Jesus's mission on earth or to question his motives. Only a few high and corrupt officials among his own people condemned him for their own material gain.

Now, as in those days, our society uses money as the medium of exchange. Money is power. And like all power, money can be used for good or evil. You're reading this book because I claim that the techniques and principles explained here can help you to make money. In your quest for financial success and independence you must not lose sight of the *Golden Rule.* An aid to this end is a thorough understanding of the Ten Basic Motives. You'll want to memorize them and be true to them. You should be aware of your motives at all times, and strive to recognize the true motives beyond the actions of others. Remember that all thoughts are ultimately translated into their material counterparts. Through the miracle of the human mind you have the privilege of largely determining your own destiny and freeing yourself from undesirable motives. You've heard the familiar saying, "Actions speak louder than words." Remember also, that it is not so much what you say as it is the TONE and MANNER in which you say it that gives one a clue as to your motives. If you react to slights, verbal injuries, alleged unfairness, or imagined fears and anxieties with suspect motivation and an "eye for an eye" philosophy, you must pay through the loss of your ability to influence others.

Remember these key points:

SELF-PRESERVATION

1. You are not entitled to live at the expense of someone else.

LIFE AFTER DEATH

2. Life after death, if it exists, is available to all humans on the face of the earth.

(cont.)

FREEDOM OF BODY AND MIND

3. Freedom of body and mind is a grant from the Creator and not from man himself.

SELF-EXPRESSION

4. Everyone is entitled to self-expression, but not at the expense of injury to his fellow man.

MATERIAL GAIN

5. When you share with others a part of what you have, that which remains multiplies and grows.

LOVE

6. Love is man's greatest defense against the spears of hate and anger and his most skillful tool to open the hearts of other men.

FEAR

7. Fear, once overcome and transmuted into faith, will return to you possession of your own mind and open the way to fulfillment of your desires and the rejection of all you do not desire.

SEX

8. The cup of sensual pleasure should never be drained to the bottom, for there is always poison in the dregs.

(cont.)

ANGER

9. The fire you kindle for your enemy often burns yourself more than him.

HATE

10. Hatred is active, and envy passive dislike; there is but one step from envy to hate.

SCR (I) PT   SUCCESS RULE 7 – USE YOUR IMAGINATION

Imagination, as it is often misunderstood, is a characteristic element of the mind, manifesting itself in such image-building powers as fantasy and dreaming. For success-building purposes, of which the creative process is essential, you must understand that imagination is not only a quality, but also a faculty – a skill developable through action or practice. If, then, you can acquire imagination, and if it can be made to work for you, it can logically be termed a servant of your will. If you do not call upon this servant, it will grow lazy and inefficient, leaving your mind filled with cobwebs and open to wrong conclusions and false premises. It is therefore critical to your success that you actively develop the faculty of imagination. Poets and dramatists, of course, have acquired this faculty through performance and practice. Successful men of business and industry follow a similar creative course of action, though the products of their labor are dissimilar.

Consider Shakespeare's poem on imagination:

> And as imagination bodies forth the form . . .
> of things unknown (problems), the poet's pen (successful person)
> turns them to shape (definition and solution) and gives to airy nothing (opportunity)
> A local habitation and a name (goals; means to an end)
> Such tricks has strong imagination
> That if he would but apprehend some joy (riches),
> It comprehends some bringer of that joy (your services);
> Or in the night imagining some fear (7 basic fears),
> How easy is a bush (obstacle) supposed a bear (defeat)?

W. Clement Stone, the famous success motivator, author, and multimillionaire, suggests that your imagination first be put to use in reducing your past successes into a formula (preferably written). When failure comes around you can then take out your stores of success knowledge and tell him to get lost. The theme of this book is to help you ward off failure. I have used my imagination in this chapter to reduce certain proven success principles into a workable formula for you to follow. The key words of "SCRIPT" and "FLAME" are products of my imagination and examples of how this faculty or servant of your mind can be made to work for you in achieving wealth, independence, and peace of mind.

Imagination has always played a key role in the success of many real estate developers and investors. William Nickerson (*How I turned $1,000 into Three Million in Real Estate*) and Albert L. Lowry *(How You Can Become Financially Independent by Investing in Real Estate)* have long practiced the procedure of buying up dilapidated apartment buildings and turning them into real money-makers through imaginative renovation, management, and refinancing. Without the acquired skill of looking behind the immediate facade, beyond the immediate situation, and acting on what they've learned, they might very well be working today as average real estate salesmen. Instead, they are millionaires and substantially independent. Imagination is the principal skill I brought with me when, as an inexperienced young man, I first entered the land development business. Without imagination I could not have succeeded as I have today.

Napoleon said that imagination rules the world, and he acted upon this premise until his downfall. How many stars in the theater and the arts were projected into the filament largely through boundless imaginations that saw no limitations on their talents and abilities? How many long-running broadway musicals would still be idle ideas or story lines were it not for boundless imagination?

Disbelievers in the divinity of Christ have said that Jesus had the greatest imagination of anyone who ever lived — he imagined he was the son of God. Yet they would readily acknowledge that all history as we now know it is incomprehensible without Christ.

William Danforth, in his famous self-help book, *I Dare You*, tells the story of Henry Ford and his belief in the power of imagination. There was the time when Ford wanted to obtain unbreakable glass for his new models. His "experts" told him it couldn't be done. "Bring me younger men of imagination who know of no reason why unbreakable glass cannot be made. I want young and ambitious fellows around me who imagine nothing is impossible." Ford soon had his unbreakable glass.

All of us are imaginative in some form or another, for images (and belief) breed desire. Desire, of course, is the inspiration for action. When developing the success principle of imagination, it is necessary for you to remember this about desire, lest your imagination carry you away:

> Desires defeat their own purposes should they be too many, too confusing, or beyond a person's training to accomplish.

The development and cultivation of imaginative effort toward specific goals can often precede the acquisition of those skills and techniques required to reach the goals. Therefore, repetitive experience is necessary to acquire this "know-how." Imaginative effort in pursuit of specific goals also requires you to become knowledgeable about your field of expected accomplishment. It is simply not enough to imagine yourself as a great and wealthy person without obtaining the required skills and knowledge of your activity field. A characteristic of eccentric persons is a runaway imagination. People who have imagination without learning, have wings and no feet.

While in pursuit of this learning, remember the importance of environment in building success. It is foolhardy to imagine yourself a great explorer without going to those areas that need exploring. Actors and actresses who become famous go to New York and Los Angeles, the meccas for television and movies. And if you can imagine yourself as a rich and successful entrepreneur in real estate, it is best to first get into the profession itself, specifically within the area of your concern, be it residential real estate, apartments, commercial real estate, or rural land.

SCRI(P)T   SUCCESS RULE 8 – DEVELOP A PLEASANT PERSONALITY

(cont.)

The development and maintenance of a pleasant personality requires, first, the building of character, because no change of circumstances can repair a defect in this essential quality. And since we are all largely the product of our individual environments, we measure strength of character by different yardsticks. Assuming, however, that the ultimate test of character strength is found in the life of Jesus Christ, and that great figures such as Lincoln, Washington, and Jefferson, are supreme examples of persons with strength of character, you can, through self-discipline, strive for improvement. Coincidentally, you must realize that a pleasant personality cannot be "manufactured" like a smile and a handshake designed to help you make money off of other people. Faulty motivation, like weak mortar, will lead to the building of an imperfect structure. If you would sell yourself to others, you will find that a flawed personality repels rather than attracts people. And since there is always room for improvement in every person on earth, there is no reason why you have to be stuck for the rest of your life with certain character flaws. The following story emphasizes this point:

A turtle was on his way across the river when he encountered a scorpion.

"Help! I can't swim much longer, I'll drown," cried the scorpion.

"Are you crazy?" said the turtle. "If I stop to help you, you'll sting me and I'll die."

"What a foolish thought," gasped the scorpion. "If I were to sting you, I would surely go down with you. Now where is the logic in that?"

"Sounds right," said the turtle. "Hop on!" The scorpion climbed on the turtle's back, and halfway across the river he gave the Good Samaritan a mighty sting in the neck. As they both sank to the bottom, the turtle resignedly said:

"Would you mind telling me something before I die? You said it wasn't logical for you to sting me. Why, then, did you do it?"

"It's not a question of logic," the drowning scorpion sadly replied, "It's just my character."

A lesson to be learned here is that you must first disassociate yourself from persons of questionable character before you can effectively begin to strengthen your own personality. A helpful aid to this end is to select persons of strong character — real or imagined — whom, because of your admiration for them, you can mentally invite into a sort of cabinet. These will be your silent advisers on matters of character — individuals selected from real life, historical or contemporary figures, famous or obscure personalities, friends, relatives, casual acquaintances — whom, at appropriate moments, can be assembled in your mind and called upon for advice. These are people you admire and respect. How do you suppose they would handle the problem at hand? How would each of them react in a similar situation?

This kind of fantasizing may seem a bit strange to you at first, but believe me, it works. You can strengthen character — and begin developing a more pleasing personality — by installing such a cabinet in your mind. Talk to your cabinet in private, as you would to God in prayer. Begin to visualize yourself as being in possession of their best qualities. Confirm to yourself, both orally and in writing, that you are becoming more virtuous. Ben Franklin kept a little book where he duly recorded his daily faults as well as his virtues.

But, you say, you don't know where to begin. You may know of only two or three people whom you genuinely admire. Maybe you don't even know them personally. You may have only heard of their good and noble deeds and personal accomplishments — this from books, television, magazines, word of mouth, or other media.

The answer is to start with them. Go back to the page listing the seven invisible guards who stand behind the men who have built up great fortunes with the help of others. (Remember this: You can have a strong character and still have a lousy personality; but your chances of influencing others are greatly diminished by the imbalance. Consequently, your ability to amass wealth is jeopardized.) You want to build character with the ancillary benefit of strengthening your personality. Begin by talking to your imaginary advisers. Affirm to yourself that you are becoming more like them every day. Remember, you'll need a qualified advisor for each of the following six posts: Mental Peace, Good Health, Faith and

Hope, Financial Success, Love, and Wisdom. Here are some sample personalities you might choose: Napoleon Hill, Jesse Owens, Billy Graham, W. Clement Stone, Albert Schweitzer, or Abraham Lincoln.

One of the first observations you may make about this group of men is the fact that they have all influenced a great many people in a very positive way — they are leaders, all possessing such essential leadership qualities as self confidence, self-sacrifice, morals, paternalism, initiative, decision, fairness, and courage. Another observation is that these men are masters of self-control. When they start out to accomplish something, they don't stop until the task is finished. If you would base the strength of your personality on what these men have to say, and if you would make it a habit today of making their thoughts your thoughts, you would begin to resemble them tomorrow. Remember Napoleon Hill's famous axiom, *"Whatever the mind of man can believe, it can achieve."* Your imaginary cabinet of advisers will only work for you if you believe deeply and sincerely that such mind power is possible. This technique has worked for others far more wealthy and influential than I am. It has also worked for me. Why not for you?

Your next stop in the development of a pleasant personality is to extend more of yourself to the world around you. Pay attention to your manner of dress. Since most of us dress to please others, this must tell you something. Where can you find the courage to speak forcefully in front of others? How can you become a more agreeable person? What changes must you make in yourself to control your anger . . . to regulate yourself from openly expressing your grievances? Begin looking for the good qualities in those you meet and associate with. Compliments, when given as an outgrowth of this habit, will be genuine, since they will come from the heart. This is not some "quickie" habit that can be acquired overnight. Your loves, unlike your tastes, are not meant to change with your fortunes. If at dusk you lived from hand to mouth, lacked general confidence, and possessed a somber personality, you could not at the dawning of a new day, obtain credibility by raising a crop of sudden compliments and driving a shiny new Cadillac. Your behavior would be suspect. You may not be, now, what you used to be; but change, nevertheless, must come from the heart, and this process develops gradually. If too many of your thoughts are directed inward (because of ego), you will turn people off and lose your ability to influence them. Think about this definition of personality: *What a person has when he makes you feel the same way about him as you do about yourself.*

Dale Carnegie, whose book on personality development, *How to Win Friends and Influence People*, which is one of the all-time best sellers, stresses that the way to a new and vibrant personality lies, first, within the mind of the individual. You must be able to influence your own mind by developing a positive mental attitude before you can influence others to follow you. Carnegie says: "All I desire is dominion over myself — dominion over my thoughts; dominion over my fears; dominion over my mind and over my spirit. And the wonderful thing is that I know that I can attain this dominion to an astonishing degree, any time I want to, by merely controlling my actions, which in turn control my reactions." Referring back to Success Rule 2 on Self-confidence we see the importance of the subconscious mind in altering behavior characteristics.

Remember that you begin to influence the subconscious mind through the process of *autosuggestion* (self-hypnosis). This process is largely oral — you must habitually repeat aloud those goals and behavior characteristics you expect to reach and adopt. In the case of character development (the foundation of a pleasant personality) you make it a habit of becoming more like those you admire (your invisible cabinet of advisors). Aristotle said that a good character carries with it the highest power of causing a thing to be believed. First you must believe that you are developing a more pleasant personality through cultivation of the proper habits. Here, in summary, are the proper habits for you to develop:

1. Orally repeat to yourself your belief that you are adopting those qualities of character and behavior patterns you find admirable in others (your imaginary cabinet). Do this at least twice a day.

2. Find opportunities to speak forcefully to others on topics of interest to them. Avoid controversy at this time.

3. Learn to control your nervous system and to become more agreeable. Avoid expressing your grievances and anger in front of others.

4. Remember the importance of your outward appearance. Your dress, as well as your behavior, is your table of contents.

5. Look for the good points in others and form the habit of making compliments from the heart.

6. Stick to your resolutions. There is nothing so **fatal** to character as half-finished tasks.

7. Devote your wholehearted effort to developing a positive mental attitude.

8. Remember that a personality change cannot be brought about overnight. Begin with small things and build from there.

9. Recognize that because of the following inviolable rule, a pleasant personality can only come about through practice: *Use breeds habit and habit is stronger than nature.*

10. Don't be discouraged by occasional failures in your efforts to improve yourself. The expectations of life depend upon diligence; the mechanic who would perfect his work must first sharpen his tools.

SCRIP (T) SUCCESS RULE 9 – PRACTICE **TOLERANCE AND PATIENCE**

What do you see when you look into the eyes of a newborn child? Wickedness? Spitefulness? Cruelty? Of course not. If such characteristics were inherited, you would see signs, much like the striving of a snake to bite, or a tiny tiger to tear and claw at you. All children come into the world with nothing but innocence, gentleness, and fear. They are about as limited in their instinct toward mischief and destruction as pigeons and rabbits. Man's tendencies, such as intolerance, grow mainly from his social heredity; his activities are largely rooted in his physical heredity. I make this point about children to emphasize that, because intolerance is an acquired trait, it can, with determined effort, be "unlearned."

The principle of tolerance is essential to success because without it you will ultimately lose in the game of life – fallible beings always fail somewhere. If you can "unlearn" the tendencies to hate, to spite, and to persecute those whose views are different from your own; if you can look dispassionately at those you disagree with, you are likely to find their motives to be more pure than you thought and their judgments less biased than your mind led you to believe. You'll probably find that your adversary's reasoning is based on the same data as yours, though he may have arrived at a different conclusion. How can mankind be so intolerant of itself?

A wise observer of man's tendencies once said, "Give me the control of the child until it is twelve years old and you can teach any religion you may please after that time, for I will have planted my own religion so deeply in its mind that no power on earth could undo my work." Hitler knew this. Here was one of the most intolerant men who ever walked the face of the earth, and he perpetuated his intolerance through the Hitler Youth Movement. If he had been able to hold tight to these youths for a single generation he could have forced his warped ideals upon their minds so effectively that they could not have resisted it. In some of the world's emerging nations, you can still see the perpetuation of intolerance through ruthless leaders who — like Hitler — have gained control of the schools and the press while subverting organized religion. Since these are the three main avenues through which social heredity operates, it is easy to see how such undesirable traits as intolerance can be nurtured and kept alive in the name of nationalism.

Two men were having a conversation on the street, and one grew wearied over the other's intolerant attitude toward Jews. "Isn't that just like a Jew?" the bigot said. When the question was raised again, the more tolerant man replied, "Which Jew do you mean, Shylock or Christ?" The point was clearly made, and the bigot must have understood that such flagrant generalities about whole classes of people are open to question by those of wider vision. The next time somebody says to you, "Isn't that just like a Black?" reply by asking "Which Black do you mean, Uncle Tom or Ralph Bunche, Idi Amin or Jackie Robinson?"

Children, as a class of mankind, seem always to be serving on the front line of impatience. If you would improve your patience level, it certainly will help you to begin with them. All of us are inclined to say too often, "You kids stop making so much noise." The next time the urge to comment harshly on the noise level occurs to you, remember your urge to raise your patience level. The time will come much too soon when beside your rocking chair, you'd give all the world to hear the ringing laughter that once disturbed you.

In Dale Carnegie's perennial best-seller, *How to Win Friends and Influence People* ((c) Simon and Schuster), is reprinted this stirring essay on patience:

FATHER FORGETS
by W. Livingston Larned

Listen son: I am saying this as you lie asleep, one little paw crumpled under your cheek and the blond curls stickily wet on your damp forehead. I have stolen into your room alone. Just a few minutes ago, as I sat reading my paper, a stifling wave of remorse swept over me. Guiltily I came to your bedside.

These are the things I was thinking, son: I had been cross to you. I scolded you as you were dressing for school because you gave your face merely a dab with a towel. I took you to task for not cleaning your shoes. I called out angrily when you threw some of your things on the floor. At breakfast I found fault, too. You spilled things. You gulped down your food. You put your elbows on the table. You spread butter too thick on your bread. And as you started off to play and I made my train, you turned and waved a hand and called, "Good-bye, Daddy!" and I frowned, and said in reply, "Hold your shoulders back!"

Then it began all over again in the late afternoon. As I came up the road I spied you, down on your knees, playing marbles. There were holes in your stockings. I humiliated you before your boy friends by marching you ahead of me into the house. Stockings were expensive — and if you had to buy them you would be more careful! Do you remember, later, when I was reading in the library, how you came in, timidly, with a sort of hurt look in your eyes? When I glanced up over my paper, impatient at the interruption, you hesitated at the door. "What is it you want?" I snapped. You said nothing, but ran across in one tempestuous plunge, and threw your arms around my neck and kissed me, and your small arms tightened with an affection that God had set blooming in your heart and which even neglect could not wither. And then you were gone, pattering up the stairs.

Well, son, it was shortly afterward that my paper slipped from my hands and a terrible sickening fear came over me. What has habit been doing to me? The habit of finding fault, of reprimanding — this was my reward to you for being a boy. It was not that I didn't love you; it was that I expected too much of youth. I was measuring you by the yardstick of my own years.

And there was so much that was good and fine and true in your character. The little heart in you was as big as the dawn itself over the wide hills. This was shown by your spontaneous impulse to rush in and kiss me good-night. Nothing else matters tonight, son. I have come to your bedside in the darkness, and I have knelt there, ashamed!

It is a feeble atonement; I know you would not understand these things if I told them to you during your waking hours. But tomorrow I will be a real daddy! I will play with you, and suffer when you suffer, and laugh when you laugh. I will bite my tongue when impatient words come. I will keep saying as if it were a ritual: "He is nothing but a boy — a little boy!"

I am afraid I have visualized you as a man. Yet as I see you now, son, crumpled and weary in your cot, I see that you are still a baby. Yesterday you were in your mother's arms, your head on her shoulder. I have asked too much, too much.

Wherever you come into contact with people, remember this essay on impatience. Your job or profession may be very demanding, leaving little time for simple courtesies and consideration toward others. Who will remind you that your patience level is receding? Perhaps there will be no little boy to spring forward with his arms full of love for you despite your failings. Like the other success principles discussed in this chapter, you must work at mastering them. Become a model to yourself, rather than a critic of others. Not only do children need someone to look up to, so do most people; and it is only through the cooperation of others that you can succeed as a person.

SCRIPT and **(F) LAME**   SUCCESS PRINCIPLE 10 – LEARN TO
                               PROFIT FROM **FAILURE**

"Of all the sad words of tongue or pen, the saddest are these:
It might have been."   — Whittier

There is no more anguished plea on earth than the lament from the man who wishes his time spent revoked, that he might try again to accomplish what he might have done, to find the happiness he might have found, and to be the man he might have been. He never hurdled life's great obstacles because life's smaller obstacles held him back. If he views himself as a failure — and most men count their misgivings — it is not that the breaks were against him, but only that his determination to succeed was not strong enough. A succession of temporary defeats — if you fail to learn from them — can often be counted as failures. And the only man who never fails at anything is the man who never does anything. You succeed in life by trying not to make the same mistakes over and over again. Failure is not an undertaker — it is a teacher; it is not defeat — it is delay; it is not a dead-end street — it is a temporary detour.

In my office I have a framed sign that reads:

NEVER ADMIT DEFEAT

Failed in business	('31)
Defeated for legislature	('32)
Again failed in business	('33)
Elected to legislature	('34)
Sweetheart died	('35)
Had nervous breakdown	('36)
Defeated for Speaker	('38)
Defeated for Elector	('40)
Elected to Congress	('46)
Son died	('50)
Defeated for Senate	('55)
Defeated for V. President	('56)
Defeated for Senate	('58)
Elected President	('60)

Just a few rough spots in the life of Abraham Lincoln

On August 17, 1978, French villagers looked up from the tiny hamlet of Miserey, and watched the helium-filled balloon, Double Eagle II, float closer to its landing in Normandy. "Vive les Americains!" went the shout from the ground. Hats were tossed into the air. People abandoned their cars along the country road and sprinted toward a nearby grain field. History was in the making.

Soon three Americans named Anderson, Newman, and Abruzzo were drinking champagne atop the shoulders of ecstatic Frenchmen who shouted, "Formidable! Formidable!" Other Frenchmen scrambled to the scene and began tearing "souveniers" from the first manned balloon to cross the Atlantic Ocean. The crossing was risky. An earlier attempt had nearly cost the Americans' lives as they plunged into the freezing waters off Iceland. Seventeen earlier expeditions had failed, and five men had died in pursuit of this elusive dream. Failure gnawed relentlessly at the men aboard the Eagle II. At first their radio system went out, forcing them to rely on a crude ham radio. Then over the mid-Atlantic, the ice build-up on top of the balloon was so heavy that the balloonists lost nearly 3,000 feet in altitude. Sandbags, lead, potatoes — all precious ballast — were tossed overboard in a desperate effort to stabilize the craft. Nearing the Irish coastline, the balloon plunged 20,000 feet in a perilous brush with the sea. The men knew that if more ballast were dropped over the side they would in all probability not reach Ireland, but past failures had turned out to be blessings, because they taught the balloonists such needed lessons of perseverance, courage, self-discipline, and a well-defined power of decision. They continued to endure until the sun had warmed the balloon and caused it to rise again. Finally the wind nearly abandoned the team altogether. They quickly discarded the remainder of the ballast. As fast as the ax tore into the floorboards of the gondola, weighty timber was tossed over the side, along with cables, radio equipment, and heavy clothing.

In great attempts it is glorious even to fail, but it was doubtful that this truth could have been believed at the time. As people never thoroughly understand truth until they have challenged it, so do they shun familiarity with failure until they have suffered from one and seen themselves triumph where others have failed. When the balloonists landed in

France, the great truth about failure was brought home to them: *Every failure carries with it the seed of an equivalent benefit.* Past defeats had been a blessing to the team, for they were signaled to move at another time and place, and they acted upon that signal as if it were a detour sign and not a dead end street.

Ralph Waldo Emerson, in his great essay on compensation, wrote of the duality that underlies the nature and condition of man.

> "Every excess causes a defect; every defect an excess. Every sweet hath its sour; every evil its good. Every faculty which is a receiver of pleasure, has an equal penalty put on its abuse. It is to answer for its moderation with its life. For every grain of wit there is a grain of folly. For everything you have missed, you have gained something else; and for everything you gain, you lose something. If riches increase, they are increased that use them. If the gatherer gathers too much, nature takes out of the man what she puts in his chest; swells the estate but kills the owner. Nature hates monopolies and exceptions . . . . There is always some levelling circumstance that puts down the overbearing, the strong, the rich, the fortunate, substantially on the same ground with all others."

For every failure there is a triumph. In real life, as in fiction, the human animal is most courageous, most interesting, most respected and admired, when snatching victory from the jaws of defeat. Remember, too, that it is contrary to nature's laws to accept failure without seeking a corresponding benefit. To blame defeat on "bad luck" is to accuse nature of abridging her own laws, and this she never does.

To ensure yourself against failure you must understand the laws of the universe and adapt yourself to their habits. The words, "I can't," are, after all, merely a statement of opinion and not a fact. Nature says that anything the mind can conceive and believe can be achieved. Your only limitations are those which you set up in your mind or allow others to establish for you. If you accept an experience as a failure, then you will have failed. *But you will have failed in your mind alone!* Never accept an experience as a failure, because your mind will direct your actions toward defeat. Classify your set-backs as delays, detours, and educational experiences. Your mind will then act accordingly to extract the ultimate triumph. It matters little what others may call your experiences, because they are yours alone. You can classify them any way you choose. Yours is the only verdict that counts.

To break yourself of the habit of failure, you must first identify the root causes. You'll want to coax them out of hiding and destroy them one by one. Habits, once formed, are not easily broken, but the battle is already half won when you identify the basic causes. A list of fifty major failure habits follows. How many can you spot within yourself?

1. Lack of chief goals in life
2. Lack of self-confidence
3. Inability to take control of your own mind
4. Succumbing to any or all of the seven basic fears
5. Accepting mediocrity as a standard
6. Procrastination
7. Lack of persistent endeavor
8. Lack of a positive mental attitude
9. Sour personality
10. Lack of gratitude for life's blessings
11. Expecting something for nothing
12. Inability to make decisions
13. Lack of practical knowledge and experience
14. Over-emphasis on formal learning
15. Unwillingness to take chances
16. Impatient attitude
17. Inability to accurately judge people
18. Lack of cooperative attitude
19. Over-emphasis on material concerns
20. Loss of harmony in marriage

(cont.)

21. Loss of spirituality
22. Inability to cultivate true friendships
23. Selfishness and greed
24. Uncontrolled envy
25. Lack of the work ethic
26. Indiscriminate spending
27. Dishonesty
28. Inaccurate thinking
29. Excessive ego
30. Lack of savings and capital
31. Intolerance
32. Abuse of power
33. Lack of enthusiasm
34. Lack of a labor of love
35. Jack-of-all-trades syndrome
36. Excessive superstition and prejudice
37. Inability to discipline yourself
38. Lack of loyalty
39. Uncontrolled emotions
40. Lack of imagination
41. Inability to recognize opportunity
42. Unwillingness to do more than you're paid for
43. Vindictive attitude
44. Minding other peoples' businesses
45. Using vulgarity and slander
46. Lack of respect for constitutional authority

(cont.)

47. Unwillingness to accept advice and counsel
48. Carelessness in settling obligations with others
49. Drug abuse and alcoholism
50. Unjustified trust in people

Pick out the failure habits that you feel have held you back. Write them down on a slip of paper and tell yourself (orally) at least twice a day that you are overcoming these undesirable habits. Have your wife or a close friend rate you on the same list. You want to become a success. You want your subconscious mind to believe that you will not tolerate any of the "fatal fifty" failure habits. Remember that you reach the subconscious mind (which controls your actions) through the technique of autosuggestion, or self-hypnosis. If you repeat a statement to yourself or to others long enough, you will begin to believe it, whether it is true or not. This is true because the thought will become embedded in your subconscious mind; hence it reflects itself through your actions and attitudes. You can develop, at will, the inspiration to overcome bad habits, and once that inspiration is transformed into action you have the most important ingredient to success known to man.

Shakespeare was one of the greatest observers of man's habits, actions, and tendencies the world has ever known. When the immortal bard says, "Assume a virtue if you have it not," he is suggesting that we look the part, dress the part, and act the part of being successful as a way to circumvent feelings of failure. To become successful, you must first convince your subconscious mind that success is what you want. Here is a self-help quiz to see if you can banish feelings of failure from your life once and for all.

1. Do you know what you want out of life?
2. Do you want it badly enough?
3. Do you confidently expect to achieve your goals?
4. Are you persistently determined to reach your goals?
5. Are you willing to pay the price for achieving them?

Obviously this quiz calls for all affirmative answers. If you cannot answer *yes* to all of the questions, you will find yourself bogged down in life. Don't, however, be so recklessly bent on success that you press on without sound judgment and consideration for others. When you set a task for yourself, it is a good habit to complete it; therefore, do not harbor desires that are too many, too confusing, and beyond your training to accomplish. Difficult and impractical tasks can often cost you harmony in your business, family, and social relationships. People around you can sense when your ego has gotten out of hand. Remember this: An honest effort to understand your abilities and determination, and to improve yourself, is not the same as amassing an offensive ego.

John Paul Getty compared the process of achieving success with an experience in a fine restaurant. In his book, *The Golden Age,* he wrote:

1. Don't expect to find every dish you want on the menu.

2. You can, however, find enough variety to satisfy hunger and palate.

3. While eating, never bite off more than you can chew.

4. Take healthy mouthfuls — for any food worth taking is not to be toyed with.

Like gluttonous and unhealthy eating habits, boorishness in one's social relationships is rooted in fear of some inadequacy. Failure habits are aggravated if you talk more than you listen. Not only do you fail to gain useful knowledge, but you also disclose your plans and objectives to potential enemies who, through envy, may wish to see you cut down a notch or two. Licking the habits of failure is best done with deeds, not empty words.

SCRIPT and F(L)AME   SUCCESS PRINCIPLE 11 – LEARN TO LEAD

Someone asked a famous conductor of a great symphony orchestra which orchestral instrument he considered the most difficult to play. The conductor thought a moment, then answered: "Second fiddle. I can get plenty of first violinists. But to find one who can play second fiddle with enthusiasm — that's a problem. And if we have no second fiddles, we have no harmony!"

This story points up the necessity for learning to work with and for others before you can expect to lead them. And, as pointed out earlier in this book, the way to wealth and independence in your own life is measured by your ability to influence others. The ability to "make friends and influence people" is largely an acquired habit — leaders are made, not born. In Edgar Puryear's excellent study of leadership, *Nineteen Stars*, the author emphasizes that the great generals, Marshall, MacArthur, Eisenhower, and Patton, spent their entire military careers preparing for high command through study and through working as junior officers for the most outstanding generals. Leadership (and initiative) is but one of the fifteen essential qualities to success and, not surprisingly, the best leaders are those who have mastered the other fourteen qualities. In the military, however, effective leadership is often a matter of life and death, and its importance is not to be minimized.

The principles of leadership apply as much to the person who aspires to success in civilian life as it does to future generals. For purposes of this discussion we will assume that *leadership* and *initiative* go hand in hand. You must, first of all, know yourself, your job, and how to get yourself going in the morning before you can understand others and expect to motivate them. This wisdom is contained in an old adage about leadership: *Know your men; know your business; know yourself.*

Before getting into a definitive list of known and proven leadership qualities, it will be useful to you to assess and evaluate your own initiative. The world will, indeed, make way for, and follow, the man who knows where he is going and how to get there. Pledge to yourself that you will soon be able to answer *yes* to all of the following questions:

1. Do you have a chief goal in life? Are you adopting the proper habits to make this goal a reality?

2. Are you licking the habit of procrastination?

3. Are you acquiring the habit of doing more than is expected of you?

As you can see from the prior questions, initiative is largely a habit that can be built through conscious effort. If you're short on initiative in the big things of life, then begin by improving yourself at home and on the job. Memorize and begin to practice the success principles discussed in this book (SCRIPT and FLAME). Accomplish one small task each day that you've been putting off. Find things to do in your daily work for which you do not expect monetary compensation. Small habits seem to gather by unseen degrees, and eventually they form larger habits, much as brooks make rivers, which in turn run to the sea. As the result of practicing initiative, you'll find yourself attracting the attention of those who will place greater value on your services. Initiative, then, is the gateway to opportunity and leadership. And, understandably, initiative opens the doors to life's great riches, all of which are hallmarks of great leaders. Oddly enough these riches are not based on wealth, but have to do with yourself as a person. They are hidden in your heart and mind.

Great leaders, as a rule, have multitudes of followers, and this is true because people hope to gain in some way through their association or affiliation with the great and successful. Since you are reading this book for purposes of building wealth and independence, I think you should understand more about the attitudes and leadership qualities of those who have built great fortunes. F. Scott Fitzgerald is reported to have once remarked to Ernest Hemmingway, "You know, the rich are different from you and me." To which Hemmingway replied, "I know, they have more money."

Those who have made and perpetuated great wealth without loss of peace of mind, all understand that the virtue of money is in its use, not in its quantity. Carnegie, Rockefeller, and Ford, all came to realize this fact and gave millions away to charitable causes before they died. Their initiative, leadership, and influence was as boundless as their fortunes. At the time these men were accumulating wealth, they had more than their share of detractors; but one of life's greatest inconsistencies is the fact that most of what we believe is not true, and myth plagued these men, even after they had become philanthropists. It is true in many cases that the man without money is at the mercy of the man who has it. And the fact prevails that people will weigh you largely in the light of your bank balance, no matter who you are or what you are capable of accomplishing. The penalty of leadership, nevertheless, is often envy, hate, and suspicion from smaller minds. Great leaders have learned to practice the positive emotions, and they have no time to waste with a desire to malign or injure others. If they did, they would not be great leaders.

The accumulation of riches obviously does not go hand in hand with leadership, though initiative is certainly a blood brother of hard-won fortunes. People will rapidly, willingly, and voluntarily follow the man who shows initiative. They will not, however, follow the man who appears bent on pursuing money for its own sake and who cannot tell you what he wants out of life besides material gain. A list of life's true rewards follows. Again I want to emphasize that great leaders and the enlightened builders of great fortunes all consciously or unconsciously practice the accumulation of these "riches."

LIFE'S TRUE REWARDS

1. Freedom from fear
2. Love of one's work
3. Harmony with others
4. Definite future plans
5. Good health
6. Economic security
7. Sharing with others
8. Control of self
9. Hope for the future
10. Positive attitude toward life
11. Open mind
12. Concern and understanding for others

You'll notice that all of the above rewards are also repeated in the following list of known and proven leadership qualities. Remember, now, that effective leadership is one of the fundamental principles you need to acquire and master for the achievement of personal success. Be honest and rate yourself as being either *good, fair,* or *poor* in each of the qualities. Your goal should be to become *good* in each and every one. When you have mastered the principles of effective leadership, along with the other fourteen success principles, you will have the finest insurance policy against failure known to mankind.

EFFECTIVE LEADERSHIP QUALITIES

1. Freedom from fear
2. Control of self
3. Concern for others
4. Selflessness
5. Ability to delegate
6. Sense of justice
7. Accurate thought patterns
8. Tolerance and patience
9. Temperance
10. Integrity
11. Ability to profit from failure
12. Willingness to shoulder responsibility
13. Doing more than required
14. Attention to detail
15. Imaginative outlook
16. Humility
17. Courage to make quick and sound decisions
18. Willingness to work, study, and prepare
19. Tactful personality
20. Concentration and persistence
21. Practicing the Golden Rule
22. Taking the initiative
23. Acting with enthusiasm
24. Ability to cooperate with others
25. Ability to build a harmonious team
26. Definite goals and plans
27. Confidence in self
28. Ability to follow through
29. Dedication to duty
30. Respect for authority
31. Showmanship

SCRIPT and FL (A) ME   SUCCESS PRINCIPLE 12 - THINK ACCURATELY

"There is a principle which is a bar against all information; which is proof against all argument; and which cannot fail to keep a man in everlasting ignorance. This principle is contempt prior to examination."

Napoleon Hill

To be truly wealthy in this world you must first be at peace with yourself, and this means, essentially, knowing your own mind, taking control of it, and directing it *accurately* toward a specific goal(s). Obviously you are searching for economic success first or you would not be reading this book; and you are certainly aware of the frustrations, worry and deprivation that befall those without sufficient money in their possession. It should be obvious, too, that aside from monetary success, you also want to be free from fear, tension, self-induced illness, and ignorance. These negative forces are your enemies, and they find refuge and succor in minds plagued with similar negative attitudes. A mind dominated by accurate thoughts of success forms an impenetrable defense against these opposing forces.

Since an enemy discovered is an enemy half-whipped, let's examine the principal inaccurate thought patterns that stalk weak minds, hoping to totter them into negativism and failure.

INACCURATE THOUGHT PATTERNS

1. Needless worry and feelings of inferiority.
2. Feelings that you cannot surmount poverty and want.
3. Mental anguish brought on by suspicion and unwarranted fear.
4. Allowing fear to bring about feelings of failure.
5. Seeking something for nothing.
6. Allowing others to control your mind.
7. Dissatisfaction with (and griping about) one's work.
8. Doing no more than you are paid or obligated for.
9. Mourning over petty misfortunes.
10. Expecting rewards and benefits prior to giving them out.
11. Cultivating the negative emotions toward life and your fellow man.
12. Encouraging indolence in charitable works.
13. Making excuses for unfulfilled objectives.

These thought patterns are your enemies and you should bolster your defenses against them by clearing away the cobwebs in your mind. Clear and accurate thinking depends, first, on separating facts from information and opinions. Next, you must separate the chaff from the wheat by getting rid of that which is unimportant or irrelevant. Thirdly, you must learn to think with your mind and not your emotions. You are interested in achieving certain goals in life without sacrificing your peace of mind, for it is clear that a mind at war with itself cannot lead you to the true riches in life. To gain control of your mind, you must first identify and root out any enemies found lurking there. Your objective is to secure more accurate thought patterns and to know your own mind. Only the Creator can prevail against such a force. Begin by pinning down the following enemies and working to destroy their build-up in your mind:

ANGER	HATRED	SLANDER
CRUELTY	HYPOCHONDRIA	UNDEPENDABILITY
DECEIT	IMPATIENCE	VANITY
DISHONESTY	INDECISION	WORRY
DISLOYALTY	INJUSTICE	EGOTISM
INSINCERITY	ENVY	INTOLERANCE
FALSEHOOD	JEALOUSY	FEAR
LUST	GOSSIP	MERCILESSNESS
GREED	REVENGE	

You build income for yourself in four basic ways, all of which involve relationships with other people; and it is when you open up yourself to others that the above enemies find opportunites to infiltrate and to become entrenched in your mind.

BASIC WAYS TO INCREASE YOUR INCOME

1. Scratching each other's back in business.

2. Showing the other fellow how he can get more for his money.

(cont.)

3. Bringing the producer and the consumer closer together.

4. Saving a portion of all you earn and sharing opportunity with those of similar intent, inclination and drive.

It is not an easy task to be constantly alert for these infiltrators, and then to be battling them throughout your life, but considering the stakes — your health, wealth, independence, and peace of mind — it is well worth the effort. Here is a list of questions you should ask yourself to determine the current accuracy of your thought patterns:

1. Do you often "blow up" at people, or in other ways lose control of your emotions?

2. Do you *slander* and *condemn* people?

3. Do you seek *revenge* for any real or imagined wrongs and injustices done to you?

4. Do you often *lose your poise* under unfavorable circumstances?

5. Do you ever think that other people *"owe"* you a living, and that you *"can't"* accomplish what you want to do?

6. Do you find yourself *bragging* and *boasting* to raise your self-esteem?

7. Do you often feel as if you *have* to do something immediately, without giving it sufficient thought?

8. Are you always *griping* and *complaining* about people and things?

9. Do you express *contempt* for new ideas, proposals, and changes prior to examination?

10. Do you often feel that your life is *hopelessly* in the hands of someone else?

11. Do you harbor and openly express any racial and religious *prejudices?*

12. Is your mind filled with *fear* about anything or anyone?

13. Do you think of yourself as an *expert on all subjects?*

14. Do you readily speak about the *faults* of others?

15. Are you *slow to forgive and forget?*

(cont.)

16. Are you always in a state of *tension, worry,* and *anxiety?*

17. Are you easily led by *ideologies* foreign to you and your country?

18. Are you constantly at *war* with your family and mankind?

19. Do you make *enemies* easily?

20. Do you *begrudge* having to share your blessings?

21. Do you *draw back* from expressing gratitude to God or man?

22. Do you express *opinions* without being in possession of the facts?

23. Do you allow *negative thoughts* to enter your mind?

24. Do you allow your mind to *drift* without steering toward definite goals?

25. Are you unable to cope with *excess* in eating, drinking, and other habits?

26. Do you *wink* at transactions which are profitable to you and harmful to someone else?

27. Do you *bemoan defeat* as anything but a temporary setback?

28. Do you often see other people as *uncooperative?*

29. Do you *"play dirty"* with adversaries?

30. Do you *doubt* the existence of a power greater than yourself — a power that is available to you if you seek it diligently?

31. Do you become *morbid* and *unglued* after disappointments?

32. Are you always *apologizing* for not doing your best?

33. Are you quick to *accuse* and *blame* others?

34. Do you keep the door to the *past* open in your mind?

35. Do you *discount* the existence of certain eternal truths about mankind in relationship to his environment?

36. Do you *rationalize* about getting into debt and take repayment of your obligations lightly?

(cont.)

37. Do you make *liabilities* of adversities and defeats, rather than turning them into assets?

38. Are you excessively *disturbed* by panics and depression in the economy?

39. Do you often *wish* you were someone else?

40. Do you sense that certain classes of people *dislike* you?

41. Do you ever find yourself trying to *live someone else's life* for them?

42. Do you allow your mind to *run away* with thoughts of wealth?

43. Do you aspire to have *more money* than you can comfortably use?

44. Do you *talk about* your success to others, rather than letting your accomplishments speak for themselves?

45. Do you *forget* to extract the seed of an equivalent benefit from all your failures?

46. Are you guilty of *lazy thinking* about a major objective in life and how to obtain it?

If you can truly answer "no" to all of the above questions you could rightfully be called a genius in knowing what you want out of life and how to obtain it without losing your peace of mind. Someone once said that genius is the ability to see the pattern of things and to project those patterns. The key to accurate thought patterns lies in your ability to identify and eventually destroy those enemies of the mind mentioned earlier. When you have done this, you will find yourself in possession of amazing powers unknown to most men, and you'll know without question that the virtue of wealth is in its use, not in its quantity.

SCRIPT and FL (A) ME   SUCCESS PRINCIPLE 13 – HAVE A DEFINITE AIM IN LIFE

After graduating from college, I wandered around for a number of years in search of myself, hoping to find out what I wanted to do in life. I considered law, went to grad school, dropped out; and, along the line, tried song writing, acting, vending, ad writing, sales, horse livery, and real estate. You could easily describe me as a rudderless young man with more than his quota of frustration, melancholy, and fear — all ailments for which the cure is a *definite* labor of love or *chief goal* in life. Years later, when I began to set down goals for myself in real estate, I found success creeping up on me like the tide. *Specific desire,* of course, was my ship of fortune; while *specific goals* were my charts through the rough seas of life.

Let's review for a moment how concentrated thought on *specifics* can literally part the stormy waters of life and open up the channels of success for you. Concentrated thought, as pointed out earlier, is aimed at reaching and influencing the subconscious mind into action. Mere wishing and vague goal-setting won't work for you, since these longings and aspirations do not penetrate the depths of the mind. To successfully find your way through life, you must first conceive a grand purpose and form a deep subconscious belief; only then can the belief become the foundation of reality. Here is Napoleon Hill's proven step-by-step procedure for reaching and influencing the subconscious mind:

1. Write out a *specific* statement of your desires, such as a definite amount of money.

2. Determine in your statement *exactly* what services you intend to render in return for the money, such as vigorous and unremitting effort in some field of endeavor.

3. Establish a *definite* time frame and *specific* date in your statement for reaching your goal.

4. *Conceive* a workable plan for carrying out your desire, and *believe* you will soon achieve your goal by implementing the plan whether it is completely ready or not. Express this belief in your statement.

5. Express *gratitude* in your statement for having been given the guidance necessary to carry out your plan.

6. Proceed with *enthusiasm,* and do not be dissuaded in your efforts to reach your goal. Affirm this in your statement.

7. *Anticipate* accomplishment of your goal by repeating in your statement that you will soon be in possession of the *specified* desires.

(cont.)

8. Read your written statement aloud — at least once in the morning and again at night — and, while reading, *see, feel,* and *believe* yourself in possession of your desire.

One of life's great truths is that general desires are but weak longings, and they have the habit of leading you onward to failure after failure. When you set *definite* chief goals for yourself and come to terms with *exactly* what you want to be and *exactly* what you want from life, you'll discover your labor of love and find the ways to reach your goals. Remember this:

> Achievement of your definite aim and goals in life is directly dependent upon the degree of force, energy, will, determination, and persistence with which you pursue your objectives.
>
> You can have or be anything you want — if you only want it hard enough.

Napoleon Hill spent fourteen years analyzing more than 16,000 men and women for his Laws of Success course. He discovered that ninety-five percent of these people had to struggle almost unbearably to find happiness and the ordinary necessities of life. In other words, they could be classified as failures. Here's what Dr. Hill says of the test group:

> "One of the most startling facts brought to light by those 16,000 analyses was the discovery that the ninety-five percent who were classed as failures were in that class *because they had no definite chief aim in life,* while the five percent constituting the successful ones not only had purposes that were *definite,* but they had also *definite plans* for the attainment of their purposes."

Preceding accomplishment in any field of endeavor (your chief aim in life) must be desire, and desires must be strong and *definite* if they are to be fulfilled. Every great accomplishment of any man at any time first had to exist as a thought before it could exist, and grand desires proceed from grand thoughts. Consider this time-proven passage from an old writer, whose prose was given new life in the Robert Collier book, *The Secret of the Ages:*

"Every deed that we do, good or bad, is prompted by Desire. We are charitable because we wish to relieve our inner distress at the sight of suffering; or from the urge of sympathy, with its desire to express its nature; or from the desire to be respected in this world, or to secure a comfortable place in the next one. One man is kind because he desires to be kind — because it gives him satisfaction and content to be so. One man does his duty because he desires to do it — he obtains a higher emotional satisfaction and content from duty well done than he would from neglecting it in accordance with some opposing desires. Another man yields to the desire to shirk his duty — he obtains greater satisfaction and content from refraining from performing his duty, in favor of doing other and contrary things which possess a greater emotional value to himself.

"The religious man is religious in his actions, because his religious desires are stronger than his irreligious ones — he finds a greater satisfaction and content in religious actions than in the pursuits of the worldly-minded. The moral man is moral because his moral desires are stronger than his immoral ones — he obtains a greater degree of emotional satisfaction and content in being moral than in being immoral. Everything we do is prompted by Desire in some shape or form, high or low. Man cannot be desireless, and still act in one way or another — or in any way whatsoever. Desire is the motive factor behind all action — it is natural law of life."

From the above passage you can see how *desire precedes action.* You always do what you want to do. Now these statements may seem at first to be overly simplistic, but I mention them to emphasize that we often fail to act along certain lines because the desire is simply not there. Then we wonder why we fail to reach our objectives or to "find ourselves" in life. How, then, can you work to build desire? This is largely accomplished by *visualizing* your goals (or your chief aim in life) and allowing your subconscious mind to take over. Psychologists often refer to this process as *autosuggestion.* Reason all you want to with your subconscious mind, and you'll find yourself still motivated more by your emotions. One of the seven positive emotions is *desire*.

If, during high school and college, you wanted to be an opera singer and your father argued convincingly that you would make a better lawyer, you may have been convinced against your will, but the desire will linger still. The reason you did not act upon that desire was due to fear and disbelief. If you're still trying to find your chief aim in life (making a million in sales, franchises, etc. or becoming an actor, writer, etc.) you must first begin building desire. This requires, first, elimination of the seven basic fears (Death, Old Age, Ill Health, Pain, Lost Love, Poverty, Criticism) and any minor subsidiary fears that may be holding you back. Secondly, you must act to build *belief* as the mainstay of your desire. As with desire, belief is built largely through visualization or autosuggestion wherein you influence the subconscious mind through the steps mentioned earlier. Decide upon the belief you want (making a million for example), set it firmly in your subconscious mind, and your subconscious will thereafter instruct your conscious mind to "live up to" that belief. In short, begin to see, hear, smell, touch, live, your goals and chief objectives in life. Believe that you will receive rewards and accomplishments; then shut the door on every suggestion of fear or worry or failure. Belief in limitation is the one and only thing that causes limitation. See the things you want as already yours. Believe it. Dream it. Go out and accomplish it by following the prescribed procedure for influencing the subconscious mind.

Don't worry about things that have happened in your past. Perhaps you've failed before, and you fear criticism or poverty. Misfortune must always stay in your past and never be allowed to hinder the future. Remember that those who love to criticize are likely to be failures themselves, and failure, like other forms of misery, loves company. Instead of bemoaning your past, *visualize* yourself as on the next rung of the ladder, and the next step above that one, and upward toward the rewards and goals you have set firmly in your mind.

Contrary to popular myth, climbing the ladder of success usually requires an initial period of putting all of your eggs in one basket so that your energies are not dissipated by sidelines. Here's what Andrew Carnegie had to say about the concentration of your efforts toward a *specific aim* in life:

> "Place all your eggs in one basket and see that no one kicks it over."

Obviously Mr. Carnegie made this remark with tongue in cheek, since you cannot spend time worrying that others might kick over your basket; nor can you be plagued by mental conflicts, fears, and tensions brought about by suspicions or by any of the negative emotions. When you finally understand that the aim of life is not the accumulation of material rewards, but to live life to its fullest, your mind will then cease to concern itself excessively with the external world. And from the time you plant a definite chief aim in your mind, your mind begins, both consciously and unconsciously, to accumulate and store away the material with which you are to reach that principal goal in life.

Never forget this cardinal rule of success:

> You may have anything you want, or be anything you want, providing you know exactly what you want, want it hard enough, confidently expect to attain it, persistently determine to attain it, and are willing to pay the price for its attainment.

SCRIPT and FLA (M) E   SUCCESS PRINCIPLE 14 – GO THE EXTRA MILE

One of the most common causes of failure is the habit of quitting when one is overtaken by temporary defeat.

James J. Corbett, the famous boxer and former world heavyweight champ, once made these remarks about the value of *going that extra mile* when your mind and body tell you it's time to quit: "Fight one more round. When your feet are so tired that you have to shuffle back to the center of the ring, fight one more round. When your arms are so tired that you can hardly lift your hands to come on guard, fight one more round. When your nose is bleeding and your eyes are black and you are so tired that you wish your opponent would crack you one on the jaw and put you to sleep, fight one more round — remembering that the man who always fights one more round is never whipped."

There are many sound reasons for turning in a performance that is not required and which may not return to you an immediate reward. But perhaps the most persuasive reason for *going the extra mile* is that, on balance, once you have acquired the habit, you will outdistance the rest of the pack and claim a greater success. Your reward could come in the form of material gain and/or public acclaim, along with the personal satisfaction you receive from knowing you've done your best.

You are familiar with the worker who performs only as much as he is paid for; no more, sometimes less. Since there is nothing outstanding in his performance, there is nothing about him that will attract favorable comment. Whatever rewards he receives are based, not on merit, but solely on seniority. He gains only by default. And surely no one will recognize him as a winner in life. Consider, then, the worker who *goes the extra mile*. He stands out from those around him, and he is much in demand. Everyone seeks out his services because they realize he will yield to them a bonus in terms of his work performance. If you are in business for yourself, and you've acquired the habit of *going the extra mile,* you will end up paying the bonus to yourself, and this will be reflected in greater success and monetary reward for you. The person who has acquired the habit of *going the extra mile* also finds that he is immune to failure, because he is not overtaken by temporary defeat. When others have given up and fallen by the wayside, he continues the extra mile toward his goal. There is an unexplained law in nature that appears to yield benefits in greater measure than the effort put forth. If you try to get something for nothing, you will end up less than even — you will lose out. If your efforts are devoted to acquiring things at less than their true value, you will receive proportionately less for your efforts. But! If you have made it a habit of giving more of yourself than you have to — *going the extra mile* — you will ultimately receive, not only equal pay for equal work, but a bonus in greater proportion to the extra effort expended. Employers who abuse or violate this law are penalized by the loss of valuable employees. The self-employed are penalized for failure to reward themselves for their extra efforts through ill health, disharmony at home, loss of friends, lack of spirituality, or eventual self-destruction.

To test this law for yourself, you need only devote a half hour or an hour of your time each day to the performance of duties or services for which you cannot see immediate reward. The very fact that you are conscious of this principle of success will help it to become a habit in your life. You will ultimately be compensated. You need not be burdened with worry that your extra efforts will not in some way be given the recognition they deserve, plus a bonus. For a thorough understanding of this principle, I refer you to Emerson's Essay on Compensation, which explains the duality of every act in nature.

POOR WORK = POOR PAY

EQUAL WORK = EQUAL PAY

EXTRA WORK = EXTRA PAY

Now you can point to the unemployment compensation laws, and to the welfare laws, and claim that Emerson's "Law" is not valid. However, this is not the case, since every act is not always *immediately* rewarded or penalized. On balance, those who seek or receive something for nothing are the big losers in life, since they are continually in debt to it.

Going the extra mile, too, means helping others to get ahead, since it is not possible for you to become a rich, famous, and truly successful person without extending a hand to others. This is a difficult principle for some achievers to understand, because advice is often promulgated that you should look out for yourself first, so as not to be put down or put upon by others. The confusion here lies between foolishness and wisdom. Once you understand the definition of a fool, you have no need for the "look out for yourself first" philosophy.

> A fool may be known by six things: Anger, without cause; speech, without profit; change, without progress; inquiry, without object; putting trust in a stranger, and mistaking foes for friends.
>
> Arabian Proverb

It is not foolish to put yourself ahead in the world by first helping others to get ahead. It is, however, foolish to allow yourself to be continually stepped on. Foolish acts are penalized, never rewarded. Forgiveness, sympathy, and love are the emotions of a wise man; whereas selfishness, suspicion, and avarice are the coveted emotions of fools. Take time, then, from your aspirations for greatness to *go the extra mile* by helping others. You will be the ultimate beneficiary.

SCRIPT and FLAM (E)   SUCCESS PRINCIPLE 15 – ACT WITH ENTHUSIASM

> Every great and commanding movement in the annals of the world is the triumph of enthusiasm. Nothing great was ever achieved without it.
>
> Ralph Waldo Emerson

Enthusiasm is the key to action. Every man, woman, and child on earth has enthusiasm at times, and when that spirit takes hold, the task is done, the point is made, and that person's influence over others is measured with greater weight. An effective sales presentation requires enthusiasm, and you'll observe this fact whether you are buying a new car or listening to a sermon.

Let's consider these two concerns in your life – one involves the physical and material portion; the other deals with your spiritual requirements. You are more apt to respond favorably to either pitch if it is made with enthusiasm, because at that moment you are filled with belief, the mainstay of desire. So many times, however, our desire wanes when the enthusiasm dies down. It should be obvious that if you could be enthusiastic all of your life, you could certainly influence a great many more people than you do now. But more importantly, since belief springs from enthusiasm, you will find yourself believing that you can and will accomplish all the things you set out to do.

Benjamin Franklin tracked his enthusiasm daily by recording in a notebook his progress toward mastering the virtues. Frank Bettger (*How I raised Myself From Failure to Success In Selling*) followed Franklin's practice by recording his daily level of enthusiasm on note cards. Human resources and spiritual powers, it seems, are given to those who use what resources and powers they have. Self-discipline and faith (belief in the Creator, or in a spiritual power higher than yourself) are available to everyone. Use these resources and powers to become more enthusiastic in your own life. The penalty for not using them is apathy, inaction, and prolonged failure.

In his book, *The Secrets Of Mind Power,* Harry Lorayne, the hypnotist, suggests how to make yourself more enthusiastic through self-hypnosis or autosuggestion: "Hypnotic suggestion is merely making the subject believe implicitly that he is something he isn't (more enthusiastic) or that he can do something of which he ordinarily wouldn't be capable (earning a million)." The process of autosuggestion has already been explained to you. You need only to add to your daily statement your intent to show more enthusiasm. Since nothing great is ever achieved without enthusiasm, it is not likely that you will reach your goals or realize your chief aim in life without concentrated effort to master the success principle of acting enthusiastically. A springboard to accomplishing this is through keeping a daily record of your enthusiasm level. If you find it low, then concentrate on raising it. Of course if you're in sales, the ministry, or in the performing arts, you may not need this daily reminder to act enthusiastically. Enthusiasm goes, so to speak, with the territory. And since every act carries with it a commensurate penalty or reward, a lack of enthusiasm in these fields would be immediately penalized by inattention, disinterest, loss of faith, lost sales, empty seats, and reduced income.

The difficulty most people have with building enthusiasm is in generating the necessary "belief" power to make it work. If you find yourself in a field of work for which you are not suited, and if you tried to be enthusiastic about your job, you would doubtlessly make some progress, but you would stall out, and have to crank yourself up again and again. This is true because you will not have persuaded yourself — and subsequently your subconscious mind — that your enthusiasm is genuine. Remember Napoleon Hill's axiomatic statement:

> *Whatever the human mind can conceive, the human mind can achieve.*

If in your mind you cannot legitimately conceive of yourself as being enthusiastic about something, you will not believe it; nor, subsequently, can you achieve it. Conviction, faith, and belief, are all required for sustained enthusiasm.

Many years ago I worked in the advertising department of a world famous corporation. I had never wanted to work for big business, but nevertheless, I was still floundering around searching for my life's work, and I called my judgment into question. Off I went for a nine-month stint during which, — initially at least — I tried to be enthusiastic about my work. My heart was always elsewhere, however, and I would arise at four thirty every morning to practice the guitar in hopes that I might escape someday into the entertainment field. Still searching for a way out, I lost opportunities for advancement within the company and, eventually, I purchased a few vending machines in expectation that they would afford me a small income and a measure of independence.

After quitting my job, I learned that the vending machines were situated in the worst possible locations for generating income. Despite this disappointment, my enthusiasm remained high because the machines represented a chance to become independent — a primary and totally believable goal. In consequence of this outlook, I proceeded to transfer the machines to more desirable and lucrative locations. I remember well how I accomplished this task and how I built up a very profitable small business from which I entered the limitless opportunity field of real estate.

When approaching the owners of various business establishments, I did not walk in and "beg" them for a location. My approach was always that I had the most "fantastic" money-making machine they had ever seen. My machine would pay them a higher rate of commissions than those currently on their location, yet it would not compete with existing machines, because the commodity dispensed was not available to the customers of that establishment. My level of enthusiasm was so high that I often did not have to actually document consumer demand for the product. After a few minutes of persuasive discussion, the owner would say, "Well, if the machine is as good as you say, bring one around and we'll try it out." Once on location, I was usually there to stay.

ENTHUSIASM = BELIEF = DESIRE = ACCOMPLISHMENT

The aforementioned formula is a simplified version of how my goals were achieved. I became enthusiastic about something; I believed in it and caused others to share that belief; desire was created; I subsequently accomplished the task at hand. Any enterprising individual knows, conciously or unconsciously, that he must be audacious and vigorous in his pursuit of goals. In essence, he begins with mere possibilities and converts them into probabilities. The heart of enterprise, then, is enthusiasm.

The most enthusiastic person who ever lived was Jesus Christ. We know this to be true because his influence has spread over more people throughout history than that of any other person. The very word, *Enthusiasm*, is derived from the Greek signifying "God in us." If you, like Jesus, had God within you, and if you believed this with the utmost conviction and faith, and if you went about your work with the highest level of inspiration, zeal, dedication, and determination, you could achieve miracles. Spiritual *belief* arises from enthusiasm, as evangelists and preachers will attest. The *desire* to be "saved" is an outgrowth of this *belief.* Conversion to Christianity is the ultimate *accomplishment* resulting from *enthusiasm.*

If you're not blessed with natural enthusiasm how, then, can you best acquire it?

This question can be answered by asking yourself either or both of the following questions:

1. Are you doing the work or rendering the service that you like best?

2. If not, do you have a definite chief aim in life toward which you are striving and which will lead you to the work of your choice?

If the answer to both questions is "no" you will have to develop a career goal in life or a definite chief aim. In no other way can you begin to build enthusiasm and achieve happiness. Happiness, of course, is a state of mind, and no man is happy if he does not think himself so. However, if happiness to you means things like the home of your choice, money in the bank, vacations when you want to take them, prestige in your career field, and so on, then these things are vital ingredients of your definite chief aim in life. You can become *enthusiastic* about these things.

An exerpt from Napoleon Hill's landmark work, *The Laws of Success* follows:

> You may develop enthusiasm over your definite chief aim in life, whether you are in a position to achieve that purpose at this time or not. You may be a long way from realization of your definite chief aim, but if you will kindle the fire of enthusiasm in your heart, and keep it burning, before long the obstacles that now stand in the way of your attainment of that purpose will melt away as if by the force of magic, and you will find yourself in possession of power that you did not know you possessed.

I'll point out that happiness also lies in the future, never in the past. You build enthusiasm by setting out firm goals of achievement for yourself and working to see them fulfilled.

A wise philosopher once said, "Life is the only real counsellor; wisdom unfiltered through personal experience does not become a part of the moral tissue. And life will give you what you ask from her only if you ask long enough and plainly enough."

Another philosopher reserved these words of temperance for the success-hungry: "How small a portion of our life it is that we really enjoy! In youth we are looking forward to things that are to come; in old age we are looking backward to things that are gone past; in manhood, though we appear indeed to be more occupied in things that are present, we even then seem too often absorbed in vague determination to be vastly happy on some future date, when we have time."

If you love life, you would be wise to follow Benjamin Franklin's example and not squander time, for that is the stuff of which life is made. Those who consistently achieve their goals in life understand, too quickly, how short is the time of life; while those who constantly fail, understand too late how long it is.

In conclusion, I want to repeat the two important observations about success made at the beginning of this discussion:

1. An intangible impulse of thought can be transmuted into material rewards by the application of known principles.

2. Knowledge is only *potential* power. It becomes power only when and if it is organized into *definite* plans of action and *definite* ends.

From here it's up to you. You have been given the known principles for the attainment of material rewards and peace of mind. By repeated study of the information provided here, and diligent application of this knowledge towards *your definite* plans and *definite* ends, you will acquire the power necessary to achieve wealth and independence in your own life.

ACTION POINTS – BOOK II

1. Memorize each of the 15 success rules as you come to them and repeat to yourself *orally* — both morning and evening — your intent to practice each rule everyday. (Example: "On a daily basis, I will practice the savings habit, self-control, etc.)

2. Memorize and commit to habit the self-confidence formula contained in the word, A-D-M-I-T.

3. Learn the poem on p. 207 and repeat it to yourself daily.

4. Develop a thorough understanding of the seven basic fears and learn to conquer them all.

5. Develop an awareness of the four essential components of your life and practice daily to keep them in balance.

6. Begin to isolate the 7 negative emotions and purge them from your life.

7. Defeat *fear of criticism* by memorizing and committing to habit the procedure for setting down roots in your subconscious.

8. On a daily basis, cultivate and apply the steps required to master the success quality of *concentration*.

9. Continue your search for people with whom you are "in tune" — those who can help you by contributing to your strengths and offsetting your weaknesses.

10. Get to know the seven indispensible and invisible guards who can advance your leadership role in any "master-mind" alliance.

11. Commit the 10 basic motives to memory and develop a thorough understanding of them.

12. A runaway imagination can be self-defeating; therefore, memorize and understand the thought about *desires* on p. 229.

13. Begin to assemble in your mind a cabinet of advisors (living or dead) whom you admire. As an extension of your powers of fantasy, call on these advisors for help in building character.

14. Memorize and commit to habit the 10 steps for developing a pleasant personality.

15. Reread the essay, *Father Forgets,* until you can promptly call upon it when impatience strikes.

16. Read Ralph Waldo Emerson's great *Essay on Compensation*. You'll benefit, too, from all of his essays. See Bibliography.)

17. Identify and purge yourself of any of the 50 basic failure habits.

18. Refer to the self-help quiz on p. 243 whenever you have feelings of failure.

19. To spur your own initiative, develop a habit of answering *yes* to the three basic questions on p. 245.

20. Get to know and practice the accumulation of life's true rewards.

21. Judge yourself as being *good, fair* or *poor* in each of the effective leadership qualities. (You can also have someone else give you a rating.)

22. Memorize the principal inaccurate thought patterns and begin to eliminate them from your mind.

23. Pin down the 26 enemies of accurate thought and destroy their build-up in your mind.

24. Refer to the list of questions on pp. 251-53 to help purge your mind of inaccurate thought patterns. Cleanse your mind by learning to answer *no* to each question.

25. Check your *Statement of Physical Goals* and your *Statement of Exchange* (Lesson 3) against the eight steps for reaching and influencing the subconscious mind. If you've left out any steps, now is the time for revisions.

26. Develop a thorough understanding of the essay on *desire*.

27. Begin devoting some time out of every day toward the performance of duties or services (no matter how small) for which you cannot see immediate reward.

28. Memorize and understand the Arabian proverb about fools on p. 264.

29. Build into your daily statement your vow to become more enthusiastic. If you have not done so, include in this vow your intent to practice each of the other success principles as well.

30. Memorize and understand the enthusiasm formula on p. 263.

APPENDIX DIRECTORY

Appendix A — Frequently Asked Questions and Answers for Beginning Subdivestors ....p. 271

Appendix B — Dictionary of Real Estate, Subdivesting, and Success Terms ....p. 277

Appendix C — Bibliography and Suggested Further Reading ....p. 309

Appendix D — Federal and State Regulations Supplement ....p. 315

Appendix E — Land Acquisition Check List and Development Forms ....p. 323

Appendix F — Measurement Tables and Computation Data for Land Areas ....p. 329

Appendix G — Mapping Structure and Information for Land Procurement ....p. 331

Appendix H — Soil Legend and Sample Soil Map ....p. 335

Appendix I — Sample Protective Covenants for Subdivisions ....p. 337

Appendix J — Sales Contract Forms, Credit Applications, and Disclosure Information ....p. 343

Appendix K — Sample Deed, Deed of Trust, and Related Note .....p. 349

Appendix L — Forms and Information for Servicing Notes Receivable ....p. 355

Appendix M — Note Discount Information and Procedures ....p. 357

Appendix N — Key to U.S. and Foreign Annual Interest Rates......p. 373

APPENDIX A

FREQUENTLY ASKED QUESTIONS AND ANSWERS FOR BEGINNING SUBDIVESTORS

1. How should I take title to the land I buy?

Answer: The most common forms of business or group ownership include corporations, partnerships, syndicates, trusts, and sole proprietorships. If you're buying the property along with your wife, you may want to take title as tenants by the entireties. This form of ownership cannot be broken without the mutual consent of both parties. Tenancy-in-common is useful when two unmarried persons are buying the property. Upon the death of one, ownership passes to the heirs of the deceased, or to those designated in his will. Should one owner wish to sell his interest, he may do so whether or not the other parties agree. The seller may even bring action to have the property sold at auction, in which case the others can (1) buy back the property at the highest bid price, or (2) accept payment for their shares out of the auction proceeds. Joint tenancy with the right of survivorship can ensure the orderly transfer of ownership interests at the death of any one owner. A joint tenant may sell his interest, and the new owner becomes a tenant-in-common with the others. When you purchase a piece of land, you can usually arrange to have the deed made out in whatever form of ownership you choose. In all cases you should have competent legal advice before taking title to any real estate.

2. What are easements?

Answer: Basically, an easement on any piece of property means that someone else has the right to use the land of another person for the purpose specified. An easement appurtenant runs with the title and always involves two or more properties. You may, for example, purchase a piece of land to which access is granted over someone's farm. The farm, then, has an easement appurtenant that runs with its title. An easement in gross is the right to use the land of another, even if the party who benefits has no ownership of land. Utility easements often take this form. The restrictions you place in the deeds to your lot owners may include either type of easement.

3. *Can the government or utility companies force me to sell them land and easements?*

Answer: Under the right of eminent domain these public and semi-public bodies can move against your will providing they pay fair market value for the land or easement taken. If their idea of "fair market value" seems out-of-line with your own estimation, you may want to hire an attorney to press your case.

4. *What do I need to know about surveys?*

Answer: Whenever you purchase a piece of land you will want to be satisfied that the property is of the promised size and within the boundaries described. A recent survey is necessary before you can proceed with your *Subdivesting* plans. Depending on your area of the country, you and your surveyor will be confronted with the following systems used to describe property boundaries:

    a. **Metes and bounds (measures and directions):** An exact description, with each side of the property measured and described in feet and all directions indicated.

    b. **Monuments:** An inexact method wherein property is described by identifying its relation to tangible and intangible monuments. Natural landmarks, such as rivers, streams, large trees, springs, etc. are considered tangible. Intangible reference points could be manmade, such as fences, streets, houses, walls, etc.

    c. **Rectangular or government survey:** A system used predominantly in the west and midwest based on surveying lines running north and south, called *meridians,* and east and west, called *base lines.* Between intersections, the land has been divided into quadrangles, twenty-four miles on each side. Each quadrangle is divided into townships, six miles on a side, and containing thirty-six sections of 640 acres each. Townships are measured and numbered east and west of the *meridians* and north and south of the *base lines.*

5. How does foreclosure under a trust deed differ from that of a mortgage?

Answer: A trust deed conveys title to a trustee who is empowered to foreclose in the event of default. Lenders find this arrangement more effective, and generally quicker, if they are forced to proceed with foreclosure. Under a mortgage, the borrower (mortgagor) pledges real property directly to the lender (mortgagee) as security for the debt. Should the borrower default under a mortgage, the mortgagee has four alternatives: (1) He can legally foreclose, which in some states can be cumbersome, expensive, and slow. (2) He can foreclose by advertising the property publicly, after giving the borrower default notice of this intent. (3) He can take possession, though he must obtain the mortgagor's consent and he has no greater title than he had under the mortgage. He must account for all income and expense items and return the property to the mortgagee when the indebtedness has been satisfied. (4) He can persuade the borrowers to designate a new manager, such as a realtor, to come in and operate the property. All net income, after expenses, can then be applied to back interest, taxes, and principal payments.

6. What is a Warranty Deed?

Answer: A Warranty Deed states that (a) the grantor has the right to convey the property; (b) you have the right of undisturbed possession; (c) there are no encumbrances on the property other than those stated; (d) grantor will take all necessary steps to deliver clear title, if needed; (e) you are forever given (warranted) title and possession to the property described in the deed.

7. What is a Special Warranty Deed?

Answer: In special situations, the grantor may be unable, or prohibited by law, from granting a Special Warranty Deed. The Special Warranty Deed limits the grantor's liability to those acts coming from, by, or through him to the grantor. For example, a *Subdivestor* disposing of subdivided lots through foreclosure may be unable to obtain title insurance unless he grants a Special Warranty Deed. A Bargain and Sale Deed implies that the grantor is owner of, or has an interest in, the property he is conveying. Unless stated otherwise, a grantor makes no further claims or covenants.

8. *What is a quitclaim deed?*

Answer: Lawyers examining the title to property often discover that other persons may have valid or vague claims that have never been cleared of record. To remove these "clouds" the lawyer will often prepare a "quit-claim" deed for these persons to sign. Their signature on this document does not, however, imply or indicate that they warrant possession or any right to title.

9. *What is a purchase money mortgage?*

Answer: In cases where the property is not paid for in cash, the purchaser gives a promissory note along with a mortgage to the seller to secure the balance due. It is prior to any purchaser's liens that are in existence at the time of the sale. This instrument takes precedence over any spouse's rights with regard to the property, and in most states the spouse is not required to sign the purchase money mortgage.

10. *What is a RESPA settlement statement?*

Answer: Though this course is mainly concerned with rural land transactions, you may be faced with the re-financing of farm homes on subdivided lots. The Real Estate Settlement Procedures Act (RESPA) applies to all new financing of single family homes by financial institutions. The act requires a standardized form for the disclosure of actual settlements at closing. Your lawyer and the financing institution are capable of complying with the law in meeting the requirements of this act. The main costs to your buyer when he purchases a single family home from you (using institutional financing) are: title insurance, closing fees, appraisal report, property taxes, and home insurance.

11. *What is a homestead exemption?*

Answer: Some states have various laws on the books to exempt a home from debt and to provide a widow or widower with a home for life. Usually the area and the value to the property involved are limited. It may also be required that the exempted property be the family home and that a written exemption of homestead be filed. Homesteads meeting all requirements are thus free of general claims for debt, except liens such as taxes and mortgages.

12. *What is meant by "community property?"*

    Answer: The following states have "community property" laws: Arizona, California, Idaho, Louisiana, Nevada, New Mexico, Texas, and Washington. Under these laws the husband and wife are usually entitled to one-half of the real estate, personal property, and income of either mate. The laws are not uniform throughout the aforementioned states and the community property interest can be modified by law and by specific restrictions in the instrument of conveyance. The rights which a husband has in his wife's estate at her death (curtesy) and the opposite rights of the wife (dower) do not exist in the community property states.

13. *Can I benefit from tax deferred exchanges of real estate?*

    Answer: To qualify for non-recognition of gain or loss under current tax laws, three elements must be present in the exchange: (1) You must actually "exchange" properties (city real estate for country land) as distinguished from a sale and separate purchase. (2) The transaction must involve business or investment assets. (3) You must exchange *like* kinds of property (office building for working farm). You cannot exchange real property for personal property; nor can "dealer" real estate qualify for tax deferment when exchanged for investment real estate. Just as he must usually give up capital gains advantages, a full-time *Subdivestor* faces a difficult time qualifying for tax deferment in an exchange due to the "dealer" exclusion.

14. *What is the thirty-percent rule in an installment sale?*

    Answer: If your seller accepts your offer to purchase his property on terms, he may not wish to take more than thirty percent as a down payment. To do so would mean he must report all gain in the year of sale, thus increasing his tax bite. Additional payments beyond the thirty percent, such as payments on the mortgage and real estate taxes paid by the purchaser on behalf of the seller, could also deny the seller a tax break. Therefore, it may be critical to your operations that you legally structure the financing in such a way as to avoid burdening the seller with premature (and potentially higher) taxes. If, to release lots from the blanket mortgage, you must make additional payments to the seller, you should seek competent legal advice. Often an escrow arrangement can be set up, or the payments channeled into stocks and bonds held by a trustee on behalf of the seller. Imaginative thought along this line can make the difference between acceptance or rejection of a particular *Subdivesting* project.

15. *Is it worth taking out public liability insurance on my projects?*

Answer: You could be a *Subdivestor* for the rest of your working life and never be sued for an accident that happened on your property to someone else; or, you could be faced with a lawsuit tomorrow. For the small amount of premium money required, public liability insurance is certainly worth the trade off for peace-of-mind alone. You should arrange with your insurance agent for all new projects to be covered automatically. A periodic review of your policy is necessary to eliminate expenditures for sold-out projects.

APPENDIX B

DICTIONARY

of Real Estate, Subdivesting, and Success Terms

ABANDONMENT: To surrender or vacate use of or rights in real property.

ABSTRACT OF TITLE: A summarization or condensed history of conveyances, transfers, and relevent information pertaining to the title of a particular tract of land, including recorded encumbrances, liens, and other charges.

ACCELERATION CLAUSE: A clause or provision in a note, trust deed, mortgage, or land contract giving the lender the right to demand immediate and full payment when a particular covenant in the contract has been violated. Failure to meet installment and/or interest payments on time are cases in point.

ACCESS: The right to enter, approach, use, and leave a parcel of land, often over land belonging to others.

ACCESS AND UTILITIES: An item given a numerical score on the FEASIBILITY CHECK LIST used in Subdivesting and referring to the quality of ingress and egress and availability of utilities within a given subdivision.

ACCRETION: The addition of soil to land due to gradual changes in a water course, excessive wind, and continuous waves.

ACCURATE THOUGHT: One of the 15 principal success attributes expounded on by Napoleon Hill and found endemic in the successful men he studied.

ACTION FILE: A county-by-county breakdown of vital information used in Subdivesting to make quick decisions when pursuing prospective land deals. Assembled data include road maps, topo maps, subdivision ordinances, zoning laws, pending land use legislation, pertinent newspaper clippings, etc.

ADMIT: In success motivation, a code word comprised of key letters in a formula of six elements intended to help raise one's self-confidence, and expressed as A-D-M-I-T. The elements are: Autosuggestion, Definite Goals, Mental Attitude, the words, I Can, and Truth and Justice.

ADVERSE LAND USE: Land use having an unfavorable effect on nearby property. A junk yard in the midst of expensive country estates could be an example.

ADVERSE POSSESSION: A claim or right to land ownership against the real owner, wherein claimant, under color of title, establishes actual, open, notorious, exclusive, and continuous possession for a statutory period. This can occur on remote or abandoned properties where the absentee owners fail to correct unwarranted changes in boundary lines or to assert their required right of ownership.

ADVERTISING AND SALES PROMOTION: A specific function of marketing in business and a specific work area in Subdivesting.

AGENCY: The business of any person, firm, etc. empowered to act for another; specifically, in real estate, a fiduciary relationship between an agent/broker and the principal/owner wherein the former negotiates the sale, purchase, leasing or exchanging of property. Agency can also exist in the relationship between a broker/principal and his salesman/agent.

AGORAPHOBIA: An abnormal fear of being in open or public places.

AGREEMENT OF SALE: A written agreement or contract dealing with the transfer of real estate or personal property between buyer and seller in which the terms and conditions of sale are specified.

AMENITIES: Attractive or desirable features within a development which act to improve the quality and enjoyment of life and which are generally considered improvement features of that property. Tennis courts, swimming pools, pleasing views, etc. are examples.

AMORTIZATION: Repayment of borrowed money on a systematic basis, wherein the principal sum of a note or mortgage is reduced over its life.

ANNUAL PERCENTAGE RATE: The true interest rate charged on a given loan, specifically meant to correct misunderstandings when interest has been "added on" at the front end before computation of an amortization schedule. For example, a 6% interest rate is, in actuality, a 10.21% annual percentage rate using the "add on" form of computation. In effect, this is a 10.21% interest rate.

ANTICIPATION: A term used in real estate connoting the creation of value through future benefits. For example, the vacant lots in a subdivision will derive benefit from future homebuilding since such improvements will create added value to unimproved lots. The opposite term is regression.

APPRECIATION: A rise in the value, worth, or price of a piece of property, usually caused by economic factors such as inflation.

APPURTENANCE: In real estate, anything which has been added to or has become a part of a property and which is usually conveyed as an easement when the property is sold, leased, or bequeathed.

ASSESSED VALUE: The value placed on a property by local taxing authorities and used as a basis for taxation.

ASSESSMENT: An amount of tax, charge, or levy placed on a parcel of property, usually based on established rates.

ASSIGNEE: A person to whom a claim, right, property, etc. is transferred. Also a person empowered to act for another.

ASSIGNMENT: A transfer of any claim, right, property, etc. from one person to another.

ASSIGNOR: A person making the transfer of any claim, right, property, etc.

ASSUMPTION OF MORTGAGE: The act of taking over or co-guaranteeing the obligations of another on a mortgage in which the new purchaser or grantee assumes liability for payment of a note secured by the mortgage or deed of trust.

ATTACHMENT: A legal taking of property by court order, usually to satisfy a plaintiff or complainant seeking settlement of a debt.

ATTORNEY'S DISCLAIMER: A written form, signed by the purchaser of real estate, wherein it is acknowledged that the agreed-upon settlement attorney did not coerce, intimidate, or force the purchaser to select him as the closing attorney.

AUTOSUGGESTION: A form of self-hypnosis wherein suggestions, which have an effect on one's thinking and bodily functions, are made to the inner self.

BALLOON PAYMENT: Usually a lump sum payment of unamortized principal on a mortgage or trust deed which is greater than any preceding payment. A balloon mortgage may be amortized over 20 years, yet carry a "balloon" provision wherein the unamortized principal becomes due and payable at the end of a 10 year span. Often, re-financing at a higher interest rate then occurs.

BASE LINE: A horizontal line measured with special accuracy to provide a base for survey by triangulation. Also an imaginary line through the initial point of a principal meridian, used to establish the location of township lines in the government survey system.

BEDROCK: Solid rock beneath the soil and superficial rock.

BELIEF: In self-motivation, the conviction or acceptance that certain things are true and real; usually the outgrowth of enthusiasm and the antecedent of desire.

BILL OF SALE: A written statement certifying that the ownership of something has been transferred by sale. In real estate, the statement is used for the transfer of personal property associated with the transfer of real property.

BINDER: An acknowlegement or memorandum of earnest money deposited by a buyer to secure the right to purchase a specific property under certain terms agreed upon by both buyer and seller.

BLADED-IN ROAD: Initial stage of road construction where a tractor with blade cuts out the road course.

BLANKET MORTGAGE: A mortgage covering more than one piece of real estate. This term is frequently used in the land development industry, where a single lien "blankets" all the subdivided lots in a particular development. As the lots are sold, releases can be made from the blanket mortgage.

BLIGHT: A condition in real estate where neighborhoods and areas are in a state of decay or stunted growth, as with the slums of major cities.

BOND: A written obligation to pay specified sums, or to do or not do certain specified things. In real estate a bond can be an interest-bearing security evidencing a long-term debt, such as a mortgage.

BUFFER STRIP: A strip of land located between two types of land use areas, such as a separation between residential and industrial. Often this parcel is unimproved except for landscaping, and its primary function is to lessen friction resulting from two incompatible or inharmonious land uses.

BUILDING CODE: An ordinance, enforced by local and state governments, and designed to regulate construction, maintenance, and alterations of structures within specific jurisdictions.

BUILDING LINE: This is also referred to as a setback line. The line marks the boundary beyond which no structure may extend and is fixed at a certain distance from the front, back, and sides of a particular lot, or at specific distances from streets or roads.

BUILDING PERMIT: A document issued within certain jurisdictions granting permission to build a structure on a specific site.

BUREAU OF LAND MANAGEMENT: A federal agency with general responsibility for public lands in the United States. Its principal function is to protect these lands from improper use and poor management.

CAPITAL GAINS: Profits resulting from the sale of capital investments such as stocks, real estate, etc. which are taxed at a lower rate than other income.

CAPITALIZATION: The process of determining the present value of a property through the conversion or discounting of expected future income payments.

CASH FLOW: Cash remaining in a business after all operating expenses and debt services have been paid, but not including income taxes and deductions for depreciation.

CAVEAT EMPTOR: A Latin term meaning, Let the buyer beware, or Buy at your own risk.

CERTIFICATE OF DEPOSIT (C.D.): A banking certificate achnowledging the receipt of a specified sum of money in a special kind of time deposit drawing interest and requiring written notice for withdrawal.

CERTIFICATE OF TITLE: An attorney's written opinion as to the validity and purity of ownership on a particular piece of real estate.

CERTIORARI PROCEEDINGS: A request from a higher court to a lower court to a board or official with some judicial power requesting the record of a case for review. In real estate, this proceeding is often used by property owners protesting rises in tax assessments.

CESSPOOL: A cistern or deep hole in the ground to receive drainage or sewage. Cesspools, where found in use, are usually covered and are now widely outlawed throughout the United States.

CHAIN OF TITLE: A summary or history of a particular title to property showing out-conveyances, encumbrances, and other transactions and documents affecting the title as far back as records are available.

CHARACTER: In self-improvement, a distinctive quality, trait, or attribute, that preceeds your reputation and must be improved before a pleasant personality can be developed.

CHATTEL MORTGAGE: A mortgage against personal property as opposed to real property.

CHECK LIST ELEMENTS: In Subdivesting, the basic components of the FEASIBILITY CHECK LIST. In broad terms the elements are broken down as follows: Physical Characteristics of the Land; Location, Location, Location; and Profit and Risk Factors.

CIRCA: A Latin term used when describing an approximate time period of certain construction or particular buildings. (Circa 1890).

CISTERN: A large receptacle or tank for storing rain water. Usually the cistern is located underground and connected to drainpipes and guttering on buildings, widely used in areas where wells are impractical or too costly to drill.

CLOSING: Often used synonymously with the word, settlement, when referring to the formal conclusion of a real estate transaction. In surveying, the term can apply to the successful bringing together of boundary lines. In sales, the word can refer to the process of getting a prospect to sign a contract (close).

CLOSING SIGNALS: Subtle hints on the part of a prospect that he may be willing to purchase if the sales argument is effective and persuasive enough. Skilled salespeople can recognize these signals, often before the prospect is aware that he's ready to buy.

CLOUD ON TITLE: A condition (revealed as the result of a title search) which impairs the title to property in some way, usually minor. Court action or a quit-claim deed can often clear the defect.

CO-BROKE AGREEMENT: An agreement between commission salespeople that they will share commissions on a particular sale.

COLLATERAL: Anything, such as stocks, bonds, notes, etc. that secures or guarantees the discharge of an obligation.

COMMINGLING OF FUNDS: The illegal intermixing of a client's money with personal funds. In real estate, this can occur when a broker deposits, or transfers to his own account from escrow, any or all funds entrusted to him by his clients. Lawyers, too, are in a position to comingle funds.

COMMITMENT FEE: A charge to a prospective borrower by a lender for the lender's agreement to loan funds in the future. Usually the fee is based on a percentage of the anticipated loan.

COMMON AREAS: Land set aside for all the property owners in a particular development to enjoy and utilize. Often this land is improved with recreational facilities such as pools, tennis courts, ponds, etc. In a condominium project, the common area may also refer to parking lots, playgrounds, and waterfront adjacent to or adjoining the buildings.

COMMON THREAD OF SUCCESS: In success motivation, a common philosophy, either expressed or held in the sub-conscious by rich and successful persons, that is largely responsible for their achievements in life.

COMMUNITY PROPERTY: In certain states of the U.S., this is a term used to describe property acquired by a husband or wife, or by both, during marriage and consequently owned by both. The term does not apply to property acquired **separately** by either spouse.

COMPONENTS OF LIFE: The four distinct parts of life to which one's energies and attention are directed. The components are: Physical Concerns; Mental Attitude; Social Involvements; and Spiritual Needs.

CONCENTRATION: One of the 15 principal success attributes expounded on by Napoleon Hill and found endemic in the successful men he studied.

CONCEPTUAL THINKING: The ability to grasp an idea or thought from disjointed and unorganized material and to turn that abstract notion into productive reality, as in developing a successful concept for an advertisement.

CONDEMNATION: The act of declaring property legally appropriated for public use under the right of eminent domain. Quasi-governmental bodies can appropriate private property for the public good providing the owner is justly compensated.

CONFIDENCE IN SELF (SELF-CONFIDENCE): One of the 15 principal success attributes expounded on by Napoleon Hill and found endemic in the successful men he studied.

CONSTRUCTION LOAN: Usually short-term financing arranged by builders until the structure is completed and a permanent long-term loan can be obtained.

CONSTRUCTION LOAN DRAW: Funds drawn against the construction loan at designated stages of construction.

CONTINGENCY: Something whose occurence depends on chance or uncertain conditions, such as the sale of a house contingent upon the purchaser first selling his own home.

CONVENTIONAL LOANS: Loans considered customary or ordinary, as opposed to mortgages guaranteed by government agencies. Usually conventional loans are made by private institutions such as savings and loan associations.

CONVEYANCE: The transfer of the ownership of real property from one person to another by deed, mortgage, or lease.

COOPERATION: One of the 15 principal success attributes expounded on by Napoleon Hill and found endemic in the successful men he studied.

COST OF MONEY: Cost for loan funds or the amount of note discounts due to interest charges and the lender's required yield on invested capital.

COUNTY BOARD OF SUPERVISORS: Elected officials within a county who act as a governing body.

COVENANTS: Clauses or agreements embodied in deeds and other instruments promising certain performances, non-performances, and land uses by and on the behalf of the grantor and his assigns.

CUL DE SAC: A street with only one outlet, usually with a turnaround at the dead end.

CURTESY: The lawful right or interest that a husband has in the properties of his deceased wife.

DEBT SERVICE: The total cost of repaying a loan; the sum of principal and interest required to amortize the obligation.

DEDICATION: To devote or give away land or property for public use and the acceptance of this gift by authorized public officials.

DEED: A document under seal which, when delivered, transfers a present interest in property.

DEED RESTRICTIONS: Restrictions written into the deed limiting the use of the property.

DEED OF TRUST: A legal instrument given by the borrower to a trustee to be held on behalf of a beneficiary as security for the fulfillment of an obligation, usually a loan for the purchase of real property.

DEFEASANCE CLAUSE: A mortgage clause stating a condition which, when met, makes the instrument void. For example, upon payment of the mortgage, the mortgagee gains the right to redeem his property with no futher obligation under the mortgage.

DEFICIENCY JUDGEMENT: A judgement in favor of a mortgagee for the remainder of a debt not completely cleared by foreclosure and sale of the mortgaged property.

DEFINITE CHIEF AIM: One of the 15 principal success attributes expounded on by Napoleon Hill and found endemic in the successful men he studied.

DEMOGRAPHIC: Relating to the statistical science dealing with the distribution, density, vital statistics, etc. of populations.

DEPLETION: The gradual using up or destruction of capital assets, especially natural resources.

DEPRECIATION: A decrease in the value of property through wear, deterioration, or obsolescence and the allowance made for this in bookkeeping, accounting, etc. to amortize or write off the cost of the property over its estimated useful life.

DESIRE: In success motivation, a strong wish or craving to acquire or do something, and always the inspiration for action. Aside from being inborn and activated by human nature, desire often springs from imaginative thought and strong belief.

DIRECT MAIL ADVERTISING: To sell or call attention to a product or service through the use of a mailing package; also referred to as direct response mail advertising.

DIRECT RESPONSE AD: An advertisement in a magazine, newspaper, or on TV or radio which is designed to evoke immediate action as opposed to a potential latent reaction from an audience; also referred to as an immediate response ad.

DISCOUNTING NOTES: To sell notes receivable at less than their present value, with the reduction largely covering interest for the purchaser.

DISCOUNT POINTS: Also called a loan fee when lender charges for his services in making the loan. Generally these fees are based on a percentage of the loan and are meant to cover services such as appraisals and inspections. Discount points are not to be confused with interest points, a separate item.

DISCOUNT RATE: The percentage charge paid by member banks to the Federal Reserve when borrowing.

DISINTERMEDIATION: An outflowing of funds from thrift institutions generally precipitated by higher interest rates and yields from other investments, such as stocks, bonds, precious metals, etc.

DOWER: The part of a man's property which his widow inherits for life.

DRAINFIELDS: The area receiving drainage from a septic system.

EARNEST MONEY: Good faith money placed as a down payment on property.

EASEMENT: A right or privilege that a person or entity may have in another's land, such as a right-of-way or grant to a utility company.

EASE OF ENTRY: An item given a numerical score on the FEASIBILITY CHECK LIST used in Subdivesting and referring to the relative difficulty of getting a subdivision underway within a given jurisdiction.

EGRESS: The act or right of going out of a property.

EMERSON, RALPH WALDO: 1803-82; U.S. essayist, philosopher, and poet whose works are widely utilized and quoted by educators and success motivators.

EMINENT DOMAIN: The right of a government or quasi-governmental agency to take, or to authorize the taking of, private property for public use, with just compensation usually being given to the owner.

ENCROACHMENT: The act of advancing beyond the proper, original, or customary limits, as when a building or part of a building intrudes upon a neighboring property line or public sidewalk.

ENCUMBRANCE: A lien, charge, or claim attached to the real or personal property of another and which has the effect of lessening or limiting value.

ENDORSEMENT: A form denoting a change, as of coverage or beneficiary, written on or added to an insurance policy or a commitment for title insurance.

ENTHUSIASM: One of the 15 principal success attributes expounded on by Napoleon Hill and found endemic in the successful men he studied.

ENTHUSIASM FORMULA: A fixed form of words expressing how enthusiasm leads to accomplishment. Specifically: Enthusiasm = Belief = Desire = Accomplishment.

ENTREPRENEUR: A person who organizes and manages a business undertaking, assuming the risk for the sake of profit.

ENVIRONMENTAL IMPACT STUDY: A formal statement or official account of the impact that a particular land use will have on the local environment. The study is commonly required by many local governments and agencies to anticipate potential changes in the physical, social, legal, economic, and political make-up of a community caused by a proposed development.

EQUITY: In real estate, equity can be taken to mean an owner's invested interest in a particular property over and above the liens against it.

EQUITY OF REDEMPTION: A mortgagee's right to redeem or recover his property prior to a foreclosure sale by paying the debt. This right can also extend for a specified period after the sale.

EQUITY PARTICIPATION: Also called a kicker, this term is usually applied to a transaction where the lender, in addition to a fixed rate of interest, retains a share in the profits of the borrower's project. Brokers and syndicators also utilize this transaction in lieu of, or in addition to, their customary fees.

EROSION: The gradual wearing away or disintegration of land area through processes of nature, as by water action or winds.

ESCALATOR CLAUSE: A clause in a contract providing for increases or decreases in certain items to cover unpredictable changes such as adjustments in tax rates or operating costs.

ESCHEAT: The reverting of property to the government when there are no legal heirs, and when there is no will disposing of the property to others.

ESCROW: A written agreement (as a bond or deed) or funds, deposited to the care of a third party and not delivered or put into effect until certain conditions are fulfilled.

ESTATE: The degree, nature, extent, and quality of interest or ownership that one has in land or other property. The term can also mean a person's possessions.

ESTOPPEL CERTIFICATE: A certificate which, when signed and delivered to another person, legally prevents that person from making an affirmation or denial contrary to facts that had been set forth earlier.

EXCHANGE, TAX-DEFERRED: The trading of a business or investment property for a like-kind of property, providing both have productive use value. Economic gain or profit from the transaction is not taxed at the time of trade.

EXCLUSIVE AGENCY LISTING: An agreement between a property owner and a real estate broker that gives the broker and his agents the right to sell certain property for a specified period of time, but which reserves the owner's right to sell the property himself without paying a commission.

EXCLUSIVE RIGHT TO SELL LISTING: A listing agreement between a broker and a property owner that gives the agency exclusive rights to sell a specified property and guaranteeing a commission to the brokerage house if the property is sold by anyone else during the term of the agreement.

EXCULPATORY CLAUSE: The clause or provision in a contract, financial instrument, or argreement that frees a debtor from personal liability if he defaults. For example, a mortgage clause might release a mortgagor in default from further obligation and provide that the property is sole security for the debt.

FAILURE HABITS: In success motivation, the root causes of failure or non-achievement that are ingrained in a person and which must be spotted and destroyed if success is to be achieved. Examples are: Lack of goals, procrastination, lack of self-confidence, impatience, uncontrolled envy, etc.

FAIR MARKET VALUE: An estimation of price that a given property would bring if sold on the open market, allowing for a reasonable period of time to locate and familiarize a buyer with the property's full use value and potential.

FAITH (AND HOPE): In religion and success motivation, the unquestioned belief that you can make direct and immediate contact with God or an Infinite Intelligence; also the mainstay of a positive mental attitude.

FANNIE MAE (F.N.M.A.): A shortened name for the Federal National Mortgage Association. This is a private corporation, sponsored by the federal government, and designed to supplement private mortgage market operations by purchasing and selling FHA, VA, and conventional loans.

FARMSTEAD: The land and buildings of a farm, or a rural tract of land that suggests farm use.

FEARS (7 BASIC): Feelings of anxiety and agitation over (1) Dying (2) Growing Old (3) Becoming Ill (4) Pain (5) Lost Love (6) Poverty (7) Criticism.

FEASIBILITY CHECK LIST: In Subdivesting, a list intended for ready checking and reference that can determine whether a project is economically practicable and potentially profitable. Items include Price and Terms, Location, Soil Conditions, Development Costs, etc.

FEASIBILITY STUDY: A critical examination and investigation of a proposed plan or project to determine whether the undertaking is capable of being managed, utilized, or dealt with successfully. Specific attention is directed toward an analysis of attainable income, probable expenses, and suitability of design and function.

FEDERAL RESERVE SYSTEM (FRS): A centralized banking system in the U.S. under a Board of Governors with supervisory powers over twelve Federal Reserve Banks, each a central bank for its district, and about 6,000 member banks. The System was established in 1913 to develop a currency which would fluxuate with business demands, and to regulate the member banks of each district.

FIDUCIARY: Of, having to do with, or involving a confidence or trust, as in a broker/client relationship.

FINANCING AND ADMINISTRATION: A specific dual function in business and a specified work area in Subdivesting.

FIXTURES: Any of the fittings or furnishings of real property that is attached, annexed, or installed in the building and ordinarily considered legally a part of it. Examples are furnaces, wall-to-wall carpeting, plumbing fixtures, and hot water heaters.

FLAME: A code word formed from key letters of six proven success principles: Profiting from FAILURE, LEADERSHIP, Definite AIM, ACCURATE Thought, Going the extra MILE, and ENTHUSIASM. Nine other principles are found in the word, FLAME.

FLOOD PLAIN: A plain along a river or tributary, formed from sediment deposited by floods.

FORECLOSURE: The legal process and forced sale of property by a mortgagee or other lien creditor to deprive a mortgagor in default from redeeming the mortgage through resumption of regular payments.

FORFEITURE: The act of giving up or losing money and/or other valuable consideration through failure to comply with specified conditions in a contract, option agreement, or other legal document.

FREEHOLD: An estate in land held for life or with the right to pass it on through inheritance.

FREE LANCE: A person who is not under contract for regular work but sells his services to any buyer. Examples are writers, artists, consultants, actors, etc.

FROSTLINE: The limitation of penetration of soil by frost. In building construction, footings that do not penetrate this depth are in danger of movement.

GAP FINANCING: Loan money advanced to cover a borrower's temporary needs until permanent financing can be arranged. For example, the developer of a shopping center may be required to achieve a certain occupancy level before his lender will grant a permanent loan. Gap financing is often a solution to the developer's interim needs.

GENERAL WARRANTY DEED: A deed carrying the seller's warranty that title is good in fee, that it is free and clear of all liens and encumbrances, and giving the grantor's assurance that he will defend the title against the claims of all persons.

GOAL DEFINITION: In success motivation, a clear and concise statement of the goals one hopes to achieve over a given period of time.

GOAL ORIENTATION: Awareness of and familiarization with one's goals as they relate to a given situation or environment, specifically a mental attitude in which a goal plan is pre-eminent.

GOAL PLODDING: A term used to define vague and sluggish thinking in the establishment of a goal plan.

GOLDEN RULE: The precept that one should behave toward others as he would want others to behave toward him. (Matt. 7:12; Luke 6:31); also, one of the 15 principal success attributes expounded on by Napoleon Hill and found endemic in the successful men he studied.

GRANTEE: A person or party to whom a grant is given, as a deed to real property.

GRAVITY FLOW: The supplying of a substance (such as water) by force of gravity alone. In rural areas, a well or spring may be so positioned above the dwelling that a free flow is established, thus eliminating the need for a pump.

GRAZING RIGHTS: The legal right or privilege granted by one party to another for the grantee to feed his animals on the growing grass, herbage, or pasture of the granter.

GROSS INCOME MULTIPLIER (GIM): A figure or ratio computed by dividing the annual gross income of a rental property into the sales price. This figure, when multiplied by gross income, can also be useful in estimating market value on unsold rental properties.

HARD MONEY: A term describing cash down payments and payments on the principal portion of a loan (as opposed to interest). This money has the effect of improving the payor's equity or ownership position and is generally not tax deductible.

HEALTH PERMIT: Written authorization from the local or regional health department to proceed with the installation of a septic system or other method of sewage disposal within specified design limits and on an approved site adjacent to a dwelling or other building.

HIGHEST AND BEST USE: A land use that will legally, possibly, and probably produce the best net return or give the greatest value to a parcel of real property over a specific period of time, while preserving its utility and present element of risk.

HOMESTEAD EXEMPTION: A law exempting a homestead (real estate occupied by an owner as a house) from seizure or forced sale to meet general debts, excluding mortgages and tax liens. In certain states this law has been expanded to include exemption from some or all property taxes.

HUD: An agency of the federal government known officially as the Housing and Urban Development Agency. The Office of Interstate Land Sales Registration (OILSR) is a division of HUD.

HYPOCHONDRIA: Abnormal anxiety over one's health, often with imaginary illnesses and severe melancholy; also, a symptom of one of man's seven basic fears: Fear of Illness.

IMAGINATION: One of the 15 principal success attributes expounded on by Napoleon Hill and found endemic in the successful men he studied.

IMPOUNDS: Funds or payments taken from a mortgagor and held by a lender or fiduciary for purposes of paying property taxes, assessments and insurance. This money can be withheld from mortgage payments to further protect the mortgagee against adverse claims and increased risk resulting from non-payment of taxes or insurance.

IMPROVED LAND: Land on which construction or development work has been initiated or completed. The term can apply to land improved by roads, sewage and water lines, homes, shell cabins, and other buildings or outbuildings.

IMPROVEMENTS: A change or addition to land or real property, such as a sewer, fence, roads, etc. to make it more valuable.

INACCURATE THOUGHT PATTERNS: In success motivation and self-improvement, a series of negative attitudes resulting from fear, tension, self-induced illness, and ignorance which, if allowed to dominate the more positive attitudes, can result in personal failure.

INFINITE INTELLIGENCE: A being having mental ability beyond measure or comprehension, such as the Christian God.

INGRESS: The right or permission to enter a given property; also, access to enter.

INJUNCTION: A writ or order from a court prohibiting a person or group from carrying out a given action, or ordering a given action to be done.

INSTALLMENT NOTE: A debt instrument providing for payments at regular times over a specified period.

INTERIM FINANCING: A temporary loan, usually for construction, that is to be repaid from the proceeds of a permanent loan.

INTESTATE: A person's legal status when he has died without leaving a will or last testament.

INVOLUNTARY LIEN: A lien, such as taxes, a special assessment, or a judgement, imposed upon a property without the owner's consent.

JOINT TENANCY: One of several forms of tenure in which two or more persons hold in concurrent ownership the same estate in realty or personalty and agree that upon the death of one joint tenant the full title to the estate remains in the surviving joint tenants and finally in the last survivor.

JOINT VENTURE: An undertaking, such as an investment or property development, in which two or more persons or organizations agree to share the benefits and risks.

JUDGEMENT LIEN: A lien on property resulting from a court decree in favor of a creditor.

KICKBACK: A giving back of part of the money received as payment, commission, etc.

LABOR AND MATERIAL RELEASE: A written statement given to a developer by laborers and materialmen who agree to waive their rights under any mechanic's liens.

LAND ACQUISITION AND DEVELOPMENT: A specific function in business enterprise and a specified work area in Subdivesting.

LAND ACQUISITION CHECK LIST: In Subdivesting, a series of critical questions to be asked and answered during the land acquisition process. An evaluation of these answers is a prerequisite to sound decision-making.

LAND COST: The cost of land after deducting the estimated or real value of any buildings, appurtenances, and improvements; also, the cost of raw land, including recording fees, escrow costs, related interest, and property taxes prior to construction.

LAND DEVELOPMENT LOAN: A loan given to a developer to cover specified costs connected with land improvements. The loan is generally secured by a mortgage.

LAND HUSTLER: A derogatory term generally used to describe high-pressure land salesmen and fast-buck developers.

LAND LOAN: A loan granted to the purchaser of raw land and secured by the property.

Generally, this loan is paid off or subordinated by a construction loan.

LAND SALES CONTRACT: A contract for the purchase of land on an installment basis, with the title remaining in the seller until the purchase price of the land has been paid and the terms of the contract fulfilled.

LEACH FIELD: The ground area surrounding a septic system into which liquid waste passes before dissipating into the soil. Where drainage is not rapid, a series of ditches is dug to accept fluid through a fill of sand and stone.

LEADERSHIP: One of the 15 principal success attributes expounded on by Napoleon Hill and found endemic in the successful men he studied.

LEADERSHIP QUALITIES: The characteristic features known to exist in effective leaders. Examples are self-control, ability to delegate, sense of justice, etc.

LEGAL DESCRIPTION: The written legal representation of property that enables it to be located on approved recorded maps and government surveys.

LEVERAGE: A means of obtaining a potentially greater rate of return on capital investment through the use of borrowed funds. When purchasing real property, greater leverage is obtained when there is a comparatively low down payment relative to loan size.

LIEN: A claim on the property of another for the payment of a just debt.

LIFE ESTATE: An estate or interest in property held only during or measured by the term of the life of a specified natural person.

LIFE'S TRUE REWARDS: Those intangible benefits from life aside from material gains. Examples are: Freedom from fear, Good health, Hope for the future, Love of one's work, etc.

LIKE-KIND PROPERTY: A term largely used to describe property that can be exchanged or traded to gain exemption from capital gains taxation. Like-kind property can include all real estate, except that owned by a dealer.

LIMITED PARTNERSHIP: An association of two or more persons in a business enterprise in which some partners' contributions and liabilities are limited.

LINK: One division (1/100) of a surveyor's chain, equal to 66/100 ft.

LINKAGE: A bondage between two or more land uses that spurs the movement of goods or people between them.

LINK FINANCING: Additional financing often obtained by borrowers when lenders require compensating balances in checking accounts. For example, if a bank insists on a compensating balance of $20,000 before granting a loan of $100,000, then link financing of $20,000 may be further required by the borrower in order to obtain the loan.

LIQUIDITY: The quality or state of possessing liquid assets; also, the ease and readiness with which assets can be converted to cash relative to the value of the investment.

LIS PEN DENS: Notice that a suit is pending and that, under law, a court located where the notice has been recorded will hear the case.

LISTING: An agreement, usually in writing, between a real estate broker and a client for the sale, lease, or rent of property. Authority is defined in the type of listing agreement, such as an Exclusive Right to Sell or an Exclusive Agency. A listing can also authorize a broker to buy, lease, or locate property for a client.

LIVING TOOLS: The essential parts or qualities of a person through which he lives or operates his life. Specifically: The body, brain, heart, and soul.

LOAN COMMITMENT: The written promise from a lender to a borrower to grant a loan of a specified amount over a certain period at an agreed upon interest rate. Often there is a charge by the lender for this commitment.

LOAN FEE: Often called points, this fee is a charge by the lender for making the loan and is generally used to compensate the lender for rising money costs. Generally, this charge is based on a percentage of the loan.

LOAN TO FACILITATE: In a general sense, this is a loan given a purchaser to facilitate the purchase of reposessed property held by the lender. A thrift institution – not in the business of buying and selling property – will often grant very favorable terms to prospective buyers.

LOAN/VALUE RATIO (LVR): The proportion of a mortgage loan relative to the appraised value of the property. For example, if a property is appraised at $80,000, and a loan of $60,000 is approved, then the LVR is 75% ($60,000/$80,000).

LOCATION, LOCATION, LOCATION: An item given a numerical score on the FEASIBILITY CHECK LIST used in Subdivesting and referring to the economic value of a property to its environment or surroundings. For example, an easily accessible property, having good exposure and many desirable qualities, could be rated high in the category of Location.

LOCK-IN PERIOD: A length of time during which prepayment on a note is not allowed by the lender. During this period, a borrower is prohibited from selling or otherwise transferring the property secured by the note.

LOT: A distinct plot of ground.

M.A.I.: A designation used by appraisers who are members of the American Institute of Appraisers of the National Association of Real Estate Boards.

MARGINAL LAND: Land of questionable use value.

MARGIN OF SECURITY: The lender's margin between the amount he has loaned and the appraised value of the property.

MARKETABLE TITLE: A title free and clear of all liens and encumbrances which can be readily transferred.

MARKET ANALYSIS: A study designed to predict changes in the types and amounts of real estate facilities needed within a given community or area. For example, a market analysis for a condominium development would include information on the number of existing units, the demand for condominiums (present and future) and pricing factors.

MARKET PRICE: The amount received by a seller for his property regardless of outside pressures and influences.

MARSHLAND: A tract of soft, wet land, usually treeless and characterized by grasses and cattails.

MASTER-MIND GROUP: A team of cooperative, enthusiastic, and energetic persons assembled by a leader for purposes of accomplishing specific goals, achieving greater success, or maximizing material gains through the exchange of ideas and the concentration of effort.

MASTER PLAN: A basic comprehensive plan for dealing with the effects on a community of social and economic change. Incorporated in the plan are ways and means of adjusting to the changing situation.

METES AND BOUNDS: A method of legally describing the boundaries of land by directions and distances.

MINERAL RIGHTS: The legal right or title to all or to specified minerals in a given tract; also, the right to explore for and extract such minerals or to receive a royalty for them.

MOBILE HOME: A large trailer outfitted as a home meant to be parked more or less permanently at a location.

MORTGAGE: The pledge of real property to a creditor as security for a debt or obligation.

MORTGAGE BANKER: A person or firm in the business of making mortgage loans, frequently with the intent of selling the loans to institutional lenders, but often reserving the right to service the mortgages for a fee.

MORTGAGE BROKER: A firm or individual acting as a middleman between the borrower and lender and who receives a fee for his services.

MORTGAGE COMMITMENT: (See Loan Commitment.)

MORTGAGEE: The person or party to whom a mortgage is given; the lender.

MORTGAGE INSURANCE: Insurance obtained by or on behalf of the lender to protect him against any financial loss in the event of default.

MORTGAGOR: The person or party giving the mortgage; the borrower.

MOTIVES (10 BASIC): The 10 basic causes of human action; specifically: Self-Preservation, Life After Death, Freedom of Body and Mind, Recognition of Self-Expression, Material Gain, Emotion of Love, Emotion of Fear, Emotion of Sex, Emotion of Anger, Emotion of Hate.

MULTIPLE LISTING: A written agreement (usually an Exclusive Right to Sell) between a real estate broker and client which has been placed in a pool of listings maintained by an organization to which the listing broker belongs.

NATIONAL PARK OR FOREST: An area of special scenic, historical, scientific, or recreational importance set aside and maintained by a national government. As a rule, hunting and the harvesting of timber is not allowed in National Parks, but can be permitted in National Forests.

NEGATIVE CASH FLOW: A financial situation in income producing properties when outgo exceeds income.

NEGATIVE EMOTIONS: Strong negative feelings that can assume control of a person's mind and actions resulting in illness and personal failure. Specifically: Hate, Envy, Greed, Fear, Superstition, Revenge, and Anger.

NET LEASE: A lease under which the tenant assumes only partial responsibility for direct expenses such as taxes, insurance, and maintenance. Under a Net-Net Lease, these additional expenses are customarily paid by the lessee. A Net-Net-Net Lease implies that all expenses connected with the rental property are paid by the lessee.

NET LISTING: An agreement between a seller and his broker/agent that the agent may keep as his commission all monies obtained for the seller over and above the agreed upon selling price.

NONRECOURSE NOTE: A note signed by the debtor which carries no personal responsibility in the event of default. Whe the note is secured by real estate, the property becomes the sole security for the debt. (See Exculpatory Clause.)

NOTE: A written promise to pay a certain sum of money to a certain person or bearer on demand or on a specified date. Also called a Promissory Note, the instrument can provide for installment payments and customarily calls for a specified rate of interest.

NOTE PROCEEDS: A term generally taken to mean the sum of money left over after a note is discounted.

NOTICE OF COMPLETION: Notification by the builder that construction is complete. This notice is recorded, and any mechanic's liens must be filed within a prescribed period thereafter, generally 30 to 60 days.

NOTICE OF DEFAULT: Recorded notification that a default has occured in a mortgage or deed of trust. (See Foreclosure.)

NOTICE OF NONRESPONSIBILITY: Notification by an owner that he is not responsible for any debts owed to contractors and materialmen and that his property is thereby relieved of any mechanic's liens. If all other legal conditions are met, the property owner posts this notice on his property and records it in the county where his land is located.

NOTICE TO QUIT: An eviction notice given by a landlord or his agent.

OBJECTIVITY FACTOR: In Subdivesting, the ability to analyse deals without bias or prejudice — an acquired state of mind where decisions are reached dispassionately.

OBSOLESCENSE: Loss of value and usefulness due to economic and functional change, but not attributed to deterioration.

OFFSITE COSTS: Those raw land improvement costs not directly related to building construction; specifically: Roads, curbs, gutters, sidewalks, etc. In the sales and marketing of improved or unimproved lots, the term can be applied to those costs not incurred on or at the development itself.

OILSR (OFFICE OF INTERSTATE LAND SALES REGISTRATION): A division of HUD.

ONSITE COSTS: Generally meant to include those costs directly related to the construction of a building or buildings on raw land. In the development and sale of improved or unimproved lots, these costs can mean any and all expenses incurred on or at the development site.

OPEN-END LOAN: A secured loan that provides for the borrower to obtain additional sums of money at various times, thus allowing a continuous source of credit.

OPEN-END MORTGAGE: A mortgage or trust deed under which the borrower can increase or renew his debt at various times, with the property standing as security against the outstanding obligation.

OPEN LISTING: An agreement between a real estate broker and a client giving the broker a non-exclusive right to sell the listed property. Any number of open listings may be given out, but only the procuring broker is entitled to a commission.

O.P.M.: An acronym for OTHER PEOPLE'S MONEY.

OPTION: The right, acquired for a consideration, to buy, sell, or lease something at a fixed price; also, to sign or renew a contract within a specified time.

OPTION LISTING: A listing agreement in which the broker reserves an option to buy the property.

ORDINANCE: A local governmental statute or regulation, such as a zoning ordinance.

ORDINARY INCOME: Personal income subject to federal taxation at the regular rate; examples are: Salaries, professional fees, commissions, rents, royalties, interest, wages, and dividends not considered capital gains.

PACKAGING: The arranging for or actual performance of certain activities required to get a development off the ground. A packager will arrange for, coordinate, or handle such diverse activities as market research, land evaluation and acquisition, project design and concept, architecture, engineering, zoning, and securing financing.

PARTITION: The legal process of dividing property and giving separate title to those who previously had joint or common title.

PATENT: Title to public land granted by the U.S. Government to an individual or group.

PERCENTAGE LEASE: A lease where rent is based on the amount of business conducted by the lessee. The lease is usually structured to provide a minimum rental fee against a percentage of gross business.

PERCOLATION (PERK) TEST: A test of soil conditions, sanctioned or performed by local health authorities, to determine if the ground will readily accept and dissipate the liquid wastes from a septic system. Holes are dug at various spots and filled with water. If the rate of absorption is satisfactory, the test is generally considered positive.

PERFORMANCE BOND: Insurance, generally required by a client, that a contractor perform as agreed under the terms of his contact. Municipal authorities usually require such a bond before contracting for public construction.

PERSONAL PROPERTY: Any property that is not considered real property.

PHYSICAL CONCERNS: Generally meant to include those desires in life that satisfy the human body as opposed to the mind. These pleasures, in the broader sense, can be the main impetus behind the acquisition of material possessions such as cars, home, boat, money, etc; though, once acquired, these things continue to affect and be affected by the other components in one's life: Mental Attitude, Social Involvements, and Spiritual Needs.

PLANNING COMMISSION: A group of people, generally appointed by elected officials, who are responsible under state or local law for the preparation and adoption of measures dealing with the orderly development of land within its jurisdiction. The ultimate objective of this group is a comprehensive, long-term growth plan which will be sanctioned by local elected officials, as representatives of the public will.

PLAT: A map or plan (usually a survey) of a piece of land showing divisions (into lots), property lines, easements, etc. and entered into the public records, as for a subdivision.

PLEASANT PERSONALITY: One of the 15 principal success attributes expounded on by Napoleon Hill and found endemic in the successful men he studied.

POINTS: A term describing a loan fee. Each point represents 1% of the loan amount. (See Discount Points.)

POND: A body of standing water smaller than a lake, often artificially formed.

POPULATION DENSITY: A term relating to the average number of permanent residents within a given area, such as per-square-mile.

POSITIVE EMOTIONS: Strong positive feelings that allow you to retain control over your own mind and actions, resulting in personal achievement, happiness, success, and better mental and physical health; specifically: Desire, Faith, Love, Sex, Enthusiasm, Romance, and Hope.

POSITIVE MENTAL ATTITUDE: A frame of mind where the positive emotions exercise control.

POTABLE WATER: Water that is fit to drink.

POWER OF ATTORNEY: A written statement authorizing another person to act on one's behalf. The person using this statement is customarily called an "attorney-in-fact."

PRELIMINARY PLAT: A tentative map of a subdivision submitted by a developer to local elected and planning officials for study and approval. Often the planning officials must first approve the plan before it can be submitted to local governing officials, such as a County Board of Supervisors. The submission of a final plat follows this first approval.

PREMIUM: In land development, a reward or prize often given to prospective buyers for visiting and touring a project.

PREPAYMENT CLAUSE: A provision in a loan contract that allows the borrower to prepay on the debt under certain conditions. If this clause is described as a "prepayment privilege" then there is no penalty for early payments. Should the contract contain a "prepayment penalty" the borrower must pay a fee (usually expressed as a percent of the debt) for the right to prepay.

PRESCRIPTION: The acquirement of the title or right to something through its continued use or possession over a long period, as with a prescriptive right-of-way.

PRIMARY FINANCING: A loan on real property secured by a first mortgage or deed of trust.

PRIME RATE: The interest rate charged by commercial banks to their prime, or most valued, borrowers.

PRINCIPAL: A person who employs another to act as his agent; also, the capital amount of a loan or investment.

PROCURING CAUSE OF SALE: Where two or more brokers have shown the same property to a buyer, and they both have valid listing agreements, the first broker is generally considered to be the procuring cause of sale, though the commission may be split between them.

PROFITING FROM FAILURE: One of the 15 success attributes expounded on by Napoleon Hill and found endemic in the successful men he studied.

PROJECT COST SHEET: In Subdivesting, a record of development costs broken down into 5 principal areas: Survey and Engineering Fees, Land Preparation, Advertising and Sales, Financing, and Overhead. Cost per lot is figured by adding project costs to raw land cost and dividing by the number of lots.

PROJECT DEVELOPMENT SHEET: In Subdivesting, a record of inspections, tests, follow-ups, actual work, and approvals, from initial location of land through the final subdivision check.

PROMISSORY NOTE: (See Note.)

PROPERTY INSPECTION FORM: In Subdivesting, a form used to record property inspected and considered for purchase and development.

PRORATED EXPENSES: Those expenses such as property taxes and interest that are divided among buyer and seller and based on the actual closing date of the sale.

PUBLIC REPORT: A report issued by a state agency concerned with subdivision control.

Before the sale of lots can commence, some states require designated agencies to check the subdivision's compliance with existing law, and to report any shortcomings. A report to the public is issued when this authority is assured that the developer has installed promised improvements and facilities, or that he has made satisfactory financial arrangements for their completion. An additional concern is that property owners are protected, or made aware of their position with respect to potential default or bankruptcy on the part of the developer.

PURCHASE MONEY MORTGAGE: Essentially this is a mortgage or trust deed given by the purchaser to the seller to secure the full purchase price of the property. In the event of default, the seller can, in some states, seek a deficiency judgement against the purchaser if the property does not bring the amount owed at a foreclosure sale.

QUALITY REFERENCE SHEET: In Subdivesting, a rating system for elements on the FEASIBILITY CHECK LIST to aid in scoring a given project. The sheet explains how to score each element on a scale from Excellent to Poor and gives numerical weight to each quality.

QUIET TITLE: A court action used to clear an impaired title or to establish title.

QUIT CLAIM DEED: A deed or other legal paper in which a person relinquishes to another a claim or title to some property or right without guaranteeing or warranting such title.

RAW LAND: Land that has not been improved by any structure or other work such as roads, sewers, etc.

REAL ESTATE: Land, including the buildings and improvements on it and its natural assets such as minerals, water, etc.

REAL ESTATE INVESTMENT TRUST (REIT): A method of holding real estate in trust form, where investors can enjoy limited liability similar to a corporation. Once it has met Internal Revenue requirements, a REIT has the ability to pass profits to its investors without payment of corporate taxes. At least 100 shareholders must participate in its formation, and most of its capital must be invested in real estate loans and properties, with a substantial part of its income coming from such real estate investments.

REAL PROPERTY: The interests, benefits, and rights that one has in the ownership of real estate, as opposed to personal property. It is the package of rights that confers ownership.

REALTOR: A real estate broker, salesperson, appraiser, etc. who is a member of the National Association of Real Estate Boards.

REBATE: A return of part of an amount paid (as for goods and services) that serves as a reduction or discount.

RECONVEYANCE: The release of specific property from the lien of the mortgage or deed of trust through a deed granted by the mortgagee or trustee of a deed of trust.

RECORDING FEE: A fee charged by counties for entering legal instruments or documents, such as a mortgage or deed, into the public records.

RECOURSE NOTE: A note signed by the debtor which carries personal responsibility beyond the repossession of security or collateral in the even of default. (See Nonrecourse Note.)

RECREATIONAL PROPERTY: In land development, a term used to describe property used primarily for camping and secondary home construction; also, any parcel of real estate mainly utilized by the owner on weekends and vacations.

REDEMPTION: (See Equity of Redemption.)

REFERRAL: In real estate sales, a potential buyer who is directed by an existing property owner to a sales agent.

REFORMATION: The act of correcting mistakes and defects in a deed or document.

REFUNDABLE UTILITY CONTRACT: A written agreement between a developer and a utility company in which the utility company promises to reimburse the developer for the installation of utility extensions such as water, gas, and electric lines. Costs are generally returned from revenues received from the new users.

REGRESSION: In real estate, a term or principle alluding to the decrease in value of certain homes in a particular neighborhood caused by the expected construction or condition of inferior dwellings in that same area. Thus, regression connotes diminished value through disadvantages anticipated in the future, such as a planned low-cost housing development in an area of high-priced homes.

RELEASE CLAUSE: A provision in a deed that allows for divisions or lots to be released from the blanket lien upon payment to the lien holder of a specified amount.

REMAINDER: An estate of expectancy but not in possession, as when land is conveyed by the same deed to one person during his lifetime, and at his death to another and his heirs.

RESCISSION: To revoke, repeal, or cancel, as with a contract to purchase real estate.

RESTRICTIVE COVENANT: A provision in a deed that limits the use and occupancy of real property. Any such provision is binding on subsequent owners of the property.

RETENTIONS: Money held back by contractors or persons receiving services from billings or invoices received during construction to ensure satisfactory completion of the work.

REVERSION: The right of succession, future possession, or enjoyment, as the return of an estate to the grantor and his heirs by operation of law after the period of grant is over.

RIGHT OF SURVIVORSHIP: A distinguishing feature of joint tenancy in which the interest of a deceased joint owner can be acquired by a survivor.

RIGHT-OF-WAY: The right, established by common or statutory law, or ingress and egress over another's property; also, a strip of land set aside for utility easements, railroads, and public roads.

RIPARIAN RIGHTS: Generally, the rights of a owner whose property adjoins a watercourse such as a lake, stream, or river. The right mainly applies to the unobstructed use and enjoyment of these waters by said owner.

ROAD GRADE: The degree of rise and descent of a road surface.

SALABILITY AFTER DEVELOPMENT: An item given a numerical score on the FEASIBILITY CHECK LIST used in Subdivesting and referring to estimated demand for the finished lots and the relative ease with which they are likely to be sold.

SALE CONTRACT: A written agreement between buyer and seller transferring ownership and stipulating price, terms, rights, and obligations of all parties concerned.

SALE-LEASEBACK: The sale of property and subsequent leasing back to the seller by the purchaser.

SALES OF SUBDIVIDED LAND: A specific function in the land development business and a specified work area in Subdivesting.

SAVINGS (HABIT): One of the 15 success attributes expounded on by Napoleon Hill and found endemic in the successful men he studied.

SCENIC EASEMENT: An easement sold or granted by a property owner to a governmental authority or non-profit organization wherein the owner restricts the use of all or part of his property in favor of preserving the scenic and natural beauty. Generally, the owner agrees not to sell to development interests or to develop his property in a way that would conflict with the true intent of the easement.

SCORING KEY: In subdivesting, a table of scores revealing the maximum and recommended numerical weight for the categories Excellent, Good, Fair, and Poor, as used on the FEASIBILITY CHECK LIST and QUALITY REFERENCE SHEET.

SCRIPT: A code word formed from key letters of nine proven success principles. Together with the six principles unlocked by the word, FLAME, a complete 15 point formula of success motivation can be easily remembered and put to use. SCRIPT is the map to the treasures of success: SAVINGS Habit, Self-CONFIDENCE, Self-CONTROL,

CONCENTRATION and Persistence, COOPERATION, Golden RULE, IMAGINATION, Pleasant PERSONALITY, and TOLERANCE and Patience. FLAME, the companion word, illuminates the way to success. (See FLAME.)

SECONDARY FINANCING: A loan obtained on property that is subordinate to the first mortgage or deed of trust and as a second mortgage or trust.

SECTION OF LAND: A 640 acre parcel of land comprising one square mile.

SECURED PARTY: Any party possessing secured evidence of debt. Thus a mortgagee could be considered a secured party, as could a conditional seller or a pledgee.

SEIZIN: Legal possession, especially of a freehold estate.

SELECTIVITY: In Subdivesting, the ability to choose profitable deals; a cultivated quality requiring the absence of extraneous pressures during periods of decision.

SELF-CONFIDENCE FORMULA: (See ADMIT.)

SELF-CONTROL: One of the 15 principal success attributes expounded on by Napoleon Hill and found endemic in the successful men he studied.

SELF-HYPNOSIS: Psychic act, characterized by a sleep-like condition, in which a state of altered consciousness is self-induced and where subject is responsive to sub-conscious suggestions made to himself. (See AUTOSUGGESTION.)

SEPTIC SYSTEM CHECK LIST: Specific considerations with regard to soils, topography, and proximity to dwellings and sources of water that should be evaluated before the installation of a septic system. In most cases, the local health authorities must approve both site and plans before installation.

SEPTIC TANK: A concrete tank to collect solid wastes. The tank is buried underground and is connected to a field of individual disposal trenches. When full, the tank is pumped out by a septic tank service truck. This method of sewage disposal is called a septic system.

SETBACK LINES: The prescribed distance that a building must be setback in relation to the perimeter of the property.

SETTLEMENT COSTS: Charges that a buyer or seller must pay at closing such as insurance and tax payments, special assessments, and sales commissions. Sometimes confused with and differentiated from closing costs, which involve attorney's fees, recording and escrow fees, costs of credit reports, etc.

SHERIFF'S DEED: A deed given to a purchaser who buys at a court-ordered foreclosure sale to satisfy a judgement. At best, the grantee receives only such title as the mortgagor had at the time he originally made the obligation.

SIGNATURE CAPITAL: Money invested in a business venture for which the only collateral was a written promise to repay the loan.

SITE: Generally, a parcel of land suitable for building that fronts on a road and has access to utilities.

SOFT MONEY: Prepaid interest, forfeitable option money, and the interest portion of an installment debt; generally, any money that does not improve the equity position of the payor.

SOIL MAP: A map describing the soils within a given area, with specific emphasis on their suitability for crops, building construction, and sewage disposal.

SOURCE BOOK: In Subdivesting, a note book containing records of potential land deals and the value of property within certain areas at specified periods of time. Data can be obtained from personal contact, newspaper advertisements, or real estate agency listings.

SPECIAL ASSESSMENT: A charge against real property by a public or quasi-public authority to cover the proportionate share of improvements such as streets and sewer lines. These charges can be imposed by law or covenant.

SPECIFIC PERFORMANCE: The exact performance of a contract or a court order enjoining it.

STAGNANT WATER: Water that has become foul from lack of movement.

STANDBY COMMITMENT: A promise from a lender to make a temporary loan to a borrower if he cannot obtain an immediate permanent loan or other satisfactory financing. There is a charge for the commitment, usually based on a percentage of the loan.

STAR ROUTE: Postal route between one city or town and another over which mail is transported in bulk by a private carrier under contact.

START-UP COSTS: Those costs — usually non-recurring — connected with getting a project under way.

STATEMENT OF EXCHANGE: In success motivation, a written statement of intent to perform to the best, highest, and fullest of your ability for the benefit of those receiving your services. The statement should be repeated orally at least twice a day following your oral recitation of a STATEMENT OF PHYSICAL GOALS.

STATEMENT OF PHYSICAL GOALS: An affirmation of faith in your ability and intent to achieve certain physical or material goals within specified periods of time. The statement should be written down and orally repeated at least twice a day, preferably in the morning upon arising and at night before going to bed.

STATUTE OF LIMITATIONS: A statute limiting the period within which a specific legal action may be taken. Title to real estate by adverse possession is gained under this statute.

SUBDIVESTING: Making maximum profits from a minimum investment in the development and quick sale of rural land which, in turn, can be resold at a profit.

SUBDIVISION: A piece of land divided into smaller parcels for sale.

SUBJECT TO MORTGAGE: A term used to describe the assumption of title to real estate without any obligation to the holder of the promissory note. In the event of foreclosure, the grantee loses only that amount he has paid in. The original maker of the note is held responsible for the balance due on the mortgage.

SUBLEASE: A lease granted by a lessee to another person of all or part of the property.

SUBMERSIBLE PUMP: An electrically-operated pump installed near the bottom of a well for purposes of pumping water to ground level, often into a pressure tank from which the flow is controlled and regulated.

SUBORDINATION: The act of relinquishing a prior position on a mortgage or deed of trust, often in return for compensation or other favors. For example, the holder of a first mortgage may agree to take second position in a refinancing if he can retain a certain favorable rate of interest.

SUBROGATION: The substitution of one creditor for another, along with a transferrence of the claims and rights of the old creditor.

SULF-R WATER: In some areas of the country, well water may produce an odor and taste resembling sulf-r. Though there is usually no health hazard, this condition can usually be corrected through the use of a filter.

SUMP PUMP: A pump used to remove collected liquid from a pit, trench, or cellar.

SURETY: A person who makes himself liable for another's debts, defaults or obligations, etc.

SURVEY: To determine the location, form, or boundaries of a tract of land by measuring the lines and angles in accordance with the principles of geometry and trigonometry.

SYNDICATION: A grouping of individuals or corporations to carry out a business venture requiring capital investment, as with a real estate project.

TAKE-OUT LOAN: A permanent loan or mortgage given to finance a structure upon completition of certain improvements. Loan proceeds are used primarily to pay off the construction loan.

TAX ESCALATOR: A provision in a lease whereby tenant agrees to pay higher rent based on rising tax rates.

TAX-LOSS CARRYOVER: The amount of tax loss allowed to be carried over for three years or back for two years. The loss can be taken as a deduction against other taxable income and is computed by deducting interest paid and depreciation taken from net operating income. To gain this tax advantage, the deductions must, of cource, exceed net operating income.

TAX SALE: A forced sale of real estate by local taxing authorities to cover delinquent taxes.

TENANCY BY THE ENTIRETY: The principle that husband and wife are legally regarded as one person on matters of real estate ownership. Both must consent to any disposition of the property, and the property passes to the survivor upon the death of either one.

TENANCY IN COMMON: When two or more persons own property without the joint right of survivorship. The respective interests are undivided, yet need not be equal.

TENANT FARMER: A person who farms another's land, usually for a share of the crops; also, an individual who rents land from another for the use of land, with payment being made in cash, services, or crops.

TESTATE: Having made and left a legally valid will.

TESTATOR: A person who has made a will, especially one who has died leaving a valid will.

TITLE: Evidence of ownership rights.

TITLE INSURANCE: A policy issued by a title insurance company which offers protection against financial loss due to defects in the title to real property which were unknown or undiscovered at the time of purchase.

TITLE SEARCH: A search through the public records, laws, and court decisions, to obtain the current facts about the title to specific real estate.

TOLERANCE (and PATIENCE): One of the 15 success attributes expounded on by Napoleon Hill and found endemic in the successful men he studied.

TOPOGRAPHIC MAP: A map showing the surface features of a region.

TREASURY BILL: A short-term obligation of the U.S. Treasury, usually maturing in 91 days, bearing no interest and sold periodically on the open market on a discount basis.

TRUSTEE: A person or institution holding and administering property under a trust.

TRUSTOR: One who grants property to a trustee.

UNEARNED INCREMENT: An increase in the value of real estate due to influences beyond any effort of the owner. Increases in population or inflationary pressures could stir a rise in value.

U.S. SOIL CONSERVATION SERVICE (SCS): An agency of the Department of Agriculture. Its main purpose is to assist farmers and ranchers in land use and to help prevent soil erosion and flood loss. Other functions include soil surveys, and the development of technical plans for individual farms, including the lending of specialized equipment to carry out conservation practices. The agency also assists and advises local authorities charged with enforcing soil and erosion control legislation.

USURY: The act or practice of lending money at excessive or unlawfully high interest rates.

VISUALIZATION: The formation of mental images of things not present to the sight. This process is largely promoted by success motivators and successful people in all walks of life as essential to the achievement of goals.

VOLUNTARY LIEN: A lien placed on property with the owner's approval or as a result of a consenting act by the owner.

WAREHOUSING: An activity largely used by mortgage bankers where mortgages or trust deed notes are held in inventory for future sale. To finance this inventory, the "warehouser" borrows short term and repays from proceeds of periodic sales.

WARRANTY DEED: A deed to real estate in which grantor gives his formal assurance that he is, in fact, the legal owner. He further guarantees that he will defend the title against all adverse claims.

WATER RIGHTS: Rights granted by a property owner to another for the use of a water facility not on the grantee's land. Such uses could include livestock watering, fishing, boating, and swimming privileges, or the actual piping of water from the grantor to the grantee.

WATER TABLE: The level below which the ground is saturated with water. Often a high water table can hamper building construction and can preclude the installation of a septic system. Drilled wells are also influenced by the water level in a given area.

WRAPAROUND MORTGAGE OR TRUST DEED: A financing technique used when additional financing is obtained that overlaps any existing obligations. The new mortgage is junior to the prior loans and is secured by a debt that includes all loans combined. For example, the owner of a land development has existing loans totalling $1,000,000 secured by all the remaining lots in his development. A lender advances him an additional $250,000 and takes a "wraparound" mortgage on the entire project. In the process, the lender assumes responsibility for paying off the prior loans. The new mortgage is for $1,250,000.

YIELD RATE: The percentage rate of return expected or earned on an investment.

ZONING ORDINANCE: (See ORDINANCE.)

ZONING VARIANCE: Official permission to bypass existing zoning laws, in many cases because strict enforcement would cause undue hardship on the applicant.

APPENDIX C

SELECTED BIBLIOGRAPHY
AND
SUGGESTED FURTHER READING

How to Make Big Profits in Real Estate

Barr, *Master Guide to High-Income Real Estate Selling;* Executive Reports Corp.
Goodkin, *The Goodkin Guide to Winning in Real Estate;* David McKay Co., Inc.
Hatfield, *The Weekend Real Estate Investor;* McGraw-Hill Book Co.
Lowry, *How You Can Become Financially Independent by Investing in Real Estate;* Simon and Schuster.
Moses, *How to Use the Inside Secrets of a Super Land Salesman to Make Big Money in Any Kind of Real Estate Sales;* Executive Reports Corp.
Nickerson, *How I Turned $1,000 Into Three Million in Real Estate - - in My Spare Time;* Simon and Schuster.
Winnikoff, *How to Make a Fortune in Real Estate;* Wilshire Book Co.

How to Achieve Success and Riches in Life

Addington, *All About Goals and How to Achieve Them;* DeVorss and Co.
Carnegie, *How to Win Friends and Influence People;* Simon and Schuster.
Clason, *The Richest Man in Babylon;* Bantam Books, Inc.
Collier, *The Secret of the Ages;* Robert Collier Book Corp.
Conwell, *Acres of Diamonds;* Hallmark Editions.
Cook, *Success, Motivation, and the Scriptures;* Broadman Press.
Emerson, *Emerson's Essays: First and Second Series Complete;* Apollo.
Getty, *The Golden Age;* Robert Collier Book Corp.
Haddock, *Power of Will;* Robert Collier Book Corp.
Hill, *Grow Rich with Peace of Mind;* Fawcett Publications.
Hill, *Laws of Success;* Success Unlimited, Inc.
Hill, *The Master-Key to Riches;* Fawcett-Publications.
Hill, *Think and Grow Rich;* Hawthorn Books, Inc.
Hill, *You Can Work Your Own Miracles;* Fawcett Publications.
Hill and Keown, *Succeed and Grow Rich Through Persuasion;* Hawthorn Books, Inc.
Hill and Stone, *Success Through a Positive Mental Attitude;* Prentice-Hall, Inc.

Lorayne, *Secrets of Mind Power;* Frederick Fell Publications, Inc.
Mandino, *The Greatest Salesman in the World;* Frederick Fell Publications, Inc.
Mandino, *The Greatest Secret in the World;* Bantam Books, Inc.
Schneider, *Benjamin Franklin Autobiography and Selections From His Other Writings;* Bobbs-Merrill Co.
Schuller, *Move Ahead with Possibility Thinking;* Spire Books.
Shook and Bingaman, *Total Commitment;* Frederick Fell Publications, Inc.
Stone, *The Success System That Never Fails;* Prentice-Hall, Inc.

All You Need to Know About Country Property

Boudreau, *Buying Country Land;* Collier-Macmillan Publishers.
Kinney, *How to Find and Finance a Great Country Place;* Parker Pub. Co., Inc.
Leavy, *Successful Small Farms;* Structures Pub. Co.
Paulson, *The Great Land Hustle;* Henry Regnery Co.
Price, *Buying Country Property;* Avenel Books.
Scher, *Finding and Buying Your Place in the Country;* Collier-Macmillan Publishers.
Tobe, *Security from Five Acres;* The Provoker Press.
U.S. Department of Agriculture, *Living on a Few Acres;* U.S. Government Printing Office.

How to Build Wealth Through Raw Land Deals

Bitney, *How to Buy Recreational Land for Profit;* Prentice-Hall, Inc.
Healy, *How to Build Quick Value in Raw Land;* Executive Reports Corp.
Henry, *How to Profitably Buy and Sell Land;* John Wiley and Sons.
Nicely, *How to Reap Riches from Raw Land;* Prentice-Hall, Inc.

How to Increase Your Income Through Tax Shelters and Estate Planning

Drollinger, *Tax Shelters and Tax Free Income for Everyone;* Epic Publications, Inc.
Greer, *The Real Estate Investor and the Federal Income Tax;* Ronald Press Publications, John Wiley and Sons.
Looney, *Estate Planning for Farmers;* Doane Agricultural Service, Inc.

Nicholas, *How to Form Your Own Corporation Without a Lawyer for Under $50;* Enterprise Publishing Co.

How to Finance Real Estate and Obtain Easy Credit

Cummings, *Complete Guide to Real Estate Financing;* Prentice-Hall, Inc.
Nickerson, *Accounting Handbook for Non-Accountants;* CBI Publishing Co., Inc.
Skousen, *The 1979 Insider's Banking and Credit Almanac;* Kephart Communications, Inc.

How to Pick Men and Read People

Mar, *Face Reading;* The New American Library, Inc.
McQuaig, *How to Pick Men;* Frederick Fell Pub., Inc.
Nierenberg/Calero, *How to Read a Person Like a Book;* Hawthorn Books, Inc.
Puryear, *Nineteen Stars;* Coiner Publications, LTD.
Whiteside, *Face Language;* Frederick Fell Pub., Inc.

How to Appraise Farm Real Estate

Suter, *The Appraisal of Farm Real Estate;* Interstate Printers and Publishers, Inc.

Where to Buy Advertising Art, Copywriting, and Direct Mail Promotional Services

Bowker, *Literary Market Place;* R.R. Bowker Company.

How to Maximize Your Profits Through Effective Advertising

Baker, *Visual Persuasion;* McGraw-Hill Book Co.
Caples, *Making Ads Pay;* Dover Publications, Inc.

Caples, *Tested Advertising Methods;* Prentice-Hall, Inc.
Collier, *The Robert Collier Letter Book;* Prentice-Hall, Inc.
Della Femina, *From Those Wonderful Folks Who Brought You Pearl Harbor;* Pocket Books.
Fox/Wood, *The Best in Advertising Campaigns;* RC Publications, Inc./Watson-Guptill Publications.
Martineau, *Motivation in Advertising;* McGraw-Hill Book Co.
McLean, *The Basics of Copy;* Ed McLean.
McLean, *The Basics of Testing;* Ed McLean.
Ogilvy, *Confessions of an Advertising Man;* Dell Pub. Co., Inc.
Reeves, *Reality in Advertising;* Alfred A. Knopf.
Sackheim, *My First Sixty Years in Advertising;* Prentice-Hall, Inc.
Schwartz, *Breakthrough Advertising;* Prentice-Hall, Inc.
Stansfield, *Advertising Manager's Handbook;* The Dartnell Corp.
Stone, *Successful Direct Marketing Methods;* Crain Books.
Watkins, *100 Greatest Advertisements;* Dover Publications, Inc.
White, *John Caples: Adman;* Crain Books.

Useful Publications and Newsletters for Informed Subdivestors

Magazines

Advertising Age; Crain Communications, Inc.
Direct Marketing Magazine; Hoke Communications, Inc.
Farm Journal; Farm Journal, Inc.
Free Enterprise; Capitalist Reporter, Inc.
Progressive Farmer; The Progressive Farmer Co.
Real Estate Review; Warren, Gorham and Lamont, Inc.
Success Unlimited; Success Unlimited, Inc.
The Mother Earth News; The Mother Earth News, Inc.
U.S. News and World Report; U.S. News and World Report, Inc.

Newspapers

Selected Regional and County Newspapers
Wall Street Journal

Newsletters

Daily News Digest; Research Publications.

Doane's Agricultural Report; Doane.
Personal Finance; Kephart Communications, Inc.
World Money Analyst; WMA.

All You Need to Know About General Real Estate

Ring/Dasso, *Real Estate Principles and Practices;* Prentice-Hall, Inc.
Semenow, *Questions and Answers on Real Estate;* Prentice-Hall, Inc.

How to Preserve Your Capital During Inflation and Hard Times

Browne, *You Can Profit From a Monetary Crisis;* Macmillan.
Ruff, *How to Prosper During The Coming Bad Years;* Target Pub.
Sinclair/Schultz, *How The Experts Buy and Sell Gold Bullion, Goldstocks and Gold Coins;* Arlington House Pub.
Skousen, *Mark Skousen's Complete Guide to Financial Privacy;* Kephart Communications.

How to Win The Upper Hand Through Effective Negotiation

Nierenberg, *Creative Business Negotiating;* Hawthorn Books, Inc.
Nierenberg, *The Art of Negotiating;* Hawthorn Books, Inc.
Ringer, *Winning Through Intimidation;* Los Angeles Book Pub. Co.

Books of Inspiration That Can Change Your Life

Common *Bible* (Revised Standard); Collins; or any version.
Grant, *Jesus — An Historian's Review of the Gospels;* Charles Scribner's Sons.
McDowell, *More Than a Carpenter;* Tyndale House Publishers, Inc.
Peale, *The Power of Positive Thinking;* Revell.
Schuller, *Peace of Mind Through Possibility Thinking;* Doubleday.

Secrets of the World's Greatest Salespeople

Bettger, *How I Raised Myself From Failure to Success in Selling;* Prentice-Hall, Inc.
Christensen, *Secrets of the Hard Sell;* Parker Pub. Co., Inc.
Girard, *How to Sell Anything to Anybody;* Simon and Schuster.
Shook, *Ten Greatest Salespersons;* Harper and Row.

APPENDIX D

FEDERAL AND STATE REGULATIONS SUPPLEMENT

1. Will your project require a HUD Filing? If so, will the state accept your effective filing with the Office of Interstate Land Sales Registration (OILSR) in lieu of state filing? Are updated or annual filings required?

2. Do you know how many developed lots constitute a subdivision within your state? What are the exemptions for lot size?

3. Will state inspection of your subdivision be required, or will inspection by smaller jurisdictions be sufficient?

4. Do your buyers have a right-of-rescission period under state law? If so, how long?

5. Will you be required to submit advertising and promotional materials to your state agency for approval?

6. Does your state prohibit or restrict the incoming mailing of sales literature concerning land offerings from outside the state?

7. Can you advertise nationally if you have not registered within your state?

8. What restrictions, if any, are applied to promotions and incentives?

9. Can out-of-state telephone solicitations be made to prospects within your state?

Following is a list of agencies where you can obtain answers to the above questions and other related information:

FEDERAL

Department of Housing and Urban Development (HUD)
Office of Interstate Land Sales Registration
451 7th St. S. W. Room 4130
Washington, D.C. 20410

*STATE AND PROVINCE REGULATORY AGENCIES

United States

Alabama
License Tax Division
Department of Revenue
Montgomery, AL 36104
(205) 832-6740

Real Estate Commission
State Capitol
Montgomery, AL 36130
(205) 832-3266

Alaska
Division of Banking, Securities,
  Small Loans & Corporations
Department of Commerce
Pouch D
Juneau, AK 99801

Arizona
Real Estate Department
1645 West Jefferson
Phoenix, AZ 85007
(602) 271-4347

Arkansas
Real Estate Commission
P. O. Box 3173
101 Main Street
Little Rock, AR 72203
(501) 371-1247

California
Department of Real Estate
714 P Street, Room 1400
Sacramento, CA 95814
(916) 445-8647

Colorado
Real Estate Commission
110 State Services Bldg.
1525 Sherman Street
Denver, Co 80203
(303) 892-2633

Connecticut
Real Estate Commission
90 Washington Street
Hartford, CT 06115
(203) 566-5130

Delaware
Real Estate Commission
Margaret O'Neill Bldg.
Box 1401
Dover, DE 19901
(302) 678-4186

District of Columbia
Real Estate Commission
614 H Street, N. W.
Washington, D. C. 20001
(202) 727-3673

Florida
Division of Florida Land
  Sales & Condominiums
Johns Building
725 S. Bronough Street
Tallahassee, FL 32301
(904) 488-0712

(cont.)

*Reprinted with permission from *The Digest of State Land Sales Regulations*, 1978 Supplement. Copyright 1978 by the Land Development Institute, Ltd., 1401 16th Street, N. W., Washington, D. C. 20036.

Office of the Attorney General
Bur. of Consumer Protection
The Capitol
Tallahassee, FL 32304
(904) 488-4481

Georgia
Land Sales Division
Office of the Secy. of State
State Capitol
Atlanta, GA 30334
(404) 656-2881

State Securities Commission
State Capitol
Atlanta, GA 30334

Hawaii
Professional & Vocational
 Licensing Division
Dept. of Regulatory Agencies
P. O. Box 3469
Honolulu, HI 96801
(808) 548-6520

Idaho
Real Estate Commission
633 North Fourth Street
Boise, ID 83720
(208) 384-3285

Illinois
Asst. Commissioner of
 Land Sales
Department of Registration
 and Education
55 E. Jackson Blvd.
Room 1700
Chicago, IL 60604
(312) 341-9810

Indiana
Real Estate Commission
1022 State Office Bldg.
100 N. Senate Avenue
Indianapolis, IN 46204
(317) 633-5386

Iowa
Consumer Protection Division
Executive Hills West
1209 E. Court
Des Moines, IA 50319
(515) 281-5926

Real Estate Commission
Executive Hills
1223 E. Court
Des Moines, IA 50319
(515) 281-3183

Kansas
Division of Land Registration
Securities Commission
State Office Building
Topeka, KS 66612
(913) 296-3307

Kentucky
Real Estate Commission
100 E. Liberty Street
Suite 204
Louisville, KY 40202
(502) 583-2771

Louisiana
Real Estate Division
Department of Occupational
 Standards
P. O. Box 44095
Capitol Station
Baton Rouge, LA 70804
(504) 925-4771

(cont.)

Maine
Securities Division
Dept. of Banks & Banking
State Office Building
Augusta, ME 04330
(207) 289-2261

Maryland
Real Estate Commission
One South Calvert Street
Baltimore, MD 21202
(301) 383-2130

Division of Securities
One South Calvert Street
Baltimore, MD 21202
(301) 383-3714

Massachusetts
Board of Registration of Real Estate
100 Cambridge Street
Boston, MA 02202
(617) 727-3055

Michigan
Land Sales Division
Dept. of Licensing and Regulation
808 Southland Avenue
Lansing, MI 48910
(517) 373-7360

Securities Division
Department of Commerce
P. O. Box 30222
Lansing, MI 48909
(517) 373-8026

Minnesota
Securities Division
500 Metro Square Bldg.
St. Paul, MN 55101
(612) 296-2594

Mississippi
Real Estate Commission
754 N. President Street
Jackson, MS 39202
(601) 354-7093

Missouri
Commissioner of Securities
Office of the Secy. of State
Jefferson City, MO 65101
(314) 751-4136

Real Estate Commission
3523 N. Ten Mile Drive
Jefferson City, MO 65101
(314) 751-2334

Montana
Board of Real Estate
LaLonde Building
42½ North Main
Helena, MT 58601
(406) 449-2961

Nebraska
Real Estate Commission
P. O. Box 94667
Lincoln, NB 68509
(402) 471-2004

Nevada
Real Estate Division
111 W. Telegraph Street
Carson City, NV 89701
(702) 885-4280

Office of the Atty. General
Commerce Division
201 S. Fall Street
Carson City, NV 89710
(702) 885-4170

(cont.)

New Hampshire
Consumer Protection Division
Office of the Atty. General
State House Annex
Concord, NH 03301
(603) 271-3641

New Jersey
Real Estate Commission
Bureau of Subdivided Land
  Sales Control
201 E. State Street
Trenton, NJ 08625
(609) 292-6965 or 8326

New Mexico
Consumer Protection Division
P. O. Box 2246
Santa Fe, NM 87501
(505) 827-2844

New York
Office of the Secy. of State
270 Broadway
New York, NY 10007
(212) 488-3158

Condominium-Cooperative
  Registration Division
Department of Law
No. 2 World Trade Center
New York, NY 10047
(212) 488-3367

North Carolina
Real Estate Licensing Board
P. O. Box 266
Raleigh, NC 27602
(919) 833-2771

Consumer Protection Division
Office of the Atty. General
State Capitol
Raleigh, NC 27602
(919) 733-7741

North Dakota
Real Estate Commission
Box 727
Bismarck, ND 58501
(701) 224-2749

Ohio
Securities Division
180 East Broad Street
Columbus, OH 43215
(614) 466-3440

Oklahoma
Department of Securities
2915 N. Lincoln Blvd.
Oklahoma City, OK 73105
(405) 521-2451

Real Estate Commission
4040 N. Lincoln Blvd.
Oklahoma City, OK 73105
(405) 521-3387

Oregon
Real Estate Division
Department of Commerce
Commerce Bldg.
Salem, OR 97310
(503) 378-8422

Corporation Division
Department of Commerce
Commerce Bldg.
Salem, OR 97310
(503) 378-4387

Pennsylvania
Real Estate Commission
P. O. Box 2649
Harrisburg, PA 17120
(717) 787-2852 or 3256

(cont.)

Bur. of Consumer Protection
204 N. Market Square
Harrisburg, PA 17120
(717) 787-2338

Rhode Island
Real Estate Division
169 Weybosset Street
Providence, RI 02903
(401) 277-2255

South Carolina
Real Estate Commission
2221 Devine Street
Suite 530
Columbia, SC 29205
(803) 758-3981

Office of the Atty. General
P. O. Box 11549
Columbia, SC 29211
(803) 758-3970

South Dakota
Real Estate Commission
P. O. Box 638
Pierre, SD 57501
(605) 224-3600

Tennessee
Real Estate Commission
Capitol Hill Bldg.
Nashville, TN 37219
(615) 741-2273 or 2629

Division of Securities
204 State Office Bldg.
Nashville, TN 37219
(615) 741-2947 or 3186

Texas
Real Estate Commission
P. O. Box 12188
Capitol Station
Austin, TX 78711
(512) 475-4247

State Securities Board
P. O. Box 13167
Austin, TX 78711
(512) 475-4561

Utah
Real Estate Division
330 E. Fourth South Street
Salt Lake City, UT 84111
(801) 533-5661

Utah Securities Commission
330 E. Fourth South Street
Salt Lake City, UT 84111
(801) 533-4239

Vermont
Securities Division
Dept. of Banking & Insurance
Montpelier, VT 05602
(802) 828-3301

Real Estate Commission
7 East State Street
Montpelier, VT 05602
(802) 828-3228

Virginia
Real Estate Commission
P. O. Box 1-X
Richmond, VA 23202
(804) 786-2161

(cont.)

Washington
    Real Estate Division
    P. O. Box 247
    Olympia, WA 98504
    (206) 753-1061

West Virginia
    Securities Commissioner
    State Auditor's Office
    Charleston, WV 25305
    (304) 348-2257

    Real Estate Commission
    102 State Office Bldg. No. 3
    Charleston, WV 25305
    (304) 348-3555

Wisconsin
    Real Estate Examining Board
    1400 E. Washington Avenue
    Madison, WI 53702
    (608) 266-5450

Wyoming
    Real Estate Commission
    2219 Carey Avenue
    Cheyenne, WY 82002
    (307) 777-7660

Canada

Alberta
    Insurance & Real Estate
      Branch
    Consumer and Corporate
      Affairs
    9th Floor, Capitol Square
    10065 Jasper Avenue
    Edmonton, Alberta T5J 3B1
    (403) 427-2244

British Columbia
    Real Estate Council
    Suite 608, 626 W. Pender St.
    Vancouver, B. C. V6B 1V9
    (604) 683-9664

    Superintendent of Insurance
    The Law Courts
    Burdett Avenue
    Victoria, B. C.

Manitoba
    Registrar
    The Real Estate Brokers Act
    Room 1128 - 405 Broadway
    Winnipeg, Manitoba R3C 3L6
    (204) 942-0761

Ontario
    Foreign Lands Officer
    Real Estate and Business
      Brokers Act
    Ministry of Consumer and
      Commercial Relations
    555 Yonge Street
    Toronto, Ontario M7A 2H6
    (416) 963-0401

Saskatchewan
    Superintendent of Insurance
    Room 308, 1919 Rose St.
    Regina, Saskatchewan S4P 3P1
    (306) 527-0101

    Director
    Farm Ownership Board
    8th Street & Circle Drive
    Saskatoon, Saskatchewan

Quebec
    Superintendent
    Real Estate Brokerage Branch
    Dept. of Consumers, Coopera-
      tives & Financial Institutions
    700, Boulevard St-Cyrille Est
    Quebec, Quebec G1R 5A9

APPENDIX E

LAND ACQUISITION CHECK LIST

1. Have you spotted the property on a topo map? If so, have you photographed and enlarged that section to spot troublesome terrain features on the project?

2. Are you sure about the soil? If not, does the contract allow you an out if an abnormal amount does not perc?

3. Is any of the land floodable or subject to natural disasters? If so, have you factored this into your sales projections?

4. Are there any easements or encroachments on the property? Are they serious enough to hold up development and sales?

5. Will there be any zoning problems?

6. Are any adverse influences present in the area which could affect property values?

7. Are utilities available? If not, will there be any problems or additional expenses involved with bringing in these services?

8. Who maintains the road to the property? If not the state, then who is responsible for maintenance? If you are responsible, then do you have enough right-of-way to service them properly?

9. Can you foresee any claims of adverse possession? Do the surrounding property owners agree with the survey? If there is no survey, have there been any disagreements over existing boundaries or fence lines?

10. Are you close enough to a town or city? Shopping? Doctors? Schools? Police? Fire protection? How much will distance affect sales?

11. Is there a recent survey? If not, does seller guarantee acreage within 10% of deed description? Will he adjust price downward if shortage is revealed in new survey? (You obviously do not want to pay more for the property if there is an excess of acreage, and if this question is brought up you will argue that, as the buyer, you stand the greatest risk of not getting what you bargained for. The seller claims he has a certain amount of acreage for sale at a specified price. You have agreed to a price. Now he must deliver what he promises or adjust the price downward. In most cases the seller will not turn the argument around unless he has agreed to pay for the survey. It's certainly worth a try.)

12. Are there defects on the title? If so, can they be cleared up before closing? Can you obtain title insurance? If closing is extended, what effect will this have on your plans?

13. Is your financing lined up? Are terms and conditions spelled out clearly? If owner is holding the note, can it be prepaid at will?

14. Will you control the mineral and water rights? Is this spelled out in the contract and deed?

15. Will taxes be prorated at closing?

16. Do you have full riparian rights?

17. Are there any hidden assessments against the property? If so, what are they? What effect will they have on your plans?

18. Will there be any restrictions as to what you can do with the property? If so, can you live with them? Can your property owners live with them?

19. Is specific performance written into the contract so that the seller cannot renege? Do you have a loophole or two built into the contract so you can get out if you want to?

20. Is contract subject to obtaining approvals from local governing bodies? If so, have you allowed yourself enough time to get through the red tape?

21. Have you tried for an interest-only period at the beginning of your mortgage? If you're using other people's money to get into the project, have you allowed yourself enough time to pay them back?

22. Are release provisions built into the contract? Are they clearly spelled out? Is a portion of the property released for the down payment? Have you requested that all principal payments be applied as credit against releases? Are the releases fair to both sides?

23. Will the seller subordinate? If so, for what consideration?

24. Were you able to build an exculpatory clause into the contract to avoid personal liability? (In the event of default the lien holder considers only the land as security against the debt.)

25. Does the contract specify that all release payments are to be applied against the next principal payments due?

26. Have you protected yourself against prepayment penalties?

27. Have you deducted from the total acreage any land tied up in easements and encroachments and requested an adjustment in the purchase price?

28. Will seller agree to suspend payments during any unforeseen delay in the development process caused by governmental authority?

29. Are closing costs apportioned in accordance with legal standards?

30. Will seller allow you to name the trustee in the deed of trust securing the property? You will want quick delivery on the deeds of partial release (when you sell off lots), the deed of dedication (your protective covenants, etc.), easements, and rights-of-way. A friendly trustee can grease the slide for you.

PROPERTY INSPECTION FORM

Property: ....

Realtor
or
Owner:
Name ....

Address ....

Phone ....

Agent:
Name ....

Address ....

Phone ....

Source (lead): ....

Property Description:

Financing (terms):

Comments:

Recommendations:

Action Taken:

326 *How You Can Grow Rich Through Rural Land*

PROJECT DEVELOPMENT SHEET*

*The final commitment to purchase land for a *Subdivesting* project is subject to a number of variables. Ideally, you'll want to buy under a refundable option arrangement until you can get at least a preliminary go ahead from any required local or regional authorities.

Project: _____

	Date Initiated	Follow-up Dates	Completion Date
Locate land and preliminary scoring			
Walk land and final scoring			
Feasibility study and follow up			
Soil survey and test holes			
Preliminary Subdivision layout			
Local health and planning officials			
Buy or Exercise option on land			
Clear rights-of-way and build roads			
Survey			
Preliminary plat (Approval dates)			
Final plat			
Price lots			
Final subdivision check			

COMMENTS

PROJECT COST SHEET *

*Two Questions:
(1.) What is your *actual* land cost?
(2.) What price can you get for your lots and still sell out quickly with no cash flow problems?
(2 x lot cost = fair return; 2½ x lot cost = good return; 3 x lot cost = excellent return)

Project: _____

DEVELOPMENT COSTS	Estimated	Actual
1. Survey and Engineering Fees		
Boundary Survey		
Lot Survey		
Topographical Map Blow-up		
Perc Test Expenses		
Soil Survey		
Misc.		
2. Land Preparation		
Clearing Roads and Rights-of-Way		
Road Construction		
Drainage Pipes		
Seeding and Finishing		
Misc.		
3. Advertising and Sales		
Cost of Ads		
Commissions and Bonuses		
Premiums		
Management fees		
Misc.		
4. Financing		
Cost of Money		
Interest		
Note discounts		
Misc.		
5. Overhead		
Office rent		
Personnel		
Utilities		
Misc.		
Purchase Price		
Cost of raw land per acre (subtract value of buildings and accompanying land)		
1. Per acre land cost (divide adjusted purchase price by remaining acreage)		
2. Average selling price per acre		

APPENDIX F

MEASUREMENT TABLES

Common Measure

Linear Measure
12 inches = 1 foot (ft.)
3 feet (ft.) = 1 yard (yd.)
36 inches = 1 yard
5½ yards = 1 rod
16½ feet = 1 rod or pole (p.)
320 rods = 1 mile (mi.)
5,280 feet = 1 mile
40 rods = 1 furlong (fur.)
3 miles = 1 statute league (l.)

Square Measure
144 square inches = 1 square foot
9 square feet = 1 square yard
30¼ square yards = 1 square rod
160 square rods or
4,840 sq. yards or
43,560 square feet = 1 acre
640 acres = 1 square mile

Surveyor's Chain Measure
7.92 inches = 1 link
100 links = 1 chain or 66 feet
100 links = 4 rods
10 chains = 1 furlong or 220 yards
80 chains = 1 statute mile

Surveyor's Square Measure
625 square links = 1 square pole
16 square poles = 1 square chain
10 square chains = 1 acre
640 acres = 1 square mile
36 square miles = 1 township

Metric System and Common Equivalents

Linear Measure
1 millimeter = 0.03937 inch
10 millimeters = 1 centimeter = 0.3937 inch
10 centimeters = 1 decimeter = 3.937 inches
10 decimeters = 1 meter = 39.37 inches
10 meters = 1 decameter = 393.7 inches
10 decameters = 1 hectometer = 328.08 feet
10 hectometers = 1 kilometer = 0.621 mile
10 kilometers = 1 myriameter = 6.21 miles

Square Measure
1 square millimeter = 0.00155 square inch
100 sq. millimeters (mm.) = 1 sq. centimeter = 0.15499 sq. inch
100 sq. centimeters (cm.) = 1 sq. decimeter = 15.499 sq. inches
100 sq. decimeters = 1 sq. meter = 1,549.9 sq. inches
or 1.196 sq. yards
100 sq. meters (m.) = 1 sq. decameter = 119.6 sq. yards
100 sq. decameters = 1 sq. hectometer = 2.471 acres
100 sq. hectometers = 1 sq. kilometer = 0.386 sq. mile or 247.1 acres

Land Measure
1 sq. meter = 1 centiare = 1,549.9 sq. inches
100 centiares = 1 are = 119.6 sq. yards
100 ares = 1 hectare = 2.471 acres
100 hectares = 1 sq. kilometer = 0.386 sq. mile or 247.1 acres

HOW TO ROUGHLY COMPUTE LAND AREAS

Occasionally you may want to quickly estimate the amount of acreage in a particular tract of land. If you can draw the rough boundaries onto a map with a specified scale, you can often "guesstimate" the acreage involved.

IF IT LOOKS LIKE THIS: *DO THIS:*

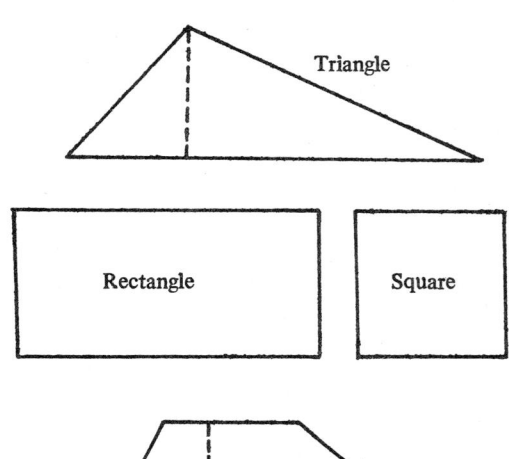

Multiply the base line (or length) by half of the height (which is determined by drawing a perpendicular line from the base line to the angle opposite this base).

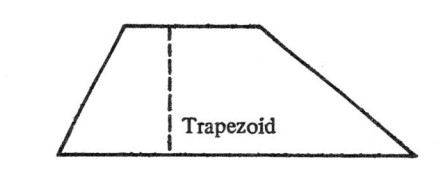

Multiply the length by the width.

Add the lengths of the two parallel sides; multiply this sum by one-half the height (the perpendicular distance between the two parallel sides).

Convert the area into two triangles (as shown). Figure the area of each triangle, then add the sums of each.

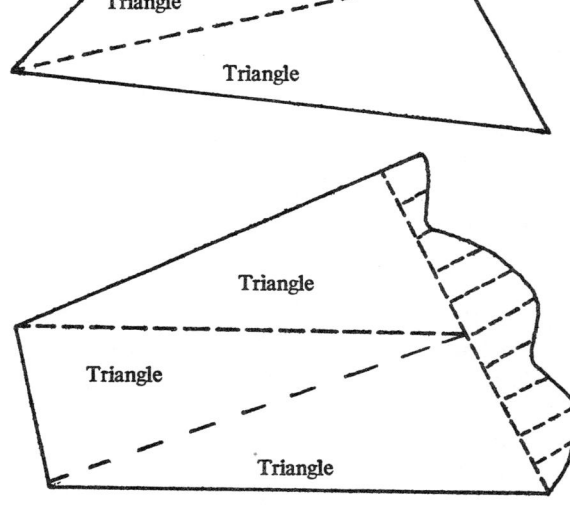

Draw a base line as close to the irregular boundary as possible, and then draw various lines from this base line, which are equidistant from each other, to the irregular boundary line. Take one-half the sum of the first and last line and add it to the sum of all the intermediate lines. Multiply this sum by the distance between the lines.

APPENDIX G

COUNTY MAP SHOWING VARIOUS ROADS, STREAMS AND OTHER PERTINENT FEATURES

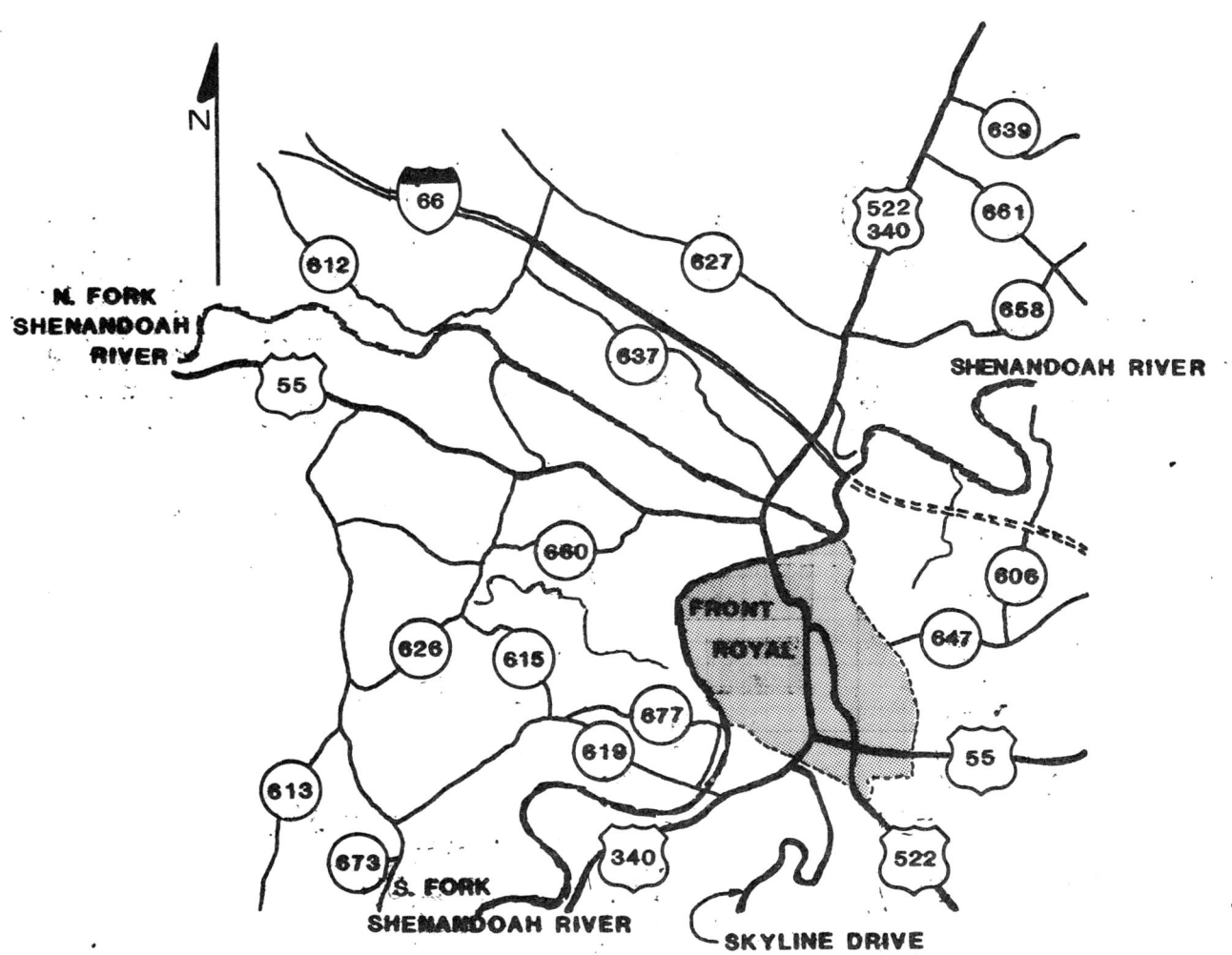

CLOSE-UP OF PREVIOUS COUNTY MAP SHOWING SPECIFIC FARM BOUNDARIES AND PERTINENT FEATURES.

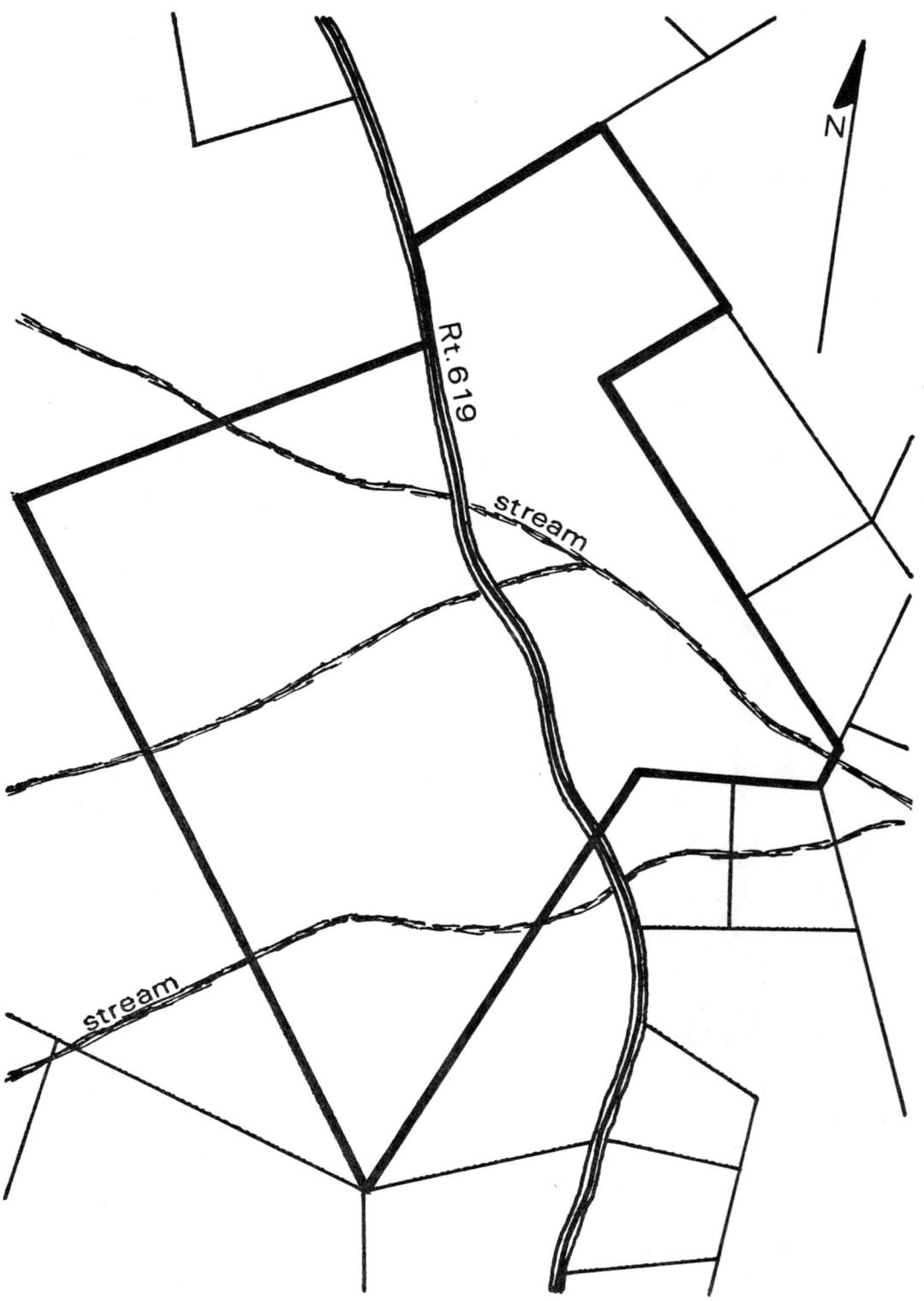

CLOSE-UP OF TOPOGRAPHICAL MAP SHOWING FARM BOUNDARIES AND PERCOLATION TEST HOLES.

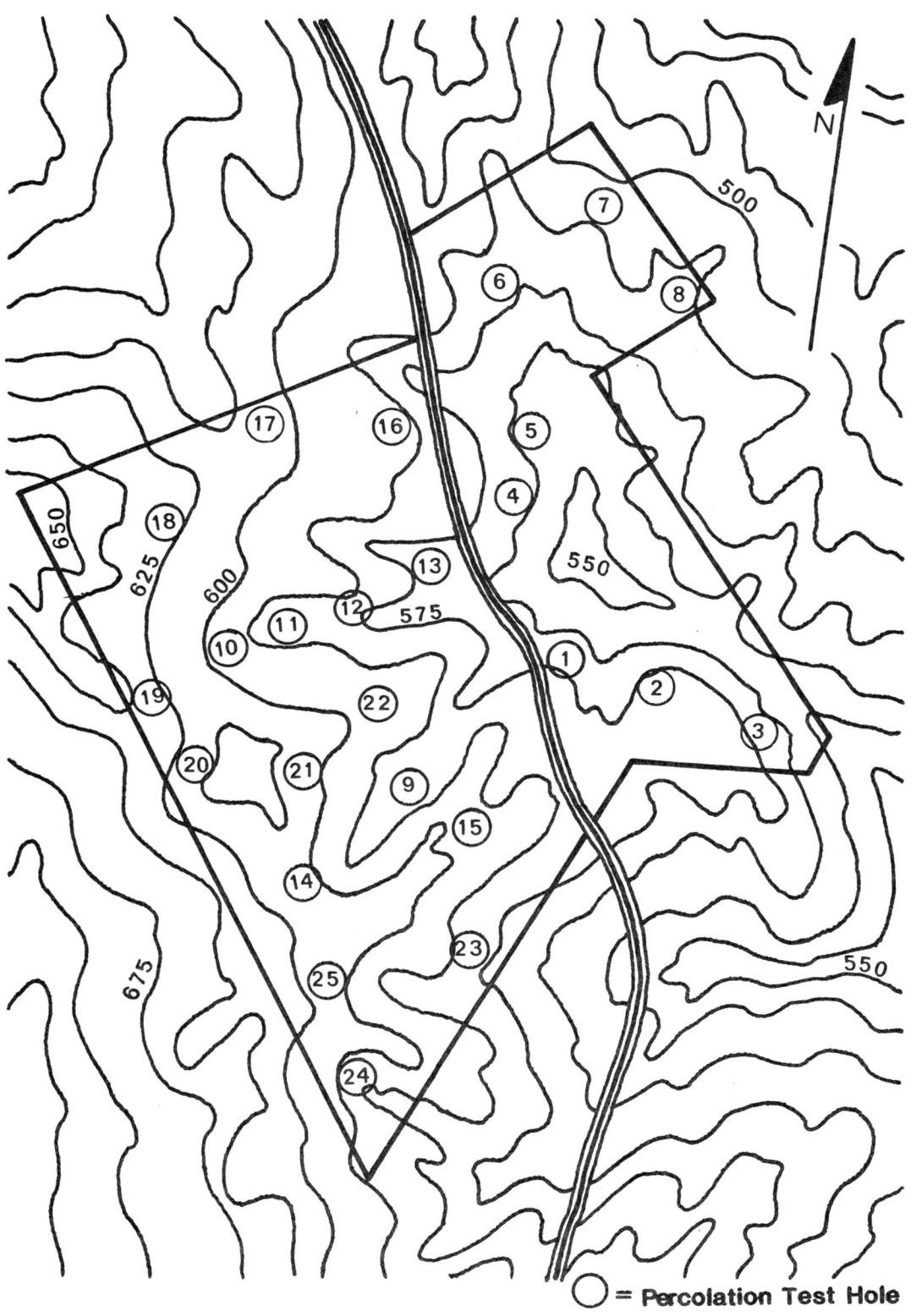

◯ = Percolation Test Hole

WHERE TO BUY TOPOGRAPHICAL MAPS

Throughout the U.S. there are many outlets where topographical maps may be purchased. The U.S. Geological Survey operates a series of information centers across the country where purchasing information can be obtained. Most of these centers also offer walk-in map purchasing. While offices are established throughout various sections of the U.S., the center in Reston, Virginia serves as headquarters for all of these offices and may be consulted for information for any part of the country.

Following is a list of information centers for the United States:

National Cartographic Information Center (NCIC)
507 U.S. Geological Survey
National Center Building
Reston, VA 22092
(703) 860-6045

NCIC - Mid-Continent Mapping Center
U.S. Geological Survey
1400 Independence Rd.
Rolla, MO 65401
(314) 364-3680

NCIC - Rocky Mountain Mapping Center
U.S. Geological Survey
Stop 504 Denver Federal Center
Denver, CO. 80225
(303) 234-2326

NCIC - Western Mapping Center
U.S. Geological Survey
345 Middlefield Rd.
Menlow Park, CA 94025
(415) 328-8111

NCIC - National Space Technology Laboratories
U.S. Geological Survey
NSTL Station, MI 39529
(601) 688-3544

APPENDIX H

U.S. Department of Agriculture
Soil Conservation Service

SOIL LEGEND

The first letter, always a capital, is the initial letter of the soil name. The second letter is a capital if the mapping unit is broadly defined; otherwise, it is a small letter. The third letter, always a capital, A, B, C, D, or E, shows the slope. Most symbols without a slope letter are those of nearly level soils, but some are for broadly defined units that have a fair to considerable range of slope. A final number, 2 or 3, in the symbol shows that the soil is eroded or severely eroded.

SYMBOL	NAME
AbB	Abell fine sandy loam, 2 to 7 percent slopes
AnB2	Appling sandy loam, 2 to 7 percent slopes, eroded
AnC2	Appling sandy loam, 7 to 15 percent slopes, eroded
ApB3	Appling sandy clay loam, 2 to 7 percent slopes, severely eroded
AsB	Ashlar sandy loam, 2 to 7 percent slopes
AsC	Ashlar sandy loam, 7 to 15 percent slopes
AsC3	Ashlar sandy loam, 7 to 15 percent slopes, severely eroded
AsD	Ashlar sandy loam, 15 to 25 percent slopes
AV	Ashlar-Manteo-Rock outcrop complex
CcB2	Cecil sandy loam, 2 to 7 percent slopes, eroded
ClB	Colfax fine sandy loam, 2 to 7 percent slopes
DuB	Durham fine sandy loam, 2 to 5 percent slopes
GrB2	Grover sandy loam, 2 to 7 percent slopes, eroded
GrC2	Grover sandy loam, 7 to 15 percent slopes, eroded
GvC3	Grover sandy clay loam, 7 to 15 percent slopes, severely eroded
MaB2	Madison sandy loam, 2 to 7 percent slopes, eroded
MaB3	Madison sandy loam, 2 to 7 percent slopes, severely eroded
MaC2	Madison sandy loam, 7 to 15 percent slopes, eroded
RoB	Roanoke silt loam, local alluvium, 2 to 7 percent slopes
WH	Wehadkee-Chewacla complex

This soil legend is designed to be used with the map on the following page. In most instances, each county will provide a different legend for the soil maps for that area. To obtain the soil legend and maps for your area, contact your local SCS office.

SCS SOIL MAP SHOWING SYMBOLS FOR SOIL TYPES, SLOPE PERCENTAGES, AND EROSION MARKINGS

APPENDIX I

(SAMPLE COVENANTS)
Vacation Subdivision

DECLARATION OF PROTECTIVE COVENANTS
FOR
BEND OF THE RIVER

This property shall be subject to the following covenants, which covenants are to run with the land.

(1) The grantors may assess each property owner the sum of fifty dollars ($50.00) per year, per tract, for the use, upkeep and maintenance of the roads and common areas. *Any assessment made pursuant to this paragraph shall constitute a lien on this property until paid,* and payment of said assessment and levy shall be payable on or before the 31st day of January next following the purchase of this property, and on or before the 31st day of each year thereafter. Lots 1-7 exempt from road maintenance fee.

The grantors assume responsibility for collection of fund monies and maintenance of roads and common areas until March 15, 1976, or until all lots are sold, whichever is first. At that time the rights and responsibilities as created by this paragraph will be delegated by the grantors to a committee of property owners. The property owners, offically known as the Bend of the River Property Owners Association will assume full responsibility for collection of funds and maintenance of roads and common areas.

The property owners association shall have the power to raise or lower the annual road fees if it is deemed necessary or desirable. A poll of all lot owners must be taken, with 75% of the owners voting in the affirmative, before any action may be taken. The fee may not be raised more than 10% per year without 100% cooperation of the lot owners. In the event of resale of a lot or lots, then the obligation to pay said maintenance fee shall be binding on the purchaser or purchasers of said lots without any provision therein specifically so provided.

(2) The grantors reserve unto themselves, their heirs or assigns, the right to erect and maintain telephone and electric light poles, conduits, equipment, sewer, gas, and water lines, or to grant easements or rights of way therefore, with the right of ingress and egress for the purpose of erection or maintenance on, over, or under a strip of land fifteen (15) feet wide any any point along the side, rear, or front lines of any of said property.

(3) No building of a temporary nature shall be erected or placed on this property except those customarily erected in connection with building operations; and in such cases, for a period not to exceed four months.

(4) Not more than one residence shall be erected on any one tract unless specifically approved, in writing, by the Louisa County Health Department, and said residence shall contain a minimum of 480 square feet on the main floor. This shall not include basement, garage, porch, or carport. All exterior construction

must be completed and closed in within eight (8) months of the commencement of construction.

(5) This property, except as hereinafter provided, shall be used for residential purposes only, and any garage or barn must conform generally in appearance and material with any dwelling on the property. The following uses shall be permitted:
- (a) Home occupations conducted by the occupant;
- (b) Agricultural uses, including indicental uses and the construction of accessory buildings;
- (c) Dairying, including the raising of milk cows and the processing and sale of milk and milk products at either wholesale or retail, provided that such uses conform to State Health Department requirements and provided that the person or persons so using the property obtain a special use permit from the applicable authorities;
- (d) All other farm related uses; and
- (e) Agricultural uses shall include, but not be limited to, the business of raising and training horses and riders and related activities.

(6) No signs, billboards, or advertising of any nature shall be erected, placed or maintained on this property, nor upon any building erected thereon, except directional and information signs of grantors. However, individual lot owners may erect signs naming or identifying their particular lot or lots, provided that such signs comply with the Louisa County ordinances relating to the erection of such signs.

(7) No building shall be erected closer than 35 feet to any street or road, nor closer than 20 feet to the side or rear of the property line, with the exception that where two or more tracts are used together for the consideration of one dwelling, then said 20 feet set back shall apply only to outside lines.

(8) All toilets constructed on said property shall conform to the regulations of the appropriate county and State Health Department, and be placed in a secluded area whenever possible.

(9) The use of trailers are unauthorized unles specifically approved in writing by Haynes-Anderson Associates or the Bend of The River Property Owners Association, except for the use of temporary camping trailers.

(10) 12" diameter culverts must be used in all driveways leading from main roads.

(11) No trucks, buses, old cars or unsightly vehicles of any type or description may be left or abandoned on said property.

(12) Haynes-Anderson Associates reserves a right-of-way for itself and it's successors and interests over the roads shown on the plat of subdivision, and Haynes-Anderson Associates further reserves the right to grant and convey to each lot owner a right-of-way over all of the roads shown on the plat of subdivision.

(13) If the parties hereto, or any of them, or their heirs or assigns, shall violate or attempt to violate any of the covenants herein, it shall be lawful for any other person or persons owning any real estate situated in said parcel to prosecute any proceedings at law or in equity against the person or persons violating or attempting to violate any such covenant either to prevent him or them from so

doing or to recover damages or other dues for such violation.

(14) Invalidation of any one of these covenants by judgement or Court order, shall in nowise affect any of the other provisions which shall remain in full force and effect.

(SAMPLE COVENANTS)
Residential Subdivision

DECLARATION OF PROTECTIVE COVENANTS

FOR

HAYNES-ANDERSON TRUST PROPERTY

(1) The Trustees of Haynes-Anderson Trust, their successors and assigns, may assess each property owner the sum of Fifty Dollars ($50.00) per tract, per year, for the use, administration and maintenance of the roads, rights of way and common areas subject to any increase as provided below. Any assessment made pursuant to this paragraph, including late fee of Five Dollars ($5.00) interest at the rate of nine percent (9%) per annum from the date of delinquency and reasonable attorney's fees incurred in the collection thereof, shall constitute a lien on this property until paid and the execution of this deed to bind themselves, their heirs and successors in title to this lien and to the covenants hereinafter written. This lien is expressly inferior and subordinate to any first lien deed of trust presently or hereafter encumbering the property affected by these protective covenants. This lien shall be payable beginning and prorated as of the date of the conveyance of this property, and on or before the 1st day of January of each year thereafter.

Haynes-Anderson Trust assumes the responsibility for the collection of the monies due under this lien assessment and for the maintenance of the roads, rights of way and common areas until January 31, 1979 or until all the property has been sold, whichever is first. Road fees shall not apply to any unsold lots. At that time the rights and responsibilities as created by this Declaration of Protective Covenants will be delegated by the Grantors to a committee of property owners who shall assume full responsibility for collection of the lien and the maintenance of the roads, rights of way and common areas. This committee shall be known as the Property Owners Association and each property owner of record of Thunderbird Farms shall have the privilege of becoming a member of this association without the payment of any additional monies except for the lien hereinbefore mentioned.

The Property Owners Association shall have the power to raise or lower the annual assessment lien if it is deemed necessary or desirable. The fee may not be raised by more than ten percent (10%) per year without the written affirmative vote of at least 66 2/3 % of the property owners. No property owner who is in default on the payment of the annual assessment lien as of May 1st of any year shall be entitled to vote.

(2) There shall be no further resubdivision of lots.

(3) The grantors reserve unto themselves, their heirs or assigns, the right to construct or erect, operate, and maintain roads, telephone and electric light

poles, conduits, equipment, sewer, gas, and water lines, or to grant easements or rights of way thereof, with the right of ingress and egress for the purpose of erection or maintenance on, over, or under a strip of land 50 feet wide at any point along the front lines and 20 feet wide at any point along the side or rear lines of any of said property.

(4) No building of a temporary nature shall be erected or placed on this property except those customarily erected in connection with residence building operations; and in such cases, for a period not to exceed four months.

(5) Not more than one single family residence shall be erected on any one tract unless specifically approved, in writing, by the Warren County Zoning Administration, and said residence shall contain a minimum of 850 square feet on the main floor. This shall not include basement, veranda, patio, garage, porch, or carport. All exterior construction must be completed and closed in within eight (8) months of the commencement of construction. No exterior construction siding or masonry block or cinder block shall be permitted.

(6) This property, except as hereinafter provided, shall be used for residential purposes only, and any garage, barn, or other outbuilding must conform generally in appearance and material with any dwelling on the property. The following uses shall also be permitted, subject to applicable state and local law;

    a. Home occupations conducted by the occupant;

    b. Agricultural and farming, including incidental uses and buildings related thereto.

    c. Agricultural uses shall include, but not be limited to, the business of raising and training horses and riders and related activities.

(7) No signs, billboards, or advertising of any nature shall be erected, placed or maintained on this property, nor upon any building erected thereon, except directional and information signs of grantors. However, individual property owners or their agents may erect signs naming or identifying their particular property or house occupation or notifying the public that the property is offered for sale, provided that such signs comply with the Warren County ordinances relating to the erection and size of such signs.

(8) No building shall be erected closer than 35 feet to any road right-of-way, nor closer than 20 feet to the side or rear of the property line, with the exception that where two or more tracts are used together for the consideration of one dwelling, then said 20 feet set back shall apply only to outside lines.

(9) All sanitation facilities constructed or placed on said property shall conform to the regulations of the Warren County and Virginia Health Departments.

(10) No house trailer or mobile home shall be placed upon the property and the use of temporary camping trailers shall be only in accordance with the Warren County and Virginia state laws.

(11) Minimum 15" diameter culverts must be used in all driveways entering upon all Thunderbird Farms roads.

(12) No vehicles of any type or description which are unlicensed or inoperable may be left or abandoned on said property unless stored in a building permitted by these covenants.

(13) *Haynes-Anderson Trust* reserves the right-of-way for itself and its successors in interest over the roads shown on the plat of subdivision, and *Haynes-Anderson Trust* further reserves the right to grant and convey to each property owner a right-of-way over all the roads shown on the plat of subdivision. It is to be expressly understood that all roads within the 1400 acre property commonly known as Thunderbird Farms not currently maintained by the Virginia Department of Highways shall be private and usable by the property owners and their invitees only.

(14) No use of firearms, except for self-defense, shall be permitted.

(15) If the owner of any property encompassed by these covenants or any of their heirs or successors shall violate or attempt to violate any of the covenants herein, it shall be lawful for any other person or persons owning any real estate situated in said parcel to prosecute any proceedings at law or in equity against the person or persons violating or attempting to violate any such covenants either to prevent him or them from so doing or to recover damages or other due for such violation.

(16) Invalidation of any one of these covenants by judgment of court order, shall in nowise effect any of the other provisions which shall remain in full force and effect.

(17) These covenants shall run with the land and shall be binding upon all the parties hereto, including their invitees, heirs, successors in title, and all parties claiming through them until October 11, 1986, at which time these covenants shall be automatically extended for incremental periods of ten years unless changed in whole or in part by written vote of a majority of the then property owners of record of Haynes-Anderson Trust Property.

(18) In all instances pertaining to the alteration of one or all of the provisions of these covenants wherein a written vote is required that there shall be only one vote per tract recorded by Haynes-Anderson, Trustees, their successors and assigns, as Thunderbird Farms.

.... (Trustee)

.... (Trustee)

APPENDIX J

TITLE:
Tenants by int. _____
Individual _____

Title Insurance _____ _____
                yes   no

B. K. HAYNES CORPORATION
501 S. ROYAL AVENUE
FRONT ROYAL, VIRGINIA 22630

Sales Office
Phone: 555-1212

REAL ESTATE SALES CONTRACT

Date: _____, 19 _____

THIS DAY RECEIVED FROM _____
_____ a deposit of ($ _____)
_____ DOLLARS to be applied as part payment in the purchase of
lot(s) _____ in the subdivision known as _____,
_____ Magisterial district, _____ County, Virginia.
The undersigned purchaser(s) agree(s) to buy and the undersigned owner agrees to sell upon the following terms and conditions as noted below:

PRICE: ($ _____) _____ DOLLARS

BASIC TERMS OF CREDIT SALE

The total "Time Price" and the TOTAL OF PAYMENTS due OWNER from Purchaser, are computed and disclosed as follows: (as provided in said CONTRACT)

1. Cash Price .... $ _____
2. Less: Cash Downpayment .... $ _____
3. Trade-in:
   Description _____ Allowance $ _____
   Net due $ _____ Net trade-in equity $ _____
4. Total Downpayment .... $ _____
5. Unpaid balance of cash price .... $ _____
   (Subtract Item 4 from Item 1)
6. Other charges: None
7. Unpaid balance (include other charges) .... $ _____
8. Amount Financed (Same as No. 7) .... $ _____
9. FINANCE CHARGE: .... $ _____
10. Payments to be made in _____ Equal Installments of ..... $ _____
11. First Payment due
12. Total of payments (Sum of No. 8 and No. 9) .... $ _____
13. Deferred payment price (Sum of Nos. 1 and 9) .... $ _____
14. ANNUAL PERCENTAGE RATE: .... _____%

Please write in space below, in you own handwriting, a statement to the effect that you have read and understand the above information.

_____

Purchaser agrees that this sale is subject to approval by the Owner or other designated officer and the Purchaser(s) credit.

The Purchaser(s) covenant(s) and agree(s) that, at the option of the owner, they will pay a "late charge" of five per centum (5%) of any installment when paid more than ten (10) days after the due date thereof; said late charge to cover the extra expense involved in handling the delinquent payments.

The Purchaser(s) may pay the full amount due at any time before maturity and shall receive a partial refund of unearned precomputed interest, based upon the Rule of 78's except that $25.00 of such interest shall be retained and no rebate shall be made thereon and no rebate shall be made of less than $20.00.

Because of the security interest disclosed herein, under the law, the SELLER must furnish BUYER with a NOTICE OF RIGHT TO RESCIND if BUYER intends to use the PROPERTY purchased hereunder as BUYER'S current or future principal place of residence. Such obligation of SELLER shall not arise where a contrary intent is evidenced. BUYER evidences his intent as follows:

BUYER _____ DOES _____ DOES NOT INTEND TO USE THE PROPERTY PURCHASED HEREUNDER AS BUYER'S CURRENT OR FUTURE PRINCIPLE PLACE OF RESIDENCE.

    1. Taxes for year of sale to be prorated as of date of settlement. 2. OWNER AGREES to convey the above-described property by Special Warranty Deed, subject to Protective Covenants (copy attached), rights of way and easements of record, if any. 3. OWNER shall name the Trustees in all deeds of trust. 4. Closing costs and recordation fees to be paid by purchaser, including preparation of Deed and Deed of Trust, and credit report. 5. Purchaser agrees to pay $ _____ per lot per year for the maintenance of roads and any facilities dedicated to Lot Owners in Common. 6. Purchaser agrees to furnish seller with certificate of insurance in amount of at least $ _____ on any property improvements. 7. On financed purchases, BLANKET ENCUMBRANCE, if any, shall be released by Deed of Release as to above lot(s) upon payment of the deed of trust note/or the balance of the purchase price.

TITLE to the above property is to be good of record and in fact free of encumbrance, except as above stated, subject to all covenants running with the land, restrictions, and easements of record.

WITHIN _____ DAYS from the date of acceptance hereof by the Owner, the Owners and Purchaser(s) are required to agree and make full settlement in accordance with the terms at the office of _____
_____ ; on the _____ day
of _____, 19 _____, at _____ A.M./P.M.

IF the Purchaser(s) shall fail to make settlement, the deposit herein provided for will be forfeited by the Purchaser(s) and the Owner may avail himself of any legal or equitable rights he may have under this contract.

THIS CONTRACT, MADE IN QUADRUPLICATE, WHEN RATIFIED, CONTAINS THE FINAL AND ENTIRE AGREEMENT BETWEEN THE PARTIES HERETO (AND THEY SHALL NOT BE BOUND BY ANY TERMS, CONDITIONS, STATEMENTS, OR REPRESENTATIONS, ORAL OR WRITTEN, NOT HEREIN CONTAINED).

WE, hereby ratify, accept and agree to the above memorandum of sale and acknowledge it to be our sole contract.

WITNESS the following signatures and seals:

Estimated closing costs _____

_____ (Seal)

REFERENCE _____ No. of Acres _____

_____ (Seal)

_____ Customer
_____ Direct Mail
_____ Newspaper

_____ (Seal)

HAYNES - ANDERSON, TRUSTEES

Day _____
Classified _____ Salesman: _____
Display _____

BY: _____ (Seal)

_____ (Seal)

B. K. HAYNES CORPORATION
501 S. ROYAL AVENUE
FRONT ROYAL, VIRGINIA 22630

NOTICE OF RIGHT OF RESCISSION

_____
(Identification of Transaction)

_____ Pursuant to the Truth in Lending Act and Regulations,
Name of Customer   we are delivering to you two copies of the Notice and
                             the important information set forth below.
_____
Street
                             By _____
_____   Name and Title of Officer
City   State   Zip

Notice To Customer Required By Federal Law:

You have entered into a transaction on _____ which may result in a lien, mortgage, or other security interest on your home. You have a legal right under Federal Law to cancel this transaction if you desire to do so, without any penalty or obligation within three business days from the above date or any later date on which all material disclosures required under the Truth in Lending Act have been given to you. If you so cancel the transaction, any lien, mortgage, or other security interest on your home arising from this transaction is automatically void. You are also entitled to receive a refund of any downpayment or other consideration if you cancel. If you decide to cancel this transaction, you may do so by notifying:

_____
(Name of creditor)

at _____
(Address of creditor's place of business)

by mail or telegram sent not later than midnight of _____
                                                         (Date)

You may also use any other form of written notice identifying the transaction if it is delivered to the above address not later than that time. This notice may be used for that purpose by dating and signing below.

I hereby cancel this transaction.

_____   _____
(Date)   (Customer's signature)

EFFECT OF RESCISSION. When a customer exercises his right to rescind under the above paragraph, he is not liable for any finance or other charge, and any security interest becomes void upon such a rescission. Within 10 days after receipt of a notice of rescission, the creditor shall return to the customer any money or property given as earnest money, downpayment, or otherwise, and shall take any action necessary or appropriate to reflect the termination of any security interest created under the transaction. If the creditor has delivered any property to the customer, the customer may retain possession of it. Upon the performance of the creditor's obligations under this section, the customer shall tender the property to the creditor, except that if return of the property in kind would be impracticable or inequitable, the customer shall tender its reasonable value. Tender shall be made at the location of the property or at the residence of the customer, at the option of the customer. If the creditor does not take possession of the property within 10 days after the tender by the customer, ownership of the property vests in the customer without obligation on his part to pay for it.

RECEIPT

I hereby acknowledge receipt of two copies of the "Rescission Notice" and the "Effect of Rescission" information set forth above.

_____
(Customer's Signature)

_____   _____
(Date of Receipt)   (Customer's Signature)

B. K. HAYNES CORPORATION

501 South Royal Avenue   Front Royal, Virginia 22630

CREDIT APPLICATION INFORMATION

Date ....

Name .... Age ....

Name of Spouse .... Age ....

Address .... For ..... years

.... Phone ....
Former
Address .... For ..... years

....

Number of Dependants ..... Ages ....

EMPLOYMENT RECORD

Employed by .... Phone ....

    Address..

    Length of Employment .... Position ....
    Formerly
    Employed By .... Phone ....

    Address..

    Length of Employment .... Position ....

Spouse Employed By .... Phone ....

Address..

Length of Employment .... Position ....

PERSONAL REFERENCES

  1. Name..
     Address...
  2. Name..
     Address...

Cash On Hand
    1. Checking Account $ .... Account No..........
                                       1. Bank ....
    2. Savings Account   Location ....
                                       2. Bank ....
                                       Location ....

Real Estate Owned:

Location	Balance Owed	Market Value
1.	$............	$............
2.	$............	$............
3.	$............	$............

Total Value of Stocks Owned $............................

FINANCIAL INFORMATION

Income
1. Monthly Income $............
2. Monthly Income of Spouse $............
3. Other Monthly Income $............
   Total Monthly Income $............

Expenditures per month:
1. Amt. of Rent or Mtg. Payments $............
   Payable to: Name..............................
                        Address............................

2. Automobile Loan Payments (Total Amount) $............
   Payable to: Name..............................
                        Address............................
                        Name..............................
                        Address............................

3. Monthly Payments on Charge Accounts (include account numbers)
   Payable to:

	Pmts.	Bal.	Acct. No.
a.	$.......	$.......	$........
b.	$.......	$.......	$........
c.	$.......	$.......	$........

4. Other Outstanding Loans or Obligations:
   Payable to:

	Payments	Balance
a.	$............	$............
b.	$............	$............
c.	$............	$............

TOTAL MONTHLY PAYMENTS $............
TOTAL LIFE INSURANCE IN FORCE $............

Signed: ....
              ....

FOREIGN INVESTOR DISCLOSURE INFORMATION

It is important for Subdivestors to be familiar with the Agricultural Foreign Investor Disclosure Act of 1978 which may require aliens to make specific disclosures on certain types of land. A subdivestor who is familiar with this act can provide important information to foreign clients.

Under the Agricultural Foreign Investment Disclosure Act of 1978, any foreign person who acquires or transfers any interest other than a security interest in agricultural land is to submit a completed ASCS - 153 to the Secretary of Agricultural not later than 90 days after the date of acquisition or transfer. Forms are available from county ASCS offices where they should be returned upon completion.

Any foreign person who holds, acquires, or transfers any interest in agricultural land who the Secretary of Agriculture determines to have failed to submit a Report ASCS - 153 or who knowingly submitted a report which is incomplete, misleading or false is subject to civil penalty not to exceed 25 percent of the fair market value of the land on the date of the assessment of the penalty.

The reports shall be analyzed by the United States Department of Agriculture Agency Staff to develop reports for the Secretary of Agriculture for issue to Congress and the Department of Agriculture in each state. The reports and the analysis shall be available for public inspection at the Department of Agriculture located in the District of Columbia.

The U.S. Department of Agriculture requires that this filing be made on any tract of more than one acre used in agricultural, forestry, or timber production; idle land must also be reported. Small plots such as household gardens are normally excluded from this act; but if an alien produces more than one thousand dollars in gross agricultural value from any plot, this must be reported.

Further information may be obtained on foreign disclosures through local ASCS offices.

APPENDIX K

(SAMPLE DEED)

THIS DEED, made this 12th day of May, 1978, by and between John D. Jones and Mary M. Jones, husband and wife, parties of the first part, and B.K. HAYNES CORPORATION, a Virginia Corporation, party of the second part,

WITNESSETH

That for and in consideration of the sum of TEN DOLLARS ($10.00) cash in hand paid, and other good and valuable consideration, the receipt of which is hereby acknowledged, the parties of the first part do hereby GRANT, BARGAIN, SELL and CONVEY, with GENERAL WARRANTY and ENGLISH COVENANTS OF TITLE unto the party of the second part the following described property, to-wit:

All that certain lot or parcel of land together with all improvements thereon and appurtenances thereunto, lying and being situate in the Monro Magisterial District of Greene County, Virginia, containing 3.57 acres more or less, and designated as Lot 49 on a plat of Flattop Mountain Subdivision made by J.R. Nicely, C.L.S., dated February 21, 1973, and recorded in the Clerk's Office of the Circuit Court of Greene County, Virginia, in Plat Book 3, at Pages 83-85.

This is the same property which was conveyed to the parties of the first part by deed of B.K. Haynes Corporation, a Virginia Corporation, dated April 10, 1976, and of record in the aforesaid Clerk's Office in Deed Book 97, at Page 347.

This conveyance is made subject to certain restrictions, and protective covenants set forth in the Statement of Protective Covenants, Conditions and Reservations of Flattop Mountain which is of record in the aforesaid Clerk's Office in Deed Book 67, at Page 3, and the Statement of Additional Protective Covenants, Conditions and Reservations of record in the aforesaid Clerk's Office in Deed Book 70, at Page 276.

The conveyance is further subject to all easements and rights of way of record, all of which are incorporated by reference into this deed.

The said Protective Covenants, include a $60.00 per lot per year road maintenance fee which is payable to, "Lot 49, Flattop Mountain Road Maintenance Fee" on or before the 31st day of January of each year.

WITNESS the following signatures and seals.

_____ (SEAL)
John D. Jones

_____ (SEAL)
Mary M. Jones

STATE OF VIRGINIA
COUNTY OF WARREN, to-wit:

I, Charles E. Smith, a Notary Public in and for the State of County aforesaid, do hereby certify that John D. Jones and Mary M. Jones, husband and wife, whose names are signed to the foregoing writing, bearing date on the 12th day of May, 1978, have acknowledged the same before me in my State and County, aforesaid.

Given under my hand this the 26th day of May, 1978.

_____
NOTARY PUBLIC

My Commission Expires:

This Deed of Trust

Made and entered into this   day of
by and between

part   of the first part, and
Trustee   , part   of the second part;

Witnesseth

That for and in consideration of the sum of Ten Dollars ($10.00) cash in hand paid, receipt of which is hereby acknowledged, the part   of the first part do   hereby grant and convey unto the part   of the second part, the following described piece, parcel or tract of land lying and being in

IN TRUST, to secure the prompt payment of the principal sum of
                                                                                                        Dollars
($), together with interest thereon at the rate of   per cent per annum; said indebtedness being evidenced by one certain promissory note of even date herewith, executed by

and made payable to the order of

at any bank or trust company; payable in monthly installments of at least
                                                                                            Dollars ($)
each, with the privilege of making larger payments in any amount; the first of said installments being due and payable on the   day of   , 19   , and one of said installments being due and payable on the   day of each and every month thereafter until

The said installments, when so paid, shall be first applied to the payment of the interest then due on the principal of the note, and the balance shall be applied to the payment of the said principal.

This is a purchase money deed of trust.

This deed is made under the provisions of Section 55-59, 55-60 of the Code of Virginia of 1950, and shall be construed to impose and confer upon the parties hereto and the beneficiary hereunder all of the duties, rights and obligations prescribed in Section 55-59 and in short form as Section 55-60 provides: "Exemptions waived; subject to all upon default; renewal or extension permitted; insurance required $

WITNESS the Following signature   and seal   :

_____ (SEAL)   _____ (SEAL)

_____ (SEAL)   _____ (SEAL)

_____ OF _____

_____ OF _____, to-wit:

I, a Notary Public in and for the   aforesaid, in the do hereby certify that

whose name   signed to the foregoing deed of trust dated   day of   19
have personally appeared before me in my   aforesaid and acknowledged the same.

GIVEN under my hand and seal this   day of   19
My commission expires on the   day of   , 19

_____
Notary Public

$_____, _____, _____, _____, 19_____

For value received and without offset, _____ jointly and severally promise to pay to the order of _____
_____ Dollars
with interest from date at the rate of _____% per annum, until paid, negotiable and payable at any bank or trust company in _____ installments of $_____ each, or as much more as makers choose to pay; the first of said _____ installments shall become due and payable on the _____ day of _____, 19_____, and thereafter a _____ installment of $_____ shall be due and payable on the _____ day of each and every succeeding _____ until the principal of this note and the interest thereon shall be paid in full; payments shall first be applied toward the payment of the interest then due on the unpaid principal, and the balance shall be applied as a credit on the principal.

Upon default in the payment of any _____ installment due on this note, the entire unpaid principal together with interest shall at once become due and payable without notice at the option of the holder of this note. Failure to exercise this option shall not constitute a waiver of the right to exercise the same in the event of any subsequent default.

The undersigned and all endorsers, sureties and guarantors of this note hereby severally waive presentment, protest, notice of protest, notice of maturity, notice of dishonor or non-payment at maturity, and demand for payment at maturity; and the undersigned and all endorsers, sureties and guarantors of this note hereby severally waive the benefit of homestead and all other exemptions as to this debt.

In case payment of this note shall not be made at maturity, the undersigned and all endorsers, sureties and guarantors agree to pay attorney's fee of ten per cent on the unpaid principal hereof if this note is placed in the hands of an attorney for collection.

Witness the following signatures and seals:

Address _____   _____ (SEAL)
_____   _____ (SEAL)
_____   _____ (SEAL)
_____   _____ (SEAL)

This note is secured by that certain deed of trust of even date herewith recorded in the Clerk's Office of the Circuit Court of _____ County, _____, conveying to the trustee identifying this note _____ Trustee(s)

Identified by: _____

DATE OF PAYMENT	INT. PAID TO	CR. INTEREST	CR. PRINCIPAL	BALANCE PRINCIPAL DUE	DATE OF PAYMENT	INT. PAID TO	CR. INTEREST	CR. PRINCIPAL	BALANCE PRINCIPAL DUE

SAMPLE LETTER PLACING NOTES FOR COLLECTION AT BANK

September 17, 1978

Senior Vice President
Mr. William Doe
Citizens Bank
Preston, VA 22844

Dear Bill:

We would appreciate your setting up the following Deed of Trust Notes for collection to B.K. Haynes Corporation, account number 6-484-124410.

Maker	Note Amount	Annual % Rate	Monthly Pmt.	1st Pmt. Due
Edward R. Smith 14304 Green Hill Drive Rockville, MD 20853	$10777.32* 6900.00	11.09	$99.79	8-24-78
Frank C. Jones 73 Knob Hill Rd.	$5889.60 3900.00	9.46	$49.08	9-1-78

We are also enclosing Mr. Jone's September payment and Mr. Smith's August and September payments.

Thank you for your cooperation.

Sincerely,

Bradley K. Haynes

Enclosure

BKH/kld

*Note: Top figure under Note Amount is balance owed, *including* interest if note goes to full term.

Appendix K 353

DELINQUENT ACCOUNT NOTICES (EXAMPLES)

FROM: The Citizen Bank
P. O. Box 3122
Preston, VA. 22844   (Dealer 22F)

DID YOU FORGET?

According to our records, the payment due on your account is now past due. Perhaps it has been overlooked. If the payment has been sent please disregard this notice. Otherwise please pay the full amount as shown below.

Preston Office   —Consumer Loan Department

Acct. Number	Unpaid Balance of Account	Amount Past Due	Unpaid Late Charge	Late Charge Assessed	Please Pay This Amount	Date of Notice
1-984-01-4428	$3,452.22	63.93	23.16	3.20	90.29	2/20/79 Date Due 2/10/79

TO: Mr. William R. Wilson
137 Braddock St.
Dundee, CA. 91342

....

CITIZEN BANK
Preston, VA. 22844
February 17, 1979

Mr. Robert G. Dempsey   RE: Loan 1-29-101-31489
41 Mance Ave.   Payment $68.84
Lorton, VA. 23505

Dear Mr. Dempsey:

In reviewing our installment loans, I find that your account is seriously delinquent. January's payment is past due and February's payment will be due on the 20th.

It has now become a serious matter in that if your loan should reach two months past due, your credit rating could be permanently damaged. Your payments are now expected within 7 days.

Sincerely yours,

Paul R. Godfrey
Assistant Vice President

LEDGER SHEET FOR NOTE COLLECTIONS

MORTGAGOR'S NAME				AMOUNT			
ADDRESS				PAYEE			
LOCATION OF PROPERTY				ACRES			
INTEREST RATE				INTEREST DUE			
DATE OF LOAN				LOAN DUE			
DATE PAID	INTEREST	PRINCIPAL	BALANCE	DATE PAID	INTEREST	PRINCIPAL	BALANCE

APPENDIX L

WHAT YOU NEED TO KNOW ABOUT SERVICING YOUR NOTES RECEIVABLE

After you have sold a lot in your project, you will be scheduling the closing with a local attorney. (I usually try to use the individual or firm handling my legal affairs in that area.) At closing, your installment purchaser signs a mortgage or deed of trust pledging his property as security for the balance owed to you. He also signs a note or bond by which he promises to pay the amount stated on the instrument. If you've sold him a lot with improvements, such as a home, cabin, or barn, he should be required to carry adequate fire and hazard insurance, and this provision should be included in the mortgage or deed of trust. The note or bond states specifically how much is owed, the rate of interest, the amount and frequency of installment payments, and the rights and remedies of both parties in the event of default. After settlement, the closing attorney records the deed and mortgage or deed of trust, in the official records of the county in which the lot is located. You'll receive the recording receipts, a copy of the settlement statement, and the note or bond. The mortgage or deed of trust will be returned to you at a later date by the county clerk or appointed official in the courthouse.

Ledger Sheet or Mortgage Card — This is your accounting record of the loan, showing the date each payment was received, proportionate amounts applied to principal and interest, and the amortized balance. If the loan is being collected in-house (as opposed to bank collection), you will supply the mortgagor with an amortization schedule or payment book on which he will record the monthly activity of his loan. If your loan is placed with a bank for collection on your behalf, the bank will supply the note maker with a payment book or an amortization schedule.

More than likely the bank will have various fees connected with the servicing of your loans. Start-up fees and monthly collection fees are examples. You should establish a separate collection account for your notes receivable and, when appropriate, transfer funds to your other accounts. If not needed for immediate operating expenses, these collected funds should be moved into interest-bearing accounts soon after receipt. Late charges, patterned after standard banking practices in your area, should be assessed upon your delinquent note makers. If your operations involve the collection of large numbers of notes, your accountant may find it advisable to computerize your collection procedures.

Document and Correspondence File — The first item in this file is usually a copy of the original contract of purchase. The credit report, original note (if not held in the bank), recording receipts, and the mortgage or deed of trust soon follow. In some cases the file will contain a copy of the plat on which the lot is located, a title opinion on the individual lot, insurance records, and possibly an appraisal of the property. A chronological record of correspondence connected with the loan can be kept in the same file or transferred to a separate correspondence file. Your original documents are important to you. They should be protected against fire and natural calamities; but copies are available on record in the local courthouse and in the office of your closing attorney.

Delinquent tax card file — If a mortgagor becomes delinquent in paying his property taxes, a lien prior to your mortgage could be placed on the property. Unpaid taxes could force the lot to be sold at public auction and, of course, this would concern you. Therefore, you should become familiar with the technical methods used by the local taxing authority and periodically review the tax status of each lot on which you hold a mortgage or deed of trust. A sub category in this file could be the hazard insurance on lots with improved structures. Where you hold a lien against the property, you will want immediate notification from the insurance company if any policy has been cancelled or marked past due.

APPENDIX M

HOW TO FIGURE YOUR PROCEEDS WHEN DISCOUNTING YOUR NOTES

Let's say you find yourself in need of cash. You're fishing for a note from your various projects, and you hook a fine-looking first mortgage specimen having the markings of good credit, prompt payment, and accumulated equity. This particular note pays you $139.35 per month, or $1,672 a year ($139.35 X 12).

The face amount of the note (balance due) is $10,000, and the annual interest rate is 9% simple. (Note history: You sold a lot for $11,000, receiving $500 down and a note for $10,500. Since then, through installment payments, $500 has been applied toward principal. The note, originally made for 10 years, has nine years to run. Now you want to sell it.)

All right, let's say your banker tells you what you already know: Money is tight. He says he has to have a 15% yield. O.K., O.K., you say; that's fine. How much can I get on the note? At this point the banker whips out his financial calculator and begins to fine-tune the deal. To tell you how much he can pay for the note he must obtain more data.

Question No. 1: *What is the finance charge per $100 of amount financed?*

Go to Table A. Read across on the 108 payment line (9 year remaining life in your note) to the annual percentage rate of your note (9.0% simple interest).

Finance charge per $100 of amount financed equals **$46.26**.

Question No. 2: *What is the amount of remaining interest (finance charge) if note goes to full term?*

Multiply the face amount of note by above finance charge. Remaining interest (finance charge) equals **$4,626**.

Question No. 3: ***What are total proceeds if note goes to full term?***

Add total finance charge to face amount of note (balance owed). ($4,626.00 + $10,000)

Total proceeds = $14,626.00

Question No. 4: ***What are my proceeds at banker's expected yield rate?***

Go to Table A. Read across on the 108 payment line to the banker's expected yield rate (15%).

Finance charge per $100 of amount financed at banker's expected yield rate equals **$82.78**.

Covert the above figure to divisor by moving decimal two places left and adding the whole number "1" (82.78 = 1.8278).

Divide total proceeds of note by above divisor.
$$\frac{\$14,626.00}{1.8278} = \$8,001.97$$

Your proceeds from sale of note =   **$8,001.97**

Question No. 5: ***What is the percentage rate of discount on this note at an expected 15% yield rate?***

Divide your proceeds by face amount of note.
$$\frac{\$8,001.97}{\$10,000.00} = 80\% = 100\% - 80\% = 20\%$$

The discount rate on your note
if sold to bank =   **20%**

An example follows showing one method of precisely determining the proceeds from a discounted note when you know the expected yield rate and "add-on" interest rate.

EXAMPLE

Your partnership has a note to sell with a face amount of $10,000 and bearing an annual percentage rate of 9.08%. Your conversion tables show you that this A. P. R. equals 5.25% "add-on." The note has ten years to run.

You have excess funds sitting in a savings and loan bank drawing 7.5% per annum in six month certificates. Renewal time is coming up, and you inform your partners that you will buy the note if you can get a 15% yield. You're aware that the note maker has good credit, substantial equity, and an excellent payment record. Further, to ensure that his property would not be threatened by a potential developer bankruptcy, the note maker made a sufficient down payment when he purchased the lot to release his property from the blanket mortgage. All-in-all, it looks like a sound investment for you. Income from the note will be used to further your children's education.

Here's how you analyze how much you will have to pay for the note:

(1) Multiply the face amount by the interest rate (add-on) by the term of the note. This will give you the amount of interest to be "added on."

($10,000 X 5.25% X 10 yrs. = $5,250)

Total interest if note goes to full term = $5,250

(2) Add above interest to face amount of note.

($10,000 + $5,250 = $15,250)

"Add-on" face amount of note = $15,250

(3) Go to Table A. Read across on the 120 payment line (10 year life) to your expected yield rate (15%). Convert this figure to divisor by moving decimal 2 places left and adding the whole number "1". (93.60 = 1.9360).

Divide face amount of note by above divisor.
$$\frac{\$15,250.00}{1.9360} = \$7,877.07$$

Amount you will pay for note = $7,877.07

WHAT IF YOUR NOTE MAKER PREPAYS?

On a simple interest note, the matter is cut and dry. Your note maker is paying interest based on the balance owed. Prepayments on "add-on" notes require special computations to determine a pay-off figure. Appendix C of the "Truth in Lending — Regulation Z" publication explains how to compute unearned finance charges associated with prepayments on "add-on" notes.

ANALYSIS OF DISCOUNT OFFERS VS. YIELD RATES

Let's say that one of your note makers is planning some home improvements on his primary dwelling. You sold him a lot as a second home site and now he wants to mortgage that lot as part of his financing arrangements. The bank, before they will agree to the deal, wants first position. Now, let's assume that you are in first place, having paid off the original mortgage when you developed the property and sold the lots. Your note maker comes to you and offers to pay off his note in full if you'll give him a 15% discount. At the time he made you that offer, you were planning to discount his note at your own bank to yield them 15%.

Which alternative would leave you with more proceeds?

EXAMPLE

The note in question pays you $103.52 per month and has eight years to run. The face amount is $7,500 at an interest rate of 9.5% simple. If you let this note go to the maker, you'll pick up $6,375 ($7500 X .85). Will you come out better by discounting the note to your bank?

Question No. 1: *What is the finance charge per $100 of amount financed?*

Go to Table A. Read across on the 96 payment line (8 year remaining life in your note) to the annual percentage rate of your note (9.5% simple interest).

Finance charge per $100 of amount financed equals $43.14.

Question No. 2: *What is the amount of remaining interest (finance charge) if note goes to full term?*

Divide face amount of note by 100.

Multiply quotient by above finance charge (75 X $43.14).

Remaining interest (finance charge) equals $3,235.50.

Question No. 3: *What are total proceeds if note goes to full term?*

Add total finance charge to face amount of note (balance owed). ($3,235.50 + $7,500)

Total proceeds = $10,735.50

Question No. 4: *What will be my proceeds at banker's expected yield rate?*

Go to Table A. Read across on the 96 payment line to the banker's expected yield rate (15%).

Finance charge per $100 of amount financed at banker's expected yield rate equals **$72.28**.

Convert the above figure to divisor by moving decimal two places left and adding the whole number "1". (72.28 = 1.7228)

Divide total proceeds by above divisor.
$$\frac{\$10,735.50}{1.7228} = \$6,231.43$$

Proceeds from sale of note to bank = **$6,231.43**

Question No. 5: *What is the percentage rate of discount on this note at an expected yield rate of 15%?*

Divide your proceeds by face amount of note.
$$\frac{\$6,231.43}{\$7,500.00} = 83\% = 100\% - 83\% = 17\%$$

The discount on your note if sold to bank = **17%**

From this example you can see that you will gain proceeds by dealing with a purchaser whose yield is 2% lower than the bank's demand rate. In this case you stand to gain $143.57 ($6,375.00 − $6,231.43). There are related charges to any note sale, such as title opinion, credit check, appraisal fee, etc., and these costs would have to be figured in when evaluating your options. If the mathematics of the deal end up favoring the banker, you have another overriding consideration. This is the question of personal endorsement on the note. If, by selling this note to the bank, you were required to replace it or make it good in the event of default, it may be worth the sacrifice of 2% by selling the note to its maker.

Finally, remember the following important tactic for maximizing your proceeds from note sales. Any note that is salable to a bank is potentially salable to the maker. You may want to offer a discount for early pay-offs prior to selling these same notes to banks and other investors. This discount can be substantially lower (with a proportionately higher increase in your proceeds) than the rate you would expect from conventional note purchasers.

The following letter shows you how you might approach note makers regarding an early pay-off. In this instance, we sent along a check made out in the name of the property owner for the amount of the savings. When the note was paid off, we had the option of signing the check or accepting the note maker's check for full pay-off less the discount offered.

DISCOUNT LETTER

(Date)

Mr. John J. Smith
123 Oak Drive
Anytown, Md. 10000

Dear Mr. Smith:

Since some property owners plan to build in the near future, we wish to point out that *lending institutions will require your note to us to be paid in full before arranging mortgage financing.*

NOW WE HAVE PROFITABLE NEWS FOR YOU

If your plans call for early construction of a home or vacation cottage, it will definitely be to your advantage to withdraw money from savings or to sell stocks to pay off your note now. Here's why:

For the month of September, we are offering a significant discount to any property owner who wishes to prepay his note in advance of construction.

ALONG WITH SIZEABLE SAVINGS IN INTEREST, THERE IS A REWARDING

*10% DISCOUNT

IMPORTANT!!! YOU MUST LET US KNOW BEFORE SEPT. 30 THAT YOU WILL BE TAKING ADVANTAGE OF THIS OFFER. AFTER THAT DATE YOUR NOTE MAY BE IN THE HANDS OF A LENDER WHO WILL NOT ALLOW THIS DISCOUNT.

*A 5% discount is available for curtailments of 50% or more on your note.

Would it be worth a free set of kitchen appliances for your home or cottage, or to save the cost of having a well drilled? *Your savings could amount to this much and more!*

The total amount you will save is shown below:

Total financed	$4,950.00
Interest saved	1,531.44
10% Discount	495.00
Total saved	2,026.44

The above figures are based on the original contract and reflect your savings if your note is allowed to run to end of term. To get current figures, subtract payments that have been made. *Past experience has shown that note payoffs are frequent before expiration date because of construction, resale, and other reasons, and that this sort of discount is, of course, not allowed.*

If you can use the extra funds that this offer allows, please call me collect at 555-1212. We are holding your note in a local bank pending a reply from you.

Sincerely,

B. K. Haynes

P. S.
The enclosed check needs only to be validated by my signature. You will be charged *NO INTEREST* for September under this offer.

BKH/bam

This procedure for determining your proceeds from discounted notes should be adequate for your needs. Where interest charges per $100 financed exceed the figure $100, you simply add the whole number 2 (rather than 1) when converting the expected yield rate to divisor form.

A basic requirement when following this method is that you will utilize the monthly payment plan tables from the publication, *Truth In Lending – Regulation Z – Annual Percentage Rate Tables.* (Copies may be obtained from the Board of Governors of the Federal Reserve System, Washington D. C. 20551.) Different tables and calculations will be necessary when figuring discounts on notes having irregular or other periodic payment schedules.

Occasionally you will be confronted with an annual percentage rate that does not conform to the intervals shown in Table A (as extracted from the publication, *Truth in Lending – Regulation Z – Annual Percentage Rate Tables*). This can occur when total interest over the life of the loan is "added on" at the front end of the loan before dividing the loan into monthly installments. (Under a simple interest loan, interest is computed on the balance due at any given time.) This difference in interest computations explains, for example, how a so-called 5.25% "add-on" rate for a 10 year loan is actually an annual percentage rate of 9.08%. Here are two other examples, based on 120 month loans:

$$9.46\% \text{ A. P. R.} = 5.50\% \text{ "add-on"}$$
$$10.21\% \text{ A. P. R.} = 6.00\% \text{ "add-on"}$$

For purposes of determining your proceeds from discounted notes, you can, when dealing with these irregular annual percentage rates, read across Table A to the interval closest to the A. P. R. on the face of your note. Then you'll proceed as described in the previous problem. Bear in mind, however, that your anticipated proceeds will only be a close estimate and not an exact figure. (Directions for handling irregular and special payment schedules are given in the "Truth in Lending – Regulation Z" publication.) Bankers and other investors will precisely calculate the discount using accepted mathematical principals. As you become more sophisticated in discounting notes and figuring yield rates, you will want to refer to tables which convert "add-on" rates to annual percentage rates. You can order these tables from:

Financial Publishing, Co.
82 Brookline Ave.
Boston, MA 02215

TABLE A

ANNUAL PERCENTAGE RATE TABLE FOR MONTHLY PAYMENT PLANS
SEE INSTRUCTIONS FOR USE OF TABLES

FRB-102-M

NUMBER OF PAYMENTS	ANNUAL PERCENTAGE RATE															
	6.00%	6.25%	6.50%	6.75%	7.00%	7.25%	7.50%	7.75%	8.00%	8.25%	8.50%	8.75%	9.00%	9.25%	9.50%	9.75%
	(FINANCE CHARGE PER $100 OF AMOUNT FINANCED)															
1	0.50	0.52	0.54	0.56	0.58	0.60	0.62	0.65	0.67	0.69	0.71	0.73	0.75	0.77	0.79	0.81
2	0.75	0.78	0.81	0.84	0.88	0.91	0.94	0.97	1.00	1.03	1.06	1.10	1.13	1.16	1.19	1.22
3	1.00	1.04	1.09	1.13	1.17	1.21	1.25	1.29	1.34	1.38	1.42	1.46	1.50	1.55	1.59	1.63
4	1.25	1.31	1.36	1.41	1.46	1.51	1.57	1.62	1.67	1.72	1.78	1.83	1.88	1.93	1.99	2.04
5	1.50	1.57	1.63	1.69	1.76	1.82	1.88	1.95	2.01	2.07	2.13	2.20	2.26	2.32	2.39	2.45
6	1.76	1.83	1.90	1.98	2.05	2.13	2.20	2.27	2.35	2.42	2.49	2.57	2.64	2.72	2.79	2.86
7	2.01	2.09	2.18	2.26	2.35	2.43	2.52	2.60	2.68	2.77	2.85	2.94	3.02	3.11	3.19	3.28
8	2.26	2.36	2.45	2.55	2.64	2.74	2.83	2.93	3.02	3.12	3.21	3.31	3.40	3.50	3.60	3.69
9	2.52	2.62	2.73	2.83	2.94	3.05	3.15	3.26	3.36	3.47	3.57	3.68	3.79	3.89	4.00	4.11
10	2.77	2.89	3.00	3.12	3.24	3.35	3.47	3.59	3.70	3.82	3.94	4.05	4.17	4.29	4.41	4.52
11	3.02	3.15	3.28	3.41	3.53	3.66	3.79	3.92	4.04	4.17	4.30	4.43	4.56	4.68	4.81	4.94
12	3.28	3.42	3.56	3.69	3.83	3.97	4.11	4.25	4.39	4.52	4.66	4.80	4.94	5.08	5.22	5.36
13	3.53	3.68	3.83	3.98	4.13	4.28	4.43	4.58	4.73	4.88	5.03	5.18	5.33	5.48	5.63	5.78
14	3.79	3.95	4.11	4.27	4.43	4.59	4.75	4.91	5.07	5.23	5.39	5.55	5.72	5.88	6.04	6.20
15	4.05	4.22	4.39	4.56	4.73	4.90	5.07	5.24	5.42	5.59	5.76	5.93	6.10	6.28	6.45	6.62
16	4.30	4.48	4.67	4.85	5.03	5.21	5.40	5.58	5.76	5.94	6.13	6.31	6.49	6.68	6.86	7.05
17	4.56	4.75	4.95	5.14	5.33	5.52	5.72	5.91	6.11	6.30	6.49	6.69	6.88	7.08	7.27	7.47
18	4.82	5.02	5.22	5.43	5.63	5.84	6.04	6.25	6.45	6.66	6.86	7.07	7.28	7.48	7.69	7.90
19	5.07	5.29	5.50	5.72	5.94	6.15	6.37	6.58	6.80	7.02	7.23	7.45	7.67	7.89	8.10	8.32
20	5.33	5.56	5.78	6.01	6.24	6.46	6.69	6.92	7.15	7.38	7.60	7.83	8.06	8.29	8.52	8.75
21	5.59	5.83	6.07	6.30	6.54	6.78	7.02	7.26	7.50	7.74	7.97	8.21	8.46	8.70	8.94	9.18
22	5.85	6.10	6.35	6.60	6.84	7.09	7.34	7.59	7.84	8.10	8.35	8.60	8.85	9.10	9.36	9.61
23	6.11	6.37	6.63	6.89	7.15	7.41	7.67	7.93	8.19	8.46	8.72	8.98	9.25	9.51	9.77	10.04
24	6.37	6.64	6.91	7.18	7.45	7.73	8.00	8.27	8.55	8.82	9.09	9.37	9.64	9.92	10.19	10.47
25	6.63	6.91	7.19	7.48	7.76	8.04	8.33	8.61	8.90	9.18	9.47	9.75	10.04	10.33	10.62	10.90
26	6.89	7.18	7.48	7.77	8.07	8.36	8.66	8.95	9.25	9.55	9.84	10.14	10.44	10.74	11.04	11.34
27	7.15	7.46	7.76	8.07	8.37	8.68	8.99	9.29	9.60	9.91	10.22	10.53	10.84	11.15	11.46	11.77
28	7.41	7.73	8.05	8.36	8.68	9.00	9.32	9.64	9.96	10.28	10.60	10.92	11.24	11.56	11.89	12.21
29	7.67	8.00	8.33	8.66	8.99	9.32	9.65	9.98	10.31	10.64	10.97	11.31	11.64	11.98	12.31	12.65
30	7.94	8.28	8.61	8.96	9.30	9.64	9.98	10.32	10.66	11.01	11.35	11.70	12.04	12.39	12.74	13.09
31	8.20	8.55	8.90	9.25	9.60	9.96	10.31	10.67	11.02	11.38	11.73	12.09	12.45	12.81	13.17	13.53
32	8.46	8.82	9.19	9.55	9.91	10.28	10.64	11.01	11.38	11.74	12.11	12.48	12.85	13.22	13.59	13.97
33	8.73	9.10	9.47	9.85	10.22	10.60	10.98	11.36	11.73	12.11	12.49	12.88	13.26	13.64	14.02	14.41
34	8.99	9.37	9.76	10.15	10.53	10.92	11.31	11.70	12.09	12.48	12.88	13.27	13.66	14.06	14.45	14.85
35	9.25	9.65	10.05	10.45	10.85	11.25	11.65	12.05	12.45	12.85	13.26	13.66	14.07	14.48	14.89	15.29
36	9.52	9.93	10.34	10.75	11.16	11.57	11.98	12.40	12.81	13.23	13.64	14.06	14.48	14.90	15.32	15.74
37	9.78	10.20	10.63	11.05	11.47	11.89	12.32	12.74	13.17	13.60	14.03	14.46	14.89	15.32	15.75	16.19
38	10.05	10.48	10.91	11.35	11.78	12.22	12.66	13.09	13.53	13.97	14.41	14.85	15.30	15.74	16.19	16.63
39	10.32	10.76	11.20	11.65	12.10	12.54	12.99	13.44	13.89	14.35	14.80	15.25	15.71	16.17	16.62	17.08
40	10.58	11.04	11.49	11.95	12.41	12.87	13.33	13.79	14.26	14.72	15.19	15.65	16.12	16.59	17.06	17.53
41	10.85	11.32	11.78	12.25	12.72	13.20	13.67	14.14	14.62	15.10	15.57	16.05	16.53	17.01	17.50	17.98
42	11.12	11.60	12.08	12.56	13.04	13.52	14.01	14.50	14.98	15.47	15.96	16.45	16.95	17.44	17.94	18.43
43	11.38	11.87	12.37	12.86	13.36	13.85	14.35	14.85	15.35	15.85	16.35	16.86	17.36	17.87	18.38	18.89
44	11.65	12.15	12.66	13.16	13.67	14.18	14.69	15.20	15.71	16.23	16.74	17.26	17.78	18.30	18.82	19.34
45	11.92	12.44	12.95	13.47	13.99	14.51	15.03	15.55	16.08	16.61	17.13	17.66	18.19	18.73	19.26	19.79
46	12.19	12.72	13.24	13.77	14.31	14.84	15.37	15.91	16.45	16.99	17.53	18.07	18.61	19.16	19.70	20.25
47	12.46	13.00	13.54	14.08	14.62	15.17	15.72	16.26	16.81	17.37	17.92	18.47	19.03	19.59	20.15	20.71
48	12.73	13.28	13.83	14.39	14.94	15.50	16.06	16.62	17.18	17.75	18.31	18.88	19.45	20.02	20.59	21.16
49	13.00	13.56	14.13	14.69	15.26	15.83	16.40	16.98	17.55	18.13	18.71	19.29	19.87	20.45	21.04	21.62
50	13.27	13.84	14.42	15.00	15.58	16.16	16.75	17.33	17.92	18.51	19.10	19.69	20.29	20.89	21.48	22.08
51	13.54	14.13	14.72	15.31	15.90	16.50	17.09	17.69	18.29	18.89	19.50	20.10	20.71	21.32	21.93	22.55
52	13.81	14.41	15.01	15.62	16.22	16.83	17.44	18.05	18.66	19.28	19.89	20.51	21.13	21.76	22.38	23.01
53	14.08	14.69	15.31	15.92	16.54	17.16	17.78	18.41	19.03	19.66	20.29	20.92	21.56	22.19	22.83	23.47
54	14.36	14.98	15.61	16.23	16.86	17.50	18.13	18.77	19.41	20.05	20.69	21.34	21.98	22.63	23.28	23.94
55	14.63	15.26	15.90	16.54	17.19	17.83	18.48	19.13	19.78	20.43	21.09	21.75	22.41	23.07	23.73	24.40
56	14.90	15.55	16.20	16.85	17.51	18.17	18.83	19.49	20.15	20.82	21.49	22.16	22.83	23.51	24.19	24.87
57	15.17	15.84	16.50	17.17	17.83	18.50	19.18	19.85	20.53	21.21	21.89	22.58	23.26	23.95	24.64	25.34
58	15.45	16.12	16.80	17.48	18.16	18.84	19.53	20.21	20.91	21.60	22.29	22.99	23.69	24.39	25.10	25.80
59	15.72	16.41	17.10	17.79	18.48	19.18	19.88	20.58	21.28	21.99	22.70	23.41	24.12	24.84	25.55	26.27
60	16.00	16.70	17.40	18.10	18.81	19.52	20.23	20.94	21.66	22.38	23.10	23.82	24.55	25.28	26.01	26.75

Appendix M 367

TABLE A

ANNUAL PERCENTAGE RATE TABLE FOR MONTHLY PAYMENT PLANS
SEE INSTRUCTIONS FOR USE OF TABLES

FRB-103-M

NUMBER OF PAYMENTS	ANNUAL PERCENTAGE RATE															
	10.00%	10.25%	10.50%	10.75%	11.00%	11.25%	11.50%	11.75%	12.00%	12.25%	12.50%	12.75%	13.00%	13.25%	13.50%	13.75%
	(FINANCE CHARGE PER $100 OF AMOUNT FINANCED)															
1	0.83	0.85	0.87	0.90	0.92	0.94	0.96	0.98	1.00	1.02	1.04	1.06	1.08	1.10	1.12	1.15
2	1.25	1.28	1.31	1.35	1.38	1.41	1.44	1.47	1.50	1.53	1.57	1.60	1.63	1.66	1.69	1.72
3	1.67	1.71	1.76	1.80	1.84	1.88	1.92	1.96	2.01	2.05	2.09	2.13	2.17	2.22	2.26	2.30
4	2.09	2.14	2.20	2.25	2.30	2.35	2.41	2.46	2.51	2.57	2.62	2.67	2.72	2.78	2.83	2.88
5	2.51	2.58	2.64	2.70	2.77	2.83	2.89	2.96	3.02	3.08	3.15	3.21	3.27	3.34	3.40	3.46
6	2.94	3.01	3.08	3.16	3.23	3.31	3.38	3.45	3.53	3.60	3.68	3.75	3.83	3.90	3.97	4.05
7	3.36	3.45	3.53	3.62	3.70	3.78	3.87	3.95	4.04	4.12	4.21	4.29	4.38	4.47	4.55	4.64
8	3.79	3.88	3.98	4.07	4.17	4.26	4.36	4.46	4.55	4.65	4.74	4.84	4.94	5.03	5.13	5.22
9	4.21	4.32	4.43	4.53	4.64	4.75	4.85	4.96	5.07	5.17	5.28	5.39	5.49	5.60	5.71	5.82
10	4.64	4.76	4.88	4.99	5.11	5.23	5.35	5.46	5.58	5.70	5.82	5.94	6.05	6.17	6.29	6.41
11	5.07	5.20	5.33	5.45	5.58	5.71	5.84	5.97	6.10	6.23	6.36	6.49	6.62	6.75	6.88	7.01
12	5.50	5.64	5.78	5.92	6.06	6.20	6.34	6.48	6.62	6.76	6.90	7.04	7.18	7.32	7.46	7.60
13	5.93	6.08	6.23	6.38	6.53	6.68	6.84	6.99	7.14	7.29	7.44	7.59	7.75	7.90	8.05	8.20
14	6.36	6.52	6.69	6.85	7.01	7.17	7.34	7.50	7.66	7.82	7.99	8.15	8.31	8.48	8.64	8.81
15	6.80	6.97	7.14	7.32	7.49	7.66	7.84	8.01	8.19	8.36	8.53	8.71	8.88	9.06	9.23	9.41
16	7.23	7.41	7.60	7.78	7.97	8.15	8.34	8.53	8.71	8.90	9.08	9.27	9.46	9.64	9.83	10.02
17	7.67	7.86	8.06	8.25	8.45	8.65	8.84	9.04	9.24	9.44	9.63	9.83	10.03	10.23	10.43	10.63
18	8.10	8.31	8.52	8.73	8.93	9.14	9.35	9.56	9.77	9.98	10.19	10.40	10.61	10.82	11.03	11.24
19	8.54	8.76	8.98	9.20	9.42	9.64	9.86	10.08	10.30	10.52	10.74	10.96	11.18	11.41	11.63	11.85
20	8.98	9.21	9.44	9.67	9.90	10.13	10.37	10.60	10.83	11.06	11.30	11.53	11.76	12.00	12.23	12.46
21	9.42	9.66	9.90	10.15	10.39	10.63	10.88	11.12	11.36	11.61	11.85	12.10	12.34	12.59	12.84	13.08
22	9.86	10.12	10.37	10.62	10.88	11.13	11.39	11.64	11.90	12.16	12.41	12.67	12.93	13.19	13.44	13.70
23	10.30	10.57	10.84	11.10	11.37	11.63	11.90	12.17	12.44	12.71	12.97	13.24	13.51	13.78	14.05	14.32
24	10.75	11.02	11.30	11.58	11.86	12.14	12.42	12.70	12.98	13.26	13.54	13.82	14.10	14.38	14.66	14.95
25	11.19	11.48	11.77	12.06	12.35	12.64	12.93	13.22	13.52	13.81	14.10	14.40	14.69	14.98	15.28	15.57
26	11.64	11.94	12.24	12.54	12.85	13.15	13.45	13.75	14.06	14.36	14.67	14.97	15.28	15.59	15.89	16.20
27	12.09	12.40	12.71	13.03	13.34	13.66	13.97	14.29	14.60	14.92	15.24	15.56	15.87	16.19	16.51	16.83
28	12.53	12.86	13.18	13.51	13.84	14.16	14.49	14.82	15.15	15.48	15.81	16.14	16.47	16.80	17.13	17.46
29	12.98	13.32	13.66	14.00	14.33	14.67	15.01	15.35	15.70	16.04	16.38	16.72	17.07	17.41	17.75	18.10
30	13.43	13.78	14.13	14.48	14.83	15.19	15.54	15.89	16.24	16.60	16.95	17.31	17.66	18.02	18.38	18.74
31	13.89	14.25	14.61	14.97	15.33	15.70	16.06	16.43	16.79	17.16	17.53	17.90	18.27	18.63	19.00	19.38
32	14.34	14.71	15.09	15.46	15.84	16.21	16.59	16.97	17.35	17.73	18.11	18.49	18.87	19.25	19.63	20.02
33	14.79	15.18	15.57	15.95	16.34	16.73	17.12	17.51	17.90	18.29	18.69	19.08	19.47	19.87	20.26	20.66
34	15.25	15.65	16.05	16.44	16.85	17.25	17.65	18.05	18.46	18.86	19.27	19.67	20.08	20.49	20.90	21.31
35	15.70	16.11	16.53	16.94	17.35	17.77	18.18	18.60	19.01	19.43	19.85	20.27	20.69	21.11	21.53	21.95
36	16.16	16.58	17.01	17.43	17.86	18.29	18.71	19.14	19.57	20.00	20.43	20.87	21.30	21.73	22.17	22.60
37	16.62	17.06	17.49	17.93	18.37	18.81	19.25	19.69	20.13	20.58	21.02	21.46	21.91	22.36	22.81	23.25
38	17.08	17.53	17.98	18.43	18.88	19.33	19.78	20.24	20.69	21.15	21.61	22.07	22.52	22.99	23.45	23.91
39	17.54	18.00	18.46	18.93	19.39	19.86	20.32	20.79	21.26	21.73	22.20	22.67	23.14	23.61	24.09	24.56
40	18.00	18.48	18.95	19.43	19.90	20.38	20.86	21.34	21.82	22.30	22.79	23.27	23.76	24.25	24.73	25.22
41	18.47	18.95	19.44	19.93	20.42	20.91	21.40	21.89	22.39	22.88	23.38	23.88	24.38	24.88	25.38	25.88
42	18.93	19.43	19.93	20.43	20.93	21.44	21.94	22.45	22.96	23.47	23.98	24.49	25.00	25.51	26.03	26.55
43	19.40	19.91	20.42	20.94	21.45	21.97	22.49	23.01	23.53	24.05	24.57	25.10	25.62	26.15	26.68	27.21
44	19.86	20.39	20.91	21.44	21.97	22.50	23.03	23.57	24.10	24.64	25.17	25.71	26.25	26.79	27.33	27.88
45	20.33	20.87	21.41	21.95	22.49	23.03	23.58	24.12	24.67	25.22	25.77	26.32	26.88	27.43	27.99	28.55
46	20.80	21.35	21.90	22.46	23.01	23.57	24.13	24.69	25.25	25.81	26.37	26.94	27.51	28.08	28.65	29.22
47	21.27	21.83	22.40	22.97	23.53	24.10	24.68	25.25	25.82	26.40	26.98	27.56	28.14	28.72	29.31	29.89
48	21.74	22.32	22.90	23.48	24.06	24.64	25.23	25.81	26.40	26.99	27.58	28.18	28.77	29.37	29.97	30.57
49	22.21	22.80	23.39	23.99	24.58	25.18	25.78	26.38	26.98	27.59	28.19	28.80	29.41	30.02	30.63	31.24
50	22.69	23.29	23.89	24.50	25.11	25.72	26.33	26.95	27.56	28.18	28.80	29.42	30.04	30.67	31.29	31.92
51	23.16	23.78	24.40	25.02	25.64	26.26	26.89	27.52	28.15	28.78	29.41	30.05	30.68	31.32	31.96	32.60
52	23.64	24.27	24.90	25.53	26.17	26.81	27.45	28.09	28.73	29.38	30.02	30.67	31.32	31.98	32.63	33.29
53	24.11	24.76	25.40	26.05	26.70	27.35	28.00	28.66	29.32	29.98	30.64	31.30	31.97	32.63	33.30	33.97
54	24.59	25.25	25.91	26.57	27.23	27.90	28.56	29.23	29.91	30.58	31.25	31.93	32.61	33.29	33.98	34.66
55	25.07	25.74	26.41	27.09	27.77	28.44	29.13	29.81	30.50	31.18	31.87	32.56	33.26	33.95	34.65	35.35
56	25.55	26.23	26.92	27.61	28.30	28.99	29.69	30.39	31.09	31.79	32.49	33.20	33.91	34.62	35.33	36.04
57	26.03	26.73	27.43	28.13	28.84	29.54	30.25	30.97	31.68	32.39	33.11	33.83	34.56	35.28	36.01	36.74
58	26.51	27.23	27.94	28.66	29.37	30.10	30.82	31.55	32.27	33.00	33.74	34.47	35.20	35.95	36.69	37.43
59	27.00	27.72	28.45	29.18	29.91	30.65	31.39	32.13	32.87	33.61	34.36	35.11	35.86	36.62	37.37	38.13
60	27.48	28.22	28.96	29.71	30.45	31.20	31.96	32.71	33.47	34.23	34.99	35.75	36.52	37.29	38.06	38.83

TABLE A

ANNUAL PERCENTAGE RATE TABLE FOR MONTHLY PAYMENT PLANS
SEE INSTRUCTIONS FOR USE OF TABLES

FRB-104-M

NUMBER OF PAYMENTS	14.00%	14.25%	14.50%	14.75%	15.00%	15.25%	15.50%	15.75%	16.00%	16.25%	16.50%	16.75%	17.00%	17.25%	17.50%	17.75%
					(FINANCE CHARGE PER $100 OF AMOUNT FINANCED)											
1	1.17	1.19	1.21	1.23	1.25	1.27	1.29	1.31	1.33	1.35	1.37	1.40	1.42	1.44	1.46	1.48
2	1.75	1.78	1.82	1.85	1.88	1.91	1.94	1.97	2.00	2.04	2.07	2.10	2.13	2.16	2.19	2.22
3	2.34	2.38	2.43	2.47	2.51	2.55	2.59	2.64	2.68	2.72	2.76	2.80	2.85	2.89	2.93	2.97
4	2.93	2.99	3.04	3.09	3.14	3.20	3.25	3.30	3.36	3.41	3.46	3.51	3.57	3.62	3.67	3.73
5	3.53	3.59	3.65	3.72	3.78	3.84	3.91	3.97	4.04	4.10	4.16	4.23	4.29	4.35	4.42	4.48
6	4.12	4.20	4.27	4.35	4.42	4.49	4.57	4.64	4.72	4.79	4.87	4.94	5.02	5.09	5.17	5.24
7	4.72	4.81	4.89	4.98	5.06	5.15	5.23	5.32	5.40	5.49	5.58	5.66	5.75	5.83	5.92	6.00
8	5.32	5.42	5.51	5.61	5.71	5.80	5.90	6.00	6.09	6.19	6.29	6.38	6.48	6.58	6.67	6.77
9	5.92	6.03	6.14	6.25	6.35	6.46	6.57	6.68	6.78	6.89	7.00	7.11	7.22	7.32	7.43	7.54
10	6.53	6.65	6.77	6.88	7.00	7.12	7.24	7.36	7.48	7.60	7.72	7.84	7.96	8.08	8.19	8.31
11	7.14	7.27	7.40	7.53	7.66	7.79	7.92	8.05	8.18	8.31	8.44	8.57	8.70	8.83	8.96	9.09
12	7.74	7.89	8.03	8.17	8.31	8.45	8.59	8.74	8.88	9.02	9.16	9.30	9.45	9.59	9.73	9.87
13	8.36	8.51	8.66	8.81	8.97	9.12	9.27	9.43	9.58	9.73	9.89	10.04	10.20	10.35	10.50	10.66
14	8.97	9.13	9.30	9.46	9.63	9.79	9.96	10.12	10.29	10.45	10.62	10.78	10.95	11.11	11.28	11.45
15	9.59	9.76	9.94	10.11	10.29	10.47	10.64	10.82	11.00	11.17	11.35	11.53	11.71	11.88	12.06	12.24
16	10.20	10.39	10.58	10.77	10.95	11.14	11.33	11.52	11.71	11.90	12.09	12.28	12.46	12.65	12.84	13.03
17	10.82	11.02	11.22	11.42	11.62	11.82	12.02	12.22	12.42	12.62	12.83	13.03	13.23	13.43	13.63	13.83
18	11.45	11.66	11.87	12.08	12.29	12.50	12.72	12.93	13.14	13.35	13.57	13.78	13.99	14.21	14.42	14.64
19	12.07	12.30	12.52	12.74	12.97	13.19	13.41	13.64	13.86	14.09	14.31	14.54	14.76	14.99	15.22	15.44
20	12.70	12.93	13.17	13.41	13.64	13.88	14.11	14.35	14.59	14.82	15.06	15.30	15.54	15.77	16.01	16.25
21	13.33	13.58	13.82	14.07	14.32	14.57	14.82	15.06	15.31	15.56	15.81	16.06	16.31	16.56	16.81	17.07
22	13.96	14.22	14.48	14.74	15.00	15.26	15.52	15.78	16.04	16.30	16.57	16.83	17.09	17.36	17.62	17.88
23	14.59	14.87	15.14	15.41	15.68	15.96	16.23	16.50	16.78	17.05	17.32	17.60	17.88	18.15	18.43	18.70
24	15.23	15.51	15.80	16.08	16.37	16.65	16.94	17.22	17.51	17.80	18.09	18.37	18.66	18.95	19.24	19.53
25	15.87	16.17	16.46	16.76	17.06	17.35	17.65	17.95	18.25	18.55	18.85	19.15	19.45	19.75	20.05	20.36
26	16.51	16.82	17.13	17.44	17.75	18.06	18.37	18.68	18.99	19.30	19.62	19.93	20.24	20.56	20.87	21.19
27	17.15	17.47	17.80	18.12	18.44	18.76	19.09	19.41	19.74	20.06	20.39	20.71	21.04	21.37	21.69	22.02
28	17.80	18.13	18.47	18.80	19.14	19.47	19.81	20.15	20.48	20.82	21.16	21.50	21.84	22.18	22.52	22.86
29	18.45	18.79	19.14	19.49	19.83	20.18	20.53	20.89	21.23	21.58	21.94	22.29	22.64	22.99	23.35	23.70
30	19.10	19.45	19.81	20.17	20.54	20.90	21.26	21.62	21.99	22.35	22.72	23.09	23.45	23.81	24.18	24.55
31	19.75	20.12	20.49	20.87	21.24	21.61	21.99	22.37	22.74	23.12	23.50	23.88	24.26	24.64	25.02	25.40
32	20.40	20.79	21.17	21.56	21.95	22.33	22.72	23.11	23.50	23.89	24.28	24.68	25.07	25.46	25.86	26.25
33	21.06	21.46	21.85	22.25	22.65	23.06	23.46	23.86	24.26	24.67	25.07	25.48	25.88	26.29	26.70	27.11
34	21.72	22.13	22.54	22.95	23.37	23.78	24.19	24.61	25.03	25.44	25.86	26.28	26.70	27.12	27.54	27.97
35	22.38	22.80	23.23	23.65	24.08	24.51	24.94	25.36	25.79	26.23	26.66	27.09	27.52	27.96	28.39	28.83
36	23.04	23.48	23.92	24.35	24.80	25.24	25.68	26.12	26.57	27.01	27.46	27.90	28.35	28.80	29.25	29.70
37	23.70	24.16	24.61	25.06	25.51	25.97	26.42	26.88	27.34	27.80	28.26	28.72	29.18	29.64	30.10	30.57
38	24.37	24.84	25.30	25.77	26.24	26.70	27.17	27.64	28.11	28.59	29.06	29.53	30.01	30.49	30.96	31.44
39	25.04	25.52	26.00	26.48	26.96	27.44	27.92	28.41	28.89	29.38	29.87	30.36	30.85	31.34	31.83	32.32
40	25.71	26.20	26.70	27.19	27.69	28.18	28.68	29.18	29.68	30.18	30.69	31.19	31.69	32.19	32.69	33.20
41	26.39	26.89	27.40	27.91	28.41	28.92	29.44	29.95	30.46	30.97	31.49	32.01	32.52	33.04	33.55	34.08
42	27.06	27.58	28.10	28.62	29.15	29.67	30.19	30.72	31.25	31.78	32.31	32.84	33.37	33.90	34.44	34.97
43	27.74	28.27	28.81	29.34	29.88	30.42	30.96	31.50	32.04	32.58	33.13	33.67	34.22	34.76	35.31	35.86
44	28.42	28.97	29.52	30.07	30.62	31.17	31.72	32.28	32.83	33.39	33.95	34.51	35.07	35.63	36.19	36.76
45	29.11	29.67	30.23	30.79	31.36	31.92	32.49	33.06	33.63	34.20	34.77	35.35	35.92	36.50	37.08	37.66
46	29.79	30.36	30.94	31.52	32.10	32.68	33.26	33.84	34.43	35.01	35.60	36.19	36.78	37.37	37.96	38.56
47	30.48	31.07	31.66	32.25	32.84	33.44	34.03	34.63	35.23	35.83	36.43	37.04	37.64	38.25	38.86	39.46
48	31.17	31.77	32.37	32.98	33.59	34.20	34.81	35.42	36.03	36.65	37.27	37.88	38.50	39.13	39.75	40.37
49	31.86	32.48	33.09	33.71	34.34	34.96	35.59	36.21	36.84	37.47	38.10	38.74	39.37	40.01	40.65	41.29
50	32.55	33.18	33.82	34.45	35.09	35.73	36.37	37.01	37.65	38.30	38.94	39.59	40.24	40.89	41.55	42.20
51	33.25	33.89	34.54	35.19	35.84	36.49	37.15	37.81	38.46	39.12	39.79	40.45	41.11	41.78	42.45	43.12
52	33.95	34.61	35.27	35.93	36.60	37.27	37.94	38.61	39.28	39.96	40.63	41.31	41.99	42.67	43.36	44.04
53	34.65	35.32	36.00	36.68	37.36	38.04	38.72	39.41	40.10	40.79	41.48	42.17	42.87	43.57	44.27	44.97
54	35.35	36.04	36.73	37.42	38.12	38.82	39.52	40.22	40.92	41.63	42.33	43.04	43.75	44.47	45.18	45.90
55	36.05	36.76	37.46	38.17	38.88	39.60	40.31	41.03	41.74	42.47	43.19	43.91	44.64	45.37	46.10	46.83
56	36.76	37.48	38.20	38.92	39.65	40.38	41.11	41.84	42.57	43.31	44.05	44.79	45.53	46.27	47.02	47.77
57	37.47	38.20	38.94	39.68	40.42	41.16	41.91	42.65	43.40	44.15	44.91	45.66	46.42	47.18	47.94	48.71
58	38.18	38.93	39.68	40.43	41.19	41.95	42.71	43.47	44.23	45.00	45.77	46.54	47.32	48.09	48.87	49.65
59	38.89	39.66	40.42	41.19	41.96	42.74	43.51	44.29	45.07	45.85	46.64	47.42	48.21	49.01	49.80	50.60
60	39.61	40.39	41.17	41.95	42.74	43.53	44.32	45.11	45.91	46.71	47.51	48.31	49.12	49.92	50.73	51.55

TABLE A

ANNUAL PERCENTAGE RATE TABLE FOR MONTHLY PAYMENT PLANS
SEE INSTRUCTIONS FOR USE OF TABLES

FRB-202-M

NUMBER OF PAYMENTS	6.00%	6.25%	6.50%	6.75%	7.00%	7.25%	7.50%	7.75%	8.00%	8.25%	8.50%	8.75%	9.00%	9.25%	9.50%	9.75%
					(FINANCE CHARGE PER $100 OF AMOUNT FINANCED)											
61	16.27	16.98	17.70	18.41	19.13	19.85	20.58	21.31	22.04	22.77	23.50	24.24	24.98	25.72	26.47	27.22
62	16.55	17.27	18.00	18.73	19.46	20.19	20.93	21.67	22.41	23.16	23.91	24.66	25.41	26.17	26.93	27.69
63	16.82	17.56	18.30	19.04	19.79	20.53	21.28	22.04	22.79	23.55	24.31	25.08	25.85	26.62	27.39	28.16
64	17.10	17.85	18.60	19.36	20.11	20.87	21.64	22.40	23.17	23.95	24.72	25.50	26.28	27.06	27.85	28.64
65	17.38	18.14	18.90	19.67	20.44	21.22	21.99	22.77	23.55	24.34	25.13	25.92	26.71	27.51	28.31	29.12
66	17.65	18.43	19.21	19.99	20.77	21.56	22.35	23.14	23.94	24.73	25.54	26.34	27.15	27.96	28.78	29.59
67	17.93	18.72	19.51	20.30	21.10	21.90	22.70	23.51	24.32	25.13	25.95	26.77	27.59	28.41	29.24	30.07
68	18.21	19.01	19.81	20.62	21.43	22.24	23.06	23.88	24.70	25.53	26.36	27.19	28.02	28.86	29.71	30.55
69	18.49	19.30	20.12	20.94	21.76	22.59	23.41	24.25	25.08	25.92	26.77	27.61	28.46	29.32	30.17	31.03
70	18.77	19.59	20.42	21.25	22.09	22.93	23.77	24.62	25.47	26.32	27.18	28.04	28.90	29.77	30.64	31.51
71	19.05	19.88	20.73	21.57	22.42	23.27	24.13	24.99	25.85	26.72	27.59	28.47	29.34	30.22	31.11	32.00
72	19.32	20.18	21.03	21.89	22.75	23.62	24.49	25.36	26.24	27.12	28.00	28.89	29.78	30.68	31.58	32.48
73	19.60	20.47	21.34	22.21	23.09	23.96	24.85	25.74	26.63	27.52	28.42	29.32	30.23	31.14	32.05	32.96
74	19.89	20.76	21.64	22.53	23.42	24.31	25.21	26.11	27.01	27.92	28.83	29.75	30.67	31.59	32.52	33.45
75	20.17	21.06	21.95	22.85	23.75	24.66	25.57	26.48	27.40	28.32	29.25	30.18	31.11	32.05	32.99	33.94
76	20.45	21.35	22.26	23.17	24.09	25.01	25.93	26.86	27.79	28.73	29.67	30.61	31.56	32.51	33.47	34.43
77	20.73	21.65	22.57	23.49	24.42	25.35	26.29	27.23	28.18	29.13	30.08	31.04	32.00	32.97	33.94	34.91
78	21.01	21.94	22.87	23.81	24.76	25.70	26.65	27.61	28.57	29.53	30.50	31.47	32.45	33.43	34.42	35.40
79	21.29	22.24	23.18	24.14	25.09	26.05	27.02	27.99	28.96	29.94	30.92	31.91	32.90	33.89	34.89	35.90
80	21.58	22.53	23.49	24.46	25.43	26.40	27.38	28.36	29.35	30.34	31.34	32.34	33.35	34.36	35.37	36.39
81	21.86	22.83	23.80	24.78	25.76	26.75	27.74	28.74	29.74	30.75	31.76	32.78	33.79	34.82	35.85	36.88
82	22.14	23.13	24.11	25.11	26.10	27.10	28.11	29.12	30.14	31.16	32.18	33.21	34.25	35.28	36.33	37.38
83	22.43	23.42	24.42	25.43	26.44	27.46	28.48	29.50	30.53	31.56	32.60	33.65	34.70	35.75	36.81	37.87
84	22.71	23.72	24.74	25.75	26.78	27.81	28.84	29.88	30.92	31.97	33.03	34.08	35.15	36.22	37.29	38.37
85	23.00	24.02	25.05	26.08	27.12	28.16	29.21	30.26	31.32	32.38	33.45	34.52	35.60	36.68	37.77	38.86
86	23.28	24.32	25.36	26.41	27.46	28.51	29.58	30.64	31.72	32.79	33.87	34.96	36.05	37.15	38.26	39.36
87	23.57	24.62	25.67	26.73	27.80	28.87	29.94	31.03	32.11	33.20	34.30	35.40	36.51	37.62	38.74	39.86
88	23.85	24.92	25.99	27.06	28.14	29.22	30.31	31.41	32.51	33.61	34.73	35.84	36.97	38.09	39.23	40.36
89	24.14	25.22	26.30	27.39	28.48	29.58	30.68	31.79	32.91	34.03	35.15	36.28	37.42	38.56	39.71	40.86
90	24.43	25.52	26.61	27.71	28.82	29.93	31.05	32.18	33.31	34.44	35.58	36.73	37.88	39.04	40.20	41.37
91	24.71	25.82	26.93	28.04	29.16	30.29	31.42	32.56	33.70	34.85	36.01	37.17	38.34	39.51	40.69	41.87
92	25.00	26.12	27.24	28.37	29.51	30.65	31.79	32.95	34.10	35.27	36.44	37.61	38.80	39.98	41.18	42.38
93	25.29	26.42	27.56	28.70	29.85	31.00	32.17	33.33	34.51	35.68	36.87	38.06	39.26	40.46	41.67	42.88
94	25.58	26.72	27.87	29.03	30.19	31.36	32.54	33.72	34.91	36.10	37.30	38.51	39.72	40.94	42.16	43.39
95	25.87	27.03	28.19	29.36	30.54	31.72	32.91	34.11	35.31	36.52	37.73	38.95	40.18	41.41	42.65	43.90
96	26.16	27.33	28.51	29.69	30.88	32.08	33.29	34.50	35.71	36.94	38.16	39.40	40.64	41.89	43.14	44.41
97	26.45	27.63	28.83	30.02	31.23	32.44	33.66	34.88	36.12	37.35	38.60	39.85	41.11	42.37	43.64	44.91
98	26.74	27.94	29.14	30.36	31.58	32.80	34.03	35.27	36.52	37.77	39.03	40.30	41.57	42.85	44.13	45.43
99	27.03	28.24	29.46	30.69	31.92	33.16	34.41	35.66	36.93	38.19	39.47	40.75	42.04	43.33	44.63	45.94
100	27.32	28.55	29.78	31.02	32.27	33.52	34.79	36.06	37.33	38.61	39.90	41.20	42.50	43.81	45.13	46.45
101	27.61	28.85	30.10	31.36	32.62	33.89	35.16	36.45	37.74	39.03	40.34	41.65	42.97	44.29	45.63	46.96
102	27.90	29.16	30.42	31.69	32.97	34.25	35.54	36.84	38.14	39.46	40.78	42.10	43.44	44.78	46.13	47.48
103	28.19	29.46	30.74	32.02	33.31	34.61	35.92	37.23	38.55	39.88	41.21	42.56	43.91	45.26	46.63	48.00
104	28.49	29.77	31.06	32.36	33.66	34.98	36.30	37.63	38.96	40.30	41.65	43.01	44.38	45.75	47.13	48.51
105	28.78	30.08	31.38	32.69	34.01	35.34	36.68	38.02	39.37	40.73	42.09	43.47	44.85	46.23	47.63	49.03
106	29.07	30.38	31.70	33.03	34.36	35.71	37.06	38.41	39.78	41.15	42.53	43.92	45.32	46.72	48.13	49.55
107	29.37	30.69	32.03	33.37	34.72	36.07	37.44	38.81	40.19	41.58	42.97	44.38	45.79	47.21	48.64	50.07
108	29.66	31.00	32.35	33.70	35.07	36.44	37.82	39.21	40.60	42.01	43.42	44.84	46.26	47.70	49.14	50.59
109	29.96	31.31	32.67	34.04	35.42	36.81	38.20	39.60	41.01	42.43	43.86	45.29	46.74	48.19	49.65	51.11
110	30.25	31.62	33.00	34.38	35.77	37.17	38.58	40.00	41.43	42.86	44.30	45.75	47.21	48.68	50.15	51.64
111	30.55	31.93	33.32	34.72	36.13	37.54	38.97	40.40	41.84	43.29	44.75	46.21	47.69	49.17	50.66	52.16
112	30.84	32.24	33.64	35.06	36.48	37.91	39.35	40.80	42.25	43.72	45.19	46.67	48.17	49.66	51.17	52.69
113	31.14	32.55	33.97	35.40	36.83	38.28	39.73	41.20	42.67	44.15	45.64	47.14	48.64	50.16	51.68	53.21
114	31.44	32.86	34.29	35.74	37.19	38.65	40.12	41.60	43.09	44.58	46.09	47.60	49.12	50.65	52.19	53.74
115	31.73	33.17	34.62	36.08	37.54	39.02	40.50	42.00	43.50	45.01	46.53	48.06	49.60	51.15	52.70	54.27
116	32.03	33.48	34.95	36.42	37.90	39.39	40.89	42.40	43.92	45.45	46.98	48.53	50.08	51.64	53.22	54.80
117	32.33	33.80	35.27	36.76	38.26	39.76	41.28	42.80	44.34	45.88	47.43	48.99	50.56	52.14	53.73	55.33
118	32.63	34.11	35.60	37.10	38.61	40.14	41.67	43.21	44.75	46.31	47.88	49.46	51.04	52.64	54.24	55.86
119	32.93	34.42	35.93	37.45	38.97	40.51	42.05	43.61	45.17	46.75	48.33	49.92	51.53	53.14	54.76	56.39
120	33.22	34.74	36.26	37.79	39.33	40.88	42.44	44.01	45.59	47.18	48.78	50.39	52.01	53.64	55.28	56.92

TABLE A

ANNUAL PERCENTAGE RATE TABLE FOR MONTHLY PAYMENT PLANS
SEE INSTRUCTIONS FOR USE OF TABLES

FRB-203-M

NUMBER OF PAYMENTS	10.00%	10.25%	10.50%	10.75%	11.00%	11.25%	11.50%	11.75%	12.00%	12.25%	12.50%	12.75%	13.00%	13.25%	13.50%	13.75%
	(FINANCE CHARGE PER $100 OF AMOUNT FINANCED)															
61	27.97	28.72	29.48	30.24	31.00	31.76	32.53	33.29	34.07	34.84	35.62	36.39	37.18	37.96	38.75	39.54
62	28.46	29.22	29.99	30.76	31.54	32.32	33.10	33.88	34.67	35.45	36.25	37.04	37.84	38.63	39.44	40.24
63	28.94	29.72	30.51	31.29	32.08	32.88	33.67	34.47	35.27	36.07	36.88	37.69	38.50	39.31	40.13	40.95
64	29.43	30.23	31.03	31.83	32.63	33.44	34.25	35.06	35.87	36.69	37.51	38.33	39.16	39.99	40.82	41.66
65	29.92	30.73	31.54	32.36	33.18	34.00	34.82	35.65	36.48	37.31	38.15	38.98	39.83	40.67	41.52	42.37
66	30.41	31.24	32.06	32.89	33.73	34.56	35.40	36.24	37.09	37.93	38.78	39.64	40.49	41.35	42.21	43.08
67	30.91	31.74	32.58	33.43	34.28	35.13	35.98	36.83	37.69	38.56	39.42	40.29	41.16	42.04	42.91	43.79
68	31.40	32.25	33.11	33.97	34.83	35.69	36.56	37.43	38.30	39.18	40.06	40.95	41.83	42.72	43.61	44.51
69	31.89	32.76	33.63	34.50	35.38	36.26	37.14	38.03	38.92	39.81	40.70	41.60	42.50	43.41	44.32	45.23
70	32.39	33.27	34.16	35.04	35.93	36.83	37.72	38.63	39.53	40.44	41.35	42.26	43.18	44.10	45.02	45.95
71	32.89	33.78	34.68	35.58	36.49	37.40	38.31	39.23	40.14	41.07	41.99	42.92	43.86	44.79	45.73	46.67
72	33.39	34.30	35.21	36.13	37.05	37.97	38.90	39.83	40.76	41.70	42.64	43.59	44.53	45.49	46.44	47.40
73	33.89	34.81	35.74	36.67	37.60	38.54	39.48	40.43	41.38	42.33	43.29	44.25	45.21	46.18	47.15	48.13
74	34.39	35.32	36.27	37.21	38.16	39.12	40.07	41.03	42.00	42.97	43.94	44.92	45.90	46.88	47.87	48.86
75	34.89	35.84	36.80	37.76	38.72	39.69	40.66	41.64	42.62	43.60	44.59	45.58	46.58	47.58	48.58	49.59
76	35.39	36.36	37.33	38.31	39.29	40.27	41.26	42.25	43.24	44.24	45.25	46.25	47.26	48.28	49.30	50.32
77	35.89	36.88	37.86	38.85	39.85	40.85	41.85	42.86	43.87	44.88	45.90	46.92	47.95	48.98	50.02	51.06
78	36.40	37.40	38.40	39.40	40.41	41.43	42.45	43.47	44.49	45.52	46.56	47.60	48.64	49.69	50.74	51.79
79	36.90	37.92	38.93	39.95	40.98	42.01	43.04	44.08	45.12	46.17	47.22	48.27	49.33	50.39	51.46	52.53
80	37.41	38.44	39.47	40.51	41.55	42.59	43.64	44.69	45.75	46.81	47.88	48.95	50.02	51.10	52.19	53.27
81	37.92	38.96	40.01	41.06	42.11	43.17	44.24	45.31	46.38	47.46	48.54	49.63	50.72	51.81	52.91	54.02
82	38.43	39.49	40.55	41.61	42.68	43.76	44.84	45.92	47.01	48.11	49.21	50.31	51.41	52.53	53.64	54.76
83	38.94	40.01	41.09	42.17	43.26	44.35	45.44	46.54	47.65	48.76	49.87	50.99	52.11	53.24	54.37	55.51
84	39.45	40.54	41.63	42.73	43.83	44.93	46.05	47.16	48.28	49.41	50.54	51.67	52.81	53.96	55.11	56.26
85	39.96	41.07	42.17	43.28	44.40	45.52	46.65	47.78	48.92	50.06	51.21	52.36	53.51	54.67	55.84	57.01
86	40.48	41.59	42.72	43.84	44.98	46.12	47.26	48.41	49.56	50.72	51.88	53.05	54.22	55.39	56.58	57.76
87	40.99	42.12	43.26	44.41	45.55	46.71	47.87	49.03	50.20	51.37	52.55	53.73	54.92	56.12	57.31	58.52
88	41.51	42.65	43.81	44.97	46.13	47.30	48.48	49.66	50.84	52.03	53.22	54.42	55.63	56.84	58.06	59.28
89	42.02	43.19	44.36	45.53	46.71	47.90	49.09	50.28	51.48	52.69	53.90	55.12	56.34	57.57	58.80	60.03
90	42.54	43.72	44.91	46.10	47.29	48.49	49.70	50.91	52.13	53.35	54.58	55.81	57.05	58.29	59.54	60.80
91	43.06	44.26	45.46	46.66	47.87	49.09	50.31	51.54	52.77	54.01	55.26	56.51	57.76	59.02	60.29	61.56
92	43.58	44.79	46.01	47.23	48.46	49.69	50.93	52.17	53.42	54.68	55.94	57.20	58.48	59.75	61.04	62.32
93	44.10	45.33	46.56	47.80	49.04	50.29	51.54	52.80	54.07	55.34	56.62	57.90	59.19	60.49	61.79	63.09
94	44.62	45.87	47.11	48.37	49.63	50.89	52.16	53.44	54.72	56.01	57.30	58.60	59.91	61.22	62.54	63.86
95	45.15	46.40	47.67	48.94	50.21	51.49	52.78	54.07	55.37	56.68	57.99	59.31	60.63	61.96	63.29	64.63
96	45.67	46.94	48.22	49.51	50.80	52.10	53.40	54.71	56.03	57.35	58.68	60.01	61.35	62.69	64.05	65.40
97	46.20	47.49	48.78	50.08	51.39	52.70	54.02	55.35	56.68	58.02	59.37	60.72	62.07	63.44	64.80	66.18
98	46.72	48.03	49.34	50.66	51.98	53.31	54.65	55.99	57.34	58.69	60.06	61.42	62.80	64.18	65.56	66.95
99	47.25	48.57	49.90	51.23	52.57	53.92	55.27	56.63	58.00	59.37	60.75	62.13	63.52	64.92	66.32	67.73
100	47.78	49.12	50.46	51.81	53.17	54.53	55.90	57.27	58.66	60.05	61.44	62.84	64.25	65.67	67.09	68.51
101	48.31	49.66	51.02	52.39	53.76	55.14	56.53	57.92	59.32	60.72	62.14	63.56	64.98	66.41	67.85	69.30
102	48.84	50.21	51.59	52.97	54.36	55.75	57.16	58.57	59.98	61.40	62.83	64.27	65.71	67.16	68.62	70.08
103	49.37	50.76	52.15	53.55	54.95	56.37	57.79	59.21	60.65	62.09	63.53	64.99	66.45	67.91	69.39	70.87
104	49.91	51.31	52.72	54.13	55.55	56.98	58.42	59.86	61.31	62.77	64.23	65.70	67.18	68.67	70.16	71.66
105	50.44	51.86	53.28	54.71	56.15	57.60	59.05	60.51	61.98	63.45	64.93	66.42	67.92	69.42	70.93	72.45
106	50.98	52.41	53.85	55.30	56.75	58.22	59.69	61.16	62.65	64.14	65.64	67.14	68.66	70.18	71.70	73.24
107	51.51	52.96	54.42	55.88	57.36	58.84	60.32	61.82	63.32	64.83	66.34	67.87	69.40	70.93	72.48	74.03
108	52.05	53.52	54.99	56.47	57.96	59.46	60.96	62.47	63.99	65.52	67.05	68.59	70.14	71.69	73.26	74.83
109	52.59	54.07	55.56	57.06	58.56	60.08	61.60	63.13	64.66	66.21	67.76	69.32	70.88	72.46	74.04	75.62
110	53.13	54.63	56.13	57.65	59.17	60.70	62.24	63.78	65.34	66.90	68.47	70.04	71.63	73.22	74.82	76.42
111	53.67	55.18	56.71	58.24	59.78	61.32	62.88	64.44	66.01	67.59	69.18	70.77	72.37	73.98	75.60	77.23
112	54.21	55.74	57.28	58.83	60.39	61.95	63.52	65.10	66.69	68.29	69.89	71.50	73.12	74.75	76.39	78.03
113	54.75	56.30	57.86	59.42	61.00	62.58	64.17	65.76	67.37	68.98	70.61	72.24	73.87	75.52	77.17	78.83
114	55.30	56.86	58.43	60.02	61.61	63.21	64.81	66.43	68.05	69.68	71.32	72.97	74.63	76.29	77.96	79.64
115	55.84	57.42	59.01	60.61	62.22	63.84	65.46	67.09	68.73	70.38	72.04	73.71	75.38	77.06	78.75	80.45
116	56.39	57.99	59.59	61.21	62.83	64.47	66.11	67.76	69.42	71.08	72.76	74.44	76.13	77.83	79.54	81.26
117	56.93	58.55	60.17	61.81	63.45	65.10	66.76	68.43	70.10	71.79	73.48	75.18	76.89	78.61	80.34	82.07
118	57.48	59.11	60.75	62.41	64.06	65.73	67.41	69.09	70.79	72.49	74.20	75.92	77.65	79.39	81.13	82.89
119	58.03	59.68	61.34	63.01	64.68	66.37	68.06	69.76	71.48	73.20	74.93	76.66	78.41	80.17	81.93	83.70
120	58.58	60.25	61.92	63.61	65.30	67.00	68.71	70.44	72.17	73.90	75.65	77.41	79.17	80.95	82.73	84.52

TABLE A

ANNUAL PERCENTAGE RATE TABLE FOR MONTHLY PAYMENT PLANS
SEE INSTRUCTIONS FOR USE OF TABLES

FRB-204-M

NUMBER OF PAYMENTS	14.00%	14.25%	14.50%	14.75%	15.00%	15.25%	15.50%	15.75%	16.00%	16.25%	16.50%	16.75%	17.00%	17.25%	17.50%	17.75%
	(FINANCE CHARGE PER $100 OF AMOUNT FINANCED)															
61	40.33	41.12	41.92	42.72	43.52	44.32	45.13	45.94	46.75	47.56	48.38	49.20	50.02	50.84	51.67	52.50
62	41.05	41.86	42.67	43.48	44.30	45.12	45.94	46.77	47.59	48.42	49.26	50.09	50.93	51.77	52.61	53.45
63	41.77	42.59	43.42	44.25	45.08	45.92	46.76	47.60	48.44	49.29	50.13	50.98	51.84	52.69	53.55	54.41
64	42.49	43.33	44.18	45.02	45.87	46.72	47.57	48.43	49.29	50.15	51.02	51.88	52.75	53.62	54.50	55.38
65	43.22	44.07	44.93	45.79	46.66	47.52	48.39	49.27	50.14	51.02	51.90	52.78	53.67	54.56	55.45	56.34
66	43.95	44.82	45.69	46.57	47.45	48.33	49.22	50.10	51.00	51.89	52.79	53.69	54.59	55.49	56.40	57.31
67	44.68	45.56	46.45	47.35	48.24	49.14	50.04	50.95	51.85	52.76	53.68	54.59	55.51	56.43	57.36	58.29
68	45.41	46.31	47.22	48.13	49.04	49.95	50.87	51.79	52.71	53.64	54.57	55.50	56.44	57.38	58.32	59.26
69	46.14	47.06	47.98	48.91	49.84	50.77	51.70	52.64	53.58	54.52	55.47	56.41	57.37	58.32	59.28	60.24
70	46.88	47.82	48.75	49.69	50.64	51.58	52.53	53.49	54.44	55.40	56.36	57.33	58.30	59.27	60.25	61.22
71	47.62	48.57	49.52	50.48	51.44	52.40	53.37	54.34	55.31	56.29	57.27	58.25	59.23	60.22	61.22	62.21
72	48.36	49.33	50.30	51.27	52.24	53.22	54.21	55.19	56.18	57.17	58.17	59.17	60.17	61.18	62.19	63.20
73	49.10	50.09	51.07	52.06	53.05	54.05	55.05	56.05	57.05	58.06	59.08	60.09	61.11	62.14	63.16	64.19
74	49.85	50.85	51.85	52.85	53.86	54.87	55.89	56.91	57.93	58.96	59.99	61.02	62.06	63.10	64.14	65.19
75	50.60	51.61	52.63	53.65	54.67	55.70	56.74	57.77	58.81	59.85	60.90	61.95	63.00	64.06	65.12	66.19
76	51.35	52.38	53.41	54.45	55.49	56.53	57.58	58.64	59.69	60.75	61.82	62.88	63.95	65.03	66.11	67.19
77	52.10	53.14	54.19	55.25	56.31	57.37	58.43	59.50	60.58	61.65	62.73	63.82	64.91	66.00	67.10	68.19
78	52.85	53.91	54.98	56.05	57.13	58.20	59.29	60.37	61.46	62.56	63.66	64.76	65.86	66.97	68.09	69.20
79	53.61	54.69	55.77	56.86	57.95	59.04	60.14	61.25	62.35	63.46	64.58	65.70	66.82	67.95	69.08	70.22
80	54.36	55.46	56.56	57.66	58.77	59.88	61.00	62.12	63.25	64.37	65.51	66.64	67.78	68.93	70.08	71.23
81	55.12	56.24	57.35	58.47	59.60	60.73	61.86	63.00	64.14	65.29	66.44	67.59	68.75	69.91	71.08	72.25
82	55.89	57.02	58.15	59.29	60.43	61.57	62.72	63.88	65.04	66.20	67.37	68.54	69.72	70.90	72.08	73.27
83	56.65	57.80	58.95	60.10	61.26	62.42	63.59	64.76	65.94	67.12	68.30	69.49	70.69	71.89	73.09	74.29
84	57.42	58.58	59.75	60.92	62.09	63.27	64.46	65.65	66.84	68.04	69.24	70.45	71.66	72.88	74.10	75.32
85	58.18	59.36	60.55	61.74	62.93	64.13	65.33	66.54	67.75	68.96	70.18	71.41	72.64	73.87	75.11	76.35
86	58.95	60.15	61.35	62.56	63.77	64.98	66.20	67.43	68.65	69.89	71.13	72.37	73.62	74.87	76.12	77.39
87	59.73	60.94	62.16	63.38	64.61	65.84	67.08	68.32	69.57	70.82	72.07	73.33	74.60	75.87	77.14	78.42
88	60.50	61.73	62.97	64.21	65.45	66.70	67.95	69.21	70.48	71.75	73.02	74.30	75.58	76.87	78.16	79.46
89	61.28	62.52	63.78	65.03	66.30	67.56	68.84	70.11	71.39	72.68	73.97	75.27	76.57	77.88	79.19	80.50
90	62.05	63.32	64.59	65.86	67.14	68.43	69.72	71.01	72.31	73.62	74.93	76.24	77.56	78.89	80.22	81.55
91	62.83	64.12	65.40	66.70	67.99	69.30	70.60	71.92	73.23	74.56	75.88	77.22	78.56	79.90	81.25	82.60
92	63.62	64.92	66.22	67.53	68.84	70.17	71.49	72.82	74.16	75.50	76.84	78.20	79.55	80.91	82.28	83.65
93	64.40	65.72	67.04	68.37	69.70	71.04	72.38	73.73	75.08	76.44	77.81	79.18	80.55	81.93	83.32	84.71
94	65.19	66.52	67.86	69.21	70.56	71.91	73.27	74.64	76.01	77.39	78.77	80.16	81.55	82.95	84.36	85.77
95	65.98	67.33	68.68	70.05	71.41	72.79	74.17	75.55	76.94	78.34	79.74	81.15	82.56	83.98	85.40	86.83
96	66.77	68.14	69.51	70.89	72.28	73.67	75.06	76.47	77.88	79.29	80.71	82.14	83.57	85.00	86.44	87.89
97	67.56	68.94	70.34	71.74	73.14	74.55	75.96	77.39	78.81	80.24	81.68	83.13	84.58	86.03	87.49	88.96
98	68.35	69.76	71.17	72.58	74.00	75.43	76.87	78.31	79.75	81.20	82.66	84.12	85.59	87.06	88.54	90.03
99	69.15	70.57	72.00	73.43	74.87	76.32	77.77	79.23	80.69	82.16	83.64	85.12	86.61	88.10	89.60	91.10
100	69.95	71.39	72.83	74.28	75.74	77.21	78.68	80.15	81.64	83.12	84.62	86.12	87.62	89.14	90.65	92.18
101	70.75	72.21	73.67	75.14	76.62	78.10	79.59	81.08	82.58	84.09	85.60	87.12	88.65	90.18	91.71	93.26
102	71.55	73.03	74.51	76.00	77.49	78.99	80.50	82.01	83.53	85.06	86.59	88.13	89.67	91.22	92.79	94.34
103	72.35	73.85	75.35	76.85	78.37	79.89	81.41	82.94	84.48	86.03	87.58	89.13	90.70	92.27	93.84	95.42
104	73.16	74.67	76.19	77.71	79.25	80.78	82.33	83.88	85.43	87.00	88.57	90.14	91.73	93.31	94.91	96.51
105	73.97	75.50	77.03	78.58	80.13	81.68	83.25	84.81	86.39	87.97	89.56	91.16	92.76	94.37	95.98	97.60
106	74.78	76.33	77.88	79.44	81.01	82.58	84.17	85.75	87.35	88.95	90.56	92.17	93.79	95.42	97.05	98.69
107	75.59	77.16	78.73	80.31	81.90	83.49	85.09	86.70	88.31	89.93	91.56	93.19	94.83	96.48	98.13	99.79
108	76.40	77.99	79.58	81.18	82.78	84.39	86.01	87.64	89.27	90.91	92.56	94.21	95.87	97.54	99.21	100.89
109	77.22	78.82	80.43	82.05	83.67	85.30	86.94	88.59	90.24	91.90	93.56	95.23	96.91	98.60	100.29	101.99
110	78.04	79.66	81.29	82.92	84.56	86.21	87.87	89.54	91.21	92.88	94.57	96.26	97.96	99.66	101.38	103.10
111	78.86	80.50	82.14	83.80	85.46	87.13	88.80	90.49	92.18	93.87	95.58	97.29	99.01	100.73	102.46	104.20
112	79.68	81.34	83.00	84.67	86.36	88.04	89.74	91.44	93.15	94.87	96.59	98.32	100.06	101.80	103.55	105.31
113	80.50	82.18	83.86	85.55	87.25	88.96	90.67	92.40	94.12	95.86	97.60	99.35	101.11	102.88	104.65	106.43
114	81.33	83.02	84.73	86.44	88.15	89.88	91.61	93.35	95.10	96.86	98.62	100.39	102.17	103.95	105.74	107.54
115	82.15	83.87	85.59	87.32	89.06	90.80	92.55	94.31	96.08	97.86	99.64	101.43	103.23	105.03	106.84	108.66
116	82.98	84.72	86.46	88.21	89.96	91.73	93.50	95.28	97.06	98.86	100.66	102.47	104.29	106.11	107.94	109.78
117	83.82	85.57	87.33	89.09	90.87	92.65	94.44	96.24	98.05	99.86	101.68	103.51	105.35	107.20	109.05	110.91
118	84.65	86.42	88.20	89.98	91.78	93.58	95.39	97.21	99.04	100.87	102.71	104.56	106.43	108.28	110.15	112.03
119	85.48	87.27	89.07	90.87	92.69	94.51	96.34	98.18	100.02	101.88	103.74	105.61	107.49	109.37	111.26	113.16
120	86.32	88.13	89.94	91.77	93.60	95.44	97.29	99.15	101.02	102.89	104.77	106.66	108.56	110.46	112.37	114.29

APPENDIX N

The Wall Street Journal
Tuesday, March 6, 1979

MONEY RATES

The key U. S. and foreign annual interest rates below are a guide to general levels but don't always represent actual transactions.

PRIME RATE: 11 1/2 to 11 3/4%. The charge by large U. S. money center banks to their best business borrowers.

FEDERAL FUNDS: 10 5/16% high, 9 1/2% low, 10 1/16% closing bid, 10 3/16% offered. Reserves traded among commercial banks for overnight use in amounts of $1 million or more.

DISCOUNT RATE: 9 1/2%. The charge on loans to member commercial banks by the New York Federal Reserve Bank.

CALL MONEY: 10 3/4% to 11 1/4%. The charge on loans to brokers on stock exchange collateral.

COMMERCIAL PAPER: Placed directly by a major finance company: 9 1/4%, 30 to 179 days; 9 1/2%, 180 to 270 days.

COMMERCIAL PAPER: High-grade, unsecured notes sold through dealers by major corporations in multiples of $1,000: 9.80%, 30 days; 9.95%, 60 days; 10.05%, 90 days.

CERTIFICATES OF DEPOSITS: 9 5/8%, one month; 9.80%, 60 days; 10.10%, three months; 10.55%, six months; 10.30%, one year. Top rates paid by major banks on new issues of negotiable C. D.'s in units of $100,000 or more.

BANKERS ACCEPTANCES: 9.85%, 30 days; 9.90%, 60 days; 9.90%, 90 days; 10%, 120 days; 10.10%, 150 days; 10.15%, 180 days. Negotiable, bank-backed business credit instruments typically financing an import order.

EURODOLLARS: 10 3/8% to 10 5/16%, one month; 10 5/8% to 10 1/2%, two months; 10 11/16% to 10 5/8%, three months; 10 7/8% to 10 3/4%, four months; 11% to 10 7/8%, five months; 11 1/16% to 11%, six months. The rates paid on U. S. dollar deposits in banks in London, usually on amounts of $100,000 or more.

FOREIGN PRIME RATES: Canada, 12%; Germany, 5.5%; Japan, 5.47%; Switzerland, 5%; Great Britain, 14 1/2%. These rate indications aren't directly compatible; lending practices vary widely by location.
Source: Morgan Guaranty Trust Co.

TREASURY BILLS: Results of the Monday, March 5, 1979 auction of short-term U. S. government bills sold at a discount from face value in units of $10,000 to $1 million: 9.364%, 13 weeks; 9.415%, 26 weeks.

INDEX

Abruzzo, 239. *See also* Failure (Profiting from)

Access and Utilities: how to rate when buying and developing land, 56. *See also* FEASIBILITY CHECK LIST

Accurate thought: enemies of, 249; success rule, 248-253; test questions, 251-253. *See also* Inaccurate thought patterns

ACTION FILE, for making quick decisions on land deals, 36, 39, 61, 62, 63, 67, 136, 184

ADMIT, 205-208. *See also* Enthusiasm, formula

Advertising: As *Subdivesting* work area, 25-26; Direct Mail Advertising, 154-166; direct mail letters, 155-165; Direct Response Ad Elements, 137; examples, 138-153; importance of, 135-136. *See also* Sales promotion

Advisors, 15, 231, 233. *See* Character, advisors

Africa, 42

Agoraphobia, 115

Alaska, 42

Amin, Idi, 235. *See also* Tolerance (and Patience)

Anderson, 239. *See also* Failure (profiting from)

Anger: basic motive, 224, 227; negative emotion, 212, 213. *See also* Motives (10 basic)

Annual Percentage Rate (Tables), Appendix M, 366-371

Appearance of lots, altering for customer appeal, 104-105

Aptitude, for career, 20

Auctions, buying land at, 73-76

Autosuggestion, 205-207, 233, 243, 256, 257, 262. *See also* Self-hypnosis; Success

Barnes, Edwin C., 6

Base investment, 87

Belief: spur to action; mainstay of desire, 257; for enthusiasm, 262. *See also* Enthusiasm, formula

Bettger, Frank: *How I Raised Myself from Failure to Success in Selling*, 261. *See also* Enthusiasm success rule

Bible, 200

Board of directors, 15

Body. *See* Living tools

Bogart, Humphrey, 19. *See also* Stability

Bonaparte, Napoleon, 182, 228. *See also* Persistence; Imagination, success rule

Brain. *See* Living tools

Building sites, considerations, 130

Bunche, Ralph, 235. *See also* Tolerance (and Patience)

Capital: from insurance companies, 93-94; Pension funds, 94; Real Estate Investment Trusts, 94-95; Real estate syndicates, 96; Savings and loan associations, 94; Trust funds, 95

Capital gains, tax considerations, 11

Caples, John, 136

Carlyle, 7

Carnegie, Andrew, 217, 246, 257-258

Carnegie, Dale: *How To Win Friends and Influence People*, 233, 236. *See also* Tolerance (and Patience)

Carribean, 42

Character: advisors, 231, 233; building of, 230

Chicago, 221

Christmas, 214

Clark, Roy, 218. *See also* Concentration

Clason, *Richest Man in Babylon, The*, 202

Client, deference to in sales, 188

Closing signals, in sales, 187-188

Collier, Robert, *The Secret of the Ages*, 256

Colorado, 42

Common thread, of success, 8

Community property, Appendix A, 275

Compensation: Emerson's Essay on, 240; law of, 260

Components of life, 212

Concentration (and Persistence): how to apply, 219; success rule, 217

Conceptual thinking, 166

Confidence, client's: in sales, 184. *See also* Self-confidence

Contracts: sample, Appendix J, 343; terminology, Appendix B, 277-308

Cooper, Gary, 204. *See also* Self-confidence, success rule

Cooperation: invisible guards, 222-223; success rule, 220-223

Corbett, James J., 258. *See also* Extra mile

Corporations: as a source of rural land deals, 35. *See also* Sources

County government, 102, 122, 123

County tax assessors, 35

County tax maps, 34

Covenants: importance of, 126-128; samples, Appendix I, 337-342

Credit application form, Appendix J, 345-346

Credit, importance of, 83-87

Criticism: fear of, 215-217. *See also* Fears (7 Basic)

Danforth, William, *I Dare You*, 228

Death: fear of, 209. *See also* Fears (7 Basic)

Deeds: quitclaim, Appendix A, 274; sample, Appendix K, 349; sheriff's, Appendix B, 303-304; special warranty, Appendix A, 273; warranty, Appendix A, 273

Deed of Trust: foreclosure under, Appendix A, 273; sample, Appendix K, 350

Definite chief aim: how to accomplish, 254; influence of subconscious, 256; lack of, 255; success rule, 253-258

Delinquent account notices, samples, Appendix K, 353

Desire: definite, 254; positive emotion, 213; precedes action, 256; self-defeating, 229

Developing the land: avoiding lot cramp, 115-116; dealing with "hard" customers, 117-119; developing recreational land, 119-122; easiest and hardest land to "hustle," 119-122; how to avoid a "lot cramp," 115-117; how to give a "nose job," 104-105; how to improve the land, 104-105; how to perform "quickie" deals, 110-113; how to provide a lot "shaft," 102-103; how to realize maximum profits, 106-110; how to "undress" a lot, 122-125; satisfying both husband and wife, 113-115; soils and building sites, 128-129

Development Costs: how to rate when buying and developing land, 56. *See also* FEASIBILITY CHECK LIST

DiMaggio, 204, 218. *See also* Self-confidence, success rule

Direct marketing, 25-26

Dirt peddler, 110

Discount letter, for notes receivable, Appendix M, 363-364

Discount rate, 86

Dobbs, Fred C., 19. *See also* Stability

Double Eagle II, 239-240

Down payments, on property, 171-172

Drainfields, 128

Eagle II, 239. *See also* Abruzzo, Anderson, Newman; Failure (profiting from)

Earnings, what amount to save, 202-204

Ease of Entry: how to rate when buying and developing land, 57. *See also* FEASIBILITY CHECK LIST

Easements, Appendix A, 271

Edison, Thomas Alva, 6, 217

Eisenhower, Dwight D., 220-221, 245. *See also* Leadership, success rule

Emerson, Ralph Waldo, 240, 260, 261

Emotions: negative, 212, 213, 222; positive, 213

England, 42

Enthusiasm: derivation of word, 264; formula, 263; how to acquire, 261, 262, 263; in selling, 183; positive emotion, 213; sessions, 216-217; spur to belief, 264; success rule, 261-266

Envy, negative emotion, 212, 213, 227

Eurydice, 183. *See also* Orpheus

Exchange, Statement of, 48-49

Expenses, 203; fixed, 87. *See also* Savings habit

Extra mile: reason for, 259-261; success rule, 258-262

Failure habits, 241-243

Failure (profiting from), success rule, 237-244

Faith (and Hope): as spur to enthusiasm, 262; guard of, 222; in personality development, 231-232; positive emotion, 213; reason for, 222. *See also* Cooperation, invisible guards; Concentration (and Persistence), how to apply

"Father Forgets" (Larned), 236-237. *See also* Tolerance (and Patience)

Fear: basic motive, 224, 226; negative emotion, 212, 213. *See also* Motives (10 Basic)

Fears (7 Basic), 209-217

FEASIBILITY CHECK LIST, 107, 115, 123, 125, 136, 184; basic elements, 54; sample, 55; scoring key, 55; evaluating possible land projects, 53-76;

FEASIBILITY CHECK LIST (continued)
    use on project, 58-70
Federal Reserve System, 86
Files: for delinquent taxes, Appendix L, 356; for documents and correspondence, Appendix L, 356. *See also* ACTION FILE
Financial success: guard of, 222; in personality development, 231-232
Financing and administration, as *Subdivesting* work area, 23-24
Financing land projects: credit with banks, 83-87; deed of trust notes, 84-87; installment contract, 91-92; insurance companies, 93-94; interest-bearing notes, 80-81, 85-86; larger pension funds, 94; importance of past performance, 106; pension funds and retirement accounts, 90-91; private individuals, 95-96; private syndicates, 96; REITS, 94-95; "release" clauses and notes, 79-83; savings and loan associations, 94; "signature" capital, 87-88; trust funds, 95
Fitzgerald, F. Scott, 246
FLAME, 206, 228; meaning, 200-201; success rules, 237-266
Floodplain, 63
Fools, Arabian Proverb, 260
Ford, Henry, 217, 221, 228-229, 246
Foreclosures, 172-174; how to advertise, 152; under deed of trust vs. mortgage, Appendix A, 273
Foreign Investment Disclosure Information, Appendix J, 347
France, 42
Franklin, Ben, 231, 261, 265
Freedom of body and mind: basic motive, 224, 226. *See also* Motives (10 Basic)
Getty, John Paul, *The Golden Age*, 244
Goals, 39-49; definition, 39; implementing goal plan, 48-49; orientation (also disorientation), 40-41, 43-44; plodding, 44; sample Statement of Physical Goals, 46-48; visualization, 45. *See also* Concentration (and Persistence), how to apply
God, 205-206, 231, 262, 264
Golden Age, The (Getty), 244
Golden Rule: example of Jesus, 224; success rule, 223-227. *See also* Motives (10 Basic)

Good health: guard of, 222; in personality development, 231-232
Government. *See* County government; HUD
Graham, Billy, 232
Gray Ghost, classic ad, 153
Great Land Hustle, The (Paulson), 119
Greatest Salesman in the World, The (Mandino), 201
Greed, negative emotion, 212, 213
Habits, 233-234
Hate: basic motive, 224, 227; negative emotion, 212, 213. *See also* Motives (10 Basic)
Health department, county, 123, 128-129
Heart. *See* Living tools
Hemmingway, Ernest, 246
Herod, 201
Hill, Napoleon: *Think and Grow Rich; You Can Work Your Own Miracles,* 6, 8, 25, 199, 201, 205, 210, 217, 221, 232, 248, 254, 255, 262, 265
Hillary, Sir Edmund, 221
Hitler, Adolph, 235. *See also* Tolerance (and Patience)
Holiday Inns, Inc., 221
Homestead Exemption, Appendix A, 274
Hope, positive emotion, 213
How I Raised Myself From Failure to Success In Selling (Bettger), 261
How I Turned $1,000 into $3 Million in Real Estate (Nickerson), 228
How To Win Friends and Influence People (Carnegie), 233
How You Can Become Financially Independent by Investing in Real Estate (Lowry), 228
HUD, 64-66
Hypochondria, Napoleon Hill's experiment, 210
I Dare You (Danforth), 228
Ideas, 7-9
Identification, with client, 186
Illness: fear of, 210. *See also* Fears (7 Basic)
Imagination: Henry Ford's quote, 229; Napoleon's quote, 228; runaway, 229; Shakespeare's poem, 227; success rule, 227-229
Inaccurate thought patterns, 249-250
Income: taxable, 90-91; ways to increase, 250-251

Inducements, in advertising, 140, 150
Installment purchases, 171-172
Installment sale, 30 percent rule, Appendix A, 275-276
Insurance, public liability, Appendix A, 276
Insurance companies: as a source of capital, 93-94. *See also* Financing land projects
Interest rate, on installment sales, 171-172
Internal Revenue Service (IRS), 90
Ireland, 42
Jefferson, Thomas, 230
Jesus, 206, 224, 228, 230, 235, 264; quoted in Matthew 7:7-8, 17:20, 219. *See also* Concentration; Tolerance (and Patience); Enthusiasm
Kickbacks: legal problems, 180. *See also* Referrals
Land acquisition: as *Subdivesting* work area, 24-25; gaining knowledge of the land, 7; seizing opportunity, 7; operating with and choosing partners, 15-25. *See also* Land development
Land Acquisition Check List, Appendix E, 323-324
Land development: as *Subdivesting* work area, 24-25; adopting a set of covenants, 126-128; appeal to husband and wife, 113-115; aesthetic improvements, 104-105; federal and state regulatory agencies, Appendix D, 316-321; Pennsylvania farm project, 106-110; "quickie" deal, 110-113; recreational land, 119-122; roads, 102-104; sewage disposal, 128-130; "shoehorned" lots, 115-117; suitable building sites, 130; "undressing" a lot, 122-126; West Virginia land project, 122-126; sample covenants, Appendix I, 337-342. *See also* Developing the land
Land "hustling," 119
Land sales contract, 80-81, 91-92, 172-173
Land Trap, ad theme, 154
Land Treasures, ad theme, 153
Larned, W. Livingston, "Father Forgets," 236-237
Leadership: effective qualities, 248; of master-mind group, 221; success rule, 244-248
Lear Jet, 45
Ledger sheet, for note collections, sample, Appendix K, 354
Life after death: basic motive, 224, 225. *See also* Motives (10 Basic)
Life's true rewards, 247
Lincoln, Abraham, 230, 232, 238
Lindberg, Charles, 204
Liquidity, importance of, 84, 202
Living tools, 213. *See also* Components of life
Location, Location, Location: critical to land acquisition, 24, 54; how to score, 56. *See also* FEASIBILITY CHECK LIST
London Sunday Times, 221
Lorayne, Harry, *The Secrets of Mind Power*, 262
Los Angeles, 229
Lost love, fear of, 212. *See also* Fears (7 Basic)
Lost profits, reasons for, 24
Love: basic motive, 224, 226; guard of, 223; in personality development, 232-232; positive emotion, 213. *See also* Motives (10 Basic)
Lowry, Albert L., *How You Can Become Financially Independent by Investing in Real Estate*, 228
MacArthur, 245. *See also* Leadership
Mandino, Og, *The Greatest Salesman in the World*, 201
Marshall, George C., 220, 245. *See also* Leadership, success rule
Master-Mind Group, 25, 221
Material gain: basic motive, 224, 226; concern with, 261. *See also* Motives (10 Basic)
Measurement tables, Appendix F, 329
Memory, 49. *See also* Lorayne, Harry
Mental attitude, 212. *See also* Components of life
Mental peace: guard of, 222; in personality development, 231-232
Mind: conscious and unconscious, 4; enemies of, 212, 213, 222; hidden powers of, 3-4; sending messages to subconscious, 4-5, 46. *See also* Emotions; Subconscious mind
Money rates, Appendix N, 373
Mortgage: foreclosure under, Appendix A, 273; related terminology, Appendix B, 294-295
Motives (10 Basic), 224-227
Mozart, 199
Nags Head, 42
Nazarene. *See* Jesus
Negative emotions, 212, 213

Newman, 230. *See also* Failure (profiting from)

Newspapers, as a source of rural land deals, 34-35, 64. *See also* Sources

Newton, Isaac, 217. *See also* Concentration

New York City, 42, 229

Nickerson, William, *How I Turned $1,000 into $3 Million in Real Estate,* 228

Nineteen Stars (Puryear), 245

Norgay, Tenzing, 221. *See also* Hillary, Sir Edmund

Note (Deed of Trust), sample, Appendix K, 351

Notes (secured by real estate): as profits, 24, 87; borrowing on, 24, 82-83, 85; buying land with, 79-81, 88-89, 92-93; discounting, 83, Appendix M, 357-363; distributing to partners, 87-88; interest-bearing (examples), 85; promissory, Appendix A, 274; "selling" to pension funds, 90-91. *See also* Financing land projects

Notes receivable, servicing, Appendix C, 355-356

OBJECTIVITY FACTOR, when making decisions on land deals, 38, 39, 61, 136

OILSR, 64-67. *See also* HUD

Old age: fear of, 209. *See also* Fears (7 Basic)

O.P.M. (Other People's Money), use of, 81-82, 88, 202

Options, 11, 62, 82

Orpheus, 183. *See also* Enthusiasm

Owens, Jesse, 232

Pain, fear of, 211. *See also* Fears (7 Basic)

Partners, 15-28; distribution of profits, 87-88.

Patience. *See* Tolerance

Patton, 245. *See also* Leadership, success rule

Paulson, Martin, *The Great Land Hustle,* 119

Pennsylvania farm deal, 106-110

Pension funds: as a source of capital, 90; benefits of, 90-91. *See also* Notes (secured by real estate)

Percolation (of soil): 54, 128-129; test holes (map), Appendix G, 333

Persistence: in sales, 181-182. *See also* Concentration, success rule

Personal goals, 40. *See also* Goals

Physical characteristics (of land): in land acquisition and development, 24, 54. *See also* FEASIBILITY CHECK LIST

Physical concerns, 212, 261. *See also* Components of life

Physical Goals, Statement of, 46-47. *See also* Goals

Planning commission, 63

Pleasant personality, success rule, 229-234

Pluto. *See* Orpheus

Positive emotions, 213

Positive mental attitude, 219. *See also* Concentration (and Persistence), how to apply

Poverty: fear of, 213; symptoms of fear, 214. *See also* Fears (7 Basic)

Preconditioning, in sales, 183-184

Premium, when substituting notes for cash in land purchases or releases, 88-89

Prepayment (on notes), Appendix M, 360

Price and Terms: how to rate when buying and developing land, 57. *See also* FEASIBILITY CHECK LIST

Prime rate, 86

Private individuals: as a source of investment capital, 95. *See also* Financing land projects

Proceeds, from discounting notes, Appendix M, 357-365

Productivity of land, 54

Profit and risk factors, in land acquisition and development, 24, 54. *See also* FEASIBILITY CHECK LIST

Profit curve, 11

Project Cost Sheet, Appendix E, 327

Project Development Sheet, Appendix E, 326

Property Inspection Form, Appendix E, 325

Property owners association, 126-128. *See also* Covenants

Prospect, deference to, 188

Protective covenants. *See* Covenants

Puryear, Edgar, *Nineteen Stars,* 245

Quality Reference Sheet, 56-57

"Quickie" development, 110-113. *See also* Developing the land; Land development

Quitclaim deed. *See* Deeds

Real estate agencies, 34, 169-171

Real estate brokers and salespeople: how to handle, 170-171; how to pay, 174-176; briefing, 177-180.

Real estate brokers and salespeople (continued)
  See also Sales, real estate agencies
Real Estate Investment Trusts, 94-95
Real estate syndicates, 96
Rebate, as sales inducement, 164
Recreational land, easiest and hardest to "hustle," 119-122
Referrals, 180. *See also* Kickbacks
Relatives, in business, 20
Release fees, 10, 79, 80, 84, 87, 88, 89; Appendix A, 276; Appendix E, 324
Rescission, notice of right of, Appendix J, 344
RESPA, Appendix A, 274
Revenge, negative emotion, 212, 213
Richest Man in Babylon, The (Clason), 202
Riparian rights, 185
Road frontage: importance of, 53; evaluating, 56
Roads, state and county requirements, 127
Robinson, Jackie, 235. *See also* Tolerance (and Patience)
Rockefeller, 246
Rockwell, Willard F. Jr., 220
Romance, positive emotion, 213
Rose, Pete, 218. *See also* Concentration (and Persistence), success rule
Salability After Development, how to rate when buying and developing land, 57. *See also* FEASIBILITY CHECK LIST
Sales: As *Subdivesting* work area, 21, 27-28; buyer's expenses, 172; commissions, 174-176; contracts, 171-173; foreclosures, 172-174; hiring and briefing salespeople, 177-179; installment basis, 171; legal expenses, 10, 172; marketing, 25-26; importance of quick turnover, 176-177; real estate agencies, 170-171, 174-175; selling your own land, 182-188
Sales contract, sample of, Appendix J, 343
Salesmanship: basic elements of, 182-188; closing signals, 187-188; deference to prospect, 188; and enthusiasm, 183; frequently asked questions, 184-186; gaining client's confidence, 184; identification with client, 186-187; persistence, 181
Sales Promotion, as *Subdivesting* work area, 25-26. *See also* Advertising

Savings accounts: importance of, 84; preservation of liquid assets, 84, 86
Savings and loan associations: as a source of capital, 94. *See also* Financing land projects
Savings habit, success rule, 202-204
Schweitzer, Albert, 232
Scoring Key, 55. *See also* FEASIBILITY CHECK LIST; QUALITY REFERENCE SHEET
Scotland, 42
SCRIPT: meaning of, 200-201; success rules, 202-237. *See also* FLAME
Secrets of Mind Power, The (Lorayne), 262.
Secret of the Ages, The (Collier), 256
Seed money, 10
SELECTIVITY, in choosing land deals, 37, 39, 61, 62, 75, 136
Self-confidence: formula, 207; success rule, 204-208. *See also* ADMIT
Self-control, success rule, 208-217. *See also* Fears (7 Basic)
Self-discipline, 262
Self-expression: basic motive, 224, 226. *See also* Motives (10 Basic)
Self-hypnosis, 205, 233, 243, 262. *See also* Autosuggestion
Self preservation, basic motive, 224, 225. *See also* Motives (10 Basic)
Septic System Check List, 129
Sex, basic motive, 224, 226; positive emotion, 213. *See also* Motives (10 Basic)
Shakespeare, William 6, 182, 210, 227, 243
Shenandoah National Park, 7
Shenandoah River, 79
Sheriff's deed. *See* Deeds
Shylock, 235. *See also* Tolerance (and Patience)
"Signature" capital, 87-88
Snead, Sam, 218. *See also* Concentration (and Persistence), success rule
Social involvements, 212. *See also* Components of life
Soil and erosion control laws, 35, 63-64
Soil Conditions (and Well Depth), how to rate when buying and developing land, 56. *See also* FEASIBILITY CHECK LIST

Soil Conservation Service (SCS), 129-130
Soil map, sample from SCS, Appendix H, 336
Soils, 128-130; SCS data, Appendix H, 335-336
Soul. *See* Living tools
SOURCE BOOK, for locating land deals, 24, 33-35, 39, 61, 136. *See also* ACTION FILE
Sources, for rural land deals, 34-36
South America, 42
Special warranty deed. *See* Deeds
Spiritual needs, 212; concern with, 261
Spiritual power, 262
Stability, in partners and key men, 19-20
Stone, W. Clement, 228, 232
Subconscious mind, 4, 5, 46, 205, 207, 243, 256-257, 262; how to reach and influence, 216-217, 233, 254
Subdivesting: definition, 11, 26; major work areas of, 21-28
Success: characteristics of, 21; and concentration, 217-219; and cooperation, 220-223; creed, 4; and definite aims, 253-258; and enthusiasm, 261-266; and following through, 47; and going extra mile, 258-261; and the Golden Rule, 223-227; and imagination, 227-229; invisible guards of, 222-223; and leadership, 244-248; and personality, 229-234; preparation for, 5; and profiting from failure, 237-244; and savings habit, 202-204; secret of, 8; and self-confidence, 204-208; and self-control, 208-217; and thinking accurately, 248-253; and tolerance (and patience), 234-237. *See also* Common thread
Suggestion: power of, 47-49. *See also* Goals, Statement of Physical Goals
Superstition, negative emotion, 212, 213
Survey methods, Appendix A, 272
Tax advantages, 85, 90, 96. *See also* Capital gains
Tax deferred exchanges, Appendix A, 275
Tax maps: as a source of rural land deals, 34. *See also* Sources
Think and Grow Rich (Hill), 6, 25, 217

Timber companies: as a source of rural land deals, 35. *See also* Corporations, sources
Tolerance (and Patience), success rule, 234-237
Topographical maps, where to buy, Appendix G, 334
Treasure of the Sierra Madre, The, 19
Trustee, for pension funds, 90
Usable Road Frontage: how to rate when buying and developing land, 56. *See also* FEASIBILITY CHECK LIST
Usable Water Frontage and/or Government Land Boundary: how to rate when buying and developing land, 56. *See also* FEASIBILITY CHECK LIST
U.S. Steel Co., 217
Utility companies, and easements, Appendix A, 271-272
Views: how to rate when buying and developing land, 56. *See also* FEASIBILITY CHECK LIST
Virginia, 81
Visualization, 45
Warranty deed. *See* Deeds.
Washington, George, 230
Water frontage: asset to lots, 122; how to rate when buying and developing land, 56; importance of, 53. *See also* FEASIBILITY CHECK LIST
Water front project, 82-83
Wealth, secret of acquiring, 8
West Virginia land project, 122-126
Whittier: quote, 237. *See also* Failure (profiting from)
Wilson, Kemmons, 221. *See also* Cooperation, success rule
Wisdom: guard of, 222, 223; in personality development, 231-232
Word of mouth: as a source of rural land deals, 35-36. *See also* Sources
Yield rate, on discounted notes, Appendix M, 357-363
You Can Work Your Own Miracles (Hill), 210
Yukon, the, 42
Zoning laws, 35